Bulawayo Burning

The Social History
of a Southern African City
1893–1960

Bulawayo Burning

The Social History
of a Southern African City
1893–1960

TERENCE RANGER

Emeritus Rhodes Professor of Race Relations
University of Oxford

WEAVER
PRESS

JAMES CURREY

James Currey
www.jamescurrey.com
is an imprint of Boydell & Brewer Ltd
PO Box 9, Woodbridge, Suffolk IP12 3DF, UK

and of

Boydell & Brewer Inc.
668 Mt Hope Avenue, Rochester, NY 14620, USA
www.boydellandbrewer.com

Weaver Press
Box A1922
Avondale, Harare
Zimbabwe

British Library Cataloguing in Publication Data

Ranger, T.O. (Terence O.)
Bulawayo burning: the social history of a southern African
city, 1893-1960
1. Bulawayo (Zimbabwe)--History--20th century.
2. Bulawayo (Zimbabwe)--Social conditions--20th century.
3. Bulawayo (Zimbabwe)--Race relations. 4. Vera, Yvonne.
Butterfly burning.
I. Title
968.9'102-dc22

ISBN 978-1-84701-020-9 (James Currey cloth)
ISBN 978-1-77922-108-7 (Weaver Press)

Typeset in 10.5/11.5 Monotype Ehrhardt
by forzalibro designs, Cape Town
Printed and bound in Great Britain by
CPI Antony Rowe, Chippenham, Wiltshire

To Yvonne,
mere prose for your poetry

Contents

7

List of Illustrations

Maps

Photographs

Introduction

Finding Bulawayo

In February 1998, having retired from my Oxford Chair, I went for three years as Visiting Professor to the University of Zimbabwe. At that moment I had two books in the press – my history of the Matopos hills, *Voices From the Rocks*, which was published in 1999, and my history of northern Matabeleland, *Violence and Memory*, researched and written with Jocelyn Alexander and JoAnn McGregor, and published in 2000. Enjoying as I did free access to the National Archives and to the field I wanted another research project. Jocelyn and JoAnn and I had so much enjoyed our collective work on Nkayi and Lupani that we planned another joint book, this time on the Zambezi valley. But they were not successful with their application for research funding. JoAnn carried through the Zambezi project on her own.[1] Jocelyn turned to her work on imprisonment and punishment. I dug about in the National Archives, Harare, and came across hitherto unused material on Labour Boards and on the relations of the Rhodesian government to the municipalities, especially to Bulawayo. I used this material to write a couple of seminar papers for the UZ Economic History Department. My audience encouraged me to carry the research further so as to explore the class character and interests of the Bulawayo City Council and the reasons why it quarrelled so fiercely with Sir Godfrey Huggins' government over African labour and housing. Some of this archival material and of these political economy questions persists in this book. I am grateful to many of the historians at UZ – to Professor Ngwabi Bhebe, to Professor Alois Mlambo, to Brian Raftopoulos and to many others – for their stimulus and encouragement. And I am grateful to research students working on urban history – particularly to Ennie Chipembere, whose richly documented doctoral draft on African labour and housing in Harare I have found invaluable.

But the real impulse for my decision to concentrate on Bulawayo came from another source. In 1998 my close friend, the brilliant novelist Yvonne Vera, published a novel set in 1946 in Makokoba township, Bulawayo.[2] The novel was dedicated to me in commemoration of 'a glorious friendship and faith'. It was a challenge to me as a historian.

---

[1] McGregor, *Crossing the Zambezi. The Politics of Landscape on a Central African Frontier*, James Currey, Oxford, 2009.

[2] *Butterfly Burning*, Baobab Books, Harare, 1998.

1

Yvonne was writing about a period seventeen years before she was born – and seventeen years after I was. She did no historical research but listened to her Luveve township grandmother's stories and listened to the township music of the late 1940s and 1950s. She also drew on some of the experiences of her mother, Ericah Gwetai.[3] When I read the novel I decided that I would make Bulawayo and its townships my major research project and that I would write about them not from the perspective of political economy but from the perspective of moral economy. If Yvonne could plumb the experience of townsmen and women in the 1940s without doing any research, what might I be able to achieve if I did lots of it? Of course I could not surpass Yvonne but I might be able to supplement her insights and put them into a longer historical context.

Bulawayo was in many ways the ideal project for a septuagenarian historian. It would not involve the restless Land Rover roaming on which my other Matabeleland books had been based. Bulawayo is manageable. It is a compact city and the guardians of its history are generous men. For much of my time there in the late 1990s and early 2000s I stayed in the gloriously anachronistic Bulawayo Club, which still did not allow women into its library or members' bar. When Yvonne first entered it while she was Director of the National Gallery in Bulawayo she gazed around in astonishment. 'We'll take this as it stands', she said, and pointing to some club members gathered round for tea, she added: 'and we'll have them too'. But the club was wonderfully situated for research. It is less than ten minutes walk away from City Hall where the Historical Reference Library was situated, with its comprehensive and invaluable collections of the Bulawayo *Chronicle* and of the African press and its endlessly helpful librarian, Peter Genje. At the City Hall, too, the Municipality stored its bound volumes of committee minutes and its subject files, going back to the 1930s. I was readily granted access to all these by the Town Clerk, Moffat Ndlovu. Across the road is the glass administrative tower where sit archives rescued by J.S. Ncube from the move of the old Council departments, among them bulging files of African Advisory Board minutes and of innumerable African Associations. The club is fifteen minutes walk away from the Tredgold Buildings, where the Bulawayo National Archives were then housed. The BNA holds a rich deposit of Municipal materials up to the 1930s, an excellent oral history collection and much more.

My friend and colleague, Mark Ncube, chief archivist in Bulawayo, put all this at my disposal.

The club, moreover, is just over twenty minutes walk away from Zimbabwe's oldest African township – the Old Location, now Makokoba, which has existed continuously since 1894. My student research colleagues, reared in other more seemly Bulawayo townships, approached Makokoba with caution and even alarm. It was, they thought, a place where you were likely to have your tape-recorder stolen or even be assaulted by a gangster. They came to love it in its current incarnation as a place of old men and women, clustering around the market; the men sitting outside the barber's in the morning with plenty of time and inclination to talk, and knowing where at that time of day everyone else was likely to be. We could read intensively in Bulawayo city and

---

[3] Yvonne's mother has published a remarkable book about her, *Petal Thoughts. Yvonne Vera. A Biography*, Mambo Press, Gweru, 2008. The first part of the book is an autobiographical memoir by Ericah Gwetai about her relations with Yvonne. She describes with extraordinary frankness her 'unwanted pregnancy' in 1964 , when she was seventeen – which she discovers by fainting at the Lobengula Street Bus Terminus and being diagnosed by the market women. She describes her unsuccessful attempts at an abortion. It is clear that Yvonne drew upon her mother's experience in her description of her heroine Phephelaphi's unwanted pregnancy and abortion in *Butterfly Burning*.

talk intensively in Makokoba. And we were given endless advice and support from Bulawayo's two great local historians, Pathisa Nyathi and Jackson Ndlovu.

So far, so good. But Bulawayo's very accessibility and hospitality, its readiness to be read and talked about, soon presented a problem. Yvonne wrote her novels in intense bursts. She would shut herself away somewhere for a few weeks and emerge with a book.[4] I was trying to respond to her with evidence. But the evidence poured in so abundantly that I became overwhelmed. Yvonne was impatient. 'Don't come near me until you have finished that book', she said. Alas, it was still unfinished when she died in 2005. This was a result of the slowness of historians but it was also a result of the contrast between writing a rural case-study – as three of my previous books had been – and an urban history.

Makokoba is a little place. For most of its existence it contained only three or four thousand people. Even in its most crowded state in 1960 it contained only twelve thousand. It is infinitely smaller and much less populated that Makoni district or the Matopos or Nkayi and Lupani about which I had previously written. But as one of our informants warned us, this little Makokoba contained a world. Even if Makokoba always had close connections with Ndebele rural society and the memories of the Ndebele state, there were people living there from all over central and southern Africa. Many languages were spoken; many different rituals were practised. It would have been very difficult for any anthropologist to say what the prevailing marriage or burial customs were. Makokoba was constantly a society in the making.

By contrast to any rural district it was much more closely monitored and administered and researched. Even when in the 1920s the Bulawayo Council cared little about the social realities of Makokoba, they were careful to list every resident, their type of house and its value. Makokoba was the site of virtually every significant African political event – and most social and cultural ones too – which took place between 1920 and 1960. From 1940 onwards political and trade union meetings were attended and reported on by the CID, producing a mass of evidence. Makokoba even threw up its own weekly newspaper, Charlton Ngcebetsha's wonderful *Home News* which began in 1953 as the organ of the Makokoba Tenants' Association. The township was the subject of many sociological inquiries and surveys. There was much more evidence for tiny Makokoba than for whole districts – reports from many officials, police and administrators instead of a single Native Commissioner and his assistant.

Moreover, the occupants of the Old Location came to enjoy a much wider range of choice than did peasants in rural areas. The Rhodesian government divided the country up into distinct denominational zones to avoid competition among mission churches. The result was that, for instance, every Protestant child educated in Mazoe became a member of the Salvation Army. But around Makokoba there grew up a ring of churches – Anglican, Catholic, Wesleyan and American Episcopal Methodist, Dutch Reformed, Brethren, Presbyterian, Lutheran, etc. By contrast to three or four missionaries reporting from a rural district, Makokoba had a dense and complex ecclesiastical history. It boasted African initiated churches, like the African Methodist Episcopal; Kenan Kamwana and other early Watch Tower preachers taught there; Mai Chaza ran a spectacular crusade there with lots of embarrassing public female confession; Maranke and Masowe Apostolics met in the open air. The Salvation Army processed through Makokoba. There was a mosque there. Behind closed

---

[4] Irene Staunton says that *Without a Name* was written in one week and revised in less than another. 'Yvonne Vera: A Memory' in Ericah Gwetai, *Petal Thoughts*, p. 135.

3

doors, in the labour compounds and in the cemeteries, 'traditional' ceremonies from all over central Africa were performed.

And there came to be as many social as religious rituals to choose from. Boxing matches were attended by a thousand people in Stanley Square, Makokoba. From the 1930s football became a mass enthusiasm. There were concerts and dances and film shows; parades of male dandies; and from the later 1940s parades of female beauties. The mix of religions, pastimes and ethnicities in Makokoba added many flavours to what had become known to young dandies by the late 1920s as 'Style Bulawayo'. It was this range of choice which increasingly attracted young migrants, male and female, from the rural areas. Despite the awful housing conditions, they wanted to know what it felt like to be participating in making the culture of a real city.

All this meant that the oral life-history evidence collected in and about Makokoba and the other townships was different from rural life histories. I had found in Makoni district, for example, that most people regarded 'history' as being about chiefly dynasties and regarded their own life stories as of little historical significance.[5] In the township oral tradition we found no trace of such chiefly histories. The culture which was reflected was the contested and changing culture of the townships rather than rural 'tradition'. There were certainly myths but they were urban myths of youth and survival and strangeness and of sporting and political heroism. They were expressed in life histories rather than in collective history-scapes.[6] My research associates – Busani Mpofu, Hloniphani Ndlovu, Lynette Nyathi and the rest – collected over two seasons hundreds of rich first-person testimonies. We would gather twice a week in the club to review progress. We quickly found that set questions about well-known events – like the 1948 general strike – brought formulaic answers. People really wanted to talk about their own lives, often in surprising ways. Readers will see from the abundant use I have made of their interviews in this book that Mpofu, Ndlovu and Nyathi are more its joint authors than research assistants.

In short, there was a superabundance and rich variety of evidence. I soon realized that I could not carry my study forward to the present as I had done with my rural case-studies. So this book covers a period of 67 years and ends in 1960. Someone else will have to write the second volume from 1960 to 2010. (I hope that might be Busani Mpofu, who was so exhilarated by the interviews he did for our book that he dedicated himself to becoming a historian, returned to UZ to take a Special Honours year and an MA, and is now completing his doctoral thesis on Bulawayo since 1960 at Edinburgh University.)

I chose 1960 as the ending point because this book is called *Bulawayo Burning* as a direct response to Yvonne Vera's novel. But I wanted some real historical burnings as well as imaginative literary ones. So the book begins in 1893 with the burning at Lobengula's orders of his capital at Bulawayo and ends in 1960 with the burning of shops and beer halls in the townships during the *Zhii* riots. In the middle come the fires of December 1929 when the goods of the irritatingly modernizing Manyika were burnt in great piles in the railway compounds and the Location. These burnings provide dramatic set pieces which give this book something of the character of a novel.

[5] Terence Ranger, *Chingaira Makoni's Head: Myth, History and the Colonial Experience*, Indiana University, Bloomington, 1988.
[6] Terence Ranger, 'Myth and Legend in urban oral memory: Bulawayo, 1930–60', in Ranka Primorac, (ed.), *African City Textualities*, Routledge, Abingdon, 2010.

The Character & Sequences of the Book

The richness and subjectivity of my evidence allows me to write a historian's response to Yvonne. I too can write about experience and memory and aspiration and frustration. So I have decided to make this book in many ways like fiction, though without inventing anything. Of course I have not tried to write in Yvonne's style. My dedication offers her 'mere prose for your poetry', though I have quoted quite a bit from *Butterfly Burning*, which raises the literary level. Nor have I taken the licence she enjoyed to invent. So far as I have been able to make it so, everything in this book is factual or actual, though the life histories which I quote are full of invention. Of course, this gives Yvonne great advantages over me. To take only one example, she was able to invent and embody a heroine for a period in which the written sources usually don't even offer up the names of the women to which they refer. In Chapter 4 I have been able to tell the story of a man, Sipambaniso Manyoba, who matches Yvonne's hero, Fumbatha. But my sources, both written and oral, merely give me his wife's name as Mrs Manyoba. And Yvonne was able to write rapidly, producing a fluid oil painting, while my book is made up of thousands of little pieces of evidence, painstakingly pieced together like a mosaic. How to make it move has been my problem.

Yvonne knowingly toyed with history. She wilfully subverted chronology. Her first novel, *Nehanda*, compressed the birth, youth, ministry and old age of her heroine into the six years between 1890 and 1896.[7] Even the much more realistic and located *Butterfly Burning* allows itself to draw into the year 1946 features of Bulawayo life that had by that time disappeared – like the ban on Africans walking on the pavements which had in fact been overturned in the courts in the late 1930s. It also extends forwards to incorporate aspects of black urban culture which had not yet developed. I have no desire to compress whole lives into a few years. I have tried to avoid anachronisms – though in using life-history testimony it is probably impossible to avoid them altogether.

But I have allowed myself to be influenced by some aspects of Yvonne's treatment of time. She often wrote between the lines of history. The opening words of *Butterfly Burning* are: 'There is a pause. An expectation.' The story takes place before the 1948 general strike when all the frustrations of her characters are building up but can find no public expression. (They find a tragic personal one in Phelephelaphi's self-abortion and suicide by fire.) I am by nature a ruthlessly narrative historian. I have been fighting for a long time against the postmodernist description of narrative as something intrusively male and colonial.[8] Like John Peel, I regard narrativity as a precious possession of African societies and of African individuals, both male and female. I want this book to present a narrative which is not hegemonic.

But the idea of a pause in the narrative, even one filled with expectation, is an attractive one. So is the idea that a narrative does not foreordain its outcome. One ought not to rush ahead from 1946 to 1948 as though the general strike was the inevitable climax of the tension. One ought to strive for a history in which no one is quite sure what will

---

[7] Yvonne Vera, *Nehanda*, Baobab Books, Harare, 1993.
[8] Terence Ranger, 'No Missionary: no exchange: no story? Narrative in Southern Africa', mss., All Souls seminar, June 1992. In this paper I was debating with Jean and John Comaroff's call for a 'dissolution of linear narrative' and for a 'revolutionary break with the (repressive) ideology of story-telling.'

happen next – a process of *Becoming Zimbabwe*, as the title of Brian Raftopoulos and Alois Mlambo's new one-volume history has it,[9] rather than *The Road to Zimbabwe*. And so in this book I have tried to avoid knowing what is to follow. In Chapter 7, for example, I treat Joshua Nkomo's political, trade union and business activities in the 1950s in deliberate ignorance that he was to become a hero, and stoutly resist his insistence in his autobiography that he had already achieved heroic status. I sternly make him wait until the end of 1960. Nkomo's emergence as a hero, surrounded by urban folk myth, is a climax of this book but not its resolution. The reader by this time knows quite enough about Nkomo's ambiguities to realize that after 1960 there is plenty of time for him to fall out of hero-hood and to regain it several times.

And I have adopted the Vera pause, a break in the narrative where the scene is set up and we wait to see what will happen within it. I have used fictional, or dramatic, terminology for the divisions in this book. It begins with a long Prelude which carries the backstory from the fires and explosions of 1893 up to 1930. Then comes the pause chapter, Chapter 1, which describes the landscapes of Bulawayo town and of its Location – white and black Bulawayo – mapping them according to the grid layout of the European town, with its frontier streets on its eastern and western borders, their houses on only one side of the road, looking east to settler civilization and west to barbarism – and to the Location. This is the stage on which the coming drama is to be set. I have tried to sketch both European and African perceptions of the town and of the Location, where self-built circular African kraals were giving way to enforced municipal straight lines. And I have tried to set both town and Location within two concentric rings, first the Commonage and outside that a surrounding ring of countryside in which thousands of Africans lived, in still-existing Ndebele villages or as rent-paying tenants on white-owned farms.

All the while, as I have said, I have kept my eye open for fires. Chapter 2 is the first moment when the dramatic narrative speeds up, devoting itself to the events of a few days, while the Prelude dealt with 37 years. Chapter 2 is called 'The First Fires, December 1929'. It deals with the so-called 'faction fights'. Ian Phimister and Charles Van Onselen have famously analysed these as an exercise in political economy. I analyse them as an exercise in moral economy. The confused movements of phantom armies and the wild rumours arose in my view out of a struggle for who should determine 'Style Bulawayo! O, Style Bulawayo!', those words which young Manyika migrants proclaimed in ecstasy as they paraded along the Location streets in their finery. The flames arose from veritable 'bonfires of the vanities'; as Manyika bicycles, suits, books and savings were piled up and set alight in railway compounds and outside township houses. The first 'character' of the book emerges from the chaos of the 'faction fights' – appropriately enough, a character whose name and reputation is given by myth. He is James Mampara (Scoundrel), a real man obscured as much as illuminated by the legends of his agility, strength, smartness and genius as a cyclist and boxer.

But then, as the flames died down and the chaos recedes, I am really able in Chapter 3 to adopt Yvonne's technique of illuminating structures through the interaction of characters. This chapter is called 'City versus State, 1930-1946'. The characters are white – the Prime Minister and archetypal Englishman, Godfrey Huggins, versus Bulawayo's city boss and archetypal Lowlands Scot, Donald Macintyre. The issues in their debate are huge, no less than the role of Africans in towns and the implica-

---

[9] *Becoming Zimbabwe*, Weaver Press, Harare, and Jacana Media, Johannesburg, 2009.

tions this has for citizenship. It is justifiable to narrate the controversy in terms of personality because of the small scale of Rhodesian municipal and national politics, with parliaments of thirty or so members and municipalities of fifteen or so councillors. It was easy for one strong man to dominate such assemblies. Rich verbatim sources exist for the hard-hitting and sometimes scurrilous exchanges between the two men – parliamentary *Hansards*, the full records of Municipal Association meetings, minutes of Bulawayo Council and committee meetings, records of testimony to Labour Boards and Commissions of Inquiry. When I gave an early version of this chapter to the Economic History seminar at UZ, Government Phiri exclaimed: 'I thought this was going to be a sober examination of parochial politics but it is like a chapter out of Charles Dickens!' I was, of course, delighted. Macintyre was a mass of contradictions – a Scottish craft unionist and an industrialist rhetorically in favour of state-run industry; parliamentary leader of the Southern Rhodesian Labour Party; a master-baker of legendary frugality; an advocate of the employment of short-term 'bachelor' African migrant labour; and a bitter enemy of African 'stabilization' in towns. Huggins was equally contradictory – an apostle of ideal segregation whose legislation brought about permanent African urban settlement.

This chapter is the 'whitest' history I have ever written. So in Chapter 4 I play a bit with chronology myself and go over the same period, 1930 to 1948, from the perspective of African experience. This is the world of Yvonne's major male character, Fumbatha (the clenched fist), a man whose hands are in every building in Bulawayo. Fumbatha is an uptight man who keeps his secrets. I needed someone much more expressive. So for 'Mr Black Bulawayo, 1930–1948', my fourth chapter, I chose Sipambaniso Manyoba Khumalo, through whose life it is possible to narrate the sporting, cultural, ethnic, industrial and political life of black Bulawayo in this period. The chapter is focused on him. I don't narrate the 1945 railway strike except in so far as Sipambaniso was involved – as he was both during and after as an adviser to the railwaymen. I don't narrate the 1948 general strike, of which he was the main spokesman, except in so far as he was involved. I discuss football and boxing because he was the best footballer and boxer. I discuss Bulawayo's modern musical life because he ran the best dance band and choir. I discuss Ndebele royal ritual and memorialization because he organized them; I discuss trade unionism because he was the mainstay of the Bulawayo Federation of African Trade Unions; I discuss national and township politics because he was on the executive of the Bantu National Congress, was elected to the Makokoba Advisory Board and helped set up the Makokoba Tenants' Association. I find him a man perfectly consistent across all these activities. Born in the Location of aristocratic Ndebele parents; a member of the Ndebele royal clan; educated and living all his life in Makokoba; a CID man and a welfare officer – Sipambaniso perfectly represented the long-term residents of the Location (especially the Ndebele ones) and consistently expressed their interests.

Taking the whole of a man's life like this cuts across the problematic of political economy. What class was Sipambaniso? As a trade unionist he spoke for 'proletarians', men dependent on wage labour, the Fumbathas of this world. As a Khumalo he walked with chiefs and princes. As a musician and master of ceremonies he represented the modern elite, though he lived all his life in the 'slum' township of Makokoba. As a footballer he represented Black Bulawayo. It makes no sense to call him 'petty bourgeois' and little more to call him 'middle class'. Classes are collectivities. Few individuals fit into them.

With a character like Sipambaniso, and still more with the young women who figure in Chapter 5 on the feminization of black Bulawayo, 1948–1960, I run into a problem that I can share with Yvonne. Once I was talking about my Bulawayo research after a day's workshop in Philadelphia. Unexpectedly a Zimbabwean arose at the end. He turned out to be a member of the UZ English department. 'We teach *Butterfly Burning* at UZ,' he said. 'Of course we admire its skill. But it is too frivolous. Joy keeps breaking in. All one needs to know about urban Africans during colonialism is that they were smears under the white man's boot. And if your book is going to be entertaining it will be of no use to us whatsoever.' His judgement would have been surprising to many commentators on Yvonne's novel. Chioma Opara, for example, has written an article entitled 'Not a scintilla of light: darkness and despondency in Yvonne Vera's *Butterfly Burning*'. She writes of 'the grossly traumatized and colonized humanity in Makokoba, a microcosm of Southern Africa' who 'represent a scathing human condition'.[10] Yet Yvonne used to call *Butterfly Burning*, despite the abortion and the suicide, her 'light book'. It is filled with music; joy *does* keep breaking in.

The point is yet more clearly made in Yvonne's 'Introduction' to the catalogue of the 1999 *Thatha Camera, The Pursuit for Reality* exhibition of Bulawayo township photographs curated by her at the National Gallery. Many of the photographs are of young women from the 1950s and 1960s recently come to join 'the grossly traumatized and colonized humanity in Makokoba'. Yet Yvonne writes:

> The evocation of desire, the invention of the desirable object is at the basis of some of the most compelling photographs in 'Thatha Camera' … a single woman sitting with legs clad in high heels; a mini-skirt, an alluring look; fingers curling delicately over a raised knee; the shoulder turned provocatively toward the viewer; a hat held on the edge of the forehead; a wig split in the middle invitingly; high cheek-bone, translucent, polished with skin-lightening creams. Each of these gestures celebrates a new found urban sensibility …
>
> Desire is the tone of self-expression in the late 60s and 70s in the township. The photographed individual is firmly convinced of the desirability of a modern lifestyle; the fulfilling absorption of modern styles … The body is fashionable; in vogue. It is a thing in itself … This is Bulawayo. This is the city. This is me.

Our interviews with women who came to Makokoba in the 1950s strike exactly this note. Conditions were terrible, they say, but Bulawayo was wonderful. In Chapter 5, on the feminization of black Bulawayo, I draw upon these oral life histories to reveal the world of the young female immigrants and runaways as they arrived in the township. They came to Makokoba because it was the only place in the 1950s from which unmarried women were not expelled. They had to stay with relatives or lovers in rooms so crowded that they slept on the floor under beds where couples were making love. But they were young; they had the opportunity to earn money as factory workers or nannies or shebeen girls; they were able to buy stiff petticoats and high-heeled shoes; they were able to dance and to enter beauty competitions. After decades when township girls were dowdy peahens and the young men were the peacocks, quite suddenly the African press was full of photos of stunning young women. As our oral informants, now old, boast, they were '*seen*, really *seen*'. Much of this chapter is like a footnote to *Butterfly Burning* but there is room in it for other women too – the staunch Christian matrons of the uniformed church movements who formed power-

[10] *Tydskrif vir Letterkunde*, Spring 2008.

ful township associations; the girls who, unlike Yvonne's heroine, managed to become nurses.

In a way *Bulawayo Burning* is *my* light book, though it contains the fires and racist repression and slum conditions. But Sipambaniso, with his sense of fun and his sense of responsibility, came out of all that. And joy does keep breaking in to my narrative, especially in the oral life histories. People don't wish to remember their lives as mere smears. Somehow one had to balance in a history, as Yvonne does in her novel and still more in the introduction to *Thatha Camera*, the memory of a dreadful poverty with the memory of a sort of personal freedom.

Then the narrative moves on beyond Yvonne's novel and into the vexed 1950s, to Chapter 6 on black Bulawayo transformed. Here, with the story of the rapid multiplication of townships and the establishment of nationalism, there can be no single representative character – no Sipambaniso. There have to be several. One is Hugh Ashton, who became Director of African Administration in Bulawayo and transformed its reputation from reactionary to progressive; another – at Yvonne's special request – is her uncle, Jerry Vera, the social and sporting Mr Bulawayo of the 1950s. Yet another is Charlton Ngcebetsha, the short, feisty and provocative editor of the *Home News*. A fourth is a sort of articulate embodiment of Yvonne's hero Fumbatha, the building union trade unionist and radical nationalist, J.Z. Moyo. And the fifth is the hero-in-waiting, Joshua Nkomo, pupil and friend of Ashton, close friend of Jerry Vera, trade unionist.

In the complex sixth chapter I trace the explosive growth of Bulawayo's townships in the 1950s, as Ashton's building programme creates a dozen townships instead of one, and as leasehold and site-and-service schemes create a residential pattern based on class. Makokoba remained as it has always been – overcrowded, impoverished, full of women. I trace the emergence of a fractured nationalism, based on the resentments of poverty in Makokoba and on the frustrated aspirations of leaseholders in the 99-year leasehold scheme in Mpopoma. At the end of 1959 a feeling of restlessness pervaded black Bulawayo – fractious pause and an uneasy expectation. The banning of Congress in February 1959 and the arrest of all its Bulawayo leaders, J.Z. Moyo among them (Ashton's friends and responsible men), left a vacuum which in Matabeleland was not filled by the founding of the National Democratic Party on 1 January 1960. Nkomo was away in exile in London. There was no one to hold nationalism together. Unemployment turned the poorest against women working in industry and against workers from outside Southern Rhodesia. Ngcebetsha feared an ethnic explosion like 1929.

So comes the final chapter, Chapter 7, as the pause ended and the forebodings were realized. It is another chapter of compressed narrative in which history runs fast and slow at the same time – 'Black Bulawayo Burns, 1960'. Here, indeed, are the fires again, as during four days of riot – *Zhii* – at the end of July 1960, every store and every beer hall in the townships is set alight; looters scurry between the flames; twelve Africans are killed. Here both the old and new landscapes of Bulawayo come into play. The white town shrinks behind Lobengula Street, its western boundary since 1895, now lined with bayonets. The townships are left to themselves in all their newly variegated social complexity. Rioters from Makokoba and other poor areas attack not only stores and municipal property but also the newly built houses of the wealthy in Pelendaba and Pumula. Great cleavages open up within black society, as leaseholders demand to be given arms to protect themselves against the poor, and between black and white society as 'moderate' Africans denounce a government which has left them to their fate. Married women denounce 'single' men as animals; 'bachelors' denounce the African elite as inhumane. Township 'community' was being torn apart. The chapter, and the book, ends with Nkomo's triumphant return from exile in November 1960 and the NDP's sweeping victory in the Advisory Board elections in December.

The book's ending is a cliff-hanger, leaving many questions unresolved. Could Nkomo's ambiguities – trade unionist, businessman, populist, capitalist, Methodist, the chosen one of the High God shrines in the Matopos – prove effective in holding Bulawayo nationalism together? Could Nkomo and Ashton work together to avoid a long stalemate as the new nationalist Advisory Boards demanded a majority on Council and dissolved themselves? Could the feminization of black Bulawayo withstand the patriarchalism of nationalism? Could the vitality of Bulawayo musical and sport culture survive the coming long years of Rhodesia Front repression? Would there be more fires?

These are questions for whoever writes the second volume to answer. In this book there is a very brief Postlude tracing the subsequent careers of the major characters and suggesting some possible patterns. After 1960 there was never again an upheaval like *Zhii*, or at least not until the post-independence violence in Entumbane in 1980 and 1981. Urban musical and dramatic culture atrophied as singers and actors migrated north. Stanley Hall and Stanley Square in Makokoba ceased to be the focus of Matabeleland's political life. Bulawayo's life was muffled. Nkomo and J.Z. Moyo spent most of the years between 1960 and 1980 in detention, prison or exile. J.Z. Moyo was killed by a bomb in Lusaka. Jerry Vera dwindled into a discredited and ignored old age. Charlton Ngcebetsha, contrary as ever, was eventually arrested, detained and sent to join Nkomo at Gonakudzingwa. Ashton, however, remained Director of African Administration in Bulawayo until his retirement. During the 1960s and 1970s there was renewed tension between the city and the state, as the Bulawayo Council, under Ashton's influence, remained committed to freehold and African membership of the Council while the Rhodesia Front government sought to deny both. Ashton managed, with Nkomo's support, to set up a single Advisory Board for all the townships, with committees which shadowed those of the Council. It acted as a Council-in-waiting so that after 1980 there was a smooth and effective Africanization of Bulawayo local government. But this meant a further, and violent, instalment of city/state tension as an efficient ZAPU Bulawayo Council presented a challenge to Mugabe's government in the 1980s. Meanwhile, Makokoba remains as disreputable and feisty as ever, resisting all demands that it be knocked down for redevelopment or turned into a tourist theme park.

Bulawayo in the Urban History of Southern Africa

Yet another difference between working on Bulawayo and researching a rural district case-study is that many people have worked on Bulawayo already. In Makoni and the Matopos I had the field to myself. But in Bulawayo I found at least three layers of previous interpretation. The first was the sociological layer of all those surveys and inquiries which reached their climax during Ashton's regime. In these, the problematic was de-tribalization. Africans were thought of as essentially rural people, traumatized by town life. The question was how to help them adapt. The second was the political economy focus of the 1970s. This found its fullest expression in Stephen Thornton's research for a Manchester doctorate in the late 1970s. His draft thesis, unfortunately never revised and submitted, bears the neutral title: 'A History of the African Population of Bulawayo'. But a better idea of its thrust can be gained from the title of the one chapter which has been published – 'The struggle for profit and participation by an emerging petty-bourgeoisie in Bulawayo, 1893-1933.'[11] Thornton's draft thesis is the story of an internal class struggle between African lumpen, proletarian and petty bourgeois elements, and of the relentless pressure of colonial capitalism on all of them.[12] The third interpretation was advanced in 1989 by Dr Ossie Stuart in his London dissertation, 'Good Boys, Footballers and Strikers: African Social Change in Bulawayo, 1933–1953.' Stuart was critical both of the materialist focus of the political economy approach and of the sociological assumption that urban Africans were culturally helpless. He focused on African self-assertions, as much in sport and popular culture as in commerce, trade unionism and politics. His thesis, none of which has been published, was an early statement of a cultural economy approach. A much more recent book, with an emphasis on urban African agency in post-independence Zimbabwe, is Ortrude Nontobeko Moyo's *Trampled No More: Voices From Bulawayo's Townships about Families, Life, Survival and Social Change*.[13]

My relationship to these three interpretations will, I hope, be clear. I don't think that Location Africans lacked cultural confidence or initiative. Indeed, my book is the story of how from the very beginning they sought to construct a 'style Bulawayo', and how this was internally contested as well as externally repressed. The sociological surveys assumed that Africans were regional men, unable to create a local identity or to draw upon global culture. My view is that urban Africans were pre-eminently both local and global, drawing upon global influences in religion, sport, fashion, music and film to fashion their own styles and values.[14] Though I draw heavily on the richness of Thornton's research I don't see class identities as the key to the earlier history of the Location. I don't interpret the December 1929 violence in class terms. On the other hand I do see *Zhii* in July 1960 as an upheaval exposing the class ambiguities of nationalism. I have sought to develop the insights of Ossie Stuart and I extend Moyo's emphasis on township agency back into the colonial period. Zimbabwean historians are now re-emphasizing ethnicity as a key factor in the history of Bulawayo.[15] My agreements and disagreements with them will emerge in this book. Indeed, I look forward to the rapid development of Bulawayo's historiography, as M. Chikowero

---

[11] In B. Raftopoulos and T. Yoshikuni (eds), *Sites of Struggle*, Baobab Books, Harare, 1999.

[12] Stephen Thornton has gone on to a distinguished career in health management and provision. When he abandoned his doctorate he gave me permission to make use of the draft. I have taken full advantage of this in this book.

[13] University Press of America, Maryland, 2007.

[14] I have argued this in a forthcoming chapter, 'Reclaiming the African City: The World and the Township', in Ulrike Freitag and Achim von Oppen (eds), *Translocality. The Study of Globalising Processes from a Southern Perspective*, Brill, Leiden, 2010.

[15] Enocent Msindo, 'Ethnicity in Matabeleland, Zimbabwe: A Study of Ndebele-Kalanga relations, 1800s–1990s', doctoral thesis, Cambridge, 2004; 'Ethnicity, not class? The 1929 Bulawayo Faction Fights Reconsidered', *Journal of Southern African Studies*, 32, 3, September, 2006; 'Ethnicity and Nationalism in urban colonial Zimbabwe: Bulawayo, 1950–1963', *Journal of African History*, 48, 2007; Sibelo Ndlovu-Gatsheni, 'For the Nation to Live, the Tribe must Die: The Politics of Ndebele Identity and Belonging in Zimbabwe', in Bahru Zewde (ed.), *Society, State and Identity in African History*, Forum for Social Studies, Addis Ababa, 2008.

describes the politics of electricity in the city and Muchaparara Musemwa describes the politics of water.[16]

Had I managed to finish this book before 2005 I should have delighted Yvonne. It would also have appeared rather more innovative than it does five years later. In September 2004, after all, the South African novelist, Achmat Dangor, was appealing for a more imaginative invocation of the township – and giving Yvonne as an example of how it could be done. As a young man Dangor himself 'wrote poems and stories set in the city, in the dusty township, trying to find beauty in dimly lit streets and the hard echo of asphalt.' But to the rest of his generation the topic was 'the savannah, the idyllic peaceful village'. For them:

> the city was transiently evil, a gigantic asphalt salt mine into which Africans had been thrust after imperial Europe had wrenched them from their rural innocence.

By 2004 Dangor had:

> observed with some relief how other African writers have taken to the streets, as it were. Yvonne Vera beautifully evokes Bulawayo ... African writers are starting to reclaim the African city from the colonialists who by their association with it had poisoned it as a centre of culture.[17]

If it had appeared in 2004 this book might have been hailed as the pioneering work of a historian 'taking to the streets'.

But the delay has meant that it now appears as part of a more general trend in southern African urban history. In 2004, after all, Belinda Bozzoli's magnificent study of the 1984 Alexandria rebellion appeared. It too follows a literary model, as its title *Theatres of Struggle and the End of Apartheid* makes clear.[18] It too has a chapter on urban landscape and one on 'nationalism and theatricality'. It too has pauses and scenes of frenzied action. It has remarkable characters. It too insists that 'nothing entered the township without being given local meaning'.[19] It insists, as I would insist for Makokoba, that any study of Alexandria must be particular, its history understood as different from that of any other South African township and quite different from that of any other southern African town. This means that one cannot suggest that Makokoba and Alexandria were similar to each other, merely that they can both be best understood by means of a similar approach.

As I was writing the last pages of this book in December 2009 and had just noted the formation in Makokoba in 1989 of the Nostalgic Actors and Singers Association, I received as a gift from my friend Professor Elizabeth Gunner a copy of Jacob Dlamini's *Native Nostalgia*.[20] Dlamini's is a call to novelists and historians even more urgent than Dangor's. Dlamini draws upon his childhood memories of Katlehong township and a hundred interviews with residents of Thandukukhanya township, exploring the violence which took place there in 2009. His book is a thoroughgoing

---

[16] M. Chikowero, 'Subalternating Currents: Electrification and Power Politics in Bulawayo, Colonial Zimbabwe, 1894–1939', *Journal of Southern African Studies*, 33, 2, 2007; Muchaparara Musemwa, 'A Tale of Two Cities: The Evolution of Bulawayo and Makokoba Township under Conditions of Water Scarcity, 1894–1953', *South African Historical Journal*, 55, 1, 2006; 'The Politics of Water in Post-colonial Zimbabwe, 1980–2007', African Studies Centre, Leiden, June 2008.

[17] Achmat Dangor, 'Another Country', *The Guardian*, 25 September 2004.

[18] International African Library, Edinburgh University Press, 2004.

[19] Bozzoli, p. 27.

[20] Jacana Media, Johannesburg, 2009.

assault on those commentators, both black and white, who depict township life under apartheid as totally anomic and alienating, destructive of values. He insists that in such repressive townships were nurtured the conviction that apartheid was immoral and the courage to oppose it. Sentence after sentence in his book resonated with me:

> Nostalgia does not have to be a reactionary sentiment. There is a way to be nostalgic about the past without forgetting that the struggle against apartheid was just. In fact, to be nostalgic is to remember the social orders and networks of solidarity that made the struggle possible in the first place. (p. 17) ... This social order bears writing about because townships tend to be seen as zones of deprivation that can only be defined in a negative sense, in terms of what they do not possess. In the telling of most histories, townships are poor places, full of poor people who often make poor choices in life ... They desperately 'need' development and lack any order. But ... there is nothing 'natural' about space or time. In fact these categories of measurement are also products of everyday practices and they are always constitutive of human exchange. (p. 105) ... If you think that townships are zones of deprivation and are nothing but vast labour camps, how can you remember such places with longing? But nostalgic about townships most people are ... Townships were (and are) dynamic places where attention to local detail (the music, the colours, the sounds, the smells) is what gave Katlehong, in my case, its distinct flavour and made it possible for me to tell it apart from the neighbouring township ... Listen to the music. Think of the different dance styles with which we grew up. Cast your mind back to the street games ... This is not to mention the role that our elders played in teaching us wrong from right. (pp. 108-9) ... The township is no stranger to thought. It has lent its name to a popular movement called township art, inspired musical genre such as township jazz ... The township was also the metaphorical black home in whose living room the post-apartheid imaginary was largely conceived by a revolutionary movement. (p. 160)

Dlamini ends his book with an injunction to readers, and to scholars. His book, he says, will have succeeded 'it if helps the reader realize that a lot of what passes for common sense about townships is in fact cant'. It is only by understanding 'the historical, political and cultural geography of South Africa ... that we can understand why blacks would remember their part under apartheid with fondness. There is no other way.'[21] I would have liked this book to be startlingly original. But I would be proud to have it seen as standing in the tradition of Bozzoli and as responding to Dlamini's call for 'a historical, political and cultural geography' of Bulawayo.[22]

---

[21] Dlamini, p. 161.

[22] Dlamini does in fact draw on South African historians and other scholars to sustain his argument. Thus he quotes Phillip Bonner and Noor Nieftagodien, *Kathorus: A History*, Longman, Cape Town, 2001; David Coplan, *In Township Tonight! South Africa's Black City Music and Theatre*, Jacana Media, Johannesburg, 2007; Achille Mbembe and Sarah Nuttall (eds), *Johannesburg: The Elusive Metropolis*, Witwatersrand University Press, Johannesburg 2008.

Prelude
Bulawayo, 1893–1930

Royal Bulawayo Burns

There have been three Bulawayos, two established by Lobengula and a third established by Cecil Rhodes. Lobengula's Bulawayos both ended in flames. The actual and metaphorical fires in colonial Bulawayo form the subject of this book.

Lobengula's first Bulawayo was burnt as part of royal custom. Whenever an Ndebele King moved his town the previous site was burnt to the ground. Royal towns were ritually fortified at various places – around the King's house, at the palisade, etc. The medicines could not be allowed to fall into the hands of witches and so everything was fired when the King left. The site of KoBulawayo (Old Bulawayo), which today is being restored and rebuilt, was abandoned by King Lobengula in 1881 and was set on fire by Induna Magwegwe Fuyane just after full moon on 15 September. As the Jesuit missionaries reported:

> Makwekwe set about burning the King's palace, the queens' huts, all the buildings in the royal kraal, sheds, coach-houses, stables and even old King Mosilikatsi's wagons.[1]

The burning of New Bulawayo twelve years later at the climax of the 1893 Matabele War was less ceremonial and more spectacular. Lobengula left the town as the white column fought its way from Fort Victoria. Few whites had ever approached Bulawayo from the east and the American Scout, F.R. Burnham, was sent ahead to locate the royal town. Burnham was hoping to take his bearings from Ntabas Induna, which turned out to be 'a miserable little molehill', but eventually found a spot from which to view Bulawayo. 'From a little rise we saw through the glasses the great capital of King Lobengula. There were a great number of beautifully woven Matabele huts.'[2] But as the column advanced on the town on 3 November 1893 a huge explosion was heard and 'large columns of smoke ascended the heavens'.[3]

---

[1] H. Depelchin and C. Croonenberghs, *Journey to Bulawayo*, Books of Rhodesia, Bulawayo, 1979, p. 324, cited in Pathisa Nyathi, 'The Ethnography of Kobulawayo', International Conference on 'A View of the Land', Bulawayo, July 2000. Lobengula had lived in KoBulawayo since 1870. Charred pole stumps have been found during the current excavations.
[2] F.R. Burnham, *Scouting on Two Continents*, Heinemann, London, 1926, p. 144.
[3] Alexander Davis, *The Directory of Bulawayo and Handbook to Matabeleland, 1895–1896*, Bulawayo, 1896, p. 14.

The town was fired in four places; the huts burnt rapidly; and the ammunition store blew up. Forbes, the commander of the column, send his 'galloper', Tanner, to ride ahead:

Tanner rode right up and into the burning kraal … The kraal was lighted up by the fires burning all round, and Tanner rode into the centre of it but could see nothing but hundreds of kaffir dogs running about.[4]

When the Victoria column arrived the flames were still roaring. The fortune-hunting Burnham recorded with sorrow that the fire:

had burned up an immense amount of ivory and treasure, along with valuable hides, horns and skins that [Lobengula] had accumulated in his storehouses. We made a great effort to put out this fire, but it was impossible to do so, and we saved very little of what must have been one of the most extraordinary collections ever made.[5]

But a scavenger did find Lobengula's rhino-horn knobkerrie and presented it to Rhodes. Modern Bulawayo began as a collection of wattle and daub huts set up beside the embers and cinders of its predecessor. In November 1893 the wind scattered the ashes from the royal town over the site of what was to become its successor. The royal towns of the Ndebele Kings were never intended to be permanent. They were moved when a King died or when their surrounding environment – grass, game, water – became exhausted. The Kings often left the towns to move about the countryside or to visit other settlements. In many ways it was misleading to call Lobengula's Bulawayo his 'capital'. Rhodes and the British South African Company chose to do so, however, in order to claim that they had seized the focal point of Ndebele power and thus overthrown the state. For the same reason Rhodes chose to build his new colonial town as close as possible to the smouldering ruins of Lobengula's.[6] The new Bulawayo thus inherited the environmental disadvantages of the old – especially the problem of water – and the designed permanence of the colonial town was to make these disadvantages much worse.

There were many contemporary critics of Rhodes's choice of the site for *his* capital in Matabeleland. The transport-rider, Stanley Portal Hyatt, was scathing:

Bulawayo stands in the barren dreariness of the high veld, the bleak wind-swept central plateau. Real Empire-makers, the adventurers risking their own lives, and not merely the lives of the employees and the money of shareholders, would never have dreamed of founding a township on that forsaken stretch of veld, in an out-of-the-way corner of the country, with the Kalahari Desert to the west, the dry bush veld to the south, the dreariness of the high veld to the north. A private individual who had thought of placing the principal town of a new colony in such a location would, rightly, have been thought a lunatic. [But for Rhodes] it was a good thing to found the new settlement, the outward and visible sign of the white man's rule, on the ruins of Lobengula's old kraal.[7]

4   W.A. Wills and L.T. Collinridge, *The Downfall of Lobengula*, London, 1894, p. 126.
5   Burnham, p. 152. Wills and Collinridge have a sketch on p. 128 showing two whites viewing the ruins of Lobengula's storehouse.
6   These points are made by Julian Cobbing, 'The Ndebele under the Kumalos', PhD, Lancaster, 1977, and by Stephen Thornton in Chapter 1 of his unfinished PhD thesis at Manchester, 'Changing Patterns of Coercive Control – the African Experience in Bulawayo, 1893–1903'. This chapter was completed in November 1978.
7   Stanley Portal Hyatt, *The Old Transport Road*, Melrose, London, 1914, pp. 31, 33, 34. Patrick Fletcher, who surveyed the site for colonial Bulawayo, did not agree with its location. He would have preferred a site more central to the Colony and close to a permanent river. Jameson dismissed his anxiety over water: 'We are not Dutchmen, we will get water by sinking wells and making dams … We can leave our successors to fight that out; get on with the job.' Oliver Ransford, *Bulawayo. Historic Battleground of Rhodesia*, Balkema, Cape Town, 1968, p. 64.

The Making of a European Bulawayo

At first, 'white man's' Bulawayo was a mere shanty settlement. 'Grass Town' was made up of shelters and cabins thatched with straw taken from African huts which had survived the fire. Some of these cabins stood just below Lobengula's stockade. But soon a formal town plan on a grid pattern was laid out. Rhodes had decreed that the new town should be laid out on flat ground three miles south of Lobengula's settlement; it should be a square mile in area, like Jerusalem; it should have wide streets, a belt of parkland, and a surrounding circle of Commonage. Its surveyor, Patrick Fletcher, took some account of existing geographical and political realities. He placed the central Market Square 'where there happened to be a mealie garden which did not require stumping' and he 'took good care that the network of streets and avenues did not cross the land previously granted to John Colenbrander by Lobengula'. Otherwise the oblong grid was as regular as an ancient Roman town, or a modern American one.[8]

Its eastern and western boundaries were set with care and given names right out of a history so recent that it was almost raw. The easternmost street, with house plots only down one side of it looking east, was named after Captain Henry John Borrow, a Salisbury man who had died on the Shangani River fighting with Major Allan Wilson's patrol in pursuit of Lobengula in December 1893. (The Wilson patrol had been wiped out the day after Cecil Rhodes had given instructions for the laying out of his new town.) Borrow street looked eastward to the park, and to the Suburbs and beyond them to Mashonaland and established white civilization. The street which became the western edge of Bulawayo – and which was nearest to the capital of the dead Ndebele King whom Borrow was pursuing – was named Lobengula Street.[9] Plot holders along the eastern side of Lobengula Street looked out westward towards 'the bush', commanding a view of 'nature'. Nothing 'civilized' was planned to arise there. In practice, however, much did. Because prevailing winds blew from east to west the smelly places were built there – the abbatoir, the pound, the municipal workers compound. From the late 1890s the 'Native Location' itself (later to be called Makokoba) developed opposite and close to North Lobengula Street, divided from it only by a stretch of open land. The street became not only an edge but a border between black Bulawayo and white Bulawayo. Yet none of these western developments were thought significant in the mental image its white citizens held of the town. Until 1935 the annual Directory grid maps still showed Lobengula Street at their extreme left-hand, western edge and depicted nothing beyond it. Borrow Street, on the other hand, had moved to the centre of the grid as white Bulawayo expanded eastward beyond it.

By March 1894 stands were being auctioned, though very few were bought in Lobengula Street. A Sanitary Board was set up in May 1894. It decided that the 'straw houses' were dangerous, both symbolically and practically – symbolically because they seemed to show that whites were no different from blacks, and practically because they offered a fire hazard which threatened to send the colonial Bulawayo the same way as Lobengula's:

The fiat has gone forth, no more straw huts to be allowed in the township. The once happy

8   H. A. Peel, 'Central Bulawayo: An urban study in functional differentiation', MSc., UNISA, 1970, p. 6.
9   Ransford, *Bulawayo. Historic Battleground of Rhodesia*, pp. 65-6.

home is roofless ... How about the natives [asked the *Bulawayo Sketch* prophetically], are they too to have brick houses?[10]

Dr Jameson officially declared the new town open on 1 June 1894. In this ramshackle town everyone was gambling on the future. The settler newspaper, *The Bulawayo Sketch*, recorded how white discourse was entirely about claim rights, farm rights, loot rights:

> Everyone has rights, except the Matabele, a strange reversal of affairs in Matabeleland. [The Ndebele] wander around ... watching their dispossessors haggling over their late goods and chattels on the morning market. They watch the Auctioneer putting up farms for sale, then claims, and then loots. They smile ... at the wonderful performance and have long indabas in their homes.[11]

Within 18 months these indabas had given rise to the second Ndebele War, to attacks on white fortune-seekers scattered over the countryide and to a siege of the Bulawayo laager. But even by the time of the 1896 rising, white Bulawayo had acquired a greater permanence.

By the end of 1894 four locally produced newspapers were available to Bulawayans: the *Bulawayo Sketch* and the *Bulawayo Chronicle,* and – as an indication of the dominance of gold mining in the white imagination – the *Matabele Times and Mining Journal* and the *Matabeleland News and Mining Record.*[12] As many as sixty firms and individuals advertised in their columns. Early in 1896 there appeared a gazetteer – Davis's *Bulawayo Directory and Handbook of Matabeleland, 1895–1896.* Its pages were full of entries for mining companies, mining engineers, assessors and assayers. It reported 'phenomenally rich specimens'. (It also reported a 'monster meeting of the inhabitants to consider the water scheme'.)[13] The vigorous young men who overwhelmingly made up Bulawayo's white population bought bicycles; as early as 1895 the first cycle race was held; in 1896 the Queens Club built a cycle track 'which will remain for ever in the memories of the old riders. It was, to all intents and purposes, square, and four and one eighth laps to the mile. It banked on the "home" corner only, with the result that the riders often went over the top in Grey Street.'[14]

All this hectic activity was driven by gold fever, the traits of which replaced the straw huts with brick built houses and with much larger buildings as well. Colin Harding recalled that:

> In the early days of Bulawayo thousands of pounds were spent in building huge offices and palatial houses for mining magnates ... The alleged wealth of Matabeleland made people careless of money [though] 75% of the old workings pegged out in 1894-5 were eventually found after development to be useless properties.[15]

---

[10] *Bulawayo Sketch*, 6 October 1894.

[11] Ibid., 4 August 1894.

[12] Ransford, p. 68. These were soon joined by the *Bulawayo Observer* and the *Bulawayo Express.*

[13] A. Davis, *Bulawayo Directory and Handbook of Matabeleland, 1895–1896*, reprinted by Books of Zimbabwe, Bulawayo, 1981.

[14] D. de L. Thompson, *A History of Sport in Southern Rhodesia, 1889–1935*, Rhodesian Printing and Publishing Company, Bulawayo, 1935, p. 217. 'It is a curious fact', wrote Thompson, 'that the country's cycling activities have been confined almost entirely to Bulawayo.'

[15] Colin Harding, *Far Bugles*, Simpkin Marshall, London, 1933, p. 19. Stephen Thornton remarks that 'at the height of the boom in 1895 many of these claims, most of which were old workings scarcely deeper than six feet from the surface, were selling for 500 pounds each.'

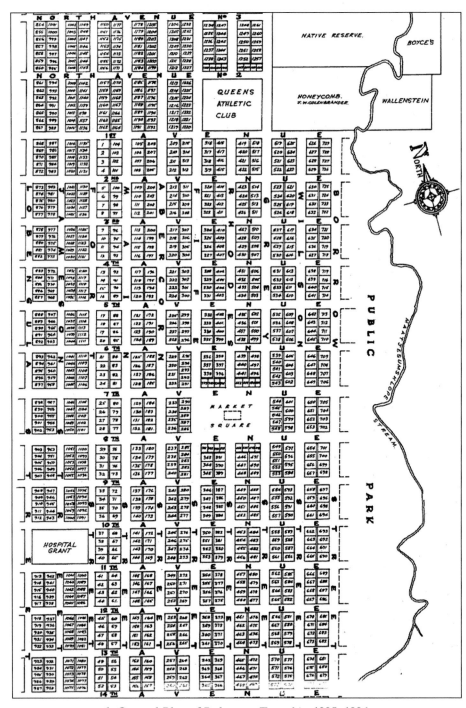

1. General Plan of Bulawayo Township, 1895–1896

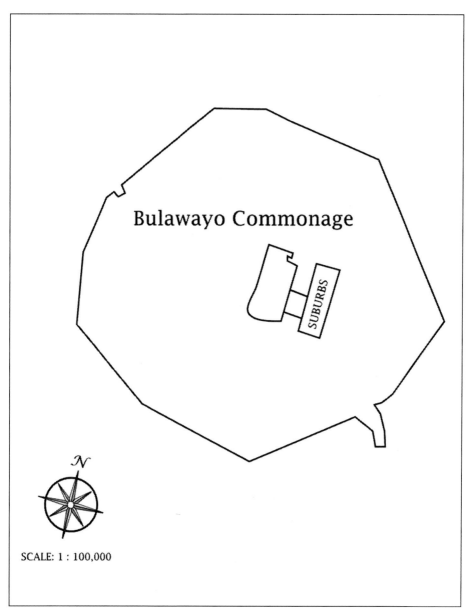

Bulawayo Commonage

SUBURBS

N

SCALE: 1 : 100,000

2. Bulawayo Commonage area before the development of townships

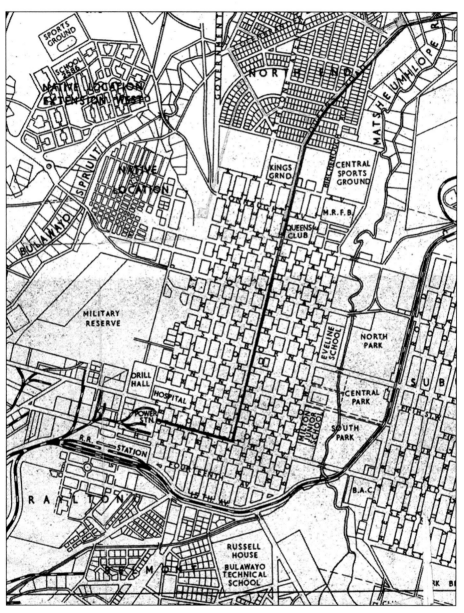

3. Bulawayo and the Location to the West, 1960s

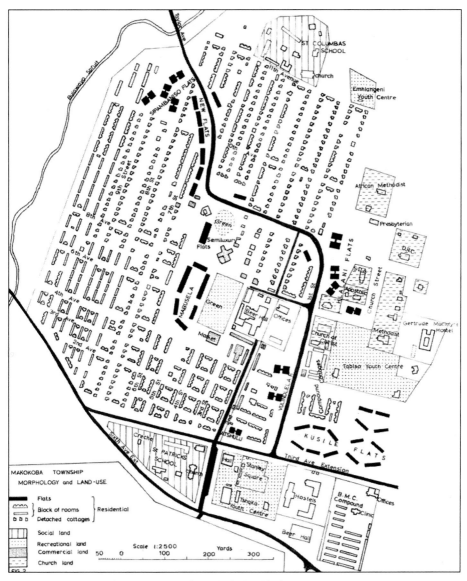

4. Makokoba, 1970

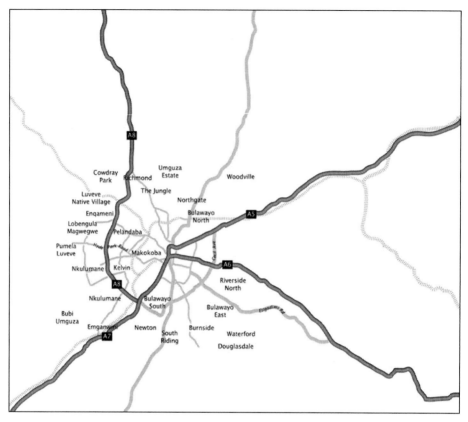

5. Bulawayo and the Western Commonage, 2010

Many of the original members of the Victoria column sold their claims to gold depos-
its, land and loot and happily left 'Grass Town'. They were replaced by men 'crowding
up from Joburg and the Transvaal, English mostly but with a good mixture of Australian, American and German'.[16] It was because Bulawayo's early white population
came from so many different places that the town insisted so strongly on proclaiming
and celebrating its British character.

Colonial Bulawayo was from the beginning a rough town. There was 'almost night-
ly violence' among whites – and until 1897 no jail in which to put white offenders.
African offenders, however, were taken to the 'Military Reserve', where they were:

> tied up to a post in front of the orderly room and whacked with a whip made of raw hippo or
> rhino hide … Every cut takes a good bit of flesh out of the niggers.[17]

Force was used too in order to provide for the town's labour needs. The Native Commissioner and police went out on raids for men. In June 1894, for instance, over a
thousand Africans were brought into Bulawayo from Gwanda, registered and allocated to 'contractors, private persons and firms, with a proportion being retained for
government works'.[18] Cattle were being seized and driven in to the bluntly named
Loot Kraal in Bulawayo.

It should have come as no surprise when in the last week of March 1896 the Ndebele rose up, killed every white outside Bulawayo, and advanced upon the town. Faced
with bankruptcy, and even with death, the white residents lashed out at nearby Africans. They sallied out from the laager to use the weapon of fire. All around Bulawayo
there were blazing villages. Fire was once again the idiom of black/white interaction.

In June 1896 the laager was relieved. Before the second Ndebele war, white Bulawayo had been 'a hearty, devil-may-care, kicking, smoking-concerting' town: during
it, Bulawayo had become 'stern, earnest, sobered, with corpses in the veld and rebels
dangling on trees'. But it was still overwhelmingly a town of young bachelors. At the
end of 1896 there were six thousand white men in Bulawayo and only a hundred white
women. 'The rowdy strain,' writes Ransford, lay 'pretty close to the surface.'[19]

It surfaced again with the coming of the railway to Bulawayo at the end of October
1897. Bulawayo was now 'Railhead'. Gold riches had proved illusory. But now Bulawayo became the town of the transport riders, during a brief period when trading
with a wagon was regarded as a manly, British adventure. As Stanley Portal Hyatt put
it in his eulogy of Bulawayo between 1897 and 1904:

> Practically the whole country was supplied from there. Scores of wagons left the town every
> day, loaded with stores of every conceivable kind, from boilers … to parcels of millinery. The
> town was flourishing as it had never flourished before, and will certainly never flourish again …
> [Around 1900] the white men could be counted in hundreds [and] tens of thousands of pounds
> worth of stuff would change hands in the morning … The transport riders dominated.

The centre of all activity was the Market Square, where goods were loaded and the
transport riders drank – and often fought – in the many bars, before going off on

[16] Henry Scott Turner to Mother, 4 May 1984, Godlonton Collection, University of Zimbabwe.
[17] Ruck to Father, 15 December 1894, RU7/1/1, National Archives, Harare.
[18] Secretary, British South Africa Company to Colonial Office, 21 July 1897, Cawston Papers, Mss. Afr. S.81,
Rhodes House, Oxford.
[19] Ransford, p. 132. The contrasting assessments of the town before and after March 1896 are quoted by Ransford from the Bulawayo Sketch.

(or after returning from) expeditions often of hundreds of miles. They argued about what kind of cattle were the best to pull their wagons, and whether it was best to employ Coloured or black South African or Ndebele team leaders. Casually dressed, they despised the government servants and the clerks in the mining officers and the assistants in the stores. Such men 'would have lost their way had they gone about three miles from the township [but they wore] riding breeches, puttee leggings and a hunting stock'.[20]

The future belonged, however, to these timid civilians. By 1904 the railway had extended beyond Bulawayo and the transport riders had departed. In Hyatt's racist eyes 'there were [then] but three real white men at the Market, in addition to the auctioneers. The rest of the crowd consisted of Greeks, coolies, half-castes and local savages. The glory of Bulawayo had departed for ever.'[21]

Bulawayo settled down to be neither a pioneer town nor a gold-rush town nor a transport rider town but a town whose business was commerce and the railway. The Bulawayo Municipality represented commerce. Meanwhile the Railways ran a virtual town within a town – their own white 'suburb', Raylton; their own, terrible, compounds for African workers. White women came in ever greater numbers. Suburban housing spread to the east of the city. Respectability was setting in.[22] But the very respectability of early twentieth-century Bulawayo made its white citizens all the more anxious to commemorate their stormy past and their eventual victory over the Ndebele. A statue of Cecil Rhodes was erected at one intersection in Main Street; facing it at another intersection was the Rebellion Monument, bearing 259 names of whites killed in 1896, and unequivocally surmounted by a Gardner machine gun, which had mown down the Ndebele fighting-men during the 1893 war. Main Street was emphatically a place in which to remember white triumph.[23] There were some five to six thousand Europeans living in Bulawayo in the early 1900s; more or less the same number of black servants and employees also lived within the boundaries of white Bulawayo.[24] But whites were determined that these African residents should 'live within the cracks', as Yvonne Vera memorably puts it. In February 1898, for example, the local journal, *Rhodesia*, expressed 'some little disgust … at the growing familiarity adopted by the natives in town, who coolly take possession of the footpaths and calmly jostle the white settlers, their wives and daughters in calm disregard of class distinction and propriety'. Responding to such protests, the City Council drafted a by-law which prohibited 'Kaffirs, Basuto, Hottentots, Bushmen and the like' from using the pavements. The Council's lawyers advised that all that was needed in the by-law was the single designation 'Native', and the measure was implemented in September 1894.[25] After 1894, as Vera writes:

20 Hyatt, pp. 30-3.
21 Ibid., p. 33.
22 Ransford remarks that 'it seemed that the old free-wheeling days were really coming to an end when a florist shop opened in Abercorn Street', and the Mayor took action against white prostitutes because ratepayers claimed their activities were lowering property values.' Ransford, p. 143.
23 It was, indeed, appropriate for Yvonne Vera to begin her township novel, *Butterfly Burning*, with a scene of hanging in 1896 and to show in the rest of her novel how this shaped the life of the township resident, Fumbatha, whose father was one of the hanged.
24 Thornton, Chapter 1, pp. 20-1, discusses the controversy in the late 1890s over shanty accommodation within European Bulawayo; the fear of epidemic and crime; and the attempted enforcement of a regulation in 1901 that only Africans employed in the town should be allowed to reside there.
25 *Rhodesia*, 12 February 1898; Coghlan and Welsh to Town Clerk, 16 September 1904, file 23.2.1R, Box 5700, National Archives, Bulawayo.

the black people learn how to move through the city with speed, and due attention, to bow their heads down and slide past walls, to walk without making the shadow more pronounced than the body or the body clearer than the shadow ... The people walk in the city without encroaching on the pavements from which they are banned.[26]

The Making of an African Bulawayo

Thus white Bulawayo proclaimed its triumph. Nevertheless, the new town was in reality very much a shared creation of whites and blacks. White masters depended on and lived cheek by jowl with black servants. Black labour built the streets and buildings of the town. (As Vera writes of her novel's hero, Fumbatha, all his life he 'has done nothing but build, and through this contact, Bulawayo is a city he understands closely, which he has held brick by brick, on his palm ... He has built. When he is dead, his hands will remain everywhere.')[27] And more than this, side by side with the white city, there grew up an African town.

It has become a truism in the urban historiography of southern Africa that towns were a colonial creation; that whites controlled place and space, movement and residence; that Africans lived in the towns on sufferance and in bewilderment. In the 1940s and 1950s there were many reports on Bulawayo which described the African Location in precisely these terms, as traumatized and chaotic. These reports argued that an overwhelming number of short-term male labour migrants, drawn from all over central Africa, had prevented the emergence of family life or common cultural institutions. The 'bachelors' remained in Bulawayo only briefly and neither understood nor desired to cultivate an urban culture. There were no leaders or spokesmen with deep roots in the town. There were few women in the Location and those that were, were there only on sufferance. White administrators and African men agreed that a woman's place was in the countryside and believed that urban women must be prostitutes or shebeen queens. I shall discuss the 1940s and 1950s and these assessments later in this book. But it is important now to emphasize that the Bulawayo Location was certainly not like this from the beginning.

Admittedly, many of the Africans who set themselves up in the mid-1890s west of the white town, in what came to be called the Location, did not stay there long. The frankly racist Hyatt described the occupants of the 'collection of hovels, many of them built of flattened out paraffin tins' as 'Kaffirs from down country – Cape half-breeds, Fingoes, Zulu and a few Basutu'; he also described how the white transport riders invaded the Location with sjamboks and drove out 'two thirds of its people, starting [them] back on the long and weary journey to Cape Colony.'[28] Among those who remained, however, were men and women who had every intention of settling in Bulawayo and who established long-lasting and influential dynasties there. There were two main kinds of African 'settlers': Ndebeles and immigrants.

Among the Ndebele who returned to the Bulawayo area soon after the fires of Lobengula's town had died down were some of his queens. One of the them, Moho, built cottages in the Location so that members of the royal family could be accom-

---

26 Yvonne Vera, *Butterfly Burning*, pp. 3-4.
27 Vera, p. 20.
28 Hyatt, p. 31. Thornton cites a trooper writing home to his mother describing how in January 1894, in order to stop a fight in the Location, he and his patrol had ridden in and 'knocked [the participants] about a bit and soon stopped it. The more you kick them the more they like you.'

modated when they visited the old centre of the Ndebele monarchy. Some informants can still remember seeing the queens:

> I can tell you whose stands these were [says Gile Ndlovu]. Can you see the corner of St Columba's? There used to be houses for King Lobengula's wives. There were four of them. When they were going into the town they wore black dresses and scarves on their head, as if they were Roman Catholic sisters. When going into town you would see them one after the other. We used to watch them as girls.[29]

But Moho was not only a traditionalist. She became an ardent Christian and patroness of an African independent church.[30] Later, as we shall see, Lobengula's sons and grandsons visited the Bulawayo Location and some of them settled there.

As well as the royals, other Khumalos also settled in the new Bulawayo and came to provide a combined traditional and modernizing leadership. One of these was Bikwapi Manyoba Khumalo, a member of the *Inzond'ebuhlungu* (painful anger) branch of the family and a direct descendant of Mzilikazi's own ancestor, Ndabezitha.[31] Bikwapi came to Bulawayo in the 1890s as a young man in his twenties and lived there for more than fifty years. Though accepted as an Ndebele aristocrat, Bikwapi was very much a modern man. He worked as an ox wagon driver and 'travelled widely throughout both Matabeleland and Mashonaland'. He was fluent in most of the African languages spoken in the Location. He was a staunch Anglican. His wife, Madhlodhlo, was 'one of the very few Africans who owned stands in the Old Location'. The house she built for her family was still standing in 1954. Bikwapi's mastery of languages, his knowledge of the outside districts from which labour migrants came, and his Khumalo identity combined to make him a power in Location politics and he held office in the first Location Advisory Board. By Madhlodhlo he had a son, Arthur Manyoba Khumalo.

As befitted an addition to the *Inzond'ebuhlungu*, the baby was given the additional name of 'Sipambaniso' ('stirrer of trouble'), by which he was to become known. The name was appropriate to a man, born in Bulawayo, who was to become from the 1920s not only the Location's foremost sportsman and its most fashionable society man, but also a politician who was able to combine imaginative appeals to Ndebele tradition with proto-nationalism and radical trade union activity.[32] By contrast to his widely roaming father, Sipambaniso was thought of as the quintessential urban man:

> Mrs Manyoba and her son [wrote Charlton Ngcebetsha] had no connection whatsoever with tribal life in the country districts seeing that Sipambaniso was born in the Location and grew up there.[33]

---

[29] Interview between Simon Mlotshwa and Gile Ndlovu, Makokoba, 25 January 2001. Gile was born in 1924.

[30] Moho's evidence to the Native Affairs Commission, March 1930, ZAN 1/1/1, National Archives, Harare. Moho complained that since the Municipality had destroyed her cottages, 'when I have visitors I am crowded out and have to share a hut with another Queen'. Moho's obituary appeared in the *Bantu Mirror*, 2 February 1946. According to this, Moho married Lobengula in 1890. After his death she lived in the Location and in the 1920s travelled to South Africa at her own expense to bring the Methodist Episcopal Church to Bulawayo.

[31] In January 2001 Bikwapi's ancestry was confirmed by the Khumalo custodian at Old Bulawayo, Gideon Joyi Khumalo, in an interview with Lynette Nyathi. The career of Ndabezitha and his place in Mzilikazi's genealogy is set out in Pathisa Nyathi, *Alvord Mabena. The Man and His Roots*, Priority Projects, Bulawayo, 2000, pp. 5, 11.

[32] An obituary of Bikwapi Manyoba Khumalo, who died 'in his seventies' on 27 October 1950, appeared in the *Bantu Mirror* of 25 November 1950. Bikwapi was reported as being able to speak Shona, Nyanja, Kalanga, and several other African languages. His funeral was attended by 'hundreds of Africans of all tribes in Bulawayo African Townships'. His son, Sipambaniso, figures largely in later chapters of this book.

[33] *Home News*, 25 December 1954.

It is strangely appropriate that Madhlodhlo is remembered today by the name of one of the township beer halls.[34]

Even if they were not able to establish homes – and political dynasties – in the Location, many other Ndebele gathered around the colonial town. As Yoshikuni writes:

> When the fin-de-siècle turmoil subsided, many Ndebele drifted back to their original home areas. They concentrated on the new Bulawayo, which emerged out of the ashes of the old Bulawayo, the centre of the Ndebele state. Many of them settled on [peri-urban] farms in Hyde Park, Rangemore and Tshabalala, and youths came into Bulawayo to work for wages. At the start of the century no less than 1,800 tax-paying indigenous males were found living in the town. The Ndebele Bulawayo was larger than any pre-colonial Ndebele settlements, and rivalled the European Bulawayo in numbers.[35]

As well as these various Ndebele, many immigrants also determined to make their future in Bulawayo. More than 50 years later, the son of such a family, J.N. Ncube, founded a Bulawayo and District African Pioneers Association, for 'those who have stayed in Bulawayo since its inception and whose parents had stands here before the Council was properly organised [and] who have no other home but Bulawayo'.[36] In 1958 Ncube declared that: 'I still call myself a Pioneer of Bulawayo and my followers call themselves so ... My parents came to Bulawayo in 1899 and built their own stand at 6th Street, now no. 1250, 6th Street, where we still live. We even had houses and rooms to let and the Bulawayo labour rented under us and pioneered Bulawayo, with our labour, our sweat, etc. in cooperation with the white man. What Bulawayo is today is because of our labour and sweat. We began stands in Bulawayo. We are truly Pioneers.'[37]

Some of these immigrant pioneers were young, unmarried women. One was the teacher, Martha, an Mfengu, who came to Bulawayo from South Africa in 1897. Martha had been trained at Lovedale and had taught for a time in South Africa. In 1897 she built herself a house on a Commonage plot near the Location and became a leading figure in its educational and political life. Like Bikwapi, she was a staunch Christian and became a deaconess in the Apostolic Faith Mission. She remained in black Bulawayo until her death more than forty years later. In 1912 she married a Mozambican migrant, James Ngano. As Martha Ngano she became famous in the 1920s. She was the spokeswoman of the Bantu Voters League and the organizer of female political protest in the Location.[38] Just as Bikwapi Khumalo enjoyed the support of non-Ndebele in the Location, so the Mfengu Martha Ngano was backed by two of Lobengula's sons, Nyamanda and Madholi.

Another remarkable young woman 'pioneer' was Elizabeth Makubalo. Elizabeth

---

[34] One of MaDhlodhlo's grandsons, Msongelwayizizwe Petros Khumalo, remembers that the Location was known as *ezitendeni* ('in the stands'). It was 'composed of people's homes made up of pole and dagga huts,' though some of these were developed into brick cottages as time went on. As well as his grandmother, many other Ndebele women owned stands – 'more than one MaKhumalo; Masibanda.' Interview with Busani Mpofu, 26 July 2000.

[35] Tsuneo Yoshikuni, 'Notes on the influence of town-country relations on African urban history before 1957: experiences of Salisbury and Bulawayo', in B. Raftopoulos and T. Yoshikuni, *Sites of Struggle. Essays in Zimbabwe's Urban History*, Weaver Press, Harare, 1999, p. 117.

[36] J.S. Ncube to Director of Native Administration, 20 November 1959, SO.8, file 178, Housing Department, Bulawayo Municipality.

[37] J.S. Ncube, Open Letter to Charlton Ngcebetsha, 2 December 1958, SO.8, Vol. 4, T Box 150.

[38] Superintendent of Natives, Bulawayo to Chief Native Commissioner, 17 May 1924, S 84/A/260, National Archives, Harare. For Martha Ngano's political career see T.O. Ranger, *The African Voice in Southern Rhodesia, 1898–1930,* Heinemann, London, 1970, Chapters 4 and 5.

was born in Kimberley in the late 1870s, where she became attached to B.B. Dabi, a strong Presbyterian. Together they took the extraordinary decision to migrate to Bulawayo in that most alarming of all years, 1896:

> The career of Mr and Mrs Dabi [wrote the *Bantu Mirror* after her death] forms the nucleus of the Presbyterian Church in Matabeleland ... They came in 1896 as ardent youths, with the pioneers from Kimberley. They went by train as far as Lobatsi, Bechuanaland, and the rest of the way by stage coach to Bulawayo. Mr Dabi was working in the Post Office in Bulawayo afterwards, and Elizabeth Makubalo as a nurse girl. They soon married and settled down in what is now Bulawayo Location. There they opened the school and then a church was opened as well. For many years the Presbyterian Church and school was referred to as 'at Dabi's'. The great work of the Presbyterian Church in Matabeleland sprang from Mr and Mrs Dabi.[39]

From the beginning of Bulawayo Location, then, there were Africans who retained a connection with the traditions of the old Ndebele state, and there were African immigrants who saw themselves as modernizing pioneers.[40] Both kinds built homes and raised families. However ramshackle it may have been, the early Location was certainly not a place only of short-term, bewildered, 'bachelor' labour migrants, unable to make sense of urban life. There were some families who maintained a sense of what Ndebele towns had been like; there were others who had experienced urban society in South Africa.[41] As the Ndebele became Christianized and the immigrants became localized, a shared sense of Bulawayo as an African town emerged. It was no accident that by far the earliest demand for an elected Advisory Board in any Southern Rhodesian town should have emanated from the Bulawayo Location a mere ten years after the founding of the colonial town. On 11 November 1903, in a beautiful copperplate hand, fourteen petitioners addressed the Mayor asking for the establishment of an elected Native Vigilance Board. They made their request 'on behalf of the residents of the Bulawayo Native Location, by their special request'. The Board would 'look after the wants of the people generally, report on the state of the Location, lay their grievances before the authorities'.[42] Needless to say, the Bulawayo Council dismissed the request out of hand. But James Mkize, Manzama, David Mavikana, Elijah Gaucha,

---

[39] *Bantu Mirror*, 21 May 1949. For the Dabis' Kimberley background see fn.37. In 1905 the Location Inspector noted the Dabis' achievement, reporting that there was 'one Mohammedan and one Presbyterian church in the Location itself; Church of England and Wesleyan on the outside'. 'Evidence' of Inspector F. Fallon, 1905, file 23/1/3R, Box 5622, National Archives, Bulawayo.

[40] There were some men from this early period who combined both experiences. One example is S.J. Mazwi, who eventually rose to become Chief Interpreter at the Bulawayo High Court, speaking Xhosa, Shona, and Tswana as well as Ndebele and English. Mazwi came from the Enhla grade of the Ndebele state. Around 1900 he was taken to South Africa by the Anglican priest, Father Wilson. There he became a teacher and married an Mfengu woman. Later he returned to Bulawayo and taught in the Location at the Anglican St Columba's mission, where Sipambaniso Manyoba Khumalo was one of his pupils. Subsequently he joined the Municipal Police and patrolled the Location. *Home News*, 23 August 1958.

[41] For reconstructions of the 'progressive' African life of Kimberley in this period, see Brian Willan, *Sol Plaatje: South African Nationalist, 1876–1932*, James Currey, London, 1988; John Comaroff, Brian Willan and Andrew Reed (eds), *The Mafeking Diaries of Sol. T. Plaatje*, James Currey, 1990. Comaroff's 'Introduction' tells of the presence in Kimberley of a 'well-established African mission-educated community ... committed Christians and church-goers [who] believed firmly in the ideals of progress, "improvement" and individual advancement through education and hard work. Among blacks in Kimberley, these principles and values fostered a fervent loyalty to the British imperial government ... and self-confident enthusiasm for exploring to the full the opportunities which Africans, individually and collectively, saw before themselves.' pp. 6-7. The supreme exemplar of Kimberley values, Sol Plaatje, later spoke in the Bulawayo Location with great effect.

[42] One of the Bulawayo Municipal files held in the National Archives, Bulawayo, deals with the Location in 1930. It contains, however, this much earlier document which has been misplaced, since it dates from 11 November 1903 rather than from 1930.

Martin Magoti, James Teke, Charles Khaka and the rest deserve to be remembered as pioneers of Zimbabwean urban consciousness. Yoshikuni goes so far as to say:

> These developments made Bulawayo's social topography unique amongst urban centres in Southern Rhodesia, or even in southern Africa as a whole. Whilst its heart was a 'European town' along the lines of Salisbury or Johannesburg, its agglomeration very much resembled the 'dual town', possessing within itself both colonial and indigenous elements. Inevitably, the town was to be haunted by the shadow of the pre-colonial traditions of the Ndebele, as well as by their voice under colonial rule ... Ndebele migrants to Bulawayo quickly developed dense networks of self-help institutions and associations in town. As early as the 1910s, formalised Ndebele self-help associations, like the Ihilo Lo'muzi (Eyes of Family) Society and the Amandebele Patriotic Society were active in Bulawayo ... Such Ndebele institutions ... also came to interlock with those of other migrant groups, a process which led to the emergence of a relatively close-knit community of associations, societies and clubs. This community fostered a spirit of solidarity among Bulawayo Africans.[43]

The early Location was a place of families committed to the development of an urban culture. Some of these pioneers, and later some of their children, offered vitally important social and political leadership. As for African women, so far from being a marginal minority, in many ways they dominated the early Location. In 1897 they were even a numerical majority. A report in May of that year revealed that 48 men lived in the Location, many of whom were engaged in the wagon trade. There were 67 women and 49 children.[44] Small though it was, the Location contained about as many black and brown women as the total number of white women in European Bulawayo. Moreover, since many of the men were away trekking, it was the women who literally constructed the African town. As we have seen, Madhlodhlo built the family home and saw to the education of her son, while Bikwapi Khumalo travelled the country.

Around 1905 the first Location Inspector, F. Fallon, estimated that there were 600 residents in the Location. The composition of the population had changed and there were now an increasing number of 'single' workers living there among the pioneer families. By this time there were more men than women. But women continued to be dominant.[45] Fallon estimated that 147 of the huts in the Location had been erected by Africans; only 32 were Council buildings. The majority of the privately erected huts were built and owned by women. Some were the homes of Ndebele and immigrant families. We have already seen how during the 1890s Lobengula's queens and Christian Ndebele and immigrant women built homes on stands in the Location. But now, in the 1900s, many women built huts to rent out to 'single' men. The economics of the business was spelt out by Fallon. The landlady paid the Council 5s a month for a stand and a 2s 4d 'lodger fee'. Two lodgers lived in one hut and there were usually two or three huts on a plot. Lodgers might pay as much as 7s 6d rent a month. A landlady with three huts and six lodgers was making thirty shillings a month profit.[46] Some women had several plots. One such was 'grandmother' Nomacela Koza, born in the

43 Yoshikuni, op.cit., pp. 117-18.
44 Thornton, Chapter 1, p. 23. The statistics are taken from a report on the proceedings of the Sanitary Board in the *Matabele Times* of 22 May 1897. The majority of the men were described as 'Colonial Natives working as wagon drivers or literate clerks'.
45 They were evidently dominant in Location feuds also. Fallon told the Town Clerk in May 1907 that 'a great disturbance by two black races took place in the Native Location ... I arrested four women and charged them at the police station.' Fallon to Town Clerk, 31 May 1907, file 23/1/3R, Box 5622, National Archives, Bulawayo.
46 'Evidence' of Inspector F. Fallon, 1905, file 23/1/3R Box 5622, National Archives, Bulawayo.

Matopos during Lobengula's reign. 'When the Location was started', ran the obituary of this notable pioneer, 'she owned three stands'; she earned enough in rents to be able to establish herself as a cattle owner and cultivator on Hyde Park farm.

Stands in the Location soon became valuable commodities. By the 1910s rights to them were being sold for several pounds each. Some women drew on their salaries as teachers; some raised the funds to buy stands by brewing beer. In 1905, for instance, women were brewing beer legally in sixty of the 179 occupied huts in the Location and selling 'large quantities'.[47] Sales of beer continued even after the Municipality had tried to ban brewing. Other women raised funds through prostitution. Thus Bakwasi, a young Basuto woman who lived in hut 34 in the Location, gave evidence to a police inquiry into sexual relations between white men and black women. Bakwasi had been born in total poverty. 'I was born in Bulawayo at the Railway Station in the same year as Cecil Rhodes died [1902].' Her father abandoned his wife and child and went to Johannesburg. But her mother was determined to obtain her own house. She went north to Wankie and lived with a white railway shunter; later she took Bakwasi to Gwelo and had sex with other whites. It was a profitable business. Black prostitutes charged white customers 20s a night: if they stayed with a white man for a time they got parting presents of several pounds cash. It was not surprising, then, that Bakwasi's mother was able to tell her that 'we had earned enough money to buy a house. My mother bought two stands in the Bulawayo Location. She paid £15 for the two. We did not [do] prostitution in Bulawayo.' The indomitable mother had risen from the railway platform to the status of home-owner and Location landlady.[48]

Even today many informants remember the names of the African landladies and recall them with equal respect, whether they began as Ndebele aristocrats or as dashing women of the town. In addition to Madhlodhlo, the litany of 'respectable' women stand-owners included MaZondo, Masuku, MaThebe, MaNcube, MaHadebe, Ma-Mkhewanazi and many more.[49] 'I heard', says Mr N. Moyo, 'that 2nd and 3rd street areas in Makokoba were earlier on occupied by women who owned stands, and that these were the people we always referred to as the real true citizens of Makokoba.'[50] But an even greater – and indeed awed – tribute is paid to a woman who is remembered for behaving with as much freedom and strength as a man, the Shona stand-owner, Mary Mutoko:

> I heard a lot about such women [says Mrs Bhetamina Ndlovu], for example Madhlodhlo, the mother of Sipambaniso. There were others like Mary Mutoko, that physically very beautiful

47 Ibid. At this time the Bulawayo Council made no attempt to prohibit brewing by women. Inspector Fallon suggested in 1905 that beer-brewing should be regulated and controlled, though he admitted that 'if allowed in small quantities I believe myself that it is very good for the Kafir as a medicine'.
48 Evidence of Bakwasi, September 1920, File 33, S.1222/1, National Archives, Harare. The many files contained in S 1222/1 are full of details of Location life; of Ndebele, Tswana, Sotho, Xhosa, and Mfengu girls, many born in the Location; of white men seeking sex; of white men falling in love and sending sentimental love letters. Some of the girls sell sex; others accept white men as their 'sweethearts'; many indignantly repudiate the suggestions of African 'procurers' that they should have sex with a white; others complain to the Location Superintendent or the Police. One stand-owner, Mary Manukwa, an unmarried Sotho woman who lived in her own house, went so far as to hide a policeman under her bed when she was propositioned by a white carpenter. The carpenter, in his dark clothes from attending a funeral, tried to have sex with her; the policeman leapt out from under the bed and told him that he should be ashamed of himself. 'He was a member of the same church as I was.' 'Complaint of Mary Manuka', file 46.
49 Interviews between Busani Mpofu and Prince Gumede, Mrs Bhetamina Ndlovu, Mrs L. Mlotshwa, Diki Maphosa, June 2000.
50 Interview between Busani Mpofu and N. Moyo, Makokoba, 24 July 2000.

lady who used to beat up men like nothing, I tell you. Mary Mutoko did not fear any man and most township men were very much afraid of her.[51]

Prince Gumede recalls Mary as 'light-skinned and very attractive ... physically very strong. Mary Mutoko was staying with her boyfriend (not really her husband) but she could go out and do whatever she wanted with other men. She always agreed to go out with other men but if they failed to give her the money she demanded such men were always given a thorough beating ... These property-owning women were very popular women at Makokoba.'[52] As we shall see, the status and position of women in the Bulawayo Location underwent a sad decline after the mid-1920s. It was good for Makokoba women in later decades to remember these powerful figures from the Location's past.

It is Gumede, again, who describes the highest mark of respect paid to these pioneers. In later years, the Bulawayo African Township Advisory Board reserved the few remaining places in the Old Cemetery for 'founders' of the Location. As they died, the women who had once owned stands were buried in the cemetery. And a year later there was performed at their graves the ceremony to bring back their spirits, the *umbuyiso*:

> For those people who had their 'roots' in the township, the *umbuyiso* ceremony for each and every one was always conducted in the township ... I can remember that a number of popular top women who had earlier on had their own stands, like MaZondo, Masuku, Sipambaniso's mother and many more had *umbuyiso* ceremonies conducted here in the township after their death ... As the new family's spirit incarnate, a daughter was always chosen [since] the deceased was a mother.[53]

The Politics of White Bulawayo

These white and black beginnings determined the nature of politics in Bulawayo before 1930. On the white side, the town was dominated not – as is often said – by mining capital, but by import-based commerce, by railway capital and by artisanal railway labour. On the black side, early political movements were the expression of all the elements which produced the Bulawayo Location – Ndebele consciousness, 'progressive' immigrant aspirations, and the dominant influence of women stand-holders. The two strands were, of course, entwined together by white racial arrogance and by black resentment.

When it began in September 1897 the Bulawayo Town Council was the mouth-piece of 'the merchants of Bulawayo represented by the Chamber of Commerce'.[54] The town's traders went through some bad times. During the depression of 1903

51 Ibid.
52 Interview between Busani Mpofu and Prince Gumede, 14 June 2000. Mary Mutoko is vividly recalled for her beauty and her beating up of men in the oral memory of Sakubva Township in Mutare as well as in Makokoba, Bulawayo. She was a woman who made a deep impression wherever she went. I owe this information to Ireen Mudeka, who is researching into the urban history of Mutare.
53 Ibid. For a more extensive discussion of these issues see T.O. Ranger, 'Dignifying Death: Burials in Bulawayo, 1900–1960', Economic History Seminar, University of Zimbabwe, September 2000.
54 Thornton, chapter 1, p. 17. Thornton is here quoting evidence given to the Martin inquiry into the causes of the 1896 revolt by a Bulawayo trader, Lothar Hope, who stressed 'the rather unique position' enjoyed by the Chamber of Commerce 'towards the Government of these territories. Whenever we have a grievance the way is open before us.' The Council was established as a result of the representations of the Chamber.

there were many trading bankruptcies and retrenchments. Many whites despaired of the future of Bulawayo. The editor of the *Bulawayo Observer* noted that:

> of all the blunders committed during the last ten years none it seems is as palpable as the establishment of the town of Bulawayo. Capital and enterprise have made it a commercial centre, but the population cannot now exist merely on sentiment.[55]

But commerce survived and gradually prospered, enjoying a period of confidence not seriously challenged again until the Depression of 1929–30. A significant number of the Town Councillors were also members of the Chamber of Commerce. They were not pioneers, scouts or transport riders. But they saw themselves, often literally, as the builders of an urban civilization.

Nowhere is this self-image more clearly expressed than in Allister Macmillan's gazetteer, published at the end of the 1930s and including a paean of romantic praise for the achievements of Bulawayo merchant capital in replacing savagery with civilization:

> The sun, dragging its fiery chariot across the heavens and plunging into the cooling earth, is a reminder of a blood-red beginning to this infant city, which lives, works, sleeps and plays in the heart of Nature undefiled ... It seems a far cry from those [pioneer] days to the Bulawayo of today but one cannot hear the beating of the tom-toms in the Location, or the shrill whistles, or watch the rhythmic beat of feet, without thinking of painted witch-doctors and wizards, quivering assegais and the savagery which made the occupation of Bulawayo more than a mere adventure.[56]

Macmillan listed the achievements of Bulawayo town councillors, taking a particular pleasure in those of his fellow Scots. ('Wherever civilisation penetrates, the Scotsman is there as a matter of course.') Councillor Ellenbogen, Mayor of Bulawayo in 1929, was the owner of Ellenbogen and Co., furnishers, on Abercorn and Selbourne:

> The influence of furniture is a subject on which much could be written ... when furniture is artistic as well as utilitarian the constant impressions received from it by the subconscious ... mind are of greater importance than enters into the philosophy of the uninitiated or unreflective ... Special interest attaches [to Ellenbogen's] accurate copies of the most notable styles of the past and present [and] clever creations that are especially adapted to Colonial necessities, customs and idiosyncrasies.[57]

Councillor Issels was from a family engineering firm established in 1894, which paid 'skilled attention to Maxims, Nordenfelds and other weapons which contributed very considerably to the establishment of law and order'. Councillor Cowden, who had been mayor for four consecutive terms, owned a building firm which had erected 'very many of the charming residences that make Bulawayo so attractive as a home town', and who were 'sewerage contractors to the Municipality'. Everywhere in their work, said Macmillan, 'there has been recognition of the essentials of beauty with utility'. Councillor Harris was a miller; Councillor Maver was an auctioneer.[58]

Maver had also been Chieftain of the Caledonian Society, whose annual Burns Night dinners were the great social and political event of Bulawayo. Another Scot-

---

55 *Bulawayo Observer*, 28 November 1903.
56 Allister Macmillan (ed.), *Eastern Africa and Rhodesia: Historical and Descriptive Commercial and Industrial Facts, Figures and Resources*, Collingridge, London, 1931, pp. 237–9.
57 Ibid., pp. 265–6. Ellenbogen's employed forty whites and its carpenters worked under the direction of 'English experts'.
58 Ibid., pp. 287–9.

tish councillor – now himself Chieftain – was John McDonald, of McDonald and Macfarlane, builders.[59] But Macmillan's most ardent hymn of praise was devoted to the business of yet another Scottish town councillor, Donald Macintyre, who was to become 'city boss' of Bulawayo. Macintyre had been trained as an apprentice in Hubbard's Bakery in Glasgow; as Master Baker he had taken over Osborn's Bakery in Bulawayo in 1920 and transformed it; by 1930 he had a café in Bulawayo, ran a sweet factory and owned bakeries in Gwelo and Salisbury:

> There are some establishments in Bulawayo which call for superlatives of expression ... Osborn's Café is delightful in its every aspect, as well as in its services and supplies. Its 100 foot of magnificent plate-glass frontage forms the finest window exhibition of the products of the baker and confectioner in Rhodesia. Its artistic interior is an object lesson in chromatic harmony, in elegance and utility [going much beyond] the satisfying of primeval requirements ... Osborn's is specialised to appease hunger and thirst or the more subtle needs that wait not upon appetite but are subservient ever to the fastidious daintiness which modern eclectism has evolved.[60]

These councillors were the men who had built, furnished and fed Bulawayo; who employed large number of whites; and who had done all this, if Macmillan were to be believed, with as much of an eye to beauty as to utility and profit. No wonder that they felt and expressed such self-confidence. But there was another side to Bulawayo politics and even to the Council's membership.

Donald Macintyre himself, the successful baker, was also a leader of the Rhodesian Labour Party, which had emerged in 1923 as a populist rather than socialist political expression of white trade unionism. Macintyre had joined the British Labour Party during his days as an apprentice in Glasgow and retained Labour sympathies in Rhodesia.

So also had another, rather more representative, figure of Bulawayo labour politics – who was to become a key figure on the Bulawayo City Council in the 1950s – James Stuart McNeillie. McNeillie had been a blacksmith's assistant in Scotland. Like Macintyre, he had a lifelong resentment of ruling-class bosses. 'Even in the army [during the First World War] I always had a little feeling of resentment when anybody was being sat on.' In 1919 he saw an advertisement for 'specialist tradesmen' on Rhodesia Railways and set off for Bulawayo. He found that:

> Pay and prospects were very much better – very, very much better, and my first month's salary on the Railway quite astonished me. It very nearly reached £60.

McNeillie continued to have 'a feeling of resentment', however. In 1922 the bosses, including the Railway's management, campaigned for union with South Africa. 'It was the workers who were in favour of Responsible Government.' The Railway's administration tried to get their white employees to vote for Union, 'but the more they tried to do that, the more I think the employees went the other way, and there were some really rough, really rowdy meetings. I can remember meetings at the old Empire Theatre [in Bulawayo] where the employer representatives came on and made the great mistake of coming in with their dinner suits on ... Tomatoes and things of that kind were thrown at these pompous looking gentlemen.' Naturally, McNeillie

---

[59]   'It is noteworthy how many Scotsmen are engaged as builders and contractors in Rhodesia', remarked Macmillan. Other Scots listed in his directory are the builders F. McGregor and A. Ogston; the hotelier, McGarry; the plumber, J.M. Adam; the blacksmith, J.H. Grieve; the watchmaker, T. Forbes.
[60]   Macmillan, pp. 277-8.

joined the white railway trade union; equally naturally, he joined the Labour Party. Yet he was, of course, a British and Rhodesian patriot and a member of the Allan Wilson Masonic Lodge.[61]

In all these ways McNeillie was typical of the white artisanal culture of Bulawayo. The town was the stronghold of white trade unionism and of the Rhodesian Labour Party because it was the centre of the railway system. Rhodesia Railways were by far the largest employer of whites (and of blacks too) in Bulawayo. As Jon Lunn puts it, 'the railways could at times resemble a state within a state, replete with its own laws, language, science, philosophy and social structure'.[62] Certainly in Bulawayo the white railway employees lived in a town within a town. Their suburb, Raylton, led its own social and athletic existence, with its sports clubs and masonic lodges; white workers shopped in their own special discount co-operative shop; Raylton constituency went on returning Labour MPs long after the party had collapsed. White railway workers were proud of their skills and saw themselves as divided by a great gulf from mere 'labourers', who in this case happened to be black. They used the language of natural rights and moral economy; they clubbed together in ex-servicemen's leagues and masonic lodges; they 'created a place for themselves in the pantheon of pioneerism [and] took pride in their own part in promoting white civilisation, progress and Empire':

> As workers [ran an editorial in the *Rhodesian Railway Review*] we have (or should have) the greater part of the formation of Rhodesia's future ... In the hands of the railwayman lies a larger part of his country's economic health.[63]

White railwaymen were prepared to take radical action if their skills were ill-rewarded by pompous managers, or if their role in creating Rhodesia, and Bulawayo in particular, was ignored. Active trade unionists arrived from Britain between 1910 and 1914 influenced by the militancy of that time. Foremost among them was Jack Keller, who arrived in Bulawayo in 1912, a year after a great railway strike in Britain in which he had been 'a rank-and-file militant'. An imperial patriot, a freemason, an orator and a demagogue, Keller came to dominate the political life of Raylton, being returned as its MP in election after election. Keller was active in the formation of the Rhodesia Railway Workers Union (RRWU) in October 1917; he organized a successful strike in February 1919 and the vastly successful strike of March 1920 which won a 25 per cent increase in pay and an eight-hour day. In 1920 Keller and the white railwaymen gained support from white postal workers and white miners. The Administrator of the Colony declared with some exaggeration that the trade unions, and especially the railwaymen, controlled the country, rather than he himself. It was even truer that white unionists dominated Bulawayo. In 1922 the RRWU backed Responsible Government, denouncing General Smuts' repression of the white worker revolt on the Rand. In 1923 the RRWU sponsored the emergence of the Rhodesian Labour Party. Labour was stronger in Bulawayo than anywhere else in Rhodesia.

Yet white labour militancy had reached its peak and throughout the 1920s the

---

[61] Interview by D. Hartridge with James Stuart McNeillie, Bulawayo, 9 February 1972, ORAL/MA5, National Archives, Harare.

[62] Jon Lunn, *Capital and Labour on the Rhodesian Railway System, 1888–1947*, St Antony's/Macmillan, London, 1997, p. 85.

[63] Ibid., p. 88, quoting the *Rhodesian Railway Review*, 6 February 1922. This paragraph is derived from Lunn's chapter on 'White Workers on the Railways'. Lunn sums up the complex 'range of identities' of the white artisans: 'identities of grade, section, department, general occupation, class, gender, ethnicity and race', p. 89.

effectiveness of the RRWU seeped away. The Railway's administration managed to detach many workers from the union and to victimize its leaders. The Labour Party soon collapsed and was only revived in 1928, when Keller and two other members were elected to parliament. On the eve of the period covered in this book there was a climactic struggle between capital and labour, which took place particularly in Bulawayo. Keller's RRWU declared a strike in February 1929 in an attempt to recapture its lost influence. Government commandeered all petrol, cars, lorries and drivers so that communications could continue; the Railways ran a skeleton service with 'loyal' workers; white citizens established a paramilitary force, and settler support for the union lapsed because of fears that the strike would encourage an African revolt. As Lunn concludes, 'it was a defeat which almost spelt the end of the union'.[64]

There was, then, a sort of white class war in Bulawayo in the 1920s. But it pitched white workers against the Railways and the mines and never took the form of tension between railwaymen and Labour Party members on the one hand and the Bulawayo Municipal Council on the other. Labour Party activists like Macintyre and H.H. Davies were elected to the Council, where together with the other councillors they took the position that city affairs should not be made a matter of party politics. Rather than too blatantly representing the interests of big commercial capital, the Council came to take the view that its duty was to represent all the whites in the town who were connected in any way to trade – as importers, processors, retailers, employees or customers. These could be personified in the concept of the ratepayer. Representatives of Bulawayo white capital and of Bulawayo white labour (whose interests were often in any case hard to disentangle) combined on the Council to proclaim the virtues of a 'ratepayers' democracy'.

The ratepayer 'citizens' of Bulawayo could be expected to finance loans for the expansion of services – roads, water, sewerage and electricity – which were gradually put into place (though in 1930 Macmillan remarked that, despite its 'wide and magnificently laid-out streets, its large and handsome buildings, and its many charming residences', Bulawayo had 'developed with a sanitary systems as old as the Zimbabwe Ruins').[65] They could be expected to finance town parks and other amenities. But the Council resolutely defended its ratepayers against two other financial demands. They could not be expected to meet the costs of services, such as education and health, which were the responsibility of central government. And they could not be expected to pay for African housing or amenities. On these issues the Council came under constant pressure from white workers, the Ratepayers Association, and businessmen and employers alike.

Macmillan, whose eulogies of Bulawayo commerce I have quoted above, also eulogized the prosperity of the white worker in 1930. He thought that new arrivals, alighting at Bulawayo Station, could learn much from the double-storied block of railway offices, where there worked 'hundreds of clerks and typists' in a kind of socialist utopia, earning good salaries and working moderate hours. White bricklayers and carpenters earned over £40 a month; 'on the railways a strong trade union, a sympathetic management, and a measure of state control' had realized the ideal of a Linotype operator earning as much as a magistrate. He found in Bulawayo a proletarian culture – the town 'consists of bars and garages ... the amount of drink consumed is great'; and among Bulawayo whites 'a lack of class distinction, a complete absence

---

[64]   Ibid., pp. 98, 99.
[65]   Macmillan, p. 303.

of unemployment and an almost complete absence of poverty'.[66]

After the struggles of February 1929 this was much too bland. There was some truth in it, nevertheless. But this degree of white unity and prosperity was founded on a shared insistence upon the marginality of Africans. Macmillan, who gave voice in poetic prose to the self-image of white Bulawayo businessmen and white Bulawayo workers, also gave voice in banal poetry to their image of blacks:

> Bantu people are unchanging; they are as they used to be
> Farmers, herdsmen, elemental, of small brain capacity ...
> All their buildings have been hutments, all their towns but kraals and camps.
> They never had mining knowledge and they had no use for lamps.[67]

Bulawayo's whites were determined that these should be self-fulfilling prophecies, and that Africans should have no chance to prove themselves to be enterprising townsmen.

The complaints of white artisans were at first directed against the African pioneers from South Africa. As early as October 1902, for instance, white building workers complained to the Council that 'colonial boys [have] recently been employed by certain contractors in town as skilled labour', and that white feeling was 'naturally very strong about the matter'.[68] The Council responded to pressure from ratepayers by dismissing black builders, foremen and wagon drivers, replacing them by whites; the Railways responded to pressure from white artisans by dismissing black firemen and clerks.

Once the South African pioneers had been dealt with, it was the turn of Ndebele townsmen, and the pattern was repeated throughout the whole period to 1930. As Stephen Thornton writes:

> The growth of a skilled [African] artisan class was strongly resisted by the Council. Fear of such a development was ever present amongst white workers and this fear reached a crescendo during the 1920s.

In the late 1920s, for instance, the Council was employing up to 22 African bricklayers, 5 carpenters, 2 painters and over 50 labourers to work on the construction of cottages in the Location. Council tried to appeal to ratepayers that it was saving them money by employing cheaper labour, but in 1927 an alliance of the white building trade unions and the Ratepayers Association forced the Council to promise that its African workers would be dismissed. The white trade union held that the Council's scheme was 'detrimental to white artisans and master builders'; the Ratepayers Association held that the employment of skilled African labour was 'entirely against the interests of the Bulawayo ratepayers'.[69]

The Council sought to deny driving licences to Africans and did everything it could to handicap African carpenters, shoemakers, etc. in the Location. Such black

---

[66] Ibid., pp. 241-2.

[67] Macmillan, 'The Gold of Ophir and the Great Zimbabwe Ruins', a poem which opens his account of Rhodesian towns. During 1929 the columns of the Bulawayo *Chronicle* were full of reports of the debate between Gladys Caton Thompson and Frobenius. Like the citizens of Bulawayo, Macmillan was outraged at archaeological theories which attributed a Bantu origin to Great Zimbabwe – 'the Great Zimbabwe Ruins, which some highbrows disavow, will be monuments of wonder in a thousand years from now'.

[68] *Bulawayo Observer*, 17 October 1902.

[69] This material is deployed by Thornton in Chapter 4 of his draft thesis, 'Patterns of Escape from Migrant Labour and the Search for Urban Permanence', pp. 9-10.

artisans were subject to licensing and control by the Council and told that they could not carry on their trades in any of the cottages it was building in the Location. Once again, these measures were not only taken to protect the interests of the white businessmen and shop-keepers so abundantly represented on the Council. They were also strongly backed by white trade unions and by the Labour Party. Councillor and Labour MP Donald Macintyre even opposed a suggestion by the Town Clerk that African tradesmen should be removed from the Location and confined to a new Native Village Settlement outside Bulawayo, where they would only serve the needs of their fellow villagers. 'When their work in the settlements was done', he warned, 'they would come into competition with Europeans.'

Labour spokesmen also opposed Africans having tenure in such new settlements: always and everywhere, they insisted, Africans should be mere 'elemental' occupants of 'hutments' rather than citizens of towns.[70] To this end, the accommodation provided by the Council itself to its own black employees should be as 'primitive' as possible. As Macintyre put it, the aim was 'the support of as many natives as possible for as little financial outlay as possible'.[71]

Africans were accommodated in equally primitive shacks at the back of businesses and houses throughout the city. As we have seen, they were banned from its pavements and condemned to its crevices. But if whites were determined that African townsmen and townswomen should not develop, they were regularly alarmed at the repressed existence of masses of unskilled Africans in their midst. There were hysterical reactions during epidemics – especially during the flu epidemic of 1918. White women arrived in the town in increasing numbers after 1900, the ratio of white men to women declining from 7:1 in 1895 to 2:1 by 1901. There were daily encounters of white housewives and black male servants, and there was the constant fear of black male sexual assault or seduction. (Meanwhile, of course, there was an even more constant series of sexual encounters between white males and black women, disapproved of but not illegal.)[72]

Hysteria about the so-called 'Black Peril' was at its height both at the beginning and at the end of the period covered by this chapter. In late 1901 the Bulawayo press was full of rumours of sexual attacks: a leading citizen, William Bain, announced that in future the women in his family would be armed and 'instructed to fire if necessary'; the editor of the *Bulawayo Chronicle* warned that if the Council did not take steps to suppress 'native ruffianism', white men would be compelled to 'take the law into their own hands'.[73] In 1902 white lynch mobs twice attacked the court house in an attempt to mete out summary justice. Throughout 1902 and 1903 large public meetings were held in Bulawayo to draw up petitions demanding the death penalty for black 'rape'; vigilante groups were formed in the suburbs, patrolling the streets at night and accosting Africans. Bowing to this pressure, a Criminal Law Amendment

---

[70] Ibid., pp. 11-13, 46-50.

[71] Ibid., Chapter 3, p. 30. Thornton quotes the Town Clerk as declaring in 1936 that 'the ratepayers would be the first to complain if the cost of labour increased because of unnecessary financial expenditure on the Municipal Compound. Its economy is its major benefit.'

[72] The files in S.1222/1 provide the main evidence of this intercourse. Most of it arises from a circular sent round by the Chief Native Commissioner in 1916 asking Native Commissioners to provide details of all white men in their district with black mistresses (or, in a few cases, wives), or from attempts by the Police in the 1920s to shame, and where possible punish, white urban offenders.

[73] *Bulawayo Chronicle*, 29 October 1901.

Act was passed in September 1903 imposing the death penalty.[74]

Such scenes were not only a feature of pioneer Bulawayo. They recurred in the 'settled and civilised' Bulawayo of 1929. In September of that year an African domestic servant, Kalonde, who worked in what the *Bulawayo Chronicle* called 'a pretty little house in First Avenue', was charged with assault on his mistress, Mrs Fredericks. Kalonde's evidence at the preliminary inquiry in October dramatized all the gender and racial tensions simmering away in white Bulawayo:

> There was a lot of washing ... I asked her what time I would finish. She said: 'Tula, you are a kafir: you must not speak to me like that.' I said: 'You must not speak to me like this as we all have the same blood.' The missis then smacked my face. I got angry and went to fetch a knife. I did not want to assault her. I wanted to kill her. I was angry because she is a woman and she struck me.

This evidence and the assault itself inflamed white Bulawayo. Some three hundred men and women gathered at night outside Bulawayo gaol: 'men and women were to be seen hurrying from all directions towards the gaol and large numbers of motor cars, motor cycles and cycles brought fresh numbers to swell the crowd every minute ... men could be heard declaring that they were determined to land hands on [the] prisoner ... It was remarkable how many women were to be seen in the centre of the crowd.' It seemed that the gaol might be stormed and Kalonde lynched: 'detachments of police, fully armed with rifles and bayonets, were speedily marched to the scene'. A speaker addressed the crowd, standing on the bonnet of a car. He told them that 'the law could be relied upon to deal adequately with the prisoner', but he was shouted down with cries of 'We want to burn him!'[75]

Soon after this incident, Macmillan was evoking the 'blood-red beginning to this infant city' in the introduction to his gazetteer. Blood and fire certainly inaugurated Bulawayo in 1893; neither was far under the surface of white Bulawayo in 1929.

The Politics of Black Bulawayo

Most Africans in Bulawayo lived in compounds and stands within the white city, as 'squatters' on the Commonage or on the farmlands which surrounded the town. The residents of the Location were a minority. In 1911, for instance, there were 2,203 Africans living in the town, 481 in the suburbs, and many hundreds more in the municipal, industrial and railway compounds. There were only 992 in the Location. The Location grew through the 1920s and 1930s but even then it contained only a minority of Africans in and around Bulawayo. Nevertheless, as we have seen, the Location represented the nearest thing to a black city. It contained numbers of long-term residents and stand-owners. Unlike all other Africans in Bulawayo, the inhabitants of the Location were even briefly allowed their own 'advisory board', formed in 1923 and consisting of two representatives from each of the twelve major 'tribes' living there.[76]

---

[74] Thornton, Chapter 1, pp. 33, 34. For similar white discourse in Gwelo at the same time see Diana Jeater, 'No Place for a Woman: Gwelo Town, Southern Rhodesia, 1894–1920', mss, June 1996, p. 9.

[75] *Bulawayo Chronicle*, 5 October 1929.

[76] Thornton, Chapter 4, pp. 64-5, discusses this first board. It was dissolved after a few months as its members began to relate to Location dwellers as constituents rather than tribesmen, and in the words of the Superintendent, 'began to presume too much' and 'assume a sort of command'. Its fate was sealed when it began to discuss rents and passes and to 'incite the whole Location against myself and my staff'. Location Superintendent to Town Clerk, 6 March 1923, B23/2/6R 5780, National Archives, Bulawayo.

All African associations in Bulawayo before 1930 were based in the Location. The frustration of compound dwellers and domestic servants only expressed itself in what Stephen Thornton has called a series of infrequent 'explosions'. Sometimes the Location associations reached out to these other Bulawayo Africans. Often, though, they were concerned mainly to defend the very existence of a black town.

The fact that the Location was the site of African politics had the effect of making the Ndebele connection continuously important. Municipal labourers, living in their own compound, were overwhelmingly Tonga; Railway labourers, living in theirs, were overwhelmingly northerners, from Northern Rhodesia and Nyasaland. Ndebele men, meanwhile, dominated jobs in the police, the post office, and as clerks, etc., replacing the earlier South African pioneers as the leaders of black urban modernization. Many of these South African migrants were, however, ready and able as Xhosa and Zulu to identify with the prestigious Ndebele identity.[77]

Thornton says that Bulawayo was 'very obviously not a Matabele town' in 1925, when there were only 4,279 indigenous African inhabitants out of a total of 10,293. But only one thousand of the indigenous were Shona, and many of the Ndebele lived in the Location.[78] Moreover, many Ndebele men still lived on agricultural land close to Bulawayo, to begin with in their original chiefdoms and eventually on 'white' farms, travelling to and from the city to work. For these reasons, we can give credence to the Chief Native Commissioner's view, expressed in 1921, that Bulawayo was still regarded as 'a historical centre by the Ndebeles, many of whom have been resident in the immediate vicinity for years'.[79]

The Ndebele connection found expression in the Bulawayo Location in three main forms. Regional movements advocating the restoration of the Ndebele monarchy or the establishment of an Ndebele homeland used the Location as their headquarters. Ndebele-speakers in the Location formed their own associations to defend black urban society. Burial societies, choirs and particularly football teams gave tangible expressions to the possibility of a modern urban culture in a peculiarly Ndebele form. All three forms gained strength from their affiliation to the heritage of the monarchy – black Bulawayo was defined as 'The City of the Kings'.

Thus when Lobengula's son, Njube – who had been educated in South Africa after his father's death – returned to Rhodesia for a brief visit in 1900 he based himself in the Bulawayo Location. *Indunas* flocked to visit him there from all over Matabeland and teachers and clerks rejoiced in the presence of an educated prince.[80] In 1908 his brother, Nguboyena, came to Bulawayo, after further education in Britain. Nguboyena sought land for the Ndebele and argued that Africans should have access to higher education and the professions. He stayed in the Location at the Wesleyan Mission with an Ndebele Christian, the Methodist teacher, Ntando. 'Nguboyena does undoubtedly receive sympathy from the educated natives (Matabele and others)', reported

[77] Ibid., p. 21. Thornton says that in 1921 there were 1,244 black railway workers and in 1931 there were 2,662, 34 per cent of the total industrial labour force of Bulawayo. The Municipality employed some 1,500 African workers at the end of the 1920s.

[78] Ibid., Chapter 3, p. 15. Memo from the Town Clerk on a census of December 1925 in B 23/3/7R 6492, National Archives, Bulawayo.

[79] Chief Native Commissioner to Administrator, 19 January 1921, N3/33/10, National Archives, Harare. By contrast, in Salisbury there were 'very few if any indigenous natives settled in the vicinity of the commonage'.

[80] T.O. Ranger, *The African Voice in Southern Rhodesia, 1898–1930*, Heinemann Educational, London, 1970, p. 32.

the Chief Native Commissioner.[81] Neither prince managed to emerge as a political leader – Njube returned to South Africa and Nguboyena, even though he remained in Bulawayo, lapsed into a silent melancholia. But the Bulawayo Location remained central to movements for the re-establishment of the monarchy and the restitution of an Ndebele 'national home'. On 10 March 1919, for instance, it was in the Location residence of another Methodist catechist, Malipe, that Lobengula's son, Nyamanda, and his nephew, Madhloli, met with South African politicians and church leaders. There they drafted a petition in the names of 'the people of the Mandabele tribe', asking that 'the so-called unalienated land [be given] to the family of the late King Lobengula in trust for the tribe'. In 1920 the Location Methodist, Ntando, travelled to Cape Town to present another petition on behalf of the royal family.[82]

In the face of repression by the Southern Rhodesian and indifference from the British governments, the royal politics movements ran out of steam. But the Location was also the base for specifically Bulawayo associations. These represented the interests of Ndebele male workers, who continued to respect the traditions of the Ndebele monarchy but whose main interest was to build and defend an Ndebele urban community. They grappled with other influential groups in the Location. Thus in 1911 the largely Ndebele Bulawayo Native Community dismissed the Union of South African Natives Association as 'representing the interests of a small section of the native community to the detriment of the rest'.[83] A few years later the Loyal Mandabele Patriotic Society, headed by a committee of 'nine earnest young men', attacked the powerful women of the Location, the landladies and the prostitutes alike. 'The Christian law and the law of Mzilikazi is being broken by prostitution', they warned in 1915. In 1916 they protested that 'in the Bulawayo Location nearly all the stands and huts are occupied by single women who should not be there at all, for the reason that these locations are established for male servants who are working in town'. They demanded that a special area be set up where settled married men could live, and that security of tenure be given to 'the more respectable class of natives'. They scorned those whites who tried to repress the emergence of long-term African urban residents and who had a vested interest in a Location made up merely of loafers and of prostitutes to whom they sought sexual access:

> In all this how can a white man boast of his being in a civilized state as he has fallen so low as to cast away his own blood? White men are supposed to be an example to natives in moral living.[84]

It was a fair enough reply to the lynch mobs of white Bulawayo.

'The more respectable class of natives' dominated the articulate politics of the Bulawayo Location, but it was more difficult for them to dominate its culture. The great cultural occasions of the Ndebele state – the annual Great Dance, the rain-making processions of Ndebele virgins through GuBulawayo– had come to an end. In the compounds of white Bulawayo and even in the Location itself other dances and rites were now performed. Tonga men in the municipal compound performed their weekly drumming and dancing; Nyasas in the railway compound marched and drilled like sol-

---

[81] Ibid., p. 35.
[82] Ibid., pp. 73-4, 82-3. Ntando expressed the pleasure of educated men in the Location 'that the sons of chiefs should be given the benefits of civilization'.
[83] CNC Bulawayo to Administrator, 30 August 1911, A3/18/4, National Archives, Harare.
[84] Ranger, p. 40; Thornton, Chapter 4, p. 22.

diers in the military *ngomas* of their home country. In the Location itself innumerable non-Ndebele rituals were performed behind closed doors or on scattered open spaces:

> You know [says Mrs Bhelamina Ndlovu] this township, Makokoba, small as it may appear, is a vast place, I tell you. It has many people of different ethnicities, of different cultures and beliefs and it is very possible to stay in Makokoba for many years without knowing that something like funeral ceremonies are held.[85]

Old residents still remember the variety of this funeral culture. The nonagenarian Msongwelwayizizwe Khumalo was born in 1910 and came to Bulawayo with his parents in 1918. He was brought up *ezitdendini*, 'in the stands of pole and dagga huts'. He remembers that:

> In the 1920s and 1930s Africans were not buried in coffins in the townships. Their bodies were just wrapped in blankets and then carried in *ithala* – a stretcherlike thing – for burial … Africans also used to dig their own graves where they buried their deceased relatives and friends. During that time people were buried according to their traditional customs. Not all people were buried facing upwards as we see now. The typical Ndebele families used to bury the body of their deceased placed sideways, facing the south where they originated from. The Ama-Nyasaranda [Nyasas] would also bury their dead according to that custom, not facing upwards. We always believed that the the AmaNyasaranda and Northern Rhodesian Africans took their dead back to their country for burials … We wondered how they did that but we later realised that they performed rituals which convinced them that they had sent their dead back home, whilst in fact they had buried him or her in Bulawayo.[86]

An old Ndebele woman, married to a Mozambican, remembers the 'traditional religion which was mostly practised by foreigners in town. People from Zambia and Mozambique would meet according to their place of origin and hold private sessions, singing their traditional songs. They would meet at certain places behind doors … honouring their ancestors and asking for protection in a foreign land.'[87]

The serious young Ndebele men of the Location associations were mainly Christians and had attended Christian schools. Christian rituals and funeral customs were eventually to become dominant in the Location. But in the 1920s they were not. Nor could the young Ndebele Christians easily dominate the secular youth culture of the Location. Apart from the drumming and the dances, the most popular competitive activity of the Location was bare-fisted boxing. There were Ndebele boxers, but these were drawn from less skilled migrants, and in any case they did not offer a serious challenge to the dominance of migrant boxers from outside Matabeleland. Bulawayo's famous boxers were Northern Rhodesians or Mozambicans or Korekore. The young Ndebele Christians had to innovate other recreational activities.

As we shall see, choirs and synchronized dancing, which eventually gave rise to the township jazz culture in Bulawayo, sprang out of the discipline and training of mission schools.[88] So also did what became the dominant version of modern Bulawayo's

[85] Interview between Busani Mpofu and Mrs Bhelamina Ndlovu, Makokoba, 24 July 2000.
[86] Interview between Busani Mpofu and Msongwelwayizizwe Khumalo, Makokoba, 26 July 2000.
[87] Interview between Hloniphani Ndlovu and Madliwayo, Pelendaba, June 2000.
[88] When the Dark Town Strutters visited Bulwayo from Johannesburg the *Bantu Mirror* exclaimed that 'the Bulawayo Community has, hitherto, seen nothing so pleasant and entertaining as what they saw being done by these Strutters. It would not be a wrong thing to advise some of the active members of the teaching profession at Bulawayo, who were privileged to see them perform, to take a cue from them and train a few boys to sing and act in the same fashion. Is such a beautiful thing not worth attempting? *Matija ako Bulawayo?* *Bantu Mirror*, 14 March 1936.

most popular sport, football. In the 1920s – and for many years earlier –[89] a sort of rough-and-ready football existed in mines and locations, largely as an opportunity for gambling. As the *Bantu Mirror* remembered in 1955:

> Football was a game associated only with survival of the fittest. Indeed the rule of the jungle prevailed, where when the lion roars, mice and rabbits, including cunning jackals, must seek shelter in the nearest hole with lightning rapidity for dear life's sake. A player could choose to enter the football field with a hunter's knife on his belt.[90]

In the Bulawayo Location in 1929 there was only one football pitch, which 'had an ugly appearance and there was hardly a blade of grass on it. There were some small stones, here and there, jutting out of the ground.'[91]

Fortunately, as the *Mirror* recalled, 'good football was found in the schools', though 'even here it meant shooting aimlessly – the harder and higher the better'. The best football was found in South Africa, at Lovedale or at Zonnebloem. In the 1920s this meant that those with the most immediate access to superior footballing skills were young men of the Ndebele aristocracy – and members of the Ndebele royal family. Jeremiah and Nsele Hlabangana went to South Africa and returned to teach in the Presbyterian School at Ntabazinduna Institute, where together with the young Mfengu teacher Charlton Ngcebetsha, they pioneered South African-style football. Meanwhile the young members of the Lobengula family were learning football in their South African colleges. Prince Njube's brother, Charles Lobengula, was centre-half and club secretary for the team at Zonnebloem.[92] Njube's sons, Albert and Rhodes, both played football in South Africa. Rhodes was particularly skilful and enthusiastic and 'formed and led a team [called Lions] at Lovedale'.[93]

After he completed his Lovedale course Rhodes Lobengula came to Bulawayo and lived in cottage 19 in the Location. He aspired to form a proper football team, once again called Lions. He could depend upon his brother Albert and upon the teachers from Ntabazinduna, Nsele and Jeremiah Hlabangana and Charlton Ngcebetsha. As Charlton recalled in 1936, these men:

> during their time as teachers at Ntabazinduna Mission some few years ago, working in concert with Rhodes Lobengula and others … started the Lions Club and since that time they have remained 'true blue' to it.[94]

The 1929 Lions team recruited Sipambaniso Manyoba Khumalo, the young descendant of the royal clan, born and educated in the Location, who was to become black Bulawayo's most famous footballer as well as its leading trade union activist. Another

---

[89] I do not have a similar early reference for Bulawayo but Diana Jeater, in her 'No Place for a Woman: Gwelo Town, Southern Rhodesia, 1894–1920', ms, 1996, p. 18, quotes a letter in the *Gwelo Times* of 22 May 1903 which speaks of the 'noticeable innovation' of football clubs among 'the town kafirs'; the writer complains that 'their playing in the town renders some of the recognised short cuts over the stands impassable'. What was true of Gwelo was presumably true also of Bulawayo.

[90] *Bantu Mirror*, 30 July 1955.

[91] *Home News*, 1 January 1954.

[92] O. Stuart, 'Players, Workers, Protestors: Social Change and Soccer in Colonial Zimbabwe', in J. MacClancy (ed.), *Sport, Identity and Ethnicity*, Berg, Oxford, 1996.

[93] *Home News*, 1 January 1954.

[94] *Bantu Mirror*, 6 June 1936. The occasion of Charlton's comments was a match between the Lions team and Ntabazibduna School. The Lions team itself, he claimed, was almost entirely composed of ex-students from the school.

Ndebele, Amos Sibanda, joined the team together with various non-royals and commoners, whose names are rendered in the sources merely as Mjuda, Willie and Magata.[95] After his death by drowning in the Great Fish River in early 1937, Rhodes was praised by the *Bantu Mirror* for 'never fixing a line of demarcation between the Matabele and non-Matabele ... hence his immense popularity'.[96] And Rhodes was certainly anxious to recruit for his team the best footballers, no matter who they might be.

Still, Ndebele royalty was at the heart of the team. A myth now widespread among the supporters of Highlanders (which descends directly from the Lions) runs that some gold coins were found in the early 1930s near the spot where Lobengula vanished. Rhodes and Nsele Hlabangana cycled 300 kilometres to the spot, claimed the money, and used it to finance the Lions. Lions/Highlanders was an inspired creation, gaining for the young Ndebele Christian townsmen the leadership of Bulawayo's fastest growing sport, and offering over the decades a symbol of Location/Makokoba Ndebele identity.[97]

Soon football as the 'civilized' sport was being widely reported, and caricatured, in the African press. The *Bantu Mirror* carried as early as October 1931 a cartoon showing male urban youths, all wearing hats and ties, downcast as 'our people are losing' or triumphant as 'our people are winning'. A report by Jeremiah Hlabangaza from the Ntabazinduna Institute in October 1932 showed the influence of school football radiating out into the nearby Reserve, with the Villagers' eleven, 'like a team of ostriches, running on one after the other in their uniform of scarlet and white'. By 1936 there were as many as 16 teams in Bulawayo's African Football League. The prestige of the Lions, however, remained pre-eminent.[98]

Young urban women, whether Ndebele or not, could not of course participate in the new civilized football. (They could and did participate in choirs.)[99] However, women remained at the heart of African politics in Bulawayo. As we have seen, their voices were not heard in the Ndebele royal movements, and the associations formed by young Ndebele urban dwellers were actively hostile to female stand-holders and to other independent women. But the interests of some women *were* voiced by their menfolk; others took the law into their own hands; and the powerful female stand-holders were mobilized in support of the supra-ethnic progressive political movements of Bulawayo.

In 1918, 62 African men, including leaders of the progressive movements like M.D. and Z. Makgatho and Thomas Mazinyane, petitioned the Bulawayo Council:

We are natives at present living in the town of Bulawayo ... By a certain Municipal Bye-Law it

---

[95] *Home News*, 1 January 1954. *Home News* was a duplicated newspaper edited by Charlton Ngcebetsha. It manifested his two preoccupations, continued from the 1920s – Ndebele tradition and football.

[96] *Bantu Mirror*, 6 February and 20 March 1937. The paper reported a meeting in the Location to raise funds for a 'monumental stone' for Rhodes and commented that it was supported by non-Ndebele and well as by Ndebele.

[97] The National Gallery in Bulawayo has had a series of exhibitions designed to celebrate township culture and particularly that of Makokoba – an exhibition of township photography and an exhibition of adorned township bicycles; in late 2001 it was showing an exhibition of photographs and posters for Highlanders, then the football champions of Zimbabwe.

[98] *Bantu Mirror*, October 1931; October 1932; 18 April 1936.

[99] In October 1921 the Amalgamated Choirs of the Location were hiring the beer hall for concerts and paying ten shillings a night extra for the use of an organ. Location Superintendent to Town Clerk, 25 October 1921, 23.2.6R, Box 5777, National Archives, Bulawayo.

is a punishable offence for a native woman to walk on the side-paths, and recently two of these, both respectable women, have been brought before the magistrate and fined for this offence. We consider this to be a very hard law for our people. Our petition to you now is that you will alter this law so that all native women shall be allowed a privilege which we believe is now conceded to native women in every town in the Union.[100]

The Police reported that over the previous four years 112 men and 12 women had been 'convicted for using the footpaths' and that it was 'only in flagrant cases that females are proceeded against. Nurses with children, etc and cases arising out of ignorance of the law are not proceeded against.' It was a reply that gave great offence. As the Methodist, John White, wrote in February 1919, 'no perversion of the English language could call these cases flagrant – before long you will be ashamed to have such a retrograde and un-British by-law on your statute book'.[101]

And if the African men of the Location thought that their women should have preferential treatment over themselves in the town centre, they also demanded the establishment of a special hospital for women during the flu epidemic of October 1918. The Municipality responded, setting up a women's hospital in the beer hall, though carefully maintaining a racial hierarchy:

The patients were placed in four rows ... Coloured women, Indians, native servants, raw kaffirs ... and children were kept separate ... The native women as a rule gave very little trouble. The more uncivilised appeared to regard their sickness as due to poison which had been adminis-tered as witchcraft ... Indian women appear to be liable to hysteria.

Despite this patronizing racism, 'the native men and women of the Location' expressed their thanks to the Council.[102]

Location men could sometimes speak out for women, then. But women were quite ready to speak out for themselves. During the 1920s they had several grievances against the Bulawayo Municipality. In the early years many Location women supple-mented their income by brewing and selling beer. At first they could do this freely and legally. Then the Council tried to suppress brewing and the police raided women's huts. The raids intensified when the municipal beer hall was opened and the beer hall itself offered what women regarded as unfair competition. The beer hall was attacked from two contrasting directions: respectable Christian women leaders like Martha

---

[100] Petition, July 1918, 23.2.1R, Box 5700, National Archives, Bulawayo. For the political careers of the Mak-gatho brothers and of Mazinyane, see T.O. Ranger, *The African Voice in Southern Rhodesia, 1898–1930*, Hei-nemann, London, 1970, Chapters 3–6.

[101] Assistant District Superintendent, Police to Town Clerk, 17 September 1918; John White to Town Clerk, 10 December 1918 and 23 February 1919, ibid. Methodist catechists in the Location had been involved in the Ndebele National Home movement. Now Methodists particularly took up the various needs of women. An increasing number of girls were being employed as domestic servants, many of them from the Baralong com-munity at Francistown; these Baralong girls reported at the Methodist Mission in the Location until they found posts; John White demanded that the Municipality should provide a hostel, and when this was not done the Methodists opened a hostel for girls in 1918 in the Location. Memorandum from G.E.P. Broderick, 16 May 1917; John White to Town Clerk, 13 June 1917; Herbert Baker to Town Clerk, 26 February 1919, ibid.

[102] E.E. Clarke, Native Women's Hospital, to Town Clerk, 23 October 1918; Native Commissioner, Bulawayo to Chief Native Commissioner, 25 October 1918; expression of thanks to Town Clerk, 18 November 1918; Report of General Committee, 19 November 1918. On 27 October Gibson Tawako and Boarder Matswelo wrote to the Town Clerk thanking him for the beer hall hospital but asking that facilities similar to those offered to women might also be made available to Location men. 23.1.8R, Box 5689, National Archives, Bulawayo.

Ngano condemned it for demoralizing Location society. But women beer-brewers tried to close it down. Mrs L. Mlotshwa remembers an event in the 1920s which I have not managed to date exactly:

> The women in Makokoba once assaulted the white superintendent of this township who was commonly known as 'Makokoba'. Women in the township were brewing a certain type of beer and so they did not want their husbands and other males to go into the Big Bhawa [municipal beer hall]. The superintendent tried to suppress those women's moves. The women in the township responded by physically assaulting the white superintendent. Two women were imprisoned for that because they were considered to be the ringleaders.[103]

But the grievance which really powered explicit women's politics in Makokoba arose from the Bulawayo Council's attempt to impose total control over the Location. The Council was determined to demolish the houses owned by the landladies and to abolish private ownership in the Location.

For a long time the Council was happy not to have to spend money on Africans, and in 1915 the Town Clerk declared himself in favour of 'leaving natives to their own resources as was the case when the Location was first started'.[104] This takeover was first seriously suggested after the flu epidemic in 1918. As the Location Superintendent wrote in June 1919:

> The condition of most of the private huts makes them uninhabitable with kitchens built of sacking ... I suggest that these places be demolished without any compensation to the owners and the Council build new places.[105]

The Superintendent was ignoring the many private houses built in brick by women before 1919, and in the 1920s there was a general movement by African stand-holders from mud to brick. Despite this, and the Council's financial hesitancy, the takeover began in the early 1920s. Use of beer hall profits encouraged the Council to begin building one- and two-room huts in the Location for 'bachelors' and families. In 1921 a new layout for the Location was drawn up which implied the destruction of most private property. The Council moved slowly – by 1923 only 24 cottages had been built. But its destructive capacity exceeded its constructive and the number of huts destroyed always exceeded the number erected. Many women no longer bothered to repair their dwellings; some despaired and left Bulawayo for the rural areas or the mines. But those who remained protested loudly. In August 1933 the acting Superintendent of Natives, Bulawayo told the Chief Native Commissioner that he was getting bitter complaints from 'not a few – especially women – who have been leasing their huts ... and deriving a substantial income in the forms of rents. Some individuals, especially the females, suffer appreciably.'[106]

The character of the Location was changing. It was no longer dominated by married families and women landladies. In the 1920s 'single' African workers poured into the Location and into municipal housing. In 1911 around 11 per cent of African workers in Bulawayo lived in the Location; by 1925 this had risen to 40 per cent. Some six thousand people lived in the Location and very many more men than women. But the

---

[103] Interview between Busani Mpofu and Mrs L. Mlotshwa, Makokoba, February 2000.
[104] Thornton, Chapter 2, p. 14. The Town Clerk was expressing his opposition to a Council-built married housing scheme.
[105] Location Superintendent to Town Clerk, B23 1/1/8R 5691, National Archives, Bulawayo.
[106] Thornton, Chapter 2, pp. 19-20.

Location's women fought the change tooth and nail and they were able to rally many others to their cause.

As Stephen Thornton writes, 'the systematic destruction of African property was the single issue which united African political groupings [and] spurred the Location inhabitants into relatively concerted attacks on the Municipal Council.'[107] The political association which gave most space for female initiative was the Rhodesian Bantu Voters Association. The RBVA was initiated by elite South African migrants in Mashonaland and Midlands but it was soon taken over by its Bulawayo branch.[108] And in turn the Bulawayo branch was taken over by Martha Ngano. She added a strong populist tone to an organization which had been started to express the interests of a handful of black landowners. Martha interpreted 'property' and its defence to mean African rights to land, and she carried the message of 'I-Vote' into the rural areas. She also steered the RBVA into the representation of the interests of the women stand-owners of Bulawayo. She attended the weekly meetings of the RBVA committee, held in Zacharia Magkatho's house in the Location. In February 1924 she moved that the RBVA should set up a 'Native Women's League ... to work for the Native Women's Uplift Morally, Socially and Educationally and advise on all matters affecting the sex'.[109]

What became the Rhodesia Bantu Women's League existed only in Bulawayo, where it had a hundred or so members. It was led by Martha Ngano, Mary Lobengula and Louisa Guqua.[110] It held public meetings attended by three to four hundred people. It protested against the eviction of 'helpless old women'; it protested against rents too high for male workers to pay; it protested against the beer hall.[111] In March 1925 the League, having 'given a lot of trouble about the destruction', went to meet the Superintendent of Natives, Bulawayo, who gave them a sympathetic ear and from then on lobbied the Council on their behalf. A little later in 1925 Martha Ngano gave evidence to the Morris Carter Land Commission. She set out the women's case:

> They say that they are not well treated there by the Superintendent of the location. He does not want them to build houses. He is having some houses built and they are rather small. He wants them to pay a lot of money, as they cannot do as they did before. They used to get a stand and they would build rooms on them which they used to let to other natives, and now they are not allowed to do that. It is very hard on them as the men cannot get sufficient money to support their wives.[112]

Despite all this, the Council's determination hardened. In 1929 it announced a ban on any further private building and a vigorous programme of destruction. The Women's League went on protesting right up to the end of 1929. They met the Superintendent of Natives again on 6 December under the Indaba Tree in the Location. He promised that he would ensure they got adequate notice and adequate compensation. It was not much satisfaction, however, and the women of the Location carried their grievances into 1930, when as we shall see, the management of Bulawayo Location became a

---

[107] Ibid., p. 18.
[108] For the RBVA see T.O. Ranger, *The African Voice in Southern Rhodesia*, Chapter 5.
[109] Constitution of RBVA enclosed in Superintendent of Natives, Bulawayo to Chief Native Commissioner, 23 May 1924, S 84/A/260, National Archives, Harare.
[110] It seems likely that Louisa was the Cape Coloured woman of the same name who is listed in November 1929 as owning four stands and four brick houses, altogether worth £29, in one of which she lived with her husband, a harness-maker; the others she let to 'coloured' boarders.
[111] List of grievances, 1924, B 23/3/3/R 5892, National Archives, Harare.
[112] Evidence of Martha Ngano, ZAH 1/1/2, pp. 607.

matter of public and indeed national concern.[113]

The Confrontation of Black & White Bulawayo: Asian Intermediaries

For many years North Lobengula Street acted not only as a frontier but also as a contact zone between black and white. As early as 1896 the Bulawayo Directory noted a 'Kaffir Store' there, owned by L. Makin. By 1910 stores in Lobengula Street supplied the Asian eating-house keepers and hawkers in the Location. These stores were owned and operated by Jewish traders – Liptz, Lazarus, Rassmer, Kirschbaum, etc. And then gradually Asian trading families themselves began to set up stores in western Bulawayo. By 1930 M.H. Naik and B.K. Patel were at 56 Lobengula Street; I. Seedat and K.R. Vashee traded there as general merchants. The 75th Anniversary Magazine of the Bulawayo Kshatriya Mandal reconstructs the experience of these pioneers. Its editor, Tuslidas Kooverji Doolabh, writes:

> In the first quarter of this century most Indians lived in small tin shacks, rented municipal housing rooms in the Location, or lived in small rooms behind their shops ... In time, Indians joined the commercial sector in great numbers and with added prosperity called their wives and children from India. They moved from their rented shacks on the outskirts of Bulawayo to the Grey/Rhodes Street, Railway Avenue and Lobengula Street areas of Bulawayo where they bought houses ... in marginal areas that provided a buffer between the blacks and the whites.[114]

As the commercial front-line, North Lobengula Street went out of its way to attract African shoppers coming out of the Location. K.M. Naki's TandaBantu store at 57a Lobengula Street – 'where everybody shops' – still stands and trades today as a survivor of this colourful past. Africans could buy basics in the Location. They came to Lobengula Street for 'fashion' and for luxuries. The street's store windows were crammed with brightly coloured clothes and accessories, including the suits and shirts and gloves and shoes to which the Location dandies aspired. African market-stalls, attached to the stores, lined the street. There was an atmosphere of carnival. 'For many of us', says Mark Ncube, Bulawayo's oral historian, 'Lobengula Street *was* Bulawayo.'[115]

In fact, Lobengula Street played the role of sucking up African customers and

---

[113] Town Clerk to Native Commissioner, Bulawayo, 4 December 1929; to Location Superintendent, 6 December 1929; to S/N/Bulawayo, 28 December 1929. Compensation was to be set by the Department of Native Affairs after inspection. It was not always a question of a few shillings. A schedule of private property drawn up in November 1929, involving 320 people, included Martha Khumalo, who had two stands and two brick houses, valued in all at £7 10s. It also included one Josephine who owned six stands, and several brick houses and brick huts. Her property was valued at £21.

[114] *75th Anniversary Commemorative Magazine, 1919–1994*, Bulawayo Kshatriya Mandal, Bulawayo, September 2001.

[115] Before she fell ill Yvonne Vera was planning an exhibition at the National Gallery in Bulawayo about the past of Lobengula Street. In her township novel, *Butterfly Burning*, p. 81, she has a vivid sketch of an African woman dealer, Zandile, who 'had a table outside Jassats' in Lobengula Street. Vera is writing about the mid-1940s, by which time African women's beauty products were much in demand. 'Zandile was a marvel in Makokoba, a pioneer advocate of a certain form of beauty ... [offering] the feel and texture of desire.' But even the bold Zandile, venturing only as far as Lobengula Street, carried 'her address written in small handwriting. One felt such a stranger in town.'

holding them away from the pavements and shops of white Bulawayo. Both Asian hawkers and eating-house keepers in the Location and the Asian stores in Loben-gula Street itself came under attack from would-be African entrepreneurs and from the mission-educated. There were widespread demands, from the Matabele Home Society and the ICU alike, for the expulsion of Asians from the Location and the grant of trading licences to Africans.[116] Christian progressives attacked the vulgarity and excess of Lobengula Street culture. Aggressive marketing exploited African gul-libility; the clothes sold in Lobengula Street, especially the clothes for young men, were caricatures of sober Christian fashion. 'How much did you spend last year on rubbish?' asked the *Native Mirror* in 1934. 'On things that were of no use? On con-certinas? Gramophones? Cheap boots that were too small? Hats that didn't fit?'[117]

In April 1933 the *Mirror* lamented:

> Natives are in the hands of store-keepers, Indian and native tailors, who supply the clothes the natives want and believe are fashionable. The result is deplorable ... outrageous plus-fours, with checks as large as soup plates, trousers so wide that they could make dresses for a whole family ... The postures, clothes and walking attitudes of these dudes is enough to make angels laugh.

But behind these attacks on Asian greed and manipulation lay a wider desire to get beyond such intermediaries and to confront white Bulawayo directly.

The Confrontation of Black & White Bulawayo: White Racism & Municipal Maladministration

By 1929 the various political interests in the Location – and beyond – were coming together to denounce the leadership of the white city. Africans in Bulawayo were united in resentment of white contempt and their own humiliation. To this day segre-gation is remembered in powerfully personalized ways. The arrogant Britishness of the dominant white culture is marvelously summed up in the larger-than-life figure of Major Gordon, whom a number of informants described:

> Around 1929 to 1930 [remembers old Diki Maphosa] there were already whites-only stores in the city where we Africans were not allowed to buy. These stores included Haddon and Sly, Railway Co-op stores, etc. You know it is also true that in the Post Office whites were always served first. In the city-centre butcheries we Africans were not allowed to use the same door as whites. You know there was also a very notorious white man by name Major Gordon who could physically assault any African he met walking on the pavement. This Major Gordon was one of the old members of the Pioneer Column. We Africans would walk on those pavements only if there was no white man in sight. As soon as you saw a white man coming you had to quickly move out of the pavement. This Major Gordon also never gave way to traffic when crossing roads. He expected the motorists to stop for him to cross. He was known to assault drivers sometimes, especially those who were not of British origins. Some Boers were assaulted by him, but his end came when he was knocked down to death by a motorcycle. You know, if you were a 'clever' African as soon as you saw Major Gordon walking you had to run to him saying, 'Nkosi! Lord!' If you did that he would dip his hand into his pockets to come up with coins which he

116 Stephen Thornton, 'The Struggle for Profit and Participation by an emerging petty-bourgeoisie in Bula-wayo, 1893–1993', in Brian Ratopoulos and Tsuneo Yoshikuni (eds), *Sites of Struggle*, Weaver Press, Harare, 1999.

117 Cited in Timothy Burke, *Lifebuoy Men, Lux Women*, Duke University Press, Durham, NC, 1996, pp. 102-3.

threw down for you to pick up. That way you won his mercy and escaped his wrath that could be expressed by physical assault.[118]

Bulawayo Africans resented the humiliation of medical examinations, when men were stripped naked; of pauper burials in which men and women were buried naked; of prison clothing, in which men wore rough gowns and no underclothes. It is no wonder that the most radical leader black Bulawayo had yet seen, Sergeant Masotsha Ndlovu, is best remembered today for his protest against these degradations.[119]

In early 1928 Ndlovu became the Secretary-General of the Industrial and Commercial Workers Union – *Ngiyakubona*. The ICU in Rhodesia was an extension of the great South African movement, founded by Kadalie. It spoke in the language of class and was active in Salisbury as well as in Bulawayo. In many senses it was a national, even a regional, movement. There has been much debate about the ICU, and historians have differed on whether it is best seen as a form of 'proto-nationalism' or as an early workers' movement. In so far as it was a workers' movement, historians have differed on whether it genuinely represented the interests of all workers or only of the 'permanent working class'.[120] Here I want to discuss it only in relation to Black Bulawayo.[121]

In many ways Ndlovu was an archetypal Location leader. His very name makes many of the connections. His last name, Ndlovu, indicates his birth as an Ndebele, in uSaba near Thekwane under chief Mphini Ndiweni. His middle name, Masotsha, indicates his father's precocious awareness of the threat of colonialism – he was born in 1890 and named for the white 'soldiers' who were entering the country with the Pioneer Column. His first name (and rank), Sergeant, was bestowed on him in an ironic appreciation of his leadership qualities by his Bulawayo employer, Thomas Meikle.[122] He represented also the South African connection, having gone down to Cape Town in 1919 where he obtained his Standard Six and English Matriculation and came into contact with Congress, the ICU and the Garveyite movement. In Cape Town he became a registered voter.

When he returned to Bulawayo in January 1928 he acquired stand 381 and a brick house in the Location, roofed with iron, with two rooms and a kitchen. Its value was assessed in 1929 as £10, making it one of the most valuable houses owned by an African man.[123] At the same time he was a new phenomenon in the Location. The

---

[118] Interview between Busani Mpofu and Diki Maphosa, Makokoba, January 2000. Resentment over the pavements by-law was expressed by the elite members of the RBVA who complained on 14 July 1924 that African clergy, teachers and voters should be accepted as 'civil enough not to block the footpaths'; the by-law is 'a great grievance'.

[119] Pathisa Nyathi, *Masotsha Ndlovu*, Longman, Harare, 1998, describes his hero's response to medical examination, prison clothing and pavements.

[120] The ICU is discussed in Chapters 7 and 8 of T.O. Ranger, *The African Voice in Southern Rhodesia*; in Stephen Thornton's draft doctoral thesis; in Ian Phimister, *An Economic and Social History of Zimbabwe, 1890–1948. Capital Accumulation and Class Struggle*, Longman, London, 1988; in Ian Phimister and Charles van Onselen, 'The Labour Movement in Zimbabwe: 1900–1945'; in Brian Raftopoulos and Ian Phimister (eds), *Keep on Knocking. A History of the Labour Movement in Zimbabwe, 1900–97*, Baobab Books, Harare, 1997; and in Pathisa Nyathi, *Masotsha Ndlovu*.

[121] In my own treatment of the ICU more than thirty years ago I focused on its challenge to the Rhodesian state and missed, or at any rate did not cite, the material deployed in this book about its challenge to the Bulawayo Council and to Bulawayo white labour.

[122] Ndlovu worked for Meikle before and during the First World War for what was then the considerable wage of £3 a month.

[123] H. Collier to Town Engineer, 22 November 1929, 23/3/7R 1930, National Archives, Bulawayo. Only

Superintendent's monthly report for April 1930 gave a list of all 'persons residing in cottages and rooms not employed in the Township'. Rhodes Lobengula was in the list as 'Government pensioner'; there was one Seventh-Day Adventist preacher; five chair-makers and carpenters; six laundrymen; eight bricklayers; three bootmakers; two wood hawkers; two hawkers; one taxi-driver; one herbalist; and one unemployed. And there was Masotsha Ndlovu as a full-time Secretary-General of the ICU.[124] There were meetings of the ICU committee twice a week in his brick house in the Location.

So far as black Bulawayo was concerned, the ICU represented a process of political expansion and democratization. The maverick white trade unionist, Bowden, put the matter clearly at an ICU meeting in the Location on 13 October 1928. Bowden was introduced as 'the working man coming from the East End of London, and therefore he knows the workers' wants. You are the working people and so is he.' Bowden indicated Martha Ngano, who spoke at this meeting as she did at many ICU gatherings:

> Five years ago the good old lady there – Mrs Ngano – asked me to speak to you on this very ground. On that day you had a rope out around you and one class was kept aside and the special class inside. That is all gone and finished today. This is one Union. Shopkeeper, blacksmith are all one.

The ICU contained peasants, builders, clerks, domestic servants, factory workers, municipal workers, miners. 'We want the railway boys to join us.'[125] In speech after speech the ICU attacked class divisions and tribal divisions equally.

In short, the ICU took much further the populist outreach which Martha Ngano and the Women's League had initiated. Ndlovu was careful to approach the educated elite of the Location and to gain their backing. He persuaded Thomas Sikaleni Mazula, who had been a 'Native Detective' and was now a Native Department Messenger, to take over the Chairmanship. (The Native Department told Mazula to resign immediately or to lose his job: he chose to continue as Chairman.) Martha Ngano and the Women's League were brought in and the ICU strongly supported the protests of the stand-owners.[126] Ngano spoke often, and at an ICU meeting on 21 April 1929 a representative of the League appeared; she was Nasi Darby, 'prostitute'.[127]

Masotsha tried hard to reach out beyond the Location. In January 1929 he raised with the Assistant Chief Native Commissioner the problem of overcrowding in the Railway Compounds in Bulawayo, claiming that 'he was authorised to make representations on this subject by the native railway workers, many of whom are members of his association'.[128] Efforts were also made to reach Africans who worked and lived

---

[123] (ctnd) Kwelekwe, with a seven-roomed house valued at £12, and Joseph with a brick house, four rooms and a verandah, valued at £15, surpassed him.

[124] Ndlovu's colleague in the ICU, Job Dumbutshena, is also listed as a full-time organizer.

[125] Report to Acting Chief Superintendent, CID, 20 October 1928, S.138 22, National Archives, Harare. The report ended with a characterization of Masotsha Ndlovu as 'an insolent, arrogant and argumentative native'.

[126] On 30 November 1929 Masotsha and Job wrote to 'the town office', Bulawayo, on behalf of 'the workers' to protest against 'the treatment exercised upon us by the council to break down our houses without giving us any notice, by taking all our privilege which was given to us by the council in the past of building our own houses in a modern European way.'

[127] Report on meeting of 20 April 1929, S.138 22. She complained that 'men and women have to be examined by a doctor – why should this be? If the Government is short of money it sends the Police to raid the Location and arrest the men who work in town.'

[128] Acting Assistant CNC to CNC, 2 February 1929, ibid. Masotsha claimed that the ICU had 300 'adult members, most of whom are educated men with families'.

in the city. Thus on 19 October 1929, shortly after the lynching attempt by the white mob at Bulawayo jail, the ICU took themselves out of the Location and held a meeting at the very centre of white Bulawayo, in the Market Square, attracting an audience of 700. 'Things have changed,' wrote an indignant white ratepayer, 'when labourers can call a mass meeting in a white man's town and are actually tolerated.'[129]

This outreach to all elements in the Location, to railway workers and to city employees, was accompanied by a shift of focus by the Bulawayo ICU. It had begun with general attacks on colonial capitalism and on the Rhodesian state, focusing on wages, on working conditions and on land. Gradually, its meetings focused on the coalition of interests which made up white Bulawayo. The ICU was naturally very interested in the demands of the white railway workers and in the abortive strike of early 1929. The 'prostitute', Nasi Darby, asked in April 1929 to be told the significance of the strike. She was not long left in doubt.

At an ICU meeting on 29 June 1929 John Mphamba, a Nyasa ex-serviceman, attacked white railway union leader, Jack Keller – 'after the Police arrested Mr Keller, Mr Keller returned and then came on the side of the Police. He told all his men to stop the strike.' Keller and Davies were asking for 'a Wages Board for every white man. We are going to fight for both peoples and demand a Wage Board for everyone.' [130] On 20 July Masotsha Ndlovu widened the attack to Labour members of parliament. 'We are the workers. We make houses and lay roads. Any reasonable person can see that we are the workers ... [yet the MPs] spoke for the white people as labour leaders. Another gentleman asked them "What about natives?" They said they are not brought to parliament by natives.' He went on to attack Bulawayo white railway workers themselves:

> I have found three cases which happened in Raylton. One of our brothers was killed on the railways. He fell from the train and the guard did not even pick him up ... Another one was killed by the Cape train. Another one was working in the Loco and fell into a tank containing boiling water ... When his friends had collected money for his coffin, they found he had already been buried. We want these cases investigated. We want to know why the guard did not stop the train at once.

And then Masotsha moved on from white workers to municipal councillors. 'The Europeans are united. In Bulawayo certain men are elected to govern the people. They are called Councillors. They make the laws to raid your Location ... The Superintendent of the Location is paid with your money.'[131]

As the Superintendent of Natives, Bulawayo, explained in June 1929:

> Not so very long ago it was the Native Commissioners who were the subject of their subversive utterances, if not the Chief Native Commissioner too; and then it was the Honourable Premier himself; and now it is the Town Location Superintendent.[132]

On 8 June, for instance, Job Dumbutshena compared Salisbury and Bulawayo Locations. 'The Salisbury Location is good and free. There is no early morning raiding. If you are a stranger you can stay with your friend without taking permission. You

---

[129] Superintendent of Natives, Bulawayo to CNC, 17 and 21 October 1929, ibid.; letter from Dan Vincent, *Chronicle*, 28 October 1929.
[130] Mphamba's speeches at this meeting are cited at length in T.O. Ranger, *The African Voice*, pp. 153-6.
[131] CID reports to Chief Superintendent, 21 July and 24 July 1929, S 138 22.
[132] Superintendent of Natives, Bulawayo to Chief Native Commissioner, 28 June 1929, ibid.

are free. There is no afternoon search. The beer [hall] is open for everyone.' But in Bulawayo, 'when you go to the beer hall, you are like prisoners. You must stand in a row like at the Pass Office. The Bulawayo treatment is very bad ... The white men put up schools and the Location beer hall and give houses, but it is all a trap. Africans should be allowed to brew beer themselves and to keep the profits.' As for compulsory medical examination, it was 'a disgrace. It shows that the black man is an animal.'[133]

A month later, on 6 July, Masotsha compared Bulawayo to Gatooma – 'a good Council':

> The Bulawayo Council treat us like thieves in our own Location. They are always sending the CID to raid us ... Do you like your women to have the blankets pulled off them? How long are you going to allow this? The white man pays rent for his house, that is his house and nobody can go into it without his permission. Why should we be raided? My blood boils to see my people so badly treated in the Location ... We don't want to live here; there is a devil here; we are like prisoners in here; we are kept here to pay money to the Council.[134]

The public meeting in the Market Square on 19 October, which whites saw as so confrontational, discussed how 'to improve conditions in the Location'.

1929 was a restless year both for black Bulawayo and for white Bulawayo. Some whites feared that the example of the white rail strike might lead to black insurrection. Even the white strikers were very much aware of their audience of 'grinning and inquisitive natives'. Bulawayo Europeans asked themselves:

> What about the natives if the white population starts rioting? What about the Matabele? Remember Bulawayo is now the railway head-quarters ... It is not such a long time since 1896. There are hundreds of Matabele living who remember the rising quite well.[135]

If whites remembered 1893 and 1896 there were Africans who remembered them too and who feared that manifestations like the lynch mob of September 1929 might lead to more general attacks on blacks. The Native Department regularly predicted that the rhetoric of the ICU would lead to open defiance. On 23 December 1929 the Chief Native Commissioner told Prime Minister Moffat that 'the gunpowder awaiting ignition ... is not an utterly remote danger ... The ICU is becoming a potential danger unless their utterances are suppressed.'[136] But as we shall see, the explosion which *did* occur at the end of December 1929 had nothing to do with the ICU or with the Women's League or with memories of the Ndebele monarchy.

---

[133] CID report to Chief Superintendent, 10 June 1929, ibid.
[134] CID report to Chief Superintendent, 6 July 1929. Mphamba added that he did not blame 'the King' or 'the Governor': 'I blame the Council because it makes our laws.'
[135] Rawdon Hoare, *Rhodesian Mosaic*, London, 1934, pp. 190-6.
[136] Chief Native Commissioner to Prime Minister, 23 December 1929, S.138 22.

1

The Landscapes of Bulawayo

The chapters which follow describe a series of more or less dramatic events. This chapter sets the scene for them by laying out the landscapes in which they took place. Southern African urban landscapes have received little attention from historians.[1] Yet a major theme in the social history of white Bulawayo in the 1930s is the inter-action of the town with a number of different surrounding landscapes. A major theme in its intellectual history is the development in Bulawayo of ideas of 'wilderness' and 'countryside'; ideas of rural, suburban and urban beauty. The creation of a black Bulawayo urban identity, moreover, was also linked to African ideas of 'the country' and of its relation with the town. These questions of landscape cannot be left out of urban history without seriously impoverishing it.

A City in the Wilderness: The Self-image of White Bulawayo in the 1930s

I have already described some of the tensions of the year 1929 in Bulawayo – the white rail strike and its repression; the lynch mob; the apprehension aroused by the ICU. Nevertheless, that August white Bulawayo was at its most urbane. Its annual Agricul-tural Show coincided for the first time with a Motor Show, the Caledonian Society Ball, a cabaret at the Grand Hotel, a local production of the musical 'Hit the Deck', and with Tarzan and Gary Cooper at the cinema. There were intellectual attractions too. No fewer than 380 scientists were due in Bulawayo from the British Association meet-ing in Johannesburg. Some of them were to lecture in the town on topics as diverse as 'Scientific Agriculture' and the meaning of rock paintings.[2]

[1] At the 'African Environments Past and Present' conference at St Antony's College, Oxford, in July 1999 there were only four papers out of seventy which dealt with urban landscapes and all of these dealt with the present and with issues of 'environmental justice'. For Zimbabwe Dr Terri Barnes has written a stimulating account of gendered landscape in Salisbury – 'Master Bedrooms, "Boys'" Kias and Old Bricks: Gender and Space in Colonial Harare, Zimbabwe', conference on 'Women and Environment', Harare, August 1999. A first version of this chapter was given as 'Towards an Environmental History of Southern African Cities. Bulawayo in the 1930s', International conference, 'A View of the Land', Bulawayo, July 2000.

[2] Throughout 1929 the *Chronicle* had carried copious reports about the 'discoveries' of the German scholar, Frobenius, and of his dispute with Gladys Caton-Thompson about the origins and antiquity of Great Zim-babwe. The proceedings of the British Association were fully covered.

An editorial in the *Chronicle* celebrated the occasion:

> Bulawayo is about to enter on its gala week of the year. The town will be packed with visitors and the residents will have as much thought for pleasure as for business. The countryman will invade the town and take possession of it, speaking in terms which will perplex the townsman. It is a good thing that there should be this periodic meeting of urban and rural dweller ... The townsman, surrounded by all the amenities which any modern town provides, may not, perhaps, appreciate to the full the tribulations of the rural dweller. On the other hand, he looks somewhat enviously at the absence of restraint and the glorious freedom which life on the land offers.[3]

Such expressions of secure urban identity, quite distinct from the life of the countryside, were in fact unusual for Bulawayo in the 1930s. The town's citizens liked instead to marvel at the very existence of the town. Tourists and more distinguished visitors were fondly quoted, admiring Bulawayo's wide streets and its modern swimming pool, and expressing astonishment that all this should exist in the veld. Thus the *Chronicle* ran a headline: 'Bulawayo Gets a Boost. A Great City in the Wilds'. It cited with pleasure a characteristic example of British press sensationalism, a story carried in the *Daily Express* about a visit to Bulawayo:

> No more than 35 years ago it was the centre of the most iniquitous despotism known in the history of South Africa ... the stage whereon twenty to thirty thousand naked savages writhed through the sensuous postures of the barbaric 'Dance of Death'. I had been prepared for the worst. I had every reason to expect something not far surpassing the tin hut villages of Uganda. But what did I find? A full-grown, prosperous twentieth-century town ... a city flung into the wilds of Central Africa.[4]

Bulawayo's citizens liked to remember how recently the town had been surrounded by bush. Sir Robert Tredgold, recalling his Bulawayo childhood, remembered 'the wild country that came to the very threshold of the town ... Whilst we lived in town, we grew up in the veld. The veld came to the very outskirts of the town and it was not necessary to travel very far to encounter big game.'[5] Allister Macmillan's account of Bulawayo in 1930 declared that 'civilised Bulawayo may be, but it is only a matter of a few minutes' drive to be in the very heart of nature. Crowds gathered at the monthly meeting of the Turf Club are not surprised when the dainty form of a steenbok or the larger and lighter-hued body of a duiker dashes away in front of their eyes.' Jackals were heard by night at Milton School; leopards were seen on the road to the Matopos; there were even giraffe in that 'rocky fastness'; and as one drove out of town 'great owls flew up from the roadway'. Arriving at Bulawayo station, wrote Macmillan, 'it is impossible to think of it as anything other than a speck in the immensity of virgin country'.[6]

Yet the white townsmen also liked to insist that the veld immediately around Bulawayo had itself been civilized. In 1930, they believed, the town was surrounded not by the 'wilderness' but by 'countryside'. Bulawayo Township formed the nucleus of a

3   *Chronicle*, 3 August 1929.
4   *Chronicle*, 15 February 1929. The paper drew the line, however, at a story which appeared in the *Observer* in January 1930 about a trek across Africa by two Australian 'explorers'. This described how the Australians entered 'the tropics' when they came to Bulawayo and that 'from Bulawayo they had to cut through unexplored forests'. The 'wilds' around Bulawayo were tamed – or at the least explored. *Chronicle*, 15 January 1930.
5   Robert Tredgold, *The Rhodesia That Was My Life*, Allen and Unwin, London, 1968, p. 44.
6   Allister Macmillan, *Rhodesia and Eastern Africa*, Collinridge, London, 1931, pp. 241, 246.

series of concentric belts. [7] Rhodes had desired that the town 'be surrounded by park-lands so that its people would never have far to walk to reach open country'. [8] In May 1930 the *Chronicle* noted that the Town Council remained true to this ideal and 'had laid it down that there is to be a belt of parkland around the town'; Macmillan found that 'the park lands completely encircle the town', never less than 150 yards across and 'widening out at the actual parks to a considerable size.'[9] When the Town Clerk wrote in December 1930 to thank the retiring Parks Curator for his 30 years of service, he told him that he had created the parks out of 'the bare veld'.[10]

The next belt around Bulawayo was the Commonage, 36 square miles in extent. The Commonage was not parkland but neither was it wild. In 1930 most of it was grazing land for large herds of cattle; parts of it constituted a Municipal Farm. On portions of the Commonage new suburbs had been marked out. These were advertised as parts of a rural landscape. Burnside, 'a new suburb of Bulawayo', was advertised as possessing 'charming scenery' and 'healthy mountain air'.[11] Then in a wider circle around the Commonage came privately owned 'European' farms. And finally, beyond all these civilized circles, there came the 'wilderness'.

There was constant exhortation that these multiple landscapes should be 'beautified'. The 'wilderness' of the Matopos was literally captured by landscape painting and by photography – the hills, wrote Eric Nobbs in the first guide to the Matopos, fitting neatly into a camera aperture. A motor road ran to the World's View and to the grave of Cecil Rhodes and many Bulawayo hotels and car firms thrived on tourists planning to make pilgrimages to the site. The Matopos had also been subordinated to Bulawayo's need for a playground. Cecil Rhodes had declared that the Matopos hills, south of Bulawayo, should be reserved for the rest and recreation of the citizens of his town. At the weekends a train ran from Bulawayo to the Matopos – its fare was 'a specially low one, intended to enable everyone to reach the Matopos from Bulawayo for a brief holiday with a minimum of expense'. Rhodes had also provided for two hotels – the Matopos Hotel and the Terminus Hotel – 'so that the people of Bulawayo may enjoy the glory of the Matopos'. As well as mountaineering and photographing and hiking in the hills, the citizens of Bulawayo could enjoy tennis, billiards, bathing and boating at the hotels. 'Dances are occasionally given', wrote Eric Nobbs in the first guide to the Matopos; 'During the holiday season the hotels

---

[7] In 1930 Bulawayo was not yet a city. The municipal area was then called the Township. The African residential area, the Location, was situated outside the Township. Later, of course, when Bulawayo became a city, the term Township came to be applied to African residential areas.

[8] Oliver Ransford, *Bulawayo. Historic Battleground of Rhodesia*, Balkema, Cape Town, 1968, p. 62.

[9] *Chronicle*, 2 May 1930; Macmillan, p. 243. Labour Party members of parliament for Bulawayo attacked the existence of this constricting 'green belt' which they held prevented low-cost housing schemes for white workers being erected close to the town centre.

[10] The Curator, J.H. Ayling, himself spoke of 'the early days of Bulawayo when the beautiful park of today was nothing more than virgin veld'. Ayling had been recruited from Natal where he had worked in the gardens of the Governor; prior to that he had worked in the gardens of a number of English stately homes. When he arrived in Bulawayo in December 1898 'there was only a small portion of ground' and 'everything was in a very primitive state'. The river flooded every rainy season and washed all the planting away. He built English-style greenhouses; laid a system of water pipes; and eventually created Central Park, 'which is today, with its green lawns, gay flower beds, rose garden and shady walks, second to none in South Africa'. From the Parks' nursery came the flowering trees which by 1930 lined the streets of the town; Parks' staff had decorated the Market Square and laid out the gardens at the swimming-pool; and 'the Parks have been responsible for the many beautiful gardens today in the Suburbs by supplying the plants, grass for lawns, etc.' *Chronicle*, 17 December 1930.

[11] *Chronicle*, 1 January 1929. Land only two and a half miles from Bulawayo was advertised as 'a very fine country estate'.

are very gay socially.'[12]

And if the 'wilderness' could be civilized, so too, surely, could the farm belt. A columnist in the *Chronicle*, one 'Sylvander', deplored the average Matabeleland farm house:

> There could be fewer greater aesthetic nightmares than the mass of Rhodesian farmhouses … Building monstrosities can be the only fitting appellation .. What can we expect from a future generation, reared in a brick box, covered with corrugated iron? When we visit the homes of the Old Dutch in the Cape we realise the debt we owe to them … What is it that we lack? Is it taste? Is it ability? One thinks that the answer must primarily lie in a lack of faith in this, our country. Most of us cannot yet settle down to considering Rhodesia our permanent home [and hence cannot build] monuments of our love for our home, our children's home and the home of our country.[13]

Thereafter the *Chronicle* regularly carried photographs of Cape Dutch architecture.

Similar exhortations were addressed to the inhabitants of the suburbs. 'The appearance of the town outside the business areas', noted a columnist, 'is dependent to a great extent on the appearance of its gardens … a well-laid-out garden can often make amends very successfully for a building that leaves something to be desired from an aesthetic viewpoint'.[14] In June 1930 suburban householders were rebuked for doing 'so much to spoil what should be the real beauty spots of Bulawayo by erecting their [sanitary] outbuildings where these are overlooked by houses on other stands'. 'There are many ugly things in our midst today', the columnist continued. It was the duty of everyone to produce a Brighter Bulawayo.[15]

The inside of houses was just as important as their exterior. The monthly reports on new buildings in Bulawayo, carried by the *Chronicle*, were illustrated with photographs of beautiful interiors, lavishly furnished. These, too, were largely derived from the Cape. As we have seen, Councillor Ellenbogen, the Mayor of Bulawayo in 1929, owned the largest furnishing store in the town. Speaking as Mayor, he praised the increasing aesthetic sense shown by the citizens of Bulawayo and urged them to buy Rhodesian landscape paintings to decorate their houses. When they could not actually get out to the Matopos, he said, they could at least sit and look at representations of them. Meanwhile Ellenbogen's regularly advertised in the *Chronicle* with photographs of magnificent suites of furniture – imported from South Africa – to deck out

---

[12] Eric Nobbs, *Guide to the Matopos*, Maskew Miller, Cape Town, 1924, pp. 2-3. The advertisements included in Nobbs' guide are instructive. Davis and Co., 'the home of beautiful books', offered reading on the Ndebele; Basch and Co. offered curios and a photographic department with 'beautiful views of the Matopos'; Ellis Allen offered 'books on the Native Language'; Puzey and Payne advertised 'motor drives to the Matopos and Rhodes's Grave'; so too did Zeederberg's and Duly's. The Palace and the Grand Hotel offered tours to the Matopos and the Victoria Falls. For Nobbs himself and for the Matopos generally, see Terence Ranger, *Voices From the Rocks. Nature, Culture and History in the Matopos*, James Currey, Oxford, 1999. Closer to a true wilderness were the forests of the Gwaii and Shangani Reserves, north of Bulawayo. For these see Jocelyn Alexander, JoAnn Mcgregor and Terence Ranger, *Violence and Memory. One Hundred Years in the 'Dark Forests' of Northern Matabeleland*, James Currey, Oxford, 2000.

[13] *Chronicle*, 12 January 1929.

[14] *Chronicle*, 24 January 1929.

[15] *Chronicle*, 17 June 1930. The main debate between Labour spokesmen and the commercial men who made up the majority on the Bulawayo Council was about the situation and the character of the town's suburbs. Labour demanded in Parliament that 'the Municipality lay out a large area on the Commonage' close to the town where land was cheap and building could be economical. Council preferred the commercial development of new suburbs like Kumalo, where there were 'high set-up prices' for land. Significantly the 30 May 1930 issue of the *Chronicle* which reported this debate, also carried a photo of 'the charming modern residence of Mr. O. Kaufman, which is one of the prettiest in the suburbs'.

the 'house beautiful'. Ratepayers could fill the interiors of their houses with the wares of their Mayor and they could fill their own interiors, and those of their guests, with the elegant delicacies sold by Councillor Macintyre's bakery.

Sometimes they were allowed to believe that Bulawayo was already Bright:

> I must confess that since the Great War I had not been inland at all [wrote the pioneer, W.E. Fairbridge] ... It was startling to look at the Bulawayo of 1930. Here I first stood in 1895 when the first buildings were like so many scattered farm beacons on a plain; and I also saw it, on and off, for fifteen years more, when its lordly streets and avenues still gaped widely for compatible mansions to grace them. Now the town is compact and continuous ... [In the suburbs] villas, large and small, line the avenues and roads, with large gardens, well-watered and cultured, supporting a mass of colour unknown in my day.[16]

The centre of the town itself was also being beautified. The ramshackle bars around the Market Square were swept away; gardens were planted; and eventually the City Hall was built. The nearby Grand Hotel advertised itself as 'the finest hotel in Rhodesia' and promised 'a magnificent lounge' and a 'beautiful Ball Room'. The British sculptor, John Tweed, designer of the statue of Rhodes which stood in Main Street and of the plaques for the Shangani Monument at World's View, visited Bulawayo for the first time in January 1929. 'He was genuinely delighted with the lay-out of Bulawayo. With such a beginning, he said, it would be a pleasure to build for the future and make a really fine town.'[17] The *Chronicle* published regular features on the new buildings going up in Bulawayo:

> What one week is an open stand, covered with grass and tree-stumps, is transformed the next into foundations, scaffolding and all the signs of busy building activity ... In the centre of the town the few remaining open spaces are rapidly filling up ... The Municipality is making gardens in Market Square, and Selbourne Avenue makes a really pleasant drive.[18]

In January 1930 the *Chronicle* reported that 'building activity in Bulawayo continues almost unabated. To gain an idea of the rate of increase it is only necessary to walk down the length of Main Street. Three years ago it consisted of a few houses separated at almost regular intervals by large vacant stands; today there is scarcely a vacant piece of ground to be found, and from Sixth Avenue to the King's Ground both sides of the road are lined with new and attractive buildings ... it is a credit to the builders and architects of the town to be able to say that there is not one which does not present a handsome frontage.'[19]

Indeed, central Bulawayo was not merely being built, it was being beautified by art. The new fire station would have 'four ten-foot entrances of an artistic design'; the Police Barracks on Selbourne would be 'artistically arched'. And so things continued. The 1930s were years of economic depression, but they were also years when the main buildings in central Bulawayo were being erected – the Bulawayo Club, the High Court, and many others gave the city a properly monumental air.

There was a class dimension to this discussion of urban aesthetics. Ellenbogen's, as a furniture store, appealed to its suburban customers by offering a comfortable

---

16 *Chronicle*, 3 July 1930.
17 *Chronicle*, 8 January 1929. Tweed made it clear, however, that he disapproved of the attempted beautification of World's View. His own design for the Shangani Memorial had been neglected and the result was a disaster.
18 *Chronicle*, 24 January 1929.
19 *Chronicle*, 24 January 1930. The paper noted that two theatres were being built; a new fire station and police barracks, clearing away 'the old shanties and ugly buildings; and a technical school hostel'.

bourgeois idea of beauty; Ellenbogen, and his successors as Mayor, were reluctant to see Bulawayo surrounded by Council estates for white workers. Certainly the rate-payers could not be expected to meet any part of the costs of cheap white housing. The Council relied on private capital and on letting by landlords. Labour spokesmen complained about high rents and overcrowding – Jack Keller in Parliament instanced a white railwayman in Bulawayo who was charged £12 10s a month rent out of a £21 monthly salary. They warned of the rise of white slums. But even Labour supporters appealed to the imperative of 'beautifying' Bulawayo. In September 1930 a corre-spondent to the *Chronicle* spelt out Labour's policy. 'There is ample ground within the immediate vicinity of the centres of the larger towns of Southern Rhodesia in the possession of the Municipality'; on this, cheap housing could be erected. If Council loans were made available then 'the individual citizen' could be transformed 'from a tenant householder to an owner with a stake in the country … affording him every incentive to beautify the surroundings in which his children are reared. The exterior styles could be varied to avoid the depressing uniformity which exists in the older countries … and each house would stand in its own acre of ground. The area selected would soon vie with the best residential areas we now have.'[20]

In short, even if white Bulawayans liked to hear visitors marvel at this city in the wilds, their image of themselves was of a highly developed town surrounded by parks, and flowers, and by charming rural scenery. The wilds had been tamed. The case of the Bulawayo lion is emblematic. For 30 years a single male lion had been an attrac-tion in Bulawayo's zoo. Stanlake Samkange, remembering his childhood in Bulawayo Location in 1929, wrote:

> Bulawayo had the country's only zoo. One went to bed or woke up to the roar of lions … no doubt a welcome assurance to new arrivals from Europe that at last they were in the heart of Africa, even though, in the streets, there was a white man whose job it was to prevent Africans from walking on the pavements.[21]

For older white inhabitants of Bulawayo, however, the lion had a different signifi-cance. When a newcomer wrote to the paper saying how wrong it was to keep a lion in a zoo rather than leaving it in the wild, a long-term resident replied:

> The old lion in our zoo is far happier where he is than he would be if he were now roaming the veld footsore and weary, ravenous with hunger, thorns and porcupine quills rotting in his feet and lips, full of despair and knowing his doom is to die a lonely, lingering and exquisitely pain-ful death. What a contrast to his present lot! Sheltered from the cold winds and rain, well cared for, and happy and contented.[22]

Rural Town & Urban Countryside

White Bulawayo preferred its nature tamed. Technological developments helped in this domestication. In the 1890s white cyclists had set off for picnics at the Umgusa

[20] *Chronicle*, 13 September 1930. See also fn15.
[21] Stanlake Samkange, *The Mourned One*, Heinemann Educational Books, London, 1975, p. 116.
[22] *Chronicle*, 7 June 1930. It could not have escaped the attention of readers that the same reply was being given to overseas 'sentimental negrophiles' who deplored the removal of Africans from their former life and their incarceration in mines and towns.

Hotel. By the 1930s motor cars had made much longer expeditions common. In the 1890s cameras had been massive and heavy, to be carried only by strong men on expeditions into the bush. Now advertisers appealed especially to white women: 'Glorious Africa. What subjects are here for your Kodak! Armed with a Kodak and a few rolls of Kodak film, you may gather pictures of all that is best in Africa as easily as a child gathers flowers.'[23] A 'countryside' and a 'wilderness playground' had been created and Bulawayo interacted intensely with both.

The interaction was economic as well as aesthetic. As we have seen, Bulawayo was quintessentially a railway town. In the future this was going to facilitate the rise of industries as sites were set aside on the Commonage close to the railway sidings. In 1930, though, the railway was important mainly for the export of agrarian rather than industrial products. Particularly important was the trade in cattle and frozen beef for the Katanga and Johannesburg markets. A major trader was the Rhodesian Export and Cold Storage Co. Ltd which, as the Town Clerk wrote on 27 November 1930, 'has recently erected large abattoirs and chilling works capable of dealing with not less than 20,000 head of stock per annum'.[24] The Cold Storage Co. rented large grazing areas on the Commonage, regularly driving in herds from their outside ranches. So too did the Rhodesian Rand Livestock Co. and the Congo-Rhodesian Ranching Co., which kept cattle in fenced paddocks near the railway sidings and regularly sent stock by train.[25] Indeed Bulawayo's economy was largely based on the production and processing of grains and animals. Fortunes could be made. In November 1929, for instance, the *Chronicle* reported that the Charter Butchery in Bulawayo had been given a contract to supply all Rhodesian Anglo American mines in Northern Rhodesia with meat, involving the slaughter of 6,000 head per year, doubling over the next 18 months. The butchery had sent agents out prospecting for cattle in Northern Rhodesia, but it would be necessary to 'send Southern Rhodesian cattle up on the hoof.'[26] 'Bulawayo's chief industries', wrote the Town Clerk in November 1931, 'are flour milling, dairy farming, poultry farming and cattle farming. Breweries are established in the town.'[27]

In other ways, too, Bulawayo's citizens had close material links with the countryside. 'If you are a resident in the town', wrote the Town Clerk in June 1933, 'you are entitled to graze two cows on the Commonage free of charge.'[28] Until February 1934 residents were allowed to maintain stables and cowsheds within Bulawayo Township area and to milk dairy cows.[29] One of Bulawayo's two cattle auctions was held at the Market Square in the very centre of the town. African drovers herded white-owned cattle to the auction ground along the town's main thoroughfare, Selbourne

[23] *Chronicle*, 5 January 1929.
[24] Town Clerk, B1/10.BR Box 18, National Archives, Bulawayo.
[25] Town Clerk to Rhodesian Rand Livestock Co., 12 March 1934; to General Manager, Congo-Rhodesian Ranching Co., 29 January 1936, B1/10/5F, National Archives, Bulawayo.
[26] *Chronicle*, 30 November 1929.
[27] Town Clerk to J.W. Robertson, 23 November 1932, B1/19/5, Box 19, National Archives, Bulawayo. There were also sugar refineries and hide processing works.
[28] Town Clerk to H. Steyn, 19 June 1933, ibid.
[29] Town Clerk to Secretary, Internal Affairs, 23 February 1934, ibid. Bulawayo's leading auctioneer was A.G. Hay, an 1893 pioneer, and President of the Bulawayo Landowners and Farmers Association. He kept a stables in town which he used for auctions: 'cattle, sheep and goats arriving by train or by road are stabled for the night pending sale'. The town's by-laws laid down that residents could only keep two cows and one calf but allowed any number of oxen or bulls. Chief Sanitary Inspector, report, 19 November 1919, 23.2.IR, Box 5700, National Archives, Bulawayo.

Avenue.[30] African pig-breeders brought their squealing animals into town and then repaired to the Location to gamble away their takings.

By 1930 there was one motor car for every five whites in Bulawayo,[31] but the Municipality itself used animal transport for most of its operations:

> We have in the service [wrote the Town Clerk in October 1935] ox transport, mule transport and motor transport, each serving the purpose for which it is required as the most economical method.

Oxen were used to cart firewood from the Commonage to municipal departments. They were used in the Location 'for rubbish collection', and on the Municipal Farm. 'In the town for rubbish removals mule transport is used ... For our night service removals we use both mules and donkeys.'[32] During 1930, when many car owners were objecting to the hazards in turning their vehicles posed by the new central lighting standards, readers wrote in to the *Chronicle* describing how ox-carts managed the manouevre perfectly.[33]

Bulawayo was a town full of animals. As we have seen, the new suburbs saw themselves as set in the countryside, with beautiful scenery and mountain air. Even the original Suburbs area, immediately east of the Park, felt itself rural rather than urban if only because of the state of the roads which linked it to the town centre. In a rare compliment to Salisbury, one 'Stave' commended its tarred suburban roads and compared them to 'the turnings which radiate from the eastern end of Selbourne Avenue ... I thought of the bumps and the marshes and the skids.'[34] The *Chronicle* waxed ecstatic about Kumalo, which 'with its position at the top of the hill and its view of a vast stretch of countryside should become Bulawayo's garden-suburb'.[35] In August 1930 a Country Club opened, seven miles along the Bulawayo-Salisbury road, its 'well elevated verandah offering a glorious view across seven miles of veld of the twinkling lights of Bulawayo.'[36]

A good stretch of this view was part of the Commonage which lay between Bulawayo and the white-owned farms and ranches. The Commonage had originally been established in 1893 to provide grazing for the horses of the Victoria Column, but leading settler and military figures had soon gained leases upon it. Some of them tried to set up farms; others held the land for speculation. With characteristic good fortune, the American adventurer, Frank Burnham, obtained a lease of land in Kumalo, which was later sold at suburban prices. In 1893 the 'coloured wagon drivers who had entered Bulawayo with Forbes' column were given one hundred acre plots'. White, Coloured and African cultivators grew vegetables on the Commonage to sell in Bulawayo Township. The original Commonage was traversed by 'the web of bushroads

---

[30] Town Clerk to Superintendent of Police, 14 March 1934. The Town Clerk sent a circular to butchers and auctioneers asking them to make sure that their herdsmen 'kept to the outskirts of the town and followed the suggested routes'. Ibid.

[31] Macmillan, p. 245.

[32] Town Clerk to Acting Town Clerk, Que Que, 2 October 1935, B1/10/5F.

[33] The District Secretary of the Automobile Association wrote to ask the Council to frame a by-law 'compelling slow-moving vehicles such as animal-drawn wagons and carts to keep the extreme left hand side of the road'. Unsympathetically, the Town Clerk replied that *all* vehicles were required to keep to the left and that inside the Township all should be slow-moving. Town Clerk to District Secretary, 11 March 1936, ibid.

[34] *Chronicle*, 1 October 1930.

[35] *Chronicle*, 23 January 1930.

[36] *Chronicle*, 11 August 1930.

which led into the surrounding countryside [and] followed tracks originally made by Lobengula's wagons'. These tracks led to African villages which in the 1890s and for many years later were occupied by their Ndebele inhabitants. They were not displaced, either by the 1893 war which had resulted in the white occupation of Bulawayo, or by the repression of the 1896 rising. Hence there were many claims on this 1890s Commonage – by the original Ndebele inhabitants; by the Bulawayo Council; by the British South Africa Company; by the white adventurers who had obtained leases; by Coloured plot-holders and by African 'squatters'.

The story of the Commonage between the 1890s and the 1930s was the achievement of municipal control and the elimination of most of the other claimants. In May 1902 the Company ceded ownership of 30,000 acres of the Commonage to the Council, though it retained mineral rights. The Council celebrated by making grants of Commonage land to the Golf Club; the Rhodesia Scottish Football Club; the Amateur Cycling Club; the Municipal Police Cricket and Football Club and other sporting bodies.[37] After the achievement of Settler Responsible Government in 1923, 'the Government granted Municipalities full title to the Commonage areas [36 square miles in total] without restriction'.[38] The Bulawayo Municipality used its new powers to squeeze all African cultivators and cattle-keepers off the Commonage and to complete the clearing away of their villages. African vegetable growers were also removed. No Africans were allowed to live on the Commonage except as Municipal Farm workers or the domestic servants of plot-holders. (Exceptionally, until her death in 1930, Martha Ngano managed to retain her Commonage stand near the Location.) The Commonage Ranger made regular patrols and raids to ensure that no African employed in the town lived on the Commonage.

The Commonage was essentially a huge 'reserved' area. Long-term municipal planning allocated some of it as industrial sites, the portion lying to the east for further European suburbs and the portion lying to the west for future African villages and locations. Little of this got under way until the late 1940s and 1950s. Today the Commonage has been swallowed up. But in the 1930s it was a huge rural zone. The Municipality ran a large farm and dairy on it, employing much African labour. The farm produced fodder for cattle and meat and cereals for the Council's African workers. The Council employed a Ranger who supervised the use of the Commonage and in particular prevented anyone from cutting wood. All firewood and charcoal produced on the Commonage went for the use of the various municipal departments.

As the Town Clerk told the Secretary of Gwelo Town Management Board in 1933, when that body was exploring the advantages of municipal status, ownership of the Commonage was a great advantage to the Council. It could set aside industrial and residential sites there and incorporate them into the rate-paying zone of the Municipality. This was largely for the future. In the meantime the Commonage was used for largely agrarian activities:

> The principal revenue from the Commonage is derived from the rent of Commonage plots. This Municipality has nearly 200 Commonage plots on lease for various businesses, such as market gardening, poultry and dairy, brickmaking and laundries. Wood is all used for Municipal purposes … Cattle grazing fees at the rate of 1s per head, per month, also provide considerable revenue. Certain parts of the Commonage have been cleared and fenced as haylands for

---

[37] Oliver Ransford, *Bulawayo. Historic Battleground of Rhodesia*, pp. 66, 68, 133, 138, 250. According to Ransford, a crocodile in the stream on the golf course was 'a recognised natural hazard'.
[38] Town Clerk to Minister of Agriculture and Lands, 17 August 1935.

Municipal transport animals … Such Municipal concerns as the dipping tanks, stockyards and abbattoirs are all established in Commonage land.[39]

Very large numbers of cattle congregated near the railway yards where the Municipality provided quarantine paddocks and water supplies, charging 2s per head a month. There were regular alarms that the Commonage was being overgrazed or that too much wood was being cut. By the 1930s the bush had largely been cleared. Cattle had driven out game from the Commonage area and overshadowed people. The majority of Bulawayo's Coloured population lived on the Commonage plots – 642 out of a total of 870. They did not pay rates but most of their houses were little more than shacks, without drainage, light, water supply or sewerage. A survey of the condition of Coloureds in Bulawayo in 1939 found that 'the lack of drainage and the proximity of cattle to the houses gave rise to numerous flies and mosquitoes, leaving the residents prone to diseases such as malaria and dysentery.'[40]

Beyond the Commonage lay the white-owned farms and ranches. There had never been Reserves within the 350,000 acres of Bulawayo District: the whole area was proclaimed as 'white' in the 1930 Land Apportionment Act. Some of the farms produced cattle for export or wheat for the Bulawayo bakeries. White farmers had close connections with the town. They came in to do their shopping, even if the terrible state of the country roads made such trips infrequent.[41] They came in every August for the annual Agricultural Show. And they flocked in for public protest meetings.

They were members of an influential lobby, the Bulawayo Landowners and Farmers Association. The Association had played an important role, along with the white railway workers, in demanding self-government in 1923. 'The really independent people in those days were the farmers so the Bulawayo Landowners and Farmers Association was the most vocal of all the bodies', campaigning against the control of land by the British South Africa Company.[42] In the late 1920s and early 1930s the Association's President was A.G. Hay. Hay symbolized the link between town and country. He was auctioneer at the Market Square, situated at the very heart of Bulawayo, to which farmers sent their cattle to be sold. Under his leadership the

[39] Town Clerk to Secretary, TMB, Gwelo, 22 August 1933.
[40] J.M. Cobb, *General Survey of the Living, Working and Housing Conditions of the Coloured Community in the Municipal Area of Bulawayo*, Bulawayo, 1939, pp. 4-5.
[41] The oral testimony of Mary Eileen Martin is interesting here. In the 1930s Martin worked at Hope Fountain Mission farm. 'We were only ten miles from Bulawayo but we rarely went into the town.' The roads were rutted and impassable in wet weather. The monthly trip to town was a great expedition. They drove in through Douglasdale, Burnside and Hillside: 'We used to get our groceries at wholesale prices at a firm called Thomas and Co. A very friendly Mr Thomas used to ask us into his office for a cup of tea while his assistants packed up groceries … We also dealt with Jaggers and Garlicks, buying bolts of material for the school there. We had accounts at Haddon and Sly … Osborne's Bakery and Doulton's tea-shop were places we went to for a mid-morning cup of tea.' They bought grapes at the auctions in Market Square. 'The bigger stores were two or three floors high but there were still many of the single-storey, iron-roofed, old shops.' Oral testimony of Mary Eileen Martin, dictated on tape 1979, National Archives, October 1985, ORAL/229.
[42] Interview with Sir Patrick Fletcher, June 1971, ORAL/FL 1, National Archives, Harare. Fletcher's father, R.A. Fletcher, was leader of the Matabeleland farmers and became Minister of Agriculture after 1923. Patrick Fletcher insists that the commercial leaders in Bulawayo would not support any political movement and depended on the patronage of the Company. But the workers were more radical. 'I always had a lot of time for Jack Keller. He was always fighting for the underdog. He was rather like a bulldog. If he got hold of a point that he thought was a good one, he never let it go.' Nevertheless, when Keller called the railway strike in 1929 and challenged the new settler Responsible Government, the farmers supported the regime against the workers. 'A lot of us were recruited during the strike,' remembers Fletcher, 'to go on picket duty on the Bulawayo station. We were given pick handles to stop the railway workers from any sabotage and to protect property.'

Association intervened in a wide range of issues, far beyond the immediate interests of agriculture. In September 1929, for instance, Hay chaired a meeting in Bulawayo to demand that government set up a 'bacteriological laboratory' in the town. And the Association took a leading part in cultivating an atmosphere of racial paranoia, adding the fears of the white country dwellers to the panics of the town.

In January 1930 Hay expressed the view of the Association that trouble 'had been simmering' between whites and blacks 'for the last two years or more'. He had seen 'a crowd of natives on the Khami Road in full war paint and carrying assegais ... having a war dance and looking for trouble'. His personal kingdom of Market Square had been invaded by the Industrial and Commercial Workers Union, who had held:

> public meetings ... at the back of the Market Square during the past few weeks and I am told on good authority that the remarks passed were more than any of you gentlemen would have stood.

Hay warned that trouble had spread from the town to the countryside – 'the days have gone by when the indunas had control of their kraals'. A farmer member of the Association warned that 'there was a sullen air among the native workers on the farms'.[43]

In March 1930 the Association organized in Bulawayo one of 'the most largely attended [meetings] for a long time' to protest against the government's appointment of a Standing Commission of Native Affairs. The 'Matabeleland Farmers' denounced the new Commission as needless, expensive and negrophilist – 'a perfect abomination'. Hay announced that:

> if they had any trouble with the natives it would devolve upon them as farmers. It would not be the townspeople and the Government who would suffer so much. Appointing such a Commission without consulting the farmers was an abomination ... I think it is high time that the farmers and miners put their foot down and saw to it that they had some say in the ruling of the native. (Loud and Prolonged Applause.)[44]

The Council had cleared the Commonage of its old African inhabitants. The members of the Bulawayo Landowners and Farmers Association were determined to clear the farmlands of any African owners. The initial idea of the Land Apportionment Act had been raised by white ranchers in Matabeleland South before the First World War.[45] Farmers in Matabeleland enthusiastically supported the idea of 'possessory segregation' in their evidence to the Carter Land Commission in 1925. Over the years, however, absentee white landowners had sold farms to Africans. As early as 1898 Maya and Gwabu, both Rozvi, bought 25 acres on the Riverside Agricultural Lots, six miles from Bulawayo, for £270. In 1904 M.D. Makgatho and D. Mogale bought 89 acres at Riverside for as much as £436; in 1916 Thomas Mazinyani bought 6 acres of Trenance Farm for £150. (Albert Nxale, about whom little is known, bought 40 acres on Trenance.) Magkatho, Mogale and Mazinyani were Sotho; their land was

---

[43] *Chronicle*, 4 January 1930.

[44] *Chronicle*, 7 March 1930.

[45] Patrick Fletcher recalled in 1971 that 'the Land Apportionment was conceived in Western Matabeleland where there was an African farm, granted in the early days, right in the middle of the European area, which developed into a ragged sort of squatter township almost ... My father was the leader of the farmers in Matabeleland and he took it up with Lord Selbourne in 1907.' R.A. Fletcher urged possessory segregation from that point onwards; introduced and carried a resolution in the Assembly in 1920; raised it with the British Government in 1923 and was responsible for the appointment of a Royal Commission. ORAL/229, National Archives, Harare.

only 6 miles away from the town; all three took prominent roles in the 'progressive' associations which met in the Bulawayo Location. Makgatho was a pastor in the African Methodist Episcopal Church which represented the aspirations of many Christian progressives in the Location.[46] But after the passage of the Land Apportionment Act in 1930 the six African landowners were dispossessed. The farming belt around Bulawayo had become a white-owned landscape and the drive was really on to transform farmhouses from 'aesthetic nightmares' to gracious homes.[47]

The Management of Space in Bulawayo Town & the Failure of Segregation

Much of the writing about urban landscapes concerns 'the management of space'. So far as southern Africa is concerned, the management of space usually means the allocation of racial residential areas in a system of segregation. As we have seen, there was indeed a drive towards segregation in Bulawayo in the 1930s. Most 'coloureds' had been placed on the Commonage and most Africans removed from it. Black farm-owners had been dispossessed. The Location itself was seen as dangerously polluting and it was separated from the town by a cordon sanitaire of open land.[48] In the 1930s many white residents of Bulawayo called for total segregation in the town itself. In February 1934, for example, a prominent Bulawayo women's leader and sympathizer with the Labour Party, Mrs McKeurtan, wrote to Prime Minister Godfrey Huggins to congratulate him on a recent speech. 'Like every other woman in Rhodesia, I have a special interest in segregation, ultimately complete and final.'[49]

The Bulawayo Municipality itself was particularly interested in the segregation of

---

[46] Robin Palmer, *Land and Racial Domination in Rhodesia*, Heinemann, London, 1977, appendix II. For M.D. Makgatho, see T.O. Ranger, *The African Voice in Southern Rhodesia, 1898-1930*, pp. 41-3, 56, 64, 72, 92-3, 114, 138, 191, 192. For Mazinyani, see pp. 92, 98, 100, 101, 117, 118, 120. For the African Methodist Episcopal Church see pp. 41-3, 51, 204.

[47] There was a landscape rhetoric associated with possessory segregation. African-owned farms were said to *look* African, like the 'ragged sort of squatter township' which developed on the African farm in western Matabeleland, with 'snaring, hunting with dogs and cutting of fences'. In fact the African landowners near Bulawayo were anxious to create a 'civilized' landscape. Maya and Gwabu built brick houses, sank wells, used irrigation and planted orchards; they owned mules, donkeys, carts, and wagons. Makgatho and Mogale established schools. Mazinyani's brick house on Trenance was valued at £200.

[48] As elsewhere in southern Africa, this discourse was stimulated by successive epidemics. It was articulated in its extreme form as early as 1908, when there was a typhoid scare. 'The Native population,' wrote the Town Superintendent in December of that year, 'is a very serious factor, their habits are entirely opposed to European ideas of sanitation ... They are responsible for the widespread pollution of the soil in the Town by using the ground for the purposes of nature.' In the Location itself all the latrines were placed on the western side. 'In consequence of this the ground bordering the Location on the Town side is greatly soiled.' Report by Town Superintendent, December 1908, 23/1/8R, Box 5689, National Archives, Bulawayo.

[49] Mrs McKeurtan to Godfrey Huggins, 2 February 1934, S.482 789/19, National Archives, Harare. It was well known that Mrs McKeurtan had a special interest in total separation of the races because her husband, a white artisan, was an inveterate hunter of black women, prostitutes and others, in the Bulawayo Location. In File 46 in the 'Immorality' series, S.1222/1, Mary Manukwa, a house-owner in Brickfields, complains that McKeurtan has been pestering her for sex; she called in the police; Constable Samuel Mahoko witnessed his attempt upon her, and told the white carpenter that 'it was no use coming after the native girls as he was well known in town and married and a white man'. Mrs McKeurtan made a statement on 14 September 1920 that 'for 17 years he has been living an immoral life ... a coloured child has been born to Mr McKeurtan who has squandered his substance'. Many previous entries concern her requests to the police to fetch her husband back from the Location. No wonder Mrs McKeurtan wanted the Location removed altogether.

Asians from both blacks and whites. It repeatedly asked the central government for authority to expel Asians from the Location:

> Native Eating houses are allowed in our location [the Town Clerk told the Secretary of a Town Management Board on 18 January 1934] but are conducted mostly by Indians, there being only two native proprietors ... No European person is allowed to carry on business in the Location and this Municipality has from time to time endeavoured to find the legal means of prohibiting Indians and Asiatics from living in the Location ...

He advised the TMB not to give permits to reside in the Location 'to persons other than natives, not even Coloured persons. Persons who are not natives follow different habits and modes of living and their actions and influence on the natives produce unsatisfactory conditions and often cause trouble.'

The Council also asked government to approve conditional leases in the new suburbs developing on the Commonage, barring either Asians or blacks from buying or renting. The Council's plan was to restrict Asian business and residence to Lobengula Street, thereby interposing a belt of Asian property between the Location and the white town.[50] But in the 1930s neither Mrs McKeurtan nor the Municipality got segregation in Bulawayo town.

When the Council approached government to approve conditional leases:

> We [were] advised by the Attorney General that the condition that the stands shall be used for European residential purposes only was invalid and that the Government must refuse to sanction the sale of the stands subject to this condition. It was stated that the proposed condition in addition to being expressly prohibited both by Common Law and by the Constitution is not in accordance with the spirit and intention of the Land Apportionment Act.[51]

At a first reading this official reply seems extraordinary. Surely the 'spirit and intention of the Land Apportionment Act' was precisely that there should be segregation. The point is, however, that the Act contained provisions for the towns as well as for the countryside. In the countryside it offered the well-known bargain: the Reserves remained entrenched in the Constitution and the remainder of the land was to be divided up between 'white' areas and the new Native Purchase Areas. Only when the NPAs were set up could 'possessory segregation' be enforced in the countryside. Under the Act a similar bargain was proposed for the towns. If Municipalities set aside a 'Native Urban Area', in which only Africans could trade, reside and lease property, *then* the rest of the town could be declared as belonging to whites only. Until such a Native Urban Area was established, the original provisions of the Constitution and Common Law would apply and formal racial discrimination could not be

---

50 For the Council's plans for a segregated 'Indian Trading Area' in Lobengula Street and for the protests of the British Indian Association against them, see Acting Town Clerk, Bulawayo, to H.W. Austin, to W.M. Goulding, to Messrs Roberts and Letts, 3 July 1930. For the Council's plans to develop segregated 'Coloured' housing on the Commonage, see Acting Town Clerk to Coghlan and Welsh, 8 August 1930; for their plans to expel all Asians from the Location, see Acting Town Clerk to Roberts and Letts, 28 August 1930; Town Clerk to Chief Native Commissioner, 23 June 1931; to Secretary, Prime Minister, 23 January 1934; on the Council's desire to have conditional leases of property see Town Clerk to Director, Lands, 11 September 1932; to Town Clerk, Gwelo, 6 January 1933. The out-letter books of the Town Clerk, Bulawayo, for the 1930s are in the National Archives, Bulawayo.

51 Town Clerk to Town Clerk, Gwelo, 6 January 1933. File S.482 789/19 in the National Archives, Harare, contains abundant correspondence on this issue. See especially the minute by the Attorney General, January 1934 and Private Secretary, Prime Minister to Town Clerk, Bulawayo, 20 April 1934.

enforced. But the Bulawayo Municipality refused for nearly two decades to apply the Land Apportionment Act to the town or to set aside a Native Urban Area.[52]

It did this because it was determined to retain total control of the Location. The Bulawayo Location was administered under regulations promulgated in 1895 which were not subject to amendment or suspension under the subsequent Native Urban Locations Ordinance of 1906. To ask that a Native Urban Area be proclaimed would bring the Location under the final authority of the government. This would enable ministers to suspend or amend municipal regulations and it would open the Bulawayo Location to the British South Africa Police rather than to the Municipality's own ramshackle force. Council were determined not to allow central government in:

> My Council feels [wrote the Town Clerk to the Municipality's legal advisors on 31 December 1930] that, although in some respects it may be advisable to bring the existing Location Regulations up to date and have them properly framed, the interference with the inhabitants of the Location by any other controlling authority would be a disadvantage from the point of view of the Superintendent's control.

The Town Clerk was instructed to reply to government in January 1931 that since 'for 35 years up to the present time satisfactory conditions have existed in the Bulawayo Location under the 1895 regulations and the Council's system of management, it must be concluded that there is no reason for a change in the law'. Ignoring the almost daily meetings in the Location protesting against municipal policies, the Town Clerk insisted that Location inhabitants themselves would not welcome change. 'It is certain that the existing easy and efficient administration will not be maintained if suspicion is aroused in the native mind that he is subject to unnecessary outside intrusion … this would lead to discontent.'[53]

I shall discuss further in a later chapter the relation of the city to the state in the 1930s and 1940s. Suffice it to say now that faced with Bulawayo's refusal to implement the Land Apportionment Act the government was in no mood to assist the Municipality in its various segregation programmes. Suburban property could not be sold or leased with racially exclusive clauses; Asians could not be expelled from the Location nor restricted to Lobengula Street. If there were African craftsmen carrying on businesses in town they could not be stopped from doing so. Legal segregation could not be established in Bulawayo until the Council finally proclaimed a Native Urban Area nearly twenty years later.

In any case, even if the Council had had the legal powers to enforce total segregation it did not have the resources to do so. In the 1920s it had built cottages in the Location for single male workers and the population of the Location had grown. It continued to do so in the 1930s. But still by 1936 the Superintendent of Natives, Bula-

---

[52] In a letter of protest to the Director of Lands on 11 September 1932 the Town Clerk tried to make the best of the situation: 'The Land Apportionment Act recognises that natives should be excluded from towns under certain conditions, and although the conditions have not yet been fulfilled by the Municipality, when setting aside areas exclusively for residential purposes it should be entitled to say by whom such areas are occupied.'

[53] Town Clerk to Secretary, Colonial Secretary, 15 January 1931. The oddly-named Colonial Secretary later became the Minister for Internal Affairs. When Salisbury did apply early in 1938 to set aside a Native Urban Area, Huggins ordered that there must be the closest supervision of all details. The Governor should approve the scale of rents, the form of leases, the size of stands, the conditions of latrines, the provision of trading facilities, the wording of Location regulations, etc. 'If we are to interfere in such matters, it will be necessary to do so now.' Secretary for Native Affairs to Prime Minister, 22 August 1938, S.1542 L5A, National Archives, Harare.

wayo, reported that only 3,897 males and 1,237 females, with 990 children, lived in the Location, out of a total male workforce of 13,866. As we shall see, very many of these workers – the Superintendent thought as many as 5,458 – lived on Private Locations on the farms around Bulawayo. But as many as 2,960 lived 'on private premises in the Municipal area'; 998 lived in the Railway Compound; 610 were accommodated in the Municipal Compound. Thus more African male workers lived in the city than in the Location.[54] Those in the Railway and Municipal Compounds lived in a controlled world which kept them away from the white residents of Bulawayo. But African employees, and their wives and friends and relatives, were everywhere in the town – in the little compounds of smaller employers, at the back of business premises, in servants' quarters in the suburbs. The centre of the town itself contained very many literal 'black spots'. Day by day whites were aware of African workers living in amongst them. To take just one example, in September 1930 a householder complained that 'the sewerage compound boys, who sleep in the compound at the north end of Grey Street, are in the habit of standing nude and bathing in full view of Mr Wheeler's household, and that, as he has a wife and children, it is most unpleasant'.[55]

The fears and fantasies which arose from living so close to those whom whites tried to repress and exclude carried on into the 1930s. In January 1932, for example, there was a panic about Africans jostling white women on the pavements. On 15 January the Town Clerk cabled the Secretary, Law, drawing his attention to what he described as a serious crisis. A Vigilantes Association had emerged in order to 'protect' white women and to demand strong action from the Council. Central government responded calmly. Statistics proved, they said, that there had been no increase in 'assaults on white women'. Indignantly the Town Clerk replied:

> While your statistical information may appear to bear out the statement contained in your letter, my Council is convinced that a far more serious intention lies behind the attempted assaults that have recently taken place in Bulawayo than has accompanied native assault cases for some time past. Considerable emotion did exist in the public mind … whatever reassuring information can be given to the public of Bulawayo by the Police Authority … would greatly assist in allaying the fears of a large number of the women of the town and of the general public.

Meanwhile, he assured the Chairman of the Vigilantes Association that 'the by-law prohibiting natives from walking on the footpaths [will be] more strictly observed.'[56]

The White Urban Landscape & Symbolic Space

The pavements by-law became more and more obviously indefensible as the 1930s wore on. But the more criticized it was the more the white inhabitants of Bulawayo demanded its stricter enforcement. It might be impossible to remove Africans from the centre of the town but at least they need not be visible on the sidewalks and in the shops. This imaginary landscape seemed more and more bizarre to outside observers. In March 1930 the *Manchester Guardian* carried a story about what it called 'one of the most amazing colonial laws ever proposed':

---

[54] Superintendent of Natives, Bulawayo to Chief Native Commissioner, 29 October 1936, S.1542 L5A.
[55] Town Clerk to Superintendent of Police, 18 September 1930, B1/10/5R, Box 18, National Archives, Bulawayo.
[56] Town Clerk to J.T. Webster, 8 February; Town Clerk to Secretary, Law, 10 February 1932, B1/9/5F, Box 19, National Archives, Bulawayo.

It is no offence if a native walking on the street is accompanied by white children, but he is liable to arrest if he is accompanied by native children. It is no offence if a native crosses the path to enter a shop to buy a hat, but it is an offence if he is caught loitering outside the shop window inspecting the goods that he is proposing to buy.

The *Chronicle* responded with indignation. It mocked the British paper for having only just discovered a by-law which had been in existence since 1904 and for casting doubts upon the legality of a measure which had been upheld by a local magistrate as 'quite in order':

There is apparently to be worked up an agitation on the grounds that natives are not allowed freedom of movement ... Around the ounce of fact that by-laws do permit natives to be kept from the side-walks there will be spoken or written a ton of fiction concerning the ill-treatment of the native by the white man.[57]

The 'ounce of fact' was hard for many people to digest. In 1930 the Council received protests about the by-law from the Conference of Christian Natives, held in the Wesleyan Church in the Bulawayo Location;[58] from the Southern Rhodesian Missionary Conference, held in the same month in the Wesleyan Hall, Bulawayo;[59] from the ICU; and from other Location associations. It even received representations from the government, which wondered if the by-law was any longer appropriate. Critics argued that the by-law had become positively dangerous now that Bulawayo's streets were full of cars and lorries, which were obliged by law to keep to the left, so that Africans had taken to walking down the centre of the road to escape danger.

On the other hand, the Council was under constant pressure from white ratepayers. 'I notice the natives are using the pavements very frequently now', wrote Annoyed in February 1930. 'One really has to give way to them as much as one has to do with coloured people in Cape Town.'[60] Sometimes, indeed, whites did not bother to write but took the law into their own hands. In March 1930 an African detective, Sanyika, was 'on special duty all night in the town [and] walking on the edge of the pavement'. He passed two whites, one of whom knocked him down without warning as a punishment for daring to be on the sidewalk. The magistrate told the assailant, John de Kock, that he had over-reacted to the 'provocation' but he was discharged with a caution.[61]

The Town Clerk was regularly addressed by bodies which wanted the by-law enforced more strictly – the Rhodesian Women's League; the Bulawayo Ratepayers Association; the Vigilantes Association; the Bulawayo Publicity Association. Council paid more attention to these constituents than it did to external, missionary or African protest. Responding to the Missionary Conference in September 1930, it placed the burden for road safety back on them:

I am directed to ask that the SRMC will draw the attention of all natives attending Mission Schools, and others if possible, to the danger of walking on the left-hand side of the road, and to arrange for schools to be instructed in the traffic regulations prevailing in towns.[62]

[57] *Chronicle*, 6 and 8 March 1930.
[58] *Chronicle*, 7 June 1930.
[59] *Chronicle*, 27 June 1930.
[60] *Chronicle*, 7 February 1930.
[61] *Chronicle*, 8 March 1930.
[62] Town Clerk to Secretary, SRMC, 8 September 1930. In July 1931 and again in December the government- and mission-sponsored *Native Mirror* printed elaborate instructions on how to walk safely in the road.

When government wrote in March and May 1931, conveying African protests about the by-law, the Town Clerk merely replied that new regulations compelling parking in the centre of the road would 'provide the side of the roads for native pedestrians'. [63] The Council was becoming more, rather than less, neurotic over its failure to control space. What one may call 'pavementia' perfectly expressed the surreal absurdity of proclaiming segregation while simultaneously demanding constant service and even bodily care from Africans.

Gendering the Urban Landscape

There was another more successful and less contested symbolic ordering of space. White Bulawayo was an intensely masculine town. Men occupied the public space at the centre of the town and the athletic space at the various sports clubs established on the Commonage. Women were largely relegated to their suburban homes. So notable was the subordination of white women that one of our township informants used it to illustrate what happened to black women in the Location in the 1930s:

> Women were less likely to go to school. They were considered useless. They were not even allowed into Bulawayo Club.[64]

The Rhodesian Women's League tried to involve white women as full citizens, campaigning for the extension of the Municipal franchise to the wives of male voters. It was pointed out in reply that women owners of property already had the vote and that if other women were to be included it would allow them to impose 'special expenditure' upon male ratepayers.[65] Women, of course, led the League and other specifically female organizations. But no women speakers are reported as addressing any of the numerous public protest meetings reported in the press.[66]

Many white women felt excluded from public space in colonial Bulawayo and left without any constructive outlet. One recent female migrant to Bulawayo complained:

> Outside [in the rural areas] I have always been happy, the small communities being forced to club together [but] here in Bulawayo I have only a few friends and they mostly live right at the other end of town. My husband cannot afford to buy a car ... Therefore when I want to pay one of my friends a visit, as about the only means of lightening the monotony of life, I have over half an hour's walk, pushing a pram over stony roads and sandy sidewalks ... Where is there to go in Bulawayo? True, one cannot expect art galleries or several sorts of museums in so young

---

[63] Town Clerk to Secretary, Colonial Secretary, 10 June 1931.

[64] Interview between Simon Mlotshwa and Noah Chakanetsa Mpofu, Nguboyena, 4 January 2001. Mpofu came to Bulawayo in 1937 to work as a driver at Northend Butchery for £5 10s a month. In 2001 the Bulawayo Club still did not allow women into its members' bar.

[65] *Chronicle*, 6 July 1929.

[66] Women did, however, write letters to the press. Often these accepted – indeed demanded – that white women be 'protected' by men. They also demanded that 'refined' women be segregated from Africans by management of ecclesiastical as well as secular space. On 19 October 1929, for instance, Mrs M. Chalmers attacked Archbishop Paget for 'the co-mingling of natives during the Church Synod services with the white people in the Church of St John'. 'If the state affords protection for us white women and our little daughters in this country, who is the Bishop to dare to take away that protection ... by eventually making it a matter of course that the native receives the solemn rites of Divine service cheek by jowl with refined white women ... The Bishop is surely becoming a spiritual communist. The white man may in instances have sold his birth-right for a mess of pottage. The white woman has not.' *Chronicle*, 19 October 1929.

a town, but after ten minutes walk around the shops one's explorations come to an end. There is the Park – so far away for many who have to walk – likewise the swimming pool … At night absolutely nothing except the pictures. This loneliness nearly broke my spirit.[67]

This correspondent did not at all live up to the ideals of Imperial Womanhood presented in the *Chronicle* a few months later. Under the heading 'The Real Dominion Builder – Woman', it reported an address by Dame Muriel Talbot. Previous empires had fallen because 'their women were not colonizers. In each of these civilizations women occupied a very inferior sphere, and when they accompanied their husbands abroad they were, more or less, disgruntled sharers of exile, mere transients who longed to get back home. How exactly contrary in character is the British woman!' She makes 'real homes'; gives her husband 'an essential sense of permanency'; brings up her children to feel equal loyalty to the new country and the old. If women realized that the permanency of the British Empire and the creation of Rhodesian identity depended upon their private, domestic tasks, they would never feel lonely or excluded.[68]

And in fact in Bulawayo white women faced a particular colonial challenge in creating 'real homes'. The masculinity of the town extended to the household, where – as Teresa Barnes tells us – the white housewife did the work of colonialism by literally putting the black male servant 'in his place'. There was a 'deadly' and daily struggle over boundaries and borderlines.[69] This could sometimes erupt into violence. During the 1929 'lynch-mob' case the trial judge warned housewives that they lived in constant danger if the 'boundaries' between mistress and manservant were overstepped. In 1930 the Federation of Women's Institutes held an inquiry into domestic service. 'There is the difficulty of sex antagonism' declared one witness. 'A European woman starts with a serious handicap. The male native is convinced that every female is an inferior creature … To be struck by the master is a misfortune; a blow from the mistress is an unforgivable insult.'[70]

In Bulawayo in the 1930s white women agonized over whether the masculinity of the town should be challenged by the employment of African women as domestics. Teresa Barnes, writing about Salisbury, says that:

> The allocation of racial space was obvious to anyone: the spacious settler bungalow fronting on to a garden of domesticated flowers, the street and the gaze of passers-by vs the small dwellings of black men … 'away up at the end of the back garden'. The 'boys' kia was squeezed away

[handwritten margin note: "Oh what a difficult decision"]

---

67 *Chronicle*, 27 July 1929. In the same issue another correspondent wrote of Bulawayo that 'a more unsociable and inhospitable crowd would be hard to find the world over, and one is quickly isolated and left to one's resources'. 'Exorbitant rents' were asked for 'wretched little houses and flats'. These letters offered a very different view of Bulawayo's urban landscape from the *Chronicle*'s usual glowing descriptions of white civic culture. The advertising view of white Bulawayo women was, of course, very different. They were crucial to beautifying Bulawayo by supervising the suburban gardens, choosing stylish furniture and producing landscape images. Photography advertising came in the 1930s to address itself almost entirely to white women, praising 'The Vanity Kodak for Smart Ladies', showing women on the Cape Town beaches filming their golden children and flappers snapping a tennis match.

68 *Chronicle*, 1 February 1930.

69 Teresa Barnes, 'Master Bedrooms, "Boys" Kias and Old Bricks: Gender and Space in Colonial Harare, Zimbabwe', Workshop on Women and the Environment, University of Zimbabwe, August 1999, pp. 14–15. Barnes writes that 'settler homes were not simply places where white women and black men played certain roles, but spaces in which they *learned to become certain kinds of people*. White women … learned slowly and sometimes painfully in the kitchens, gardens and master bedrooms to be the memsahibs of Rhodesia.'

70 Evidence of W.S. Bazeley, *Report of the Standing Committee on Domestic Service*, Federation of Women's Institutes, Bulawayo, 1930.

from the public gaze ... These were spaces where black women and girls were not allowed. Gender and race privilege were marked boldly by the fact that only 'real' men were able to live with women – the white masters in spaces 'clothed' with the presence of wives. The 'boys' supposedly lived without women in another world. But it was one only just a few steps from the master's back door.[71]

So in Salisbury few, if any, black women lived in the suburbs. Nor did they come in to work there from single women's accommodation in the Location. Barnes remarks that in Salisbury the first hostel built specifically for African women was not erected until 1953.

Things were rather different in Bulawayo. The first hostel for single women was erected there as early as 1918 and it was designed especially for the Baralong women from Francistown who had come to work as domestic servants.[72] There was considerable competition for their services. During the flu epidemic at the end of 1918 many black domestic servants were cared for in the special women's hospital and their employers delighted the doctor in charge by sending soups and other sustaining foods for their employees or angered him by trying to get him to discharge a maid before she had recovered. Through the 1920s there was a continuous minority tradition of employing African women in Bulawayo households. In 1927, when the Federation of Women's Institutes was formed, one of its first concerns was to lobby the Prime Minister against the employment of male servants in white girls' boarding schools, maternity homes and women's hospital wards. At his request they established a sub-committee to report on African female domestic service more generally, which took evidence in the first months of 1930. Two at least of the sub-committee members were strongly in favour of employing African women.[73]

Nevertheless, although Bulawayo was different from Salisbury, the old insistence on the employment of males was hard to shake. The Mayor of Bulawayo, W.H. Peard, said that it would be a long time before Location women were trained and civilized enough to be employed. Moreover, there was the problem of 'temptation in the way of young adolescent males who may be in the European houses where native girls are employed ... tending to produce the terrible problem of coloureds'. (A good many white women were more afraid of placing temptation in the way of old married males.) Other witnesses stressed the dirty conditions of Location houses and the 'immorality' of black women. Yet there were some witnesses, black and white, who challenged these assumptions.

The report of the FWI sub-committee included a testimony from an African woman domestic servant, Martha Tshologwane:

We hear a lot of talk about the badness of us native girls in towns and that there are some ladies who say that they would rather employ boys than girls in their homes. Yes, good, but ... is there

---

[71] Barnes, p. 14.

[72] The Hostel was a Methodist initiative. Giving evidence to the Native Female Domestic Labour Committee on 15 September 1932 the Methodist minister, Herbert Carter, confessed that 'the hostel system does not at all appeal to the native girl and we should far rather make an arrangement which would give her freedom and privacy. We had difficulty in Bulawayo ... and had to give up the hostel as more or less unsastisfactory.' S.235 474, National Archives, Harare.

[73] There was also a lobby in Bulawayo and elsewhere to dispense with African domestic servants altogether, male or female, and to enforce segregation in the home. This lobby argued that 'the effects upon the young European of intimate association with native adults of either sex ... are in the main bad', and that government should seek to substitute European or Coloured servants for black. Report of the Native Female Domestic Labour Committee, October 1932, S.95, National Archives, Harare.

any of you who has been done any harm by a native girl yet? It does not mean that because we are black that there are not some who have self-respect. I know some girls who have been working for many years and their mistresses had no trouble with them yet, but they are staying in town all these years, so therefore I think anybody can be good in or out of town ... Poor girls, what must we do to be good?[74]

Giving evidence to a subsequent official inquiry in August 1932, the Bulawayo representative of the Federation of Women's Institutes, Mrs Fripp, attacked the ignorance of city councillors. 'No Municipal councillor is ever elected to office because he has special knowledge of, or interest in, native affairs. No Municipal councillor ever places in his election address such specialised interest nor would he probably, if he did, gain a single white vote thereby, yet such councillors have the ultimate shaping of policy which affects all the natives under the control of a Municipality.' Government, she thought, should intervene to make the Location 'suitable for housing native female domestic servants'. After all:

Social and mental developments and opportunities are the right of every native woman, should she so wish it. These women have a right to everything which such developments connote: the pleasure of personal cleanliness, pretty clothes, etc. To make them the prize of immorality only (by denying the right to domestic service to these women) is to wrong deeply this developing native feminine life.[75]

Landscaping the Location

The last thing the Bulawayo Municipal Council intended to do in the 1930s, however, was to make the Location suitable for women workers. Their intention was to break the influence of the women stand-holders and to introduce many more male 'bachelors' into the Location. The Council refused to build houses for white workers and relied on private enterprise. They assumed that white workers would be married and would occupy family homes. So far as black workers were concerned the Council's attitude was completely the opposite. The only housing was to be provided by the Municipality and most of it was to be for 'single' men. They did not feel it necessary for African workers to be married and be family men.

The Council's insistence on ending private ownership was reiterated in October 1930 in reply to the complaints of 'a deputation of native women':

The Council issued instructions over a year ago that no further private buildings were to be allowed in the Location and resolved that its policy is to reduce the number of private dwellings and huts within the Location as much as possible ... The natives have only small quantities of bricks and by no means sufficient for additional buildings, their idea being to purchase a few at a time as money becomes available, with the result before the date on which work of this nature was prohibited, some of the buildings had been in progress for years and unsatisfactory conditions existed on account of the buildings being occupied before completion.[76]

---

74 Written evidence of Martha Tshologwane, June 1930, S.235 475, National Archives, Harare. One of Lobengula's grand-nieces, Sophie, gave evidence to the Committee on Native Female Domestic Labour on 15 September 1932. She had been trained at Hope Fountain Mission and had then worked as a domestic servant in town. 'I have been home twice since I have been working and my father is quite satisfied.'
75 Evidence of Mrs Fripp, 30 August 1932. S.94, National Archives, Harare.
76 Town Clerk to Superintendent of Natives, Bulawayo, 4 October 1930, B1/10.5R, Box 18, National Archives, Bulawayo.

The bit-by-bit process of removing women property-owners carried on right through the 1930s. In January 1936, for example, Council paid £4 to a woman, Telopo, for two huts on stand 53, 6th Street; they were at once demolished and 'two or three rows of rooms are to be erected on the space which will thus become available'.[77]

In asserting its absolute control over the Location and proceeding to reshape it, the Council had in mind a black urban landscape shaped by a few simple considerations. The Location had to be situated in an area where no whites would wish to live. Africans must be placed on the west and whites on the east of the town because the prevailing wind blew from east to west and carried with it the smoke and dust and smells. White suburbs had developed to the north and east of the town and Council was determined that no African settlements should be established except to the west. Late in 1930 the government was talking of setting up a Native Village Settlement on Willsgrove Farm, east of the Umgusa river. The Town Clerk at once responded:

> The area referred to is on the East side of town and in the direction of the prevailing wind which would be a considerable disadvantage to the inhabitants of the town ... For some time past the Council has had under consideration the question of town planning and zoning and has passed a resolution that nearly the whole of the Commonage Area to the east of the town shall be reserved as a European residential area. It is presumed that the native village settlement is intended for natives who work in Bulawayo, and as the main avenues of approach would be through the residential section of Bulawayo town, the Suburbs and Kumalo, the Council considers that the resulting stream of native traffic through quiet purely residential areas would be a constant source of annoyance and give rise to trouble. They are convinced that the residents in those parts would offer strong objections. [Moreover] misgivings have already been expressed as to the danger of epidemic outbreaks ... If the Government plans something that is merely a scattered Location then the Council foresees that many grave dangers may arise and would offer the strongest opposition.[78]

The Location itself had to be constructed as cheaply as possible and on as little land as possible – in 1930 its 5,500 people lived on only 64 acres. (By contrast the government aimed to acquire 1,000 acres for its Willsgrove Village Settlement.) There was no talk here of working-class houses each on their own acre! Nor was there to be space for cultivation or grazing. Africans were not allowed to graze their beasts outside the Location. 'My Council is strongly of the opinion', wrote the Town Clerk in December 1931, 'that it is inadvisable that any native cattle should be allowed to graze on Commonage land.'[79] White residents had the right to pasture and stable animals: blacks in the Location could keep no animals except dogs, which were regularly trapped and put down in police raids.

The municipal cottages – despite their rustic name – were small, brick boxes, packed tight together, with inadequate partitions between their two rooms, no ceilings and unplastered walls. Nevertheless, they were 'finished' and thought to look civilized in contrast to African buildings in progress. The Location was landscaped only in the sense that it was tidied up. It was laid out on a municipal plan with cottages – and roads – in straight lines on a grid pattern. African-owned buildings which

---

77 Town Clerk to Location Superintedent, 29 January 1936, B1/10/5F, National Archives, Bulawayo. On occasion, the Council acquired a private house which it did not destroy but leased out to tenants or used for other purposes.

78 Town Clerk to Private Secretary, Prime Minister, 10 November 1930 and 12 February 1931, B1/10/5R; Town Clerk to Private Secretary, Prime Minister, 9 February 1931, 23/3/8R, Box 6540, National Archives, Bulawayo.

79 Town Clerk to Assistant Director, Lands, 7 December 1931, 23/3/8R, Box 6540.

got in the way of this linear pattern were removed.[80] As the Native Affairs Commission reported early in 1930, 'successful efforts have been made of late to secure uniformity in the streets which were formerly invaded by native huts'.[81] Everything had been done, in fact, to sweep away the impression of an African landscape which the Location had presented earlier in the twentieth century, with its clusters of huts in compounds, its winding paths, its patches of maize, and its cattle grazing on the Commonage.[82]

The Location was now an urban landscape of the most basic kind. The only buildings with pretensions to grandeur, and even then of the simplest sort, were the mission churches which bordered the Location. Stanlake Samkange lived in the Methodist manse in 1929 as the young son of the minister, his father Thompson. He recalled:

> the church, a majestic red building, towering over the Location like a colossus. [It] was not far from Lobengula Street, though a small stream and a forest of miganu, mipafa and mimosa trees lay between.[83]

In much the same way the grandest street events in the Location were religious processions, like the march of the Salvation Army through its streets on 14 March 1930, with General Higgins following on in his motor car. Even then the Council only gave permission for this spectacle on condition that the 'procession must not stop'![84]

African Resistance & African Alternative Landscapes

The women stand-holders resisted the Council's reshaping of the Location as strongly as they could. In March 1930 the government-appointed Native Affairs Commission asked African organizations to give evidence on conditions in the Location.

Martha Ngano was old and ill; she died in April 1930, the Council taking the opportunity for some racial tidying-up by allocating her Commonage cottage to a Coloured man.[85] Ngano's last statement as a leader was embittered. She bemoaned the lack of African solidarity and the death of the progressive dream. A new kind of

---

[80] Thus on 15 July 1933 the Town Clerk wrote to the Superintendent of Natives, Bulawayo, about the Mayor's desire to straighten things up in the Location. 'Native buildings are interfering with the lay out of new streets and preventing the progress of the building scheme which consists of the erection of rooms and cottages.' The Town Clerk admitted that the African-owned buildings 'are in a good state of repair' and their owners were refusing compensation. He asked the Superintendent to persuade the owners to be reasonable.

[81] 'Report of the Native Affairs Commission on its Inquiry into Matters concerning the Bulawayo Native Location', 1930, S.482 789/19, National Archives, Harare.

[82] Stanlake Samkange lived in Bulawayo as a boy at the Wesleyan church, where his father Thompson was minister. In his his novel, *The Mourned One*, Samkange recalled the Location in 1929. He contrasted the remnants of the older area, where houses were 'made of traditional African materials and people lived as they did in their villages' with what he called 'the new Location' with its municipal cottages. p. 116.

[83] Samkange, ibid. For an account of Thompson Samkange's career in Bulawayo at this period, see T.O. Ranger, *Are We Not Also Men? The Samkange Family and African Politics in Zimbabwe, 1920–64*, James Currey, London, 1995, pp. 4-5.

[84] Town Clerk to Superintendent, Location, 5 September 1930, B1/10/5R, Box 18, National Archives, Bulawayo.

[85] Town Clerk to Native Commissioner, Bulawayo, 9 May 1930, B 1/10/5R, Box 17, National Archives, Bulawayo. The Town Clerk told the NC that Martha 'held this lease during the pleasure of the Council. Mary Umfolo has been allowed to remain on the plot and look after the two children until such time as Mrs Ngano's three brothers come to settle the estate. A five-roomed house on the plot was the property of the late Martha Ngano.' On 25 July 1930 the Town Clerk told the Town Engineer that the plot – and presumably the house – was to be transferred to L. Culverwell.

womanhood had arisen in the Location, as young girls from rural areas migrated to town. She recalled that she had come to Bulawayo 'thirty years ago to teach in the schools … There are some who have spoken today who received their education from me.' But despite education and despite Christianity:

> We natives have no belief … we have no real conviction as a body. We have deteriorated men-tally and morally. In the old days girls were protected by their parents until they were well matured, but nowadays it seems that they are allowed to do exactly as they please. If one asks a young girl what she is doing so far from home she will reply, 'I am a grown up' … The lures of town life attract her and she forthwith becomes immoral.

But other women members of the League were less fatalistic and more protesting. 'I was born in the Location', said Mbane, 'and have never been treated as I am now being treated. We cannot collect our own wood, we are obliged to buy it in 3d bun-dles.' Moho told the Commission that:

> previously I rented two stands on which I built two houses. Vawdrey (the recently disgraced Location Superintendent) said that when he pulled my houses down he would build again so that I would have six rooms. When he did build he built me only two rooms and a kitchen. I am one of Lobengula's queens. The members of the Khumalo family stay with me when they are in town. Vawdrey promised to supply bricks, wood and iron for my other rooms. He did nothing. Today when I have visitors I am crowded out and have to share a hut with another queen.

Manduweni complained that women who had 'lived in the town for many years and have now no desire to live in native reserves far from the towns', women who were 'detribalised and urbanised', could not live if deprived of rents from lodgers. She added that Location families exercised 'parental control'. 'The girls from the country are responsible for the immorality in the Location.'[86]

Women went on protesting after the report of the Native Affairs Commission and after the death of Martha Ngano. A deputation of women approached the Superin-tendent of Natives in September 1930, complaining that the bricks they had bought for improving and extending their houses were lying idle and getting spoilt. The Superintendent backed the women: the Council refused to let them build.[87] This became the pattern throughout the 1930s – someone would take up the case of the women, petition the Mayor, and receive a firm rebuff. One interesting example for African political history was Thompson Samkange's letter of 8 July 1931, written to the Mayor from the Weslyan Mission at the Bulawayo Location. Samkange – who was to become President of the first African National Congress – asked for an interview

---

[86] Evidence to the Native Affairs Commission, March 1930, ZAN 1/1/1, National Archives, Harare. No dates are given for the appearance of African witnesses before the Commission. European witnesses also com-mented on the dilemma of women in the Location as it had been shaped by the Municipality. Reverend G.H.B. Sketchley deplored the fact that the women now had no land to cultivate: they 'should have work to take up their time during the day'. He found that houses built by Africans 'are better cared for than those built by the Council'. In his view, 'civic pride should be encouraged'; the Council should build no more accommodation in the Location and bring in no more single men. Instead the whole area should be divided into half-acre plots on which African families could build houses and cultivate gardens. In these proposals he was putting forward the women's point of view. And he defended the reputation of Location women. There were not many 'illegal unions'; half of the women were of 'unquestionable character'. The Superintendent of Natives, Bulawayo, spoke in favour of African plot-holders. But none of these opinions were to have the slightest effect on municipal policy.

[87] Superintendent of Natives, Bulawayo to Town Clerk, 30 October 1930, 23/3/7R, National Archives, Bula-wayo.

with the Mayor so that he could urge the case of the stand-holders. He had a reply on the very next day:

> His Worship the Mayor cannot see that any useful purpose would be served by an interview … The Council's policy has been adopted in the interests of the natives themselves.[88]

On 15 October 1932 a large public meeting was held in the Location, partly to demand an Advisory Board and partly to ask that people be allowed to build their own houses. The Council turned down both requests – 'the convenience given to the natives by the improved type of buildings the Council erects, compared with native owned houses, is for the benefit of the natives' living conditions'.[89] No matter how many times Africans told the Council that they wanted to build their own houses, the Council stubbornly refused to credit that that was what they really desired.

One of the women witnesses to the Native Affairs Commission in 1930 had said that her only legal alternative to rents from lodgers was the sale of 'hop' beer. In 1934 the Council decided to ban the trade in 'hop' beer. 'A large gathering of native women from the Bulawayo Location' protested to the Superintendent of Natives, who once again backed their case, pointing out that women had brewed and sold 'hop' beer for many years.[90] The women accused the Council of trying to drive men away from Location social gatherings and into their own municipal beer hall. But the Council persisted in trying to criminalize female 'hop' brewers:

> For some time past [the Town Clerk told the Secretary, Internal Affairs] my Council has been aware of the increasing quantity of alleged 'hop' beer being brewed in the Native Location. [It] has arrived at the conclusion that this practice, because of the high alcoholic content of the liquor, tends to incidents of lawlessness and public disturbances. It is suspected, moreover, that surreptitious trading in 'hop' beer takes place at night time … In collaboration with the Police several samples of this 'hop' beer have been seized … The [Location] Superintendent secured the arrest of two native women in connection with the brewing of this 'hop' beer.[91]

Life for women in the Location was becoming more and more difficult, yet by the end of the 1930s there were still many more women living there than is ordinarily supposed. As we have seen, in 1936 there were 1,237 women and 495 girls in the Location in comparison with 3,897 men and 495 boys. More or less a third of the Location population was still female. But the status and freedom of action of the long-term women residents had been sadly diminished and the incoming women were mostly deprived and dependent. Old informants remember the change. Mrs L. Mlotshwa was born some time before 1910. In the 1920s she stayed in the Location with her aunt. She remembers that:

> We used to stay in the pole and dagga huts. There was an employee from the superintendent's office whose job was to bring clay soil to the house occupants in the old Location so that they could repair their houses. Any occupant could repair their houses when necessary … There were quite a good number of women who owned stands … Most of the houses which were built later were mainly built to accommodate male-bachelor workers … You could find at least four males sharing a room. Some got married and stayed with their women and sometimes their children under these very crowded conditions. There was hardly any form of privacy … Some

88 Town Clerk to Thompson Samkange, 9 July 1931. B1/10/5R, Box 18, National Archives, Bulawayo.
89 Town Clerk, Memo to Location Superintendent, 25 November 1932.
90 Town Clerk to Superintendent of Natives, 15 January 1924.
91 Town Clerk to Secretary, Internal Affairs, 7 April 1924.

males who were not married entertained their girl-friends in these rooms. So the situation was just a terrible provoking experience.[92]

Other old informants remember changes in the Location's relationship to the surrounding countryside. They recall that when they were children it was possible to travel on foot from the Location to Ndebele settlements close to the town. The old Location was itself rather like a village set in a landscape of villages. But now the surrounding Ndebele villages had been cleared away and the old Location was being steadily destroyed. With no cultivation or grazing rights the inhabitants of the Location were the only fully urbanized people in the Bulawayo of the 1930s. The Native Affairs Commission, after its inquiry into the Location, reported that:

> Native urban communities of heterogenous composition spring into existence in a haphazard manner to meet European labour needs. It is such communities that, under the worst possible auspices, have to bear the full brunt of the demands and attacks of an alien civilisation. That they have been able to adjust themselves under unpromising circumstances to a soil and atmosphere so alien and of so formidable a type is proof of the indestructability of which the African is compounded.

The Commission reported, quite rightly, that the Municipality were offering no services to the inhabitants of the Location, nor assisting them to adjust to so narrowly defined an urban landscape. But the Commission did not realize that what was happening was that most of the old adjustments, through which an African Bulawayo had been made, were being eroded.[93]

The struggle over space was fought right down to the 'cottages' themselves. The Council resolutely maintained that African tenants themselves preferred to live in the two-roomed, brick-built municipal accommodation. Yet every association giving evidence to the Native Affairs Commission attacked the new 'cottages' as an immoral space.

In November 1929 the Matabele Home Society had been formed, as the latest expression of the Ndebele traditionalist dimension of black Bulawayo's culture. One of its leading members was the Wesleyan teacher, Ntando, who had been involved in all the previous Ndebele nationalist movements in the Location.[94] Now the Society's spokesmen attacked the Council's management of space in the Location:

> I have been selected [said Madhlinga] by the Matabeleland Home Society to express the grievances of Location inhabitants. My people request me to ask the Commission to enquire into the question of the demolition of our buildings and the terms of occupation and the inadequacy of natives' wages in the town and the smallness of our houses. According to custom it is usual for parents to live in one hut, for our sons to live in another, and for our daughters to live in another, and for our mother-in-law to live in a fourth.

This had been achieved in the cluster of round buildings erected by families themselves on stands in the Location. But in the square municipal 'cottages' everyone had

---

92 Interview between Busani Mpofu and Mrs L. Mlotshwa, Makokoba, February 2000. A similar male account was given to Mr Mpofu by Msongelwayizizwe Petros Khumalo on 26 July 2000. Khumalo was born in 1910; he came to live in the Makokoba *ezitendini* in 1918. Many women owned stands. But 'around 1930 the Municipality had started to build some houses for workers on the western side of Makokoba', and he remembers the 'bachelors' and the girlfriends they carried in to this housing.

93 S 482 789/19, National Archives, Harare.

94 For the emergence and character of the Matabele Home Society, see T.O. Ranger, *The African Voice in Southern Rhodesia*, pp. 187-90.

to live in two rooms, imperfectly separated from each other. Madhlinga was seconded by Magavu Indebele, who complained that 'in the Location we have but two rooms, there is no door between these two rooms, only a gap in the wall, and the dividing wall does not reach the roof'.[95]

The ICU, which often criticized the Matabele Home Society for its sectionalism, agreed with it on this. Masotsha Ndlovu told the Commission that 'in our natural habitat there are always more than two sleeping rooms. When a man marries he builds a room for himself and his wife ... as his family grows he must have a room for his daughters and another room for his sons. In the Location we are not allowed to add to the buildings the Municipality built for us. If we have relatives or friends to live with us they are obliged to live in one room and we in the other. If it is necessary for persons in the inner room ... to leave that room during the night he or she is obliged to walk through the sleeping apartment of those relatives. This is against custom and public morals. When we were allowed to build our own huts on the plots we rented we could add to them to meet the needs of our growing families ... The remedy is to allow natives to build their own houses.'[96]

Naturally, the African ministers of religion from the Location also agreed. Reverend Z.C. Mtshwelo of the African Methodist Episcopal Church complained that during the 18 months he had lived in a Location cottage, 'the forced proximity of the children to me at night time I considered immoral'. The Anglican, Reverend Sagonda, contrasted the customary 'four huts' to the Location two rooms, which 'encourage immorality ... boys and girls should not sleep together'. Thompson Samkange complained that 'natives are not permitted to practice their old customs which forbade certain persons seeing each other in a state of undress.'[97]

There could hardly have been a greater clash between two notions of urban landscape. The 'civilizing' cottages of the Municipality, sitting squarely along the straight lines of the new streets, struck Africans as an undermining of the moral law. For married families the answer seemed to be to abandon the Location and start all over again. On some new space they might be able to build their own houses, cultivate their own gardens, cut their own wood. 'I am old and I grew old in the Location', said an MHS member, Jojo. 'When I am no longer able to work I shall be evicted from the Location ... In a village settlement we could live undisturbed. We ask for some land where our women can work and where we ourselves can have pastimes. In the Location there is nothing for us to do. We cannot dig, we cannot collect wood, and our women also have nothing to do.' And at the very end of the African evidence to

[95] ZAN 1/1/1, National Archives, Harare. Magavu earned 45s a month and had lived in the Location 'many years'. His wife and four children lived a hundred miles away in the Shangani Reserve. 'I could not afford to keep them in the Location.'

[96] ZAN 1/1/1. Masotsha still lived at this time in his own spacious house in the Location.

[97] Ibid. Sagonda and Samkange were able to bring their own children up in the more spacious houses attached to the mission; the Presbyterian spokesman, a Northern Rhodesian Tonga, Tshiminiya, had bought a brick house with four rooms for £35 and spent a further £18 on adding two more rooms. In his view the new model Location was suitable only 'for bachelors ... but is unsuitable for married men'. When these criticisms were repeated by the Missionary Conference in August 1930 the Location Superintendent defended the municipal cottages. They were having ceiling boards put in and enlarged fire places. In the African villages a family might have more than one hut, but 'they have not got water laid on and street lighting, wash and bath houses and sanitary conveniences'. On mine compounds, African employees only got one circular hut for their whole family. The Superintendent thought that the criticisms came from unrepresentative Africans who owned property and who wanted to go on charging lodgers more rent than the Municipality required. Location Superintendent to Town Clerk, 1 September 1930, 23/3/7R, National Archives, Bulawayo.

the Commission came a group bringing together Masotsha Nhlovu and spokesmen of the RBVA. They demanded that there should be set up at the site of the present Location a village settlement with leasehold or freehold tenure. People could improve their houses and cultivate their gardens. And 'the property of each should be counted as qualification to vote in the Legislative Assembly.'[98]

All this was in vain. The Municipality had been considering the idea of a 'village for married natives' since at least 1922.[99] Several times in the 1930s it raised the idea again. But the Council was never serious. The idea was raised either to fob off African demands or to try to prevent the government from building settlements itself around Bulawayo. In February 1932 the Council did 'not believe that there is a real necessity for the suggested native village near Bulawayo'; in September 1931, faced with detailed government plans for a village some four miles from the town centre, the Council said that it did not want to grant any Commonage ground because it *might* set up a village of its own; there was abortive negotiation with government over inadequate municipal proposals which amounted to 'little more than an extension of the existing town Location'; in February 1934 there was still haggling over whether the Council or the government should take the initiative. Prime Minister Huggins told the Council that under the Land Apportionment Act they *must* set up both a Native Urban Area and a Native Village Settlement. 'This was a scheme for ever.'[100] But still the Council did nothing and as we shall see in a later chapter, the government Native Village Settlement at Luveve was only established late in the 1930s and then with conditions which made it unattractive to potential settlers. In the 1930s those Africans who objected strongly to the way the Location was developing had no effective way of changing things. All they could do was to vote with their feet. The Location Superintendent's report for the month of July 1930 was in this respect suggestive. The Location had an Acting Headman, Jujuju. He had been dismissed for 'absenting him from duty and instead of residing in the Location was in the habit of clearing out at night and sleeping at Hyde Park'.[101]

---

[98] ZAN 1/1/1. Thornton documents earlier demands for a village settlement which would allow Africans to enjoy a mixture of rural and urban life; such demands were made regularly throughout the 1930s.

[99] Draft departmental reports towards the Mayor's Annual Minutes, June 1922, 23/2/6R, Box 5777, National Archives, Bulawayo. The then Superintendent of the Location, T.E. Vawdrey, asked for his view, thought that 'the idea [must] be to make the new location a model one and not allow it to develop into a native kraal, because, I take it, the object is to uplift the native and give him an opportunity to live as like the white race as possible'. He thought the new settlement could be called 'The Municipal Location Extension' and that it should be visited daily by the Superintendent. 'The educated native needs more discipline than the raw native. He has reached that stage of his existence which some might term half-broken, and he might take the wrong step which leads to crime and fornication.' Alternatively, in the new plans for the existing Location, with their 'straight lines', 'every class could be segregated, namely married natives, single natives, coloured people and Indians'. And, after all, 'the Location is bounded by eight churches and schools of different denominations so that the Location with such surroundings is the ideal place for those wishing to lead a virtuous and pious life'.

[100] Town Clerk to Private Secretary, Prime Minister, 9 February 1931; meeting of Land Board and City Council, 4 September 1931; Assistant Director of Native Lands to Town Clerk, 11 September 1931; Town Clerk to Assistant Director, 12 October 1931; Assistant Director to Town Clerk, 23 October 1931; Town Clerk to Assistant Director, 7 December 1931; Special meeting of Bulawayo Council with Prime Minister, 26 February 1934; Secretary, Prime Minister to Town Clerk, 4 April 1934, 23/3/R, Box 6540, subject file on Native Village scheme.

[101] Location Report, June 1930, 23/3/7R, National Archives, Bulawayo. The monthly reports by the Superintendent, H. Collier, give a vivid picture of everyday Location life. In May a man was charged with *crimen injuria* for 'peeping into a hut where native women were bathing'; a woman was arrested for bringing beer into the Location 'from the kraals'; in June a man was arrested for witchcraft and the Location Police disarmed sixty workers from the quarries who came out armed with knobsticks and axes; in July an Afro-

Hyde Park was a huge 'white' farm twelve miles north-west of Bulawayo. White farmers and ranchers in Matabeleland might be entirely in favour of the Land Apportionment Act so far as ownership of land was concerned. But it was very different so far as *use* of the land was concerned. Most of the farms in the circle around the Commonage – from six to as many as twenty miles away from Bulawayo – were inhabited by African tenants paying rent under the Private Locations Ordinance of 1908. Under the Land Apportionment Act Private Locations were supposed to be abolished. But around Bulawayo the PLs continued to exist until after the Second World War. If Africans wanted abundant gardens to cultivate and grazing for their cattle, wood to gather, and separate accommodation for their sons and daughters, the farms offered it all. Hyde Park farm itself was almost as large as the whole Commonage. Admittedly, the farms were much further away than the Location from Bulawayo town. Nor were there any buses. But Macmillan noted in 1930 that if there was one car to every five whites in Bulawayo there were 9,000 bicycles for 10,000 Africans. As Kingsley Fairbridge remarked in astonishment:

> It was startling to look at the Bulawayo of 1930 … The native servants, including delivery boys and labourers, ride good bicycles through the main thoroughfares, astonishing one who could only think back to the days when the push bike was the aristocratic preserve of the white man.[102]

The bicycle was a prestige object, but it was also an essential tool with which Africans were able to create and maintain alternative landscapes.[103]

In 1936 the Superintendent of Natives, Bulawayo, calculated that as many as 5,458 of the 13,866 African workers in the town lived out on the Private Locations. Some had been there before the Location began to be transformed into a stark urban landscape; others – like Jujuju – took refuge from the Location on the PLs. I draw here on Takavafira Zhou's excellent MA thesis.[104] Zhou calls these PLs 'satellite suburbs', 'bed-room towns', which 'housed many of the city's workers by night but were largely vacated by day'. However, the farms were very large and the environment was not urban. Housing was dispersed and the large tracts of bush made police control difficult. There were many thousands of African-owned cattle on the PLs. Wives grew vegetables and brewed beer for sale. Zhou suggests a double circle of Private Locations around Bulawayo. Roughly within the ten mile radius lived city workers and beer brewers; outside the ten-mile radius was 'the outer urban zone, characterised by small-scale capitalist farming or market gardening'.

Villages on the PLs were not survivals of the pre-colonial period but new migrant creations. They came together as 'connections of friends, compatriots and co-workers'. On some PLs every settler was Ndebele; on others the great majority were non-indigenous. Missions ran schools on the largest farms. Zhou singles out two farms as the home of 'Christian worker-peasant tenants', Hope Fountain Mission Farm and Gumtree Farm. Here, he says, many tenants 'were tailors, hotel workers and railway

---

101 ctnd American, George Haynes, was shown around the Location and told of 'the various tribes residing there'. There was a combined raid by the CID and the Location police in August, and others in September, October and November. In fact there were two in November so as to clear loafers and gamblers out before Christmas.

102 *Chronicle*, 2 July 1930.

103 For the social history of the bicycle in Bulawayo see T.O. Ranger, 'Bicycles and the Social History of Bulawayo' in *Thatha Bhasikili. An Exhibition of Adorned Bicycles in Bulawayo*, National Gallery, Bulawayo, 2001.

104 T. Zhou, 'A History of the Private Locations Around Bulawayo City, 1930–1957', MA thesis, University of Zimbabwe, April 1995.

workers, chauffeurs, carpenters, hospital orderlies and the like'; they owned donkeys, carts and wagons as well as cattle and sheep.[105]

Both oral and archival testimony allow us access to this Christian tenant elite. Mary Eileen Martin, who arrived at Hope Fountain girls' boarding school south of Bulawayo in 1936, describes both the degenerate whites and the aspiring blacks who lived close to the mission. At the nearby mines were 'poor whites … pathetic children, very uncommunicative, of low mentality. One man who came from a very respectable family had gone native and he was a horrible creature … [The Honourable Peel] had also gone native, from whose kraal a whole string of coloured children used to come to school every day'. By contrast, when she walked along the footpaths on the mission farm and explored the ruins of Old Bulawayo, she found that:

> any homes which had women who had been to school … were exceptionally well kept and furnished. Not all were as ornate as that of old Ben who had a four-poster bed in his bedroom hut … but tables and chairs, sideboards and other simple furniture were in most houses; bicycles and sewing machines were acquired.[106]

Yet more interesting was Gumtree Farm. Here was launched an experiment by the leading African Independent church in the Location, the African Methodist Episcopal Church. Long involved in progressive Location politics, the AMEC under Reverend Mtshwelo set out in the 1930s to evade the effects of the Land Apportionment Act and to escape the confinements of the new Location. Mtshwelo managed to collect enough money from members of the church to buy a lease of Gumtree from its white owner, A.J. Tomlinson. A large number of AMEC adherents moved to the farm and began to build. Then Mtshwelo applied to the Chief Native Commissioner for a licence to establish a Private Location. In 1934 it was too late for such an initiative, even though Mtshwelo had some supporters in the Native Department. Tomlinson himself argued the case of the settlers, though in a characteristically condescending manner:

> During my round of visits I found many of the natives had built substantial houses and furnished these primitively in European style. Others had well built huts of Kimberley brick and furniture – in fact they are a very decent type of native living in a semi-civilised manner, happy and comfortable as a community, the men working for the most part in Bulawayo and cycling to and from their work daily. They had spent a lot of money on their houses and in getting land in order.[107]

The application was refused, but many of the AMEC settlers stayed on as Tomlinson's tenants. The African dream of a liveable 'rurban' environment was tenacious.

An African Symbolic Victory

In the city itself, of course, there were few victories to be won. But at least one was achieved, all the sweeter for striking at the heart of the main symbol of white control of civic space. Early in 1934 Masotsha Ndlovu determined to strike down the pavement by-law. Pathisa Nyathi gives a lively account in his biography:

---

[105] Zhou, op.cit. He goes so far as to claim that 'on the urban fringe lived a class of dynamic accumulators of wealth whose operations gave rise to capitalist labour relations within the African society'.
[106] Interview with Mary Eileen Martin, 1979, ORAL/229, National Archives, Harare.
[107] A.J. Tomlison to Prime Minister, 3 January 1935, S.1542 P8, National Archives, Harare.

Masotsha and his colleagues asked for a volunteer who would defy the law and walk on the pavement. Sithupha Tshuma was willing to be used as a guinea pig ... He was asked to take a good bath and put on his Sunday best. Tshuma looked very smart indeed. He was then given £2 to buy sweets and oranges. Walking confidently on the pavement, Tshuma ate his oranges and sweets, awaiting the inevitable to happen. In no time, startled whites were upon him. 'You, kaffir, what is your business on this pavement?' asked the cheeky white policeman, hurriedly alighting from his jittery white horse ... The white policeman's lower lip was bitten white with anger at the black man who did not know his place in the streets of Bulawayo. 'Ngingumuntu,' (I am also a human being) replied Tshuma in Sindebele.[108]

Tshuma was taken before the Magistrate and fined one shilling. For once the matter did not end there. Masotsha briefed Robert Tredgold to take the case on appeal. The result was a triumph. The judge found that the by-law was repugnant to natural justice and ordered that it be withdrawn. The Council vainly groped around to find some substitute; for decades Bulawayo whites bitterly resented the loss of their pavements.[109]

To this day the victory is remembered in Makokoba oral memory in lushly ornamented versions which rub home the confounding of white sexual fears. 82-year-old Ndlovu from Mpopoma recounts a myth of Masotsha Ndlovu, accompanied by later township heroes, like Sipambaniso Manyoba Khumalo and Benjamin Burombo, walking the pavements in defiance of the whites:

Blacks were not allowed to use the pavements because it was said they would disturb 'Missus'. Masotsha would walk facing the ground on the pavements. When he bumped into a white woman he would pretend not to have noticed her. He would touch her breasts. Because of this they arrested him. [But] he worked hard until the whites agreed that blacks could walk on pavements.

Then old Ndlovu added:

But still people were not allowed into stores. They bought through the windows. That was their life. It was bad.

Even heroic myth cannot conceal from memory the realities of Bulawayo in the 1930s.[110]

---

[108] Pathisa Nyathi, *Masotsha Ndlovu*, pp. 22-3.
[109] Robert Tredgold, *The Rhodesia That Was My Life*; Town Clerk to Coghlan and Welsh, 15 and 27 June 1934.
[110] Interview between Simon Mlotshwa and Mr Ndlovu, Mpopoma, 26 January 2001.

2

The First Fires
December 1929

Introduction

At the end of an eventful 1929, and three and half years before they were deprived of their legal monopoly of the pavements, the whites of Bulawayo celebrated the glories of European urban culture. Oddly, perhaps, for a town which went to so much trouble to proclaim its Britishness and where a dour Lowland Scottish influence was strong, Christmas Eve 1929 became something like a festival. The *Chronicle* rhapsodized:

> Christmas Eve in Bulawayo. Once a year the people of Bulawayo – young and old – forget all worries and cares and remember only that it is Christmas Eve. It has been said that the Britisher is inherently incapable of really feeling the carnival spirit, but judging by the merriment and riotous fun of Christmas Eve this would seem to be scarcely applicable to Rhodesians. Streets were thronging from early in the morning until late at night with pedestrians, motor cars, motor cycles and pedal machines.

People bought paper hats, masks and false noses, entering 'these shops as ordinary citizens and as often as not coming out so altered by these artificial aids that even their best friends could not have recognised them':

> The noise made by the high-pitched whistles, the rattles and by the babble of voices and the sight of paper caps and streamers made it almost impossible to realise that the modest Bulawayo of December 23 had not been shifted bodily and replaced by a French Carnival in a sub-tropical setting. The crowds at night jostled along the footpaths and into the shops: strings of people linked arms and almost danced their way around the town.

That night Africans were nowhere to be seen in the centre of the city.[1]

They were where they were supposed to be – in the compounds or in the Location or preparing for their employers' Christmas in suburban houses. And in these places, the *Chronicle* was happy to report, it had been the quietest Christmas for

---

[1] *Chronicle*, 28 December 1929. The same issue, however, carried a story of the clash of the two worlds. On Boxing Day there was a Celebratory Bowling Match on the Green in the Park. Two rowdy Africans, pursued by the police, sought escape by running across the Green, 'to the consternation of the players'. The paper solemnly reported that 'the European detective received a check before the final kill because the ticket collector at the bowling green demanded a shilling in price of admission and refused to believe that he was merely there to arrest two disturbers of the public peace'.

years, with 'a marked absence of drunkenness and crime of any kind'. Whites were having riotous fun; blacks were being soberly law-abiding. Everything was as it should be. But the next issue of the paper on 4 January 1930 carried huge headlines of a very different sort: KNOBKERRIE WARFARE IN BULAWAYO. MATABELE AND MASHONA IN COMBAT. TWO KILLED AND FIFTY INJURED ... DEFENCE FORCE CALLED OUT. As the paper explained in its story, the violence in black Bulawayo had spilled into the white city. It was noticed first, of course, by 'residents in Lobengula Street near the town location', who reported to police that 'a large and unruly crowd of natives had gathered'. But soon the sacred pavements of white Bulawayo were being invaded:

> Charge office officials were continually answering the telephone to alarmed householders asking for the police to come and disperse natives who had gathered on the streets or on the pavements, or who were fighting.[2]

Yet the violence of December 1929 only accidentally impinged on whites, none of whom were targeted or attacked. It was a clash between elements of society in black Bulawayo and it arose out of the question of who was to determine its culture and character.

Many years later Stanlake Samkange recalled the atmosphere just before the December 1929 violence:

> The weekend was an exciting time in the Location. There was so much going on, even in the streets. There were young men, mostly Mashonas, who went about very well dressed, over-dressed in fact. They usually wore an expensive black suit; black hat, white-rimmed spectacles, white shirt, black tie, black waistcoat with a mirror on the tummy, black coat with a row of fountain pens in the top pocket, black trousers and black shoes. They carried knives and forks in a bag; white gloves and a walking-stick. In pairs or alone they strutted and pranced about the streets, saying '*Kudada panyika! Kudada panyika!*' (To be proud on earth), or 'We are style Burawayo, oh! style Burawayo!' [sic][3]

But in the transition from one kind of Location to another, what *was* to be the Bulawayo style and who was to set it?

Interpretations

More than twenty years ago the Bulawayo 'faction fight' of December 1929 was the subject of one of the classics of radical historiography, Charles van Onselen and Ian Phimister's 1979 article, 'The Political Economy of Tribal Animosity'.[4] All contemporary reporting on the faction fights treated them as an outburst of ethnic animosity – 'the Matabele and Mashona in combat'. Van Onselen and Phimister wanted to make more sense of them. Their article 'attempted to situate the specific economic grievances of differentially incorporated groups in the same wide context of Southern Rhodesia's political economy' and to confront 'any suggestions that "faction fights"

---

[2]   *Chronicle*, 4 January 1930.
[3]   Stanlake Sanakange, *The Mourned One*, p. 122. Samkange remembers that 'at Christmas time it was dangerous to walk the streets of the location ... Many Africans believed strongly and most sincerely that at Christmas one could steal, rob, assault or do anything, even commit murder and it would be all right'.
[4]   *Journal of Southern African Studies*, 6, 1, October 1979.

were and are manifestations of mindless irrational "tribal" violence'. Men did not fight each other because they belonged to different ethnic groups. They fought each other because they had different and competitive economic interests.[5]

Van Onselen and Phimister detected two phases in the violence. Between Christmas Eve and 27 December it 'took the form of gang assaults and robbery' directed against 'respectable' long-term residents of the Location. But 'from the afternoon of 27 December the nature of the conflict changed radically. Whereas formerly it had essentially been a case of "Shona" gangs assaulting workers, it now became a case of workers attacking recent migrants ... [especially] the recent influx of Shona. The conflict was now fundamentally one between "established workers" and "new immigrants".'[6] It was the assumption of their article that most 'respectable' long-term workers were 'Ndebele' and that most gangsters and recent incomers were 'Shona'.

The gangsters were 'Shona' because they 'were the most recent migrants. Many of them would have occupied, at least temporarily, the lowest of Bulawayo's socio-economic rungs, including the ranks of the petty criminals and the unemployed.' So in 1929 'the unemployed merged with the Location's lumpen-proletariat' to form gangs which terrified 'Ndebele' residents.[7] These 'Shona' migrants had flooded into Bulawayo because of the agricultural crisis of the late 1920s:

> The unemployment crisis was felt most heavily in Mashonaland, where the tobacco farms were concentrated, and obliged work-seekers to look beyond the province's boundaries. To many Shona workers ... Bulawayo must have looked especially promising.[8]

The desperate immigrants were ready to accept work at whatever wages were offered. They offered intense competition to 'Ndebele' workers. Van Onselen and Phimister sum up the predicament of the locals:

> Ndebele labourers were now in the intolerable and novel position of being squeezed from both domestic and foreign labour markets. For the first time they were vulnerable to competition or even displacement from the labour market at precisely the same time the viability of their rural areas was being noticeably eroded ... The Ndebele faced an influx of Shona migrants which must have seemed especially ominous when Ndebele migration to South Africa was threatened with curtailment.

So the 'Ndebele' workers took advantage of the 1929 violence to drive out the 'Shona'.[9]

In this interpretation, the apparently random events of late 1929 really marked a profound shift in the history of the African working class in Bulawayo. When Stephen Thornton came to write up his research on the African history of Bulawayo in the early 1980s, however, he concluded that van Onselen and Phimister had failed in their 'attempt to establish an effective linkage between their theoretical explanation and the actual events of Christmas 1929–30'. They had failed to achieve their aim to establish 'who the fighting was between, when and why'. In Thornton's view, they were too anxious to argue that the faction fights embodied new realities. Thus there was a need for them to 'invent' a 'somewhat contrived' account of the creation of peculiar conditions in 1929–30.

[5] Ibid., pp. 40-1.
[6] Ibid., pp. 38-9.
[7] Ibid., pp. 36-7.
[8] Ibid., p. 17.
[9] Ibid., p. 18.

His own research found:

> little evidence of any significant increase in the number of unemployed immigrants in Bulawayo
> in the period 1928-30 and less still for the assertion that such immigrants were predominantly
> Shona. In January 1928 it was reported that 'labour was very short and very few natives (were)
> looking for work'. By 1930 the situation had changed little. The Manager of the plumbing firm
> Dupleis, for example, in March 1930 described his 'labour problem' as 'very acute'. Similarly,
> the Council itself noted that it was experiencing difficulties in 1930 in securing labour for the
> night soil service (a job regularly abandoned by migrants in times of labour scarcity).

Moreover, Thornton finds that 'Shona made up only a small proportion of recent migrants'. He offers the example of the workers recruited for the new sewerage scheme in 1930 – an abundant source of new jobs. As many as 1,540 men were employed, of whom 825 were described as 'northern natives' and 232 as 'Portuguese'. Only 483 were 'indigenous' and of these 300 were Ndebele locals who 'leave for their kraals to plough in November'. Only 183 were Shona.[10]

In Thornton's view there was no desperate Shona influx in 1929; no new crisis for the Ndebele working class; and nothing special to explain in the violence of December 1929. To him the faction fight of that year was merely 'part of a wider pattern of faction fighting' which took place regularly throughout the inter-war years. Thornton instances such violence in May 1907; January 1920; December 1923; January 1928 and January 1929. He cites the Location Superintendent, Vawdrey, writing in December 1928 that 'there is always a tendency towards unrest between the Mashonas, the Awemba and the Matabeles and these fights generally revive at Christmas'. He would make 'the usual raid' on Christmas Eve and remove any dangerous weapons.[11] Thornton concludes that 'the 1929–30 fight was only different in its intensity and in the depth of reporting by the European press'.

The whole sequence of faction fights shows, in his view, 'that the lumpen/worker division was not the most significant division within the social structure of Bulawayo. Instead it was the engendered ethnic division amongst workers themselves which generated expressions of ethnic violence.' Workers themselves participated along with employers and with the Rhodesian state to 'imagine' urban ethnicities and to effectuate an ethnic division of labour.[12]

There the argument about the December 1929 'faction fights' rested for more than twenty-five years. But in 2006 two articles appeared which took a 'moral economy' approach rather than the 'political economy' emphasis of Thornton, van Onselen and Phimister.

One was by the young Zimbabwean historian, Enocent Msindo.[13] Msindo agrees with van Onselen and Phimister that the 1929 violence was very significant. It 'marked a turning point' in Southern Rhodesian urban history, and it is 'imperative that his-

---

[10] Stephen Thornton, 'The African Work Experience and the Patterning of Proletarian Consciousness, 1905–1935', pp. 44-5. He draws his examples from Municipal correspondence files in boxes 159 and 243 in the National Archives, Bulawayo and from the Superintendent of Natives to Chief Native Commissioner, 23 September 1930, S.138/60, National Archives, Harare.

[11] Ibid., p. 44. Thornton's citation is Location Superintendent to Town Clerk, 12 December 1928, B23/3/5R 6345, National Archives, Bulawayo. Despite Vawdrey's precautions, a fight took place at Christmas 1928, starting at the Railway Compound and ending near the Location.

[12] Ibid., p. 46.

[13] Enocent Msindo, 'Ethnicity Not Class? The 1929 Bulawayo Faction Fights Reconsidered', *Journal of Southern African Studies*, 32, 3, September 2006.

torians have a fair understanding of the 1929 Bulawayo fights ... before probing the later period'.[14] But he agrees with Thornton that they have not proved their case. 'There is no evidence [that] the Shona were the largest group of recent newcomers to Bulawayo in the late 1920s'. Nor was violence directed only against recently arrived lumpen Shona migrants. Long-established and wealthy Shona were attacked also.[15] Indeed he goes beyond Thornton, himself preoccupied with political economy and class relations, to proclaim: 'It is time ... to debunk the reductionism of the late 1970s historiography that saw "everything" in terms of specific pigeon-holes, such as "class-struggle", "labour" or other reductionist explanations.'[16]

Msindo's own interpretation is that the violence was an attempt by the Ndebele to 'regain lost moral authority over Bulawayo'. In his view, post-Lobengula black Bulawayo 'began with a foreign outlook, inhabited at its core by people of different ethnicities'. These aliens had 'an influence on Bulawayo's ethnic and moral fabric [which] helps explain the 1929 violence'. They had become 'owners' of black Bulawayo, defining its 'moral, linguistic and social tone'. It 'took a heavy and protracted struggle for the Ndebele and other inhabitants of Matabeleland to "regain" Bulawayo'. But by the late 1920s there was an 'increased Ndebele presence in town' and an 'ethnic revival'. The Matabele Home Society began to prepare to use violence against the 'insolent' and dominant Shona, mobilizing and training fighters in *amalaita* gangs and reviving the Ndebele warrior image. He emphasizes the 'high level of planning that culminated in the fight'.[17]

The other article to appear in 2006 was my own 'The Meaning of Urban Violence in Africa'.[18] I will not summarize it here because this chapter presents an extended version of its argument. Briefly, though, I concur with Msindo in pursuing a moral rather a political economy approach. The 1929 violence was about who could define 'style Burawayo' [sic]. But readers of this book will know that I do not see the earlier history of the Bulawayo African Location in the same light as Msindo. I see long-term Ndebele urban dwellers, in alliance with educated South African migrants and women property owners, as having determined the social patterns of the Location. They were challenged in the late 1920s not by a lumpen Shona invasion but by young men who claimed to represent modernity. I do not think that the explosion of violence in December 1929 had been long planned or that it was purposeful. I believe that it arose in an atmosphere of rumour and myth in which the boasts of the 'insolent' young men created a panic, with phantom armies marching through the Bulawayo bush.

I have myself seen all the evidence deployed by van Onselen and Phimister and most of the evidence deployed by Thornton.[19] To this I have been able to add much oral evidence collected in the townships by my research collaborators. As a result I agree with those historians who see the 1929 faction fighting as different in its significance from previous ethnic clashes. Our older oral informants barely recall other faction

---

[14] Ibid., p. 429.
[15] Ibid., p. 431. Msindo instances the case of a crippled Shona storekeeper in the Railway Compound who lost £21 in cash and more than £80 in goods when his property was burnt. 'So rich a man could not have been a newcomer to Bulawayo.'
[16] Ibid., p. 431.
[17] Ibid., pp. 433, 434, 445, 446.
[18] Terence Ranger, 'The Meaning of Urban Violence in Africa: Bulawayo, Southern Rhodesia, 1890–1960', *Cultural and Social History*, 3, 2006.
[19] Thornton worked more intensively than I have done on Municipal subject files for the 1920s. However, I have come across additional archival materials and also made use of oral interviews.

fights but they vividly remember 1929. The 1929 violence was regularly recalled by the African press in the 1940s and 1950s. It certainly seemed something unusual to the African residents of Bulawayo.

I shall argue that the categories 'Ndebele' and 'Shona' were still very much in the making in 1929 and that to understand what happened at the end of that year we need to disaggregate them. (We need to realize, for example, that the population of the Location and of the Railway Compounds was not simply divided between 'Shona' and 'Ndebele', but in each case was multi-ethnic.) I shall argue that perhaps the most important factor in disparate Location identities was the perceived fit between different ethnicities and particular jobs. Because of these 'fits' there were some jobs, among them some of the best as well as some of the worst rewarded, for which 'Ndebele' men did not compete. This meant that migrants not only worked as night-soil removers and unskilled labourers but also as waiters and chefs and teachers. In 1929 even more noticeable than the 'Shona' unemployed were the 'Manyika' privileged, occupying or aspiring to the best jobs and arrogantly conscious of their superior education, smartness and modernity. Men like this certainly aspired to set the 'style Burawayo', and their aspirations were resented by those who had previously shaped the culture of the black town.

This was, of course, partly a matter of generation as well as of ethnicity. As we have seen, the Location was changing. Many more young 'bachelors' were being housed in municipal cottages and were no longer dependent on long-term plot-owners and rentiers. There was great rivalry between groups of these young men, expressing itself in competitive dressing, competitive dancing, competitive boxing and in competitive fighting. There were 'Ndebele' gangs as well as 'Shona' ones. The youths of the Location interacted and competed with the young workers in the Railway compounds.

As we have seen, there were still more women in the Location than has often been supposed, including more young women. But they were certainly in a minority and their favours were competed for. Van Onselen and Phimister write that 'trouble may have begun over foreigners abusing Ndebele women'. But much more resentment was caused by 'foreigners' courting, winning and marrying Ndebele women. Here, of course, the resentment was shared by older Ndebele – by parents and uncles – as well as by young Ndebele workers. In much the same way, what was essentially at stake between the young men was the claim to represent modernity. But this claim in itself challenged black Bulawayo's sense of history and so was resented by older residents. And finally, the very definitions of modernity adopted and fought over by the young challenged the old Christian ideas of 'progress' and 'development'. The denunciations of male youth fashion carried in the pages of the elite *Native Mirror* reveal the resentment felt by the guardians of Christian progressive ideals.

There were thus several important issues at stake in the 1929 fighting, even if after it every articulate spokesman of African opinion came to denounce violence as a way of resolving them. A moral economy approach undermines any idea of 'mindless irrational tribal violence' just as profoundly as a political economy one.

In what follows I want first of all to offer a brief narrative of the late December 1929 faction fighting. Then I will examine in turn the making of ethnicity – the ethnic composition of the Location, the invocation of history, the emergence of an occupational ethnic hierarchy. I shall explore the reality of gangs and the complexities of gender. I shall then turn to the oral – and literary – memory of the faction fight and to an analysis of the flames that flared in 1929. I shall emphasize that much of the violence took place outside the Location and some of it in the Bulawayo countryside. Finally, I will explore some of the consequences of the violence and make the point that more than most violence it was a disruption rather than a reflection of the basic political patterns of the Bulawayo Location.

A Brief Narrative of the 1929 Faction Fights

It is hard to provide a coherent narrative of the 1929 violence. In 1929 there were no African newspapers and the only press source is the Bulawayo *Chronicle*, which had no correspondents in the Location or the Compounds and was thoroughly confused about ethnicity. Nor were any analytical official reports produced. In January 1930 the Superintendent of Natives, Bulawayo, suggested that an inquiry into the events and causes of the faction fighting should be the first task of the newly appointed Standing Native Affairs Commission.[20] But although the Commission did indeed take the Bulawayo Location as its first task – and produced a highly critical report on conditions there – it asked no question of either black or white witnesses about the faction fights and made no reference to them in its report. No analysis was ever published by the Municipality. There exists, however, a CID narrative report on the 'Bulawayo Native Disturbances' submitted on 4 January 1930 by Chief Superintendent J.B. Brundell[21] which can be supplemented by the day-by-day correspondence of the Native Department and the Municipality. Oral evidence is very strong on what our aged informants believe the violence to have been about, and I shall draw on it extensively below. But after this lapse of time it is no use in reconstructing a sequence of events.

Expectations of Trouble

The Native Department had been expecting trouble in Bulawayo for several months. It thought that this trouble would come from the Industrial and Commercial Workers Union under its leader, Sergeant Masotsha Ndlovu. Quite apart from the alarm caused by the ICU's criticisms of the Native Department and the Municipality, officials knew that the violent Durban Beer Hall riots of June 1929 had been preceded by months of ICU *yase Natal* protests and marches.[22] They knew that on 20 July 1929 Masotsha had commented on events in Durban to his Bulawayo audience:

> The 'good boys' will say that the ICU are the Devil's people. Do not take any notice of them. When they feel something hard they will come to us. They say that all that happened in Durban was because of the ICU. I say that it was only human feelings. It happens elsewhere too. You will hear of riots all over the world. As long as people oppress that will be there always.[23]

---

[20] S/NA/Bulawayo to Chief Native Commissioner, 9 January 1930, S.138/22, National Archives, Harare.
[21] S.482/805/39, National Archives, Harare.
[22] Paul la Hausse, 'The Struggle for the City: Alcohol, the Ematsheni and Popular Culture in Durban, 1902–1936', in Paul Maylam and Iain Edwards (eds), *The People's City. African Life in Twentieth-Century Durban*, University of Natal Press, Pietermaritzburg, 1996.
[23] CID report, 21 July 1929, S.138, National Archives, Harare.

The Native Department did not take such a philosophical view of urban riot. In November 1929 the Rhodesian and South African Ministers of Justice met in Pretoria and agreed that the ICU should be closely watched by both governments: the situation in Bulawayo might develop as it had in Durban.[24] When the fires broke out in Bulawayo in December 1929 the Superintendent of Natives, Bulawayo, Colonel Carbutt, 'from the information he had was inclined to think that the ICU had been connected with the troubles'.[25]

Other officials picked up quite different information. The Native Commissioner, Umzingwane, had been warning of impending trouble for months before the violence. 'I gather that the trouble between the Matabele and the Mashona originated in Bulawayo about a year ago,' he wrote. 'This rumour appears to have come from Bulawayo in November [1929] and that the attack would be made at Christmas time by the Mashona.'[26]

Meanwhile the Police were content to take merely routine precautions:

> There was no evidence to show that any unusual native disturbance in Bulawayo was to be anticipated but precautionary measures were taken on 23-12-29 by the seizure of 900 offensive weapons, comprising knobkerries, iron bars, sticks and assegais in the Bulawayo Location and adjoining premises and destruction of 615 gallons of kaffir beer in the neighbouring Municipal compounds.

No seizure of beer or weapons took place in the Railway Compounds. Nevertheless, the police expected no serious trouble and were made uneasy by only one thing:

> The native war-dances which have been held by the Batonka (Zambezi) natives – employed by the Bulawayo Municipal Council – in the Location area for many years and which have hitherto attracted numbers of European spectators did not take place.

Instead, the Tonga workers gathered outside their Compound on the edge of the Location, armed with sticks.[27]

The Outbreak of Fighting

The *Chronicle* only became aware of unrest on the evening of 27 December. Officials knew, however, that there had been clashes in the Location and the western streets of the town on the nights of 24, 25 and 26 December.[28] The Native Department was inclined to dismiss these as unimportant. But the Acting Location Superintendent, Collier, took a different view:

> On the 25th of December in the afternoon the [Tonga] Natives of the Bulawayo Municipal Compound were coming out in a fighting attitude and the Natives returning to the Location were afraid. Twice that afternoon I had to go out to put them back [in the Municipal Compound] as the Location Natives were congregating in large numbers to pass the Compound. On

24 *Chronicle*, 23 November 1929.
25 *Chronicle*, 4 January 1930. Carbutt was speaking to a meeting of the Bulawayo Landowners and Farmers Association.
26 Native Commissioner, Umzingwane, to S/N/Bulawayo, 9 January 1930, S.138, National Archives, Harare.
27 Report by J.B. Brundell, 4 January 1930, S 482/805/39, National Archives, Harare.
28 Ibid. S/N/Bulawayo to Chief Native Commissioner, 27 December, S.138, National Archives, Harare.

Christmas night the Native Police patrolled the Location with me till 2 am as the Natives continued to be uneasy. On the 26th instant at 7 pm small gangs of Natives were dashing [around] the Bulawayo Municipal Compound part of the Location. I got together several Police Boys and sent a few in with two of the Location Police in charge and kept the road clear ... for Natives who were coming home from work in the night. I kept certain Mashona Natives in the office for safety and personally conducted them to their rooms when things got quiet.[29]

These events, and the rumours that had preceded them, created alarm in 'the better class of Natives residing in the Location'. Next morning, 27 December, a deputation of Ndebele Location residents came to Superintendent of Natives, Carbutt. Although up to that point there had been few reports of 'Shona' taking any aggressive initiative, they assured him that 'natives from Victoria Circle [Karanga] are at the bottom of it. They have started a rumour to the effect that in consideration of £8, said to have been given to me, I have authorised them to assault Matabele natives with impunity. It is alleged that the Victoria Natives go about in gangs of five or six and that they are particularly dangerous at night.' Mangatshana, Head Messenger at the High Court, thought that these gangsters were influenced by Johannesburg: they were the type who 'wore short coats and trousers wide enough for a man to get inside'. Carbutt was warned that the attacks planned by the Shona would begin at 5 p.m. on 27 December. He alerted police and himself went to the Location.[30]

There he found that Municipal officials were also on the alert and that Africans were assembling in the streets. Collier reported later that:

At 7 pm [on the 27th] about five or six hundred natives assembled in front of the office. I instructed them to disperse and go to their homes and as they were leaving a couple of Mashona ran up the street and got out of hand and started fighting and throwing stones. Mr Rogers of the Beer Hall assisted me and the Native Police arresting a large number carrying sticks and binding up the wounded, using all the bandages and medicines in stock.[31]

Rogers's report was more dramatic. From 7.30 p.m. on the 27th to 5 a.m. the next morning, both he and Collier were 'hard at work'. 'We were the means of saving the lives of at least three natives by our knowledge of first aid and rescuing them from the crowd ... One native died while I was examining him for his injuries ... Other than a few bruises in the ribs and having one of my shins cut with stones we came out of several good fights very fortunate.'[32]

Meanwhile, violence was taking place in Railway Compound 2, south of the Location in Raylton. It was from there that a large group tried to march on the Location on the late afternoon of 27 December through the veld parallel to Lobengula Street. The *Chronicle* of 4 January 1930 described how three to four hundred men 'were seen marching across the veld ... in the direction of the Bulawayo Location, shouting and waving sticks, and generally behaving in an extremely bellicose manner'. They carried bicycle chains attached to sticks, axes, knives and bayonets. 'A crowd of Location inhabitants gathered to await the attack', but mounted police using batons broke up the march. They returned to the Railway Compound and it was there that the first fires of Christmas 1929 broke out.

29 Location Monthly Report, December 1929, Box 23/3/7R, 1930, National Archives, Bulawayo.
30 S/N/Bulawayo to Chief Native Commissioner, 27 December 1929, S.138.
31 Location Monthly Report, December 1929, Box 23/3/7R, National Archives, Bulawayo.
32 Monthly Beer Hall Report, December 1929, Box 23/3/7R, National Archives, Bulawayo.
33 *Chronicle*, 4 January 1930.

The *Chronicle* reported what happened next in high dramatic style:

Shortly before 8 o'clock [on the 27th] urgent messages were received at the Town and district police headquarters that the railway location was being burned down. A rosy glow of flame in the southern sky lent colour to this report and all available forces, with the exception of a number of troopers left on guard at the Bulawayo Location, went as quickly as possible to Raylton. As the railway compound neared, a tremendous noise of shouting and screaming could be heard and flames could be seen everywhere. On arriving at the location, it was found that all the clothing, bicycles and other belongings of some 300 to 400 Manicaland natives living in the location, had been seized by the Matabele, placed in nine or ten huge piles and set alight. In the light of the raging fires, natives could be seen dancing around, shouting war cries and threats and waving sticks, knobkerries and knives, inciting each other to kill the Mashonas. The police surrounded the compound but did not venture inside, the savage spectacle continuing until the fires had burned down.[33]

Carbutt reported that 'the Mashonas' in the Railway Compound had lost 'bedding, clothes, sewing machines and all other domestic appliances. One man alleges that he lost £21 in notes in these fires.' 'Railway property', he added, 'was not damaged in any way.'[34] Next morning, Saturday 28 December, there was 'very little trouble in the Location, most of the women packing up their property and leaving same at Beer Hall, and they left for their kraals'.[35] By this time most of 'the Mashonas' had fled from the Location and the Compounds. The deputations which came to see Carbutt, however, were 'all Matabeleland tribes' and they still insisted that 'the Mashonas … were the aggressors and instigators of the disturbances'. Carbutt then went to both of the Railway Compounds and warned the workers there that further violence would not be tolerated. At 3 p.m. he addressed over a thousand men in the Location. The speakers included not only Ndebele traditionalist spokesmen but also Masotsha Ndlovu of the ICU. There were no 'Shona' or 'Manyika' speakers:

All were very bitter against the so-called Manyika. It was alleged that they were the aggressors, led by a man named Rusere, alias James Mabala, a native of Chibi district, since arrested on charges of violence and possibly of murder.

Speakers said they were 'merely defending themselves against the Mashona'; it was unsafe to walk at night because of Shona gangs; the Mashona should be sent back to their own territory. Carbutt rebuked them and insisted that 'all tribes are equal in the eyes of the Government and have the right to pursue peaceful avocations anywhere in the Colony'. But as the meeting dispersed, there was a cry that 'Mashona' had arrived to attack the crowd. Mobs chased the supposed Shona, and police and officials intervened to save them.

Carbutt's busy day continued. He went next to the brickfields, where rumours said that Shona were massing in large numbers. He found none, but at the quarry he found 'a large number of natives aimed with assegais, fish-spears, pickhandles and other weapons, advancing on the Location through the bush'. Leaving his car, he 'intercepted and disarmed as many as I could catch'. He returned to the Location where there was still 'turmoil, natives rushing about and shouting in every direction'. He 'was informed that a concerted attack on the Location might be expected during the night from Mashonas who were assembling to the north'. The Defence Force was

---

[34] S/N/Bulawayo to CNC, 30 December 1929, S.138.
[35] Monthly Location Report, December 1929.

deployed to picket the Location but no Shona army arrived.[36]

On Sunday 29th December a company of the Defence Force 'marched down one street and up another in the Location' and then did the same thing in the Railway Compound. Fighting was displaced into the suburbs and the town and throughout the day fights took place between small groups of Africans on the sacred pavements of white Bulawayo.[37] The Acting Location Superintendent was mopping up:

> The Matabele were hunting any Mashona natives they could find and we were kept busy getting these natives away and sending them to the Police Camp for protection. About 4.50 pm the BSAP arrived with a few hundred Mashona Natives who they were bringing in to the Location. I got Colonel Carbutt on the phone and asked him to come down and have Mashonas removed as the Location Natives were getting out of hand and arming with sticks to fight. The Mashonas were then taken away. Since then everything has been quiet and a lot of women are returning to the Location.[38]

Meanwhile violence had spread to the countryside. In Umzingwane that Sunday night a party of some 30 Ndebele attacked a Shona kraal on Willsgrove Farm. 'That night there was a tense feeling along the Umguza, the Mashona expecting to be attacked and burnt out, and the Matabele thought Mashona reinforcements would arrive and attack their kraals.'[39]

On Monday 30 December, however, most men in the Bulawayo Location returned to work. Carbutt believed that this would enable 'the Mashonas. who wish to do so, to drift back to the Location'. By this time he had ceased to believe that the main root of the trouble was either ICU sedition or Ndebele fear of attack. 'The Matabele are determined to drive the Mashona out of Bulawayo and its precincts. Very strong action will have to be taken to overcome their determination ... If they are allowed to have their way with the Mashona in Bulawayo, I have no doubt that the movement will spread to the Mines and every industry in Matabeleland, resulting in the disorganization of labour, and dictatorship by the Matabele which cannot be tolerated.'[40] Strong action was being taken. On that Monday 200 men appeared in court and were summarily sentenced by Magistrate Fynn. The next day Carbutt summoned the leaders of the ICU, the Matabele Home Society and various Ndebele elders – 'apart from them there are no leaders of the natives in Bulawayo'. He told them that 'the Matabeles who are fighting may not be all members of the ICU and the MHS, but a great many of your members are joining in the disturbances. How is it that you cannot control your members but allow them to join disturbances which are entirely opposed to the professed objects of your associations?' They were to tell their members that 'the Matabele will not be allowed to drive away the Mashona. All tribes are under the protection of the Government and are equal in the eyes of the Government. There is more work here than the Matabele alone can do.' He ended with a dire threat:

> Many of your people, I know, think that the white people never kill anyone and that no matter what they do they will only be fined or go to gaol for a few months. Do not be misled. There is a limit to all things and if you carry your determination to drive the Shona out too far it can only

36 S/N/Bulawayo to CNC, 30 December 1929, S.138.
37 *Chronicle*, 4 January 1930.
38 Monthly Location Report, December 1929.
39 Native Commissioner, Umzingwane to S/N/Bulawayo, 9 January 1930. S.138.
40 Carbutt to CNC, 30 December 1930, S.138.

lead to the Government having to resort to stronger measures – even to the shooting of some of the leaders of these disturbances.[41]

Saturday 4 January marked the end of the upheaval. There was a big meeting in the Location at which representatives of the various ethnic groups spoke. Masotsha Ndlovu of the ICU spoke first. He thanked the government for restoring order 'when we are biting each other', but went on to stress that 'the trouble was just caused by confusion – we do not know the head or start of it ... All the Location was in confusion and no-one knew who had hit him except those who had been attacked in their houses.' Many had been 'convicted innocently'. The other speakers all called for unity between every ethnicity. Fingos, Zezuru, Ndebele, Manyika, Bemba, Lozi, Tonga – all deplored mindless violence and called for collaboration. Sitchela, an Ndebele, rebuked his fellows: 'You are just like two dogs who start fighting and the other dogs join in. I have never seen human beings fight without cause.'[42]

All that remained was for Carbutt to speculate on the cause of the violence, to assure the Prime Minister that steps had been taken to compensate those who had lost their property in the Railway Compound, and tell him that James Mabala, alias Rusere, had been convicted of public violence and fined £10 or three months.[43]

The Making of Ethnicity

By now the reader must be sympathizing with Masotsha Ndlovu. This is certainly a puzzling narrative, and like him we cannot be sure quite what was happening or who was doing what to whom. Maybe the trouble *was* 'just caused by confusion'.

Who were the workers from the Municipal Compound who appeared in fighting array on Christmas Day? They certainly were not either 'Ndebele' or 'Shona', neither of which groups contributed to the Municipal workforce. Who were the workers who marched on the Location from the Railway Compound? They were certainly not 'Shona', since they returned to the Compound and burnt the property of Manyika workers there. Who were the men in the bush armed with fishing-spears, which were not carried by either 'Ndebele' or 'Shona'? Indeed, where were the 'Shona' armies which so many people expected to appear? Carbutt says he was warned on 27 December that 'the Mashonas were organizing a general attack on the Location' but the only march on the Location was made by the railway workers, who were certainly not Shona. During his meeting with 1,000 Location residents on 28 December a rumour spread that armed Shona had been killing Ndebele a mile from the Location. But this turned out to be untrue. Later that same day Carbutt went to the Brickfields where it was reported that large numbers of Shona were massing. He found nobody there. The whole episode was full of ghost armies and phantom enemies. And except for the small-scale Umzingwane raid it is impossible to find Ndebele *impis* as distinct from groups in the Location. One begins to think that the term 'Ndebele/Shona faction fights', usually employed to describe the late December 1929 violence, is something of a misnomer. Certainly there were no pitched battles between 'Matabele' and 'Mashona'.

We may well ask, indeed, what did the *Chronicle* mean by 'the Matabele' and the

[41] Address to Matabele on Disturbances, 31 December 1930, S.138.
[42] Notes of a meeting in the Bulawayo Location, 4 January 1930, S.138.
[43] Carbutt to CNC, 4 March 1930, S.138.

'Mashona'? Did 'the Matabele' include the Kalanga-speakers of Plumtree, and the Banyubi of the Matopos? Or was a 'Matabele' anyone who carried a knobkerrie and performed a war dance? The *Chronicle* used the heading 'Matabele and Mashona in Combat' when it described the fires in the Railway Compound. It assumed that the Africans who were 'dancing around, shouting war cries' were Ndebele. But few Ndebele worked on the railways and few were involved in the burnings.

And what can we understand by 'Mashona' – the word constantly used by the *Chronicle* and by Native Department officials but hardly used at all by the African protagonists? On 30 December 1929 Carbutt wrote that the Ndebele 'alleged that the Mashonas, especially those from Victoria Circle, were the aggressors and instigators' but immediately added that 'locally they are all referred to as "Manyika"'. On 9 January he again noted that the term used by the Ndebele for all natives of Mashonaland was 'Manyika'. Nevertheless, in the rest of his long memorandum he himself uses the word 'Mashona'.[44] In his account of the meeting of 28 December Carbutt consistently summarizes complaints against the 'Mashona', but when the meeting breaks up in disarray it is with the cry, 'There are the Manyikas looking for us'. And at his meeting with the Ndebele representatives of the associations on 31 December, Carbutt himself told them that they could not drive out 'the Mashona', but when summarizing their own demands, reminded them that one of their speakers had said 'You must send all the Manyikas back to their country'.

It may seem that I am belabouring this point and that it can be resolved merely by saying that what the whites meant by 'Mashona' and what the blacks meant by 'Manyika' was exactly the same. But as I will argue, the connotations of 'Mashona' and 'Manyika' were very different.

There seems no doubt, in other words, that ethnicity in Bulawayo in 1929 was very much in the making and very flexible. The first urban association designed to represent 'the Matabele' as a whole did not formally emerge until November 1929, a month before the faction fights. This was the Matabele Home Society, whose objects were 'to support and build up the fallen Nation (Natives) and develop their welfare on a civilized basis'. The MHS was itself, and long remained, a schizophrenic body, not quite sure whether it represented 'true' aristocratic Ndebele, or the descendants of everyone who had been incorporated into the Ndebele state, or everyone who spoke Sindebele or everyone in Matabeleland. Its 'three abiding concerns were the conditions of life for urban dwelling Ndebele, the attempt to restore the monarchy and the question of Ndebele land'.[45] Carbutt included the leaders of the MHS in his meeting of 31 December, quoting from its constitution to the effect that it desired to 'secure the co-operation of all persons who have at heart the interests of humanity', and rebuking them for failing to ensure that their members lived up to this ideal.

As for 'the Mashona' in Bulawayo, it was not until some twenty-five years later that the Sons of Mashonaland Society emerged, with its demand that people should be proud to be 'Mashona' rather than Zezuru, or Karanga, or Korekore, or Manyika. In December 1929 there was no pan-Shona consciousness in Bulawayo. There was no 'Mashona' boxing team or football club, for example: Zezuru fought Korekore and Manyika fought Karanga. 'Mashona' identity was more imposed than proclaimed. Two factors were at play – the insulting traditional Ndebele term, *Maswina*, which made many people reluctant to be called 'Mashona'; and the insistence of the whites in call-

[44] Carbutt to CNC, 30 December 1929 and 9 January 1930, S.138.
[45] T.O. Ranger, *The African Voice in Southern Rhodesia*, pp. 187-8.

ing everyone from central and eastern Rhodesia by that name. Very many preferred to claim a name that carried an aura of prestige rather than of shame – like 'Manyika'.

The Native Commissioner, Umzingwane, recalled in January 1930 how successive faction fights in Bulawayo had been powered by mythic history:

> I understand that there was trouble in Bulawayo after the Boer War between the Xhosa and the Matabele, because the former had been on our side in the Rebellion; and a few years later between the Zambesi Natives and the Matabelele, because the former had been raided in the old days.[46]

These memories certainly don't fit with Msindo's idea of an alien Bulawayo which only saw an Ndebele resurgence in the 1920s. But these historical identities were very fluid. By December 1929 the Xhosa and the 'Zambezis' – the men with the fishing spears – were on the side of the Ndebele.

According to the Native Commissioner, a further historical myth was at play in 1929. 'The Mashona said that the Matabelele had killed their people years ago and that now they intended to kill the Matabele and had bought them from the Government.' But much more important than myth in defining 'ethnicity' in Bulawayo in December 1929 were job differentiation and 'ethnic' hierarchies of prestige. One needs a much more graduated approach than to identify the Ndebele with residence and long-term jobs and the Shona with recency and lumpen-proletarian unemployment, as van Onselen and Phimister did.

Oral Accounts of Urban Ethnicity

I was assisted in interviewing men and women long resident in Makokoba by two third-year history students, Hloniphani Ndlovu and Busani Mpofu. Our informants, both Ndebele- and Shona-speaking, presented a very complex world. They insisted on job differentiation on the basis of 'urban tribalism'; they insisted on the prosperity and modernity of many 'Shona', especially the Manyika; and they insisted on the capacity of these smart, well-educated migrants to attract local women rather than to intimidate them.

Mr Vundla of New Magwegwe insists that 'vital was how educated one was'. Workers from Northern Rhodesia and Nyasaland did the hard work on the railways, with Shona-speakers employed as clerks. Hardly any local Ndebele or Kalanga worked on the railways. Dirty municipal jobs, like 'night-soil' removal, were done by 'Zambesi boys'. The Ndebele and Kalanga, he says, were builders and ran grinding mills. 'The Manyika from Mutare wanted clean jobs as they considered themselves to be very smart, wearing suits and ties, and thus they chose to work in hotels.'[47]

When we unpack this testimony it explains many things in the narrative of December 1929. The term 'Manyika', unlike the term 'Mashona', carried prestige connotations. Jobs in hotels and offices were at the head of the early colonial job

---

[46] NC, Umzingwane to S/N/Bulawayo, 9 January 1930, S.138. The Location Inspector, T. Fallon, told the Town Clerk on 31 May 1907 that 'a great disturbance by two Bantu races took place in the Native Location on the afternoon of the 27th. I arrested four women.' General Correspondence, Bulawayo Council, 23/1/3R, Box 5622, National Archives, Bulawayo.

[47] Interview between Hloniphani Ndlovu and Mr Vundla, New Magwegwe, February 2000.

hierarchy. Manyika success was resented by men in less prestigious or less well-remunerated occupations. All over southern Africa the 'Manyika' from eastern Zimbabwe, with the educational advantage of the best mission schools and with their impressive facility in English, impressed local women and irritated local men.[48] As Vundla says, the majority of the workers in the Railway Compounds were Northern Rhodesians and Nyasas. When Carbutt took 'Mashona' workers to the No. 2 Compound on 4 January, and told the residents that there must be no more trouble, 'the crowd, who are all Northern natives, thereupon clapped their hands, signifying assent'. It was the Northerners, rather than the Ndebele, who set alight the luxury goods – clothes, sewing machines, bicycles, cash – of the resented 'Manyika'.

Workers in the Municipal Compound, who came out ready to fight on Christmas Day, were almost entirely so-called 'Zambesi-boys', who had been allocated the dirtiest jobs – street-sweeping, night-soil clearing – and who were hostile to the self-display of the young Manyika, returning to the Location from work in the city. The men Carbutt met on 28 December 'armed with fish spears' were 'Zambesis and Barotses, and undoubtedly intended to take part in the fighting had they not been checked'.[49] When Carbutt spoke to 'Mashona' leaders on 31 December they told him that 'as far as the Matabele were concerned they knew of no reason why they should not make friends and live in harmony: that the people who were still inclined to cause trouble were the Zambesis and the Barotse'.[50]

But here, too, there were many Northerners who did not live in the Municipal Compound and did not do menial jobs. They had attained status either in the Location or in the Private Locations which ringed Bulawayo. Some of them spoke at the meeting of 4 January 1930. Patrick, alias Mulenga, was a Bemba, who held the good job of Post Office messenger and was King of the Northern Rhodesian Association. He told his fellow northerners: 'You, my friends, from far away Nyasaland to Tanganyika, we did not come here to cause disturbance, but followed the European because of money.' Gibson, alias Twaka, was a Tonga shoemaker from Nyasaland, who had lived in the Location for many years. He was reluctantly caught up in the violence:

When the trouble started I was out at Hyde Park. I went to Riverside for Christmas. On my return to Bulawayo on Friday 27th I was stopped by the Police who told me that I could not go into town … I was passing the meeting – some Matabele chased the Mashonas – I ran – we ran – they all ran. I was afraid. I went out to my kraal and hid in the veld during the day. I kept hearing things from town – I expected that there would be shooting and I was ready to hide in the mountains.[51]

[48] T.O. Ranger, 'Missionaries, Migrants and the Manyika: the invention of ethnicity in Zimbabwe', in Leroy Vail (ed.), *The Creation of Tribalism in Southern Africa*, James Currey, London, 1989. See also a delightful memoir by a Cape Coloured woman, Katie Hendriks, *The Bend in the Road*, Cape Town, n.d. Katie's father, Mandisodza, was educated at Old Umtali Episcopal Methodist Mission primary school in Manicaland, where he reached Standard Five. 'He was an incurable boaster.' In about 1920 he went to Salisbury and obtained the prestigious job of head cook at a big hotel at the wage of £4 10s a month. He window-shopped in the city, feasting 'his delighted eyes on the clothes displayed in the shop windows, and then, with only a few pence in his pockets, he would walk up to the counter and ask to be shown the very best shirts and suits.' In the mid-1920s he went to Cape Town and 'wanted to try out everything in this wonderful city at once'. He got a job as cook at a Hout Bay hotel, was 'very dapper' and had an affair with 'a pretty coloured girl with little dancing feet'. Their daughter, Katie, met 'an immaculately dressed' Manyika waiter in the 1940s; he was highly educated; she married him.

[49] Carbutt to CNC, 4 March 1930, S.138.
[50] Carbutt to CNC, 2 January 1930, S.138.
[51] Notes of speeches in the Bulawayo Location, 4 January 1930, S.138.

Oral Accounts of Location Gender Relations

Immigrants from Manicaland particularly, but Shona-speakers generally, courted local girls:

> Most Shona men [says a self-identified Manyika immigrant] were comfortable with the presence of women in town as women could relieve them from the stress of hard work ... Most of the Ndebele men were not interested in women ... Shona men were comfortable with the presence of women in town as they felt they needed them constantly.[52]

A Northern Rhodesian informant, Mr Zulu, says that 'the Ndebele were not comfortable with the presence of their women in town ... Some Shona men managed to get wives from those few Ndebele women who were there. Ndebele men would go home every weekend to see their families. They were bitter about women who came to Bulawayo.'[53] The Ndebele, Mali Nyathi, agrees that 'Shona men were the only group interested in girls' because the Ndebele had wives outside town. He adds, moreover, that 'most of the ladies liked the Shona because they were generous with their money ... Ndebele were not liked because they were very stingy'.[54] Not surprisingly, perhaps, Shona-speakers agree. Tanyanywa Kadungure says that 'in those days Ndebele guys did not know how to entice girls. They were rough to ladies, they were stingy in most cases ... The direct opposite were the Shona, especially the Manyika. The Manyika knew very well how ladies should be treated. So the township singers sang songs along those lines.'[55] 'Then came a Shona man', ran one of these songs, 'and smacked me with a green [note] and said, Baby, you are smart'.[56] It is striking that both Ndebele-speaking and Shona-speaking informants insist that fights started not so much when a Shona lumpen tried to harass an Ndebele woman, but when 'an Ndebele snatched a lady from the Shona'.

In the late 1920s, so different from post-Second World War Bulawayo, it was male immigrants who dazzled by their dress. There were no Makokoba beauty queens. The young men were the peacocks of that time. Local township women rarely wore shoes – except on the day of their wedding, when they oiled their feet and practised walking in shoes for weeks beforehand. Local women in 1929 wore short skirts, not as fashionable minis, but as an urban version of the rural traditional apron. One of our informants was immediately attracted to the girl who became his wife because she wore tennis shoes. Our female informants, on the other hand, admit to being swept off their feet by the smartness and politeness of their immigrant suitors, with their black suits, and gloves and canes. Just as in the Cape Town of the 1920s, fashionable Manyika men proved irresistible.[57]

A reporter in the *Chronicle* of 4 January 1930 tells us that he accompanied a police patrol to Umzingwane where he interviewed a 'fairly well educated native'. The man gave him a mix of ethnic myth, history and gender politics:

52 Interview between Hloniphani Ndlovu and a Manyika informant who requested anonymity, January 2000.
53 Interview between Hloniphani Ndlovu and Mr Zulu, Entumbane, February 2000.
54 Interview betwen Hloniphani Ndlovu and Mali Nyathi, Magwegwe, February 2000.
55 Interview between Hloniphani Ndlovu and Tanyanyiwa Kadungure, Makokoba, January 2000.
56 M. Hove, *Confessions of a Wizard*, Mambo Press, Gweru, 1985, p. 123.
57 T.O. Ranger, 'Pictures Must Prevail: Sex and the History of Photography in Bulawayo', *Kronos*, 27, November 2001.

One must not blame the Matabele too much for the outbreaks as they are striking for what they consider their own rights. Before the British came to this country, Matabeleland was under the complete sway of the Matabele ... Whenever another tribe tried to enter the country they were attacked and killed ... Since the white man came the alien boys have slowly come into the town and taken many of the good jobs and stolen some of the Matabele's wives. They know the white man will protect them and they do not care. What the Matabele do not like, however, is the way the strangers behave. They arrive from beyond the borders and build their huts and work in the towns, and when they want a wife they court her and spoil her and they do not pay lobola.

This informant turned out to be from Manicaland![58]

Many of the 'Manyika' lived with their 'Matabele' wives in the Location. Others lived in the kraals beyond the Commonage from which they commuted to work. On Gumtree Farm, for instance, lived 'tailors, hotel waiters, chauffeurs, hospital orderlies and the like', many of them 'Manyika', whose wives engaged in peasant cultivation. This Manyika enclave was undisturbed in December 1929. But where 'Manyika' set up households with Ndebele women in the Location they were very vulnerable. One of them was Richard alias Malila who spoke at the 4 January meeting as a self-identified 'Manyika':

I did not think of trouble. I have a Matabele wife and I went to her kraal. I did not think of being assaulted. I came to Bulawayo on Friday, 27th, with my brother. I found that my windows were broken in and bricks inside my house – my crockery was broken. I thought thieves had been there. I went to the woman in the next cottage and asked her what had happened. She told me that had I been there I would have been killed.[59]

Our oral informants tell us that all the clothes and other goods from these mixed Manyika-Ndebele marriages were piled up outside the house and set on fire. 'Some of the Ndebele wives who had remained behind' when their husbands fled, 'were ordered by the Ndebele to remove all the clothes of their husbands and pile them in front of their houses. The Ndebele then poured paraffin on those clothes and set them alight.'[60] What was happening was not looting but the symbolic elimination of Manyika high fashion.

Oral Myths of the Origins of the Fighting [61]

It is in this context of Manyika, and more generally speaking Shona-speaking, over-confidence that we must understand oral memories of December 1929. We have seen that during the days of violence the 'Manyika' or the 'Mashona' did very little. According to oral evidence, however, it was what they had done *before* the violence that counted.

The central figure in the oral myth is the man who appears briefly in the white narrative (and in van Onselen and Phimister) as James 'Mabala', alias Rusere. In oral

---

[58] The informant added that the children of alien/Matabele marriages 'grow up as Matabele boys ... and they fight with the Matabelele and when their fathers say: "Come let us go to the country beyond the border", they reply: "You may go if you like, but we are Matabele and we shall stay behind."'

[59] Notes of speeches in the Location, 4 January 1930, S.138.

[60] Interview between Hlonbiphani Ndlovu and Mrs Mlotshwa, Makokoba, January 2000.

[61] For an account of the patterning of Bulawayo oral memory see T.O. Ranger, 'Myth and Legend in Urban Oral Memory: Bulawayo, 1930–60', *Journal of Postcolonial Writing*, 44, 1, March 2008.

accounts he figures as James 'Mambara' (crazy) from Shabani. He is certainly not from Manicaland but all our informants call him 'Manyika'. Mambara makes a wonderfully equivocal myth hero. As one might expect from van Onselen and Phimister's interpretation, he figures as a hero of a violently competitive youth culture; as one might expect from my own emphases, he figures as a 'Manyika' achiever. In the Bulawayo of the late 1920s Location, youth saw themselves not as part of an urban underclass but as participants in competition for modernizing prestige.

Mambara was certainly not unemployed. He worked at Meikles, the wealthiest concern in Bulawayo, as also did Masotsha Ndlovu. He was exquisitely fashionable. He was 'very well educated and spoke English like a white man'.[62] As Mike Hove sums up, on the basis of oral memory, Mambara was 'the man in town, especially among the Shona … their hero of heroes, the first and last man among men'. He was a master boxer, who had defeated hundreds of men; he was 'able to run or cycle the longest journey'; indeed his powers were more than human. He could 'race fast on a bicycle without wheels' or with square ones; he could even become invisible. Every young competitor – gang-member, boxer, cyclist – in the Location wore *mangoromera*, studded bracelets used in self-defence but at the same time giving magical power. James Mambara possessed the most powerful *mangoromera* of all, and sold such bracelets to others.[63]

Van Onselen and Phimister say that these bracelets were sold to Shona youth, 'fairly new to Bulawayo and unemployed'. But in fact the competitive youth culture in which James Mambara excelled was multi-ethnic. There were 'Matabele' gangs as well as 'Manyika' ones; 'Matabele' boxing teams as well as 'Manyika' ones. And all of them wore *mangoromera* bracelets. Van Onselen and Phimister cite a criminal case involving Bulawayo youth as evidence that Shona 'newcomers to Bulawayo, at first unemployed, were pulled into gangs', which specialized in the use of *mangoromera*.[64] But in fact the gang involved in the case was a *Kalanga* gang, allied to the Ndebele, and members testified that 'the wristlets were for hitting the Portuguese or Manyika natives at Christmas time'.[65]

The oral myth of James Mambara is set in this world of violent youth confrontation, though focusing on boxing rather than on gangs. In 1929 boxing was much more popular than football in the Location and attracted great crowds of spectators, pick-pockets and gamblers. Diki Maphosa, who arrived in the Location from the Matabeleland countryside in 1928 when he was 16, remembers boxing against James Mambara:

> I was very active in those fights. This James Mambara was a boxer. I had once played boxing games with him before those factional fights. I suffered some personal injuries.

Maphosa remembers that 'before the factional fights' there were boxing matches between Korekore, Zezuru, Karanga and Manyika teams – there was no 'Shona' team –'in the bushy area covered now by the Thokozani flats'. 'On Sundays we Ndebele always held boxing games in a bushy area around the current Barbourfields Stadium.'

---

[62] Stanlake Samkange summarizing Bulawayo oral memory in *The Mourned One*, p. 128.
[63] M. Hove, *Confessions of a Wizard*, p.124.
[64] Van Onselen and Phimister , p. 37, fn165.
[65] Evidence of Sitapi and Ndaladhlambani, 29 September 1930, S 569, 1930. The witnesses testified that they and other Kalanga marched through the Location, sometimes as many as twenty abreast, and that 'had a Manyika or a Portuguese native come between us when we marching we should have hit him'. Msindo insists that while often allied to the Ndebele these Kalanga gangs were autonomous of them.

But there was a crucial difference between the two sets of contests. 'James Mambara was leading the Shona group and the Shona boxers did not play "dry hand" boxing. They were putting on gloves'. Ndebele boxers, however, fought 'dry handed'.[66]

In the oral myth this difference between bare-hand and gloved boxing has come to stand for notions of 'Matabele' backwardness and 'Manyika' civilization. These ideas, informants insist, were mediated by the whites. Mr Mpofu tells us that white officials organized boxing matches between the Ndebele and 'the Mashona' and tried to enforce Queensbury rules:

> Trouble between the Ndebele and the Shona started from these boxing games pitting the Shona against the Ndebele. During the boxing competitions the Shona always put gloves on and the Ndebele refused to put on gloves. During the fights/games the Ndebele did not use their hands only – they resorted to head-butting their Shona opponents and also kicked them with their knees. Head-butting and kicking were not allowed in boxing games. As a result the whites who officiated in those games argued that the Ndebele were very unprofessional people. Those whites publicly declared that the Ndebele were very unprofessional in boxing and declared that the Shona were superior ... The Shona then began to view themselves as 'Kings' and challenged the Ndebele to a fist fight. The ring leader was none other than James Mambara ... The Ndebele were fighting, not competing. The whites forced them into competition with their Shona counterparts.[67]

James Mambara and his young followers swaggered about the Location as though they owned it. During 1929 rumours spread, and were reported by Carbutt, that 'the Manyika' had 'bought' the permission of the whites to attack 'the Matabelele'. As van Onselen and Phimister say, this idea was believable in a Location which had been corruptly administered for years. It was also believable, however, in the context of the Location boxing myth:

> James Mambara was the instigator of those 1929 faction fights. It's like the Shona looked down upon the Ndebeles. They under-rated the Ndebele in everything they did. They argued that they could never be defeated by the Ndebeles. We also heard that James Mambara went to the magistrate, and asked for permission to start a fight with the Ndebeles, and it is most likely that those whites privately encouraged his plans.

But, as all our oral informants say, while Mambara wanted a fist fight, the 'Matabele' went into the bushes and prepared knobkerries. 'It's like James Mambara had called for a fist fight with the Ndebele, but the Ndebele ended up using weapons to give the Shona a thorough beating.'[68]

I think all this helps to explain the odd fact that although so many people insisted in late December 1929 that the 'Manyika/Mashona' were the aggressors, it is hard to find them carrying out much aggression in the actual narrative of those days. It is clear that 'Manyika' boasting – their claim to be masters of 'style Burawayo' –

[66] Interview between Busani Mpofu and Diki Maphosa, Makokoba, January 2000.
[67] Interview between Busani Mpofu and M. Mpofu, Makokoba, 25 January 2000. This distinction between gloved Shona and bare-fisted Ndebele was not in fact made by the administration at the time. Carbutt told the Bulawayo Landowners and Farmers Association that 'the start of the trouble, silly as it may seem, was a small one. Quite recently, the "young bloods" had taken up boxing as a pastime; but they boxed without any idea of fair play or the rules of the game. No stroke was prohibited and no grip banned, and, although the matches started in a friendly way, they soon developed into strong antagonism between the tribes.' *Chronicle*, 4 January 1930.
[68] Diki Maphosa, Makokoba, January 2000.

stimulated the growth and spread of all sorts of rumours in the days immediately before the outbreak. It was believed that officials had 'sold' the 'Matabele' to the 'Manyika', who had licence to kill them;[69] that James Mambara had stabbed a young Kalanga to death in a gang affray; that James Mambara, who shared a room in the Location with a fellow Meikles employee', 'had stabbed to death his fellow worker because he was an Ndebele'.[70]

These rumours spread among 'Northern' and 'Zambesi' workers in Bulawayo as well, helping to explain why they came out in arms against 'the Manyika' at the Municipal and Railway Compounds. The *Chronicle* of 7 January reported a trial in the magistrates' court. A witness testified that he was 'a Mashona' who lived in the Railway Location. Before the violence he had 'heard two natives going about the compound among the members of the different tribes employed there, inciting them to arm themselves, as the Mashonas were coming to attack them'. The 'Northerners' were told that the 'Mashona' had bribed officials to hand over to them members of all other tribes 'for the purpose of killing them'. The 'Northerners'' march on the Location from the Railway Compound was a pre-emptive strike; frustrated there, they returned to destroy the property of workers from Manicaland.

Driven by rumour as it was, the violence when it erupted was haphazard; no one knew who was attacking whom; men were responding to phantom armies. Hove writes that:

> The whole community was socially seriously ill. As if by a harsh, sudden and devastating hail storm, people were taken by shocking surprise, unable to comprehend the events, their cause, their meaning ... three days hell for the black residents of Bulawayo. In the absence of a foolproof distinguishing mark, each side frequently attacked members of its own side, because one had to hit, or kill, first, or be hit or killed.[71]

But in all the confusion one pattern emerged. However much the swagger of the 'Manyika' young bloods may have provoked rumour and resentment, it was the 'Manyika' who lived in the Location who suffered by far the most from the violence. As Diki Maphosa remembers:

> Some Ndebele from the rural areas wanted to come and join ... You know we were moving around the Old Location trying to identify places where we could find some Shona people. Those who were found were severely assaulted. Most of them ran away from Bulawayo on foot and some of them never came back.

Ennie Ngwenya recalls that 'the Ndebele gangs went on raiding those houses in the township where they suspected the Shona were living. Any Shona caught in those raids learnt it the hard way.' Those who escaped, she says, fled as far away as Mrewa and Harare. Mrs Mlotshwa says that:

> Some of the Shona tried to catch the Harare-bound train in the evening but the Ndebele followed them to the train station and beat them up there. Some of the women in the Old Location

[69] At the Bulawayo Landowners and Farmers Association meeting a farmer, H.G.M. Hartley, said that out in the countryside 'the Matabele' were saying that whites had 'accepted money from these slaves of our tribe to come in here and kill us'. *Chronicle*, 4 January 1930.

[70] Interviews with Mr M. Mpofu and Mrs L. Mlotshwa, January 2000; circular from S/N/Bulawayo to all Native Commissioners, January 1930, S.138. Although Mambara was arrested and charged with violence, no proof of the rumoured murders was found. He was sentenced to only three months in prison.

[71] M. Hove, *Confessions of a Wizard*, pp. 122, 125.

who were married to Shona husbands followed them to their homes in Mashonaland. Some of those wives who had remained behind were ordered by the Ndebele to remove all the clothes of their Shona husbands and pile them in front of the houses. The Ndebele then poured paraffin on those clothes and set them alight.

The Aftermath of the Fighting

As the violence died away, news of it spread into the countryside, where it was greatly magnified in the telling. In Matabeleland the story was one of 'Manyika' presumption and 'Matabele' vengeance. In Manicaland itself, according to Stanlake Samkange, a very different version was current. James Mambara was said to be possessed by the great prophet, Chaminuka. He had begun the *nyonganyonga* fighting in Bulawayo not so much to kill Ndebele but to distract the attention of the whites. They would rush all their police and troops to Bulawayo and this would allow another rising in the rest of the country. Mambara (who was in fact serving his three-month sentence in jail in Bulawayo) was said to be travelling the country disguised as a teacher, making use of his perfect English to arouse people to kill missionaries and officials.[72]

Meanwhile, police and reservists marched through the Location. Mounted police 'patrolled the Location, shouting *Chosa Chipewa*, Remove your Hat! to every and any African in sight; smacked and clubbed before asking any questions; arrested and imprisoned before taking particulars, The whole town was teeming with police and police informers.'[73] Men attending an ICU meeting on 5 January 1930 were assaulted by white police troopers. They were calmed by Masotsha Ndlovu, who promised legal redress:

> Now go back to your houses and be peaceful. Go back, do not fight … We are fighting for peace but not with our fists.[74]

Throughout 1930 the police watched the Location very carefully, making regular raids on it, and intervening to stop fighting between 'Northerners' and 'Zambezis'. In June, workers at the municipal quarries 'came to the dance ground', armed with sticks and axes 'as they were going to fight with Natives working in the Brickfields'. They were disarmed by Location Police.[75] In October, police visited the football ground 'owing to a dispute having taken place the previous Sunday between the different teams'. Boxing was banned. In November, Carbutt suggested that 'the Location be raided for the loafer element twice before Christmas, which will put a stop to any trouble which might occur through these people holding gambling parties. Through these raids which have been held there has been no trouble in the Location.'

But although the police intervened in every competitive activity, irrespective of ethnicity, many Ndebele speakers believed that it was the events of December 1929 which still preoccupied Bulawayo Europeans, and they remained fearful of white retribution. Diki Maphosa says that he ran away to Johannesburg in 1932 because of 'rumours circulating in Bulawayo that the whites in the city were calling for the cas-

---

[72] Stanlake Samkange, *The Mourned One*, pp. 128-9.
[73] Ibid., pp. 125-6.
[74] Report on meeting of ICU, 5 January 1930, S.84/A/300, National Archives, Harare.
[75] Location Report for June 1930, 23/3/7R 1930, National Archives, Bulawayo.

tration of all African males in the townships following the 1929 faction fights.'[76]

The *Native Mirror* for December 1932, while revealing nothing quite so draconian, nevertheless reported strong police action designed to prevent any further Ndebele violence:

> We have received a number of letters shewing that many Africans have the strange idea that they may do wrong at Christmas time without being punished for it. This applies especially to acts of violence, fighting and so on. It will be remembered that two years ago in Bulawayo there was serious fighting in the Native Location and the Railway Compound. But all who were caught were severely punished.

The *Mirror* warned Ndebele-speakers in particular. They might think they could use violence at Christmas because it was the time of the *Inxwala* dance, when Lobengula 'used to gather his regiments together and have a big display … Perhaps when the old men talk of it it stirs the young men. But Lobengula has gone and his regiments have gone with him and such things will not be allowed again in this country. Let it be well understood that this cannot be allowed. It should be a sharp lesson to all Natives that … the police have raided the Bulawayo Location and arrested 280 boys, most of whom have been punished.'

The Faction Fights as a Disruption rather than a Reflection of Location Politics

This degree of intervention lasted until the end of the 1930s. In February 2000 Busani Mpofu interviewed Tanyanyiwa Kadungure who worked as a policeman in Bulawayo in 1940. He found his fellow Shona-speakers 'very much afraid of the Ndebele. Most of the Shona who were employed as domestic workers in white suburbs went to the Charge Office after working hours. The Police would then accompany them to the township. The then colonial government threatened the Ndebele and also threatened to empower the Police and army officials with the right to assault anyone found provoking tribalistic fights.' This was only eight years before the united workers' action of 1948.

But when the 1948 strike took place ethnic tensions were not apparent. Africans then acted as workers rather than as 'Matabele' and 'Manyika'. This was partly because the ongoing structures of Bulawayo political life had revived after the 1929 violence and were able to mediate a wider Bulawayo African consciousness. Particularly important in this were embryonic trade unionism and the politics of gender.

As we have seen, the administration had believed that the ICU would provoke violence and even, for a time, that it actually was behind the fighting in December 1929. Nothing could have been further from the truth. The fighting ran directly counter to the ICU doctrine of worker unity. Once Masotsha Ndlovu had recovered from his confusion he rapidly returned to the core message. On 5 January 1930 he spoke at a meeting in the Location:

> I hear some of you saying that the ICU caused the trouble. The ICU is not only for Matabele: it is a movement for Africans. The people who started the confusion are uneducated people who

---

[76] Interview between Busani Mpofu and Diki Maphosa, Makokoba, January 2000.

do not think before they fight. Now, gentlemen, we fight for one thing, unity. I beseech you, gentlemen, to stop this nonsense. The ICU is the gospel of peace because it unites different tribes. If you were all members of the ICU you would not have fought.[77]

The ICU picked up its activities again, campaigning especially against the Bulawayo Council's destruction of African-owned houses in the Location. On 11 January Masotsha addressed a meeting called specifically to debate 'What is wrong with the Mayor and Council and what is right with them?' Masotsha found plenty of answers to the first question and none to the second. 'We are citizens in this town but we have no privileges in this Location. Join the movement and we will cry, we will not let the Council rest or the Government rest; the Imperial Government must hear. We must have rights in this location ... our town councillors, inspectors and guards.' A resolution was passed strongly protesting 'against the fact that in the black area of Bulawayo no privileges are given us'.[78] When the Standing Native Affairs Commission took evidence there in March 1930 the ICU provided abundant testimony. No mention was made of the December 1929 violence.

At the end of March 1930 the Chief Native Commissioner made two reports to the Minister of Native Affairs. One concerned the faction fighting, saying that 'boxing contests have been tacitly abandoned' and that 'I have no doubt that the actual outbreak of the disturbances came as a surprise to the Natives themselves.' The other concerned the conscious and purposeful influence of the ICU:

> I have in former minutes dealt with subversive utterances at ICU meetings and have definitely recommended preventive legislation. The position grows more dangerous.

It was back to political business as usual.[79]

And if the faction fights had briefly swept aside the influence of the ICU, so too had they suddenly marginalized women. At the meeting in the Location on 4 January 1930 Masotsha Ndlovu asked 'men and women – leaders of different associations – [to] come out and speak'. Immediately, a beer hall employee, Gufa, retorted: 'The women must not interfere. It is not right for women to talk. This is a man's affair.' No woman did speak. And in oral memories of the violence women only appear as fugitives or as wives vainly trying to defend their husbands' property.

And yet, women had been and were again to become, outspoken participants in Location politics. Martha Ngano, founder member of the Bantu Voters Association and the Women's League, had called as early as June 1925 for the appointment of a Native Affairs Commission. Ngano spoke at the very first ICU meetings and other women also took part in them. On 15 December 1928, for instance, Ngano advised 'all natives to join the ICU'. On 20 April 1929 a meeting called by the ICU but attended by representatives of other associations, was addressed by Nasi Darby, introduced as representing the interests of prostitutes. On 27 May 1929 Martha Ngano spoke to an ICU meeting about the moral dangers to 'our girls who come to Town from

---

[77] Report of ICU meeting, 5 January 1930. On the same day Charles Mzingeli, ICU leader in Salisbury, denounced 'the trouble in Bulawayo – the Northern and Matabele Natives against the Mzeruru and the Manyika ... I wish the people who caused this should be sent to prison and given 25 cuts ... Instead of uniting they are dividing themselves.' S.84/A/300.

[78] For a fuller account of this meeting and the debate between Masotsha and the Location policeman, Solomon, see T.O. Ranger, *The African Voice in Southern Rhodesia, 1898–1930*, pp. 158-9.

[79] CNC to Minister of Native Affairs, 24 and 29 March 1930, S.138.

outside'. On 8 June 1929 'a native female' speaker objected to compulsory medical examination:

> This was written by a white lady concerning native women that we must be examined under our clothes. We women do not believe in examination. If this white lady would come near we would tell her the truth. Not all women have diseases.[80]

When Prime Minister Moffat came to Bulawayo on 7 November 1929 and received delegations from the Location, three delegates attended from the Women's League, Ngano, Moho and Regina.[81]

The key issue which concerned women in the Location, and on which they made urgent representations to the Native Department both before and after the faction fights, was the question of property in the Location. Many women owned stands there, had erected buildings and leased them out to lodgers. The Council decided that all such privately owned property should be demolished. The significant thing from the point of view of this chapter on ethnicity was that women stand-owners were a very multi-ethnic group. 'Matabele' women, Tswana women, Sotho women, Xhosa women, Coloured women and 'Mashona' women combined to argue their case against the Council. Their unity was not disrupted by the faction fights and none of them was driven out by them. No men wanted to mess with the formidable Mary Mutoko, even in December 1929.

And when the fighting was over, the women emerged again as Location activists. They complained incessantly to Carbutt. They gave evidence to the Native Affairs Commission. Faction fighting might be 'a man's affair' but women played a leading role in the struggle against the Municipality.

Finally, if the ICU and the women's voices were momentarily silenced in late December 1929 that other structural feature of Location life – the Christian churches – continued their work right through the violence. Stanlake Samkange recalls that the Wesleyan minister, his father, Thompson Samkange, and his great friend Oliver Somkence, the Anglican priest, though both 'Mashona', were able to move around the Location unmolested during the fighting.[82]

Although the ICU itself succumbed to persecution in the mid-1930s it had laid the foundations for the re-emergence of trade unionism in the 1940s. The influence of the churches and of women helped to create a sense of Location identity. Smart young men of every ethnicity had to operate within the boundaries of this moral community as 'style Burawayo' continued to be made and remade.

---

[80] Report on ICU meeting of 8 June 1929, S.138. The white woman referred to was Mrs Fripp of the Womens' Institute. Reports of all the other meetings cited: S.138.

[81] List of 'Natives who interviewed the Minister of Native Affairs in Bulawayo', November 1929, S.138. The other organisations represented were the Matabele Home Society; the Southern Rhodesian Native Welfare Association, the Bantu Voters Association; the Bantu Benefit Association; the ICU; the Northern Rhodesian Bantu Association; and the Bulawayo Location Mozambique Club.

[82] Stanlake Samkange, *The Mourned One*, p. 124. See also T.O. Ranger, *Are We Not Also Men? The Samkange Family and African Politics in Zimbabwe, 1920–64*, Baobab Books, Harare, and James Currey, London, 1995, p. 5. Thompson's wife Grace hid her children under the bed while her husband cycled around the Location.

3
City versus State
1930–1946

The Intervention of Howard Moffat

White Bulawayans had been supportive of Responsible Self-Government in the 1923 Referendum, but they were determined not to allow their elected government too much power. The town was the centre of white artisan militancy, and the white railway workers' strike of 1929 threatened to bring down the government of Howard Moffat. Long thereafter Bulawayo constituencies provided the main support for the Rhodesian Labour parties. Moreover, the commercial elites who dominated the Municipal Council joined with white worker representatives in their suspicion of the effete, bureaucratic capital city, Salisbury. White Bulawayo was determined to do its own thing.

In particular, the Council was determined to run its African Location in its own way. The Location was the oldest in the country. The regulations which governed it had been drawn up in 1895 before any government regulations had been laid down. The Location was controlled by the Council's own police force. In Bulawayo in 1930 the railway administration controlled its own 'native' compounds; various employers housed African workers on their stands; and the Municipality ran the Location. The Rhodesian government had no direct authority over urban Africans and no responsibility for their housing or conditions.

And yet what happened in the Bulawayo Location affected the Rhodesian government. Lewis Gann remarks that at the end of the 1920s Howard Moffat, the Rhodesian premier, 'for the first time found himself facing a small emergent "Africanist" movement'.[1] The most articulate of these 'Africanists' lived in the Bulawayo Location. As we have seen, the Location organizations bitterly criticized the Council and called upon the state to intervene. Martha Ngano had called for a government commission of inquiry in 1925, and in 1928 and 1929 Masotsha Ndlovu pressed urgently for Moffat to come to Bulawayo. At an ICU meeting in the Location on 15 December 1928 he proposed a resolution that the premier be invited 'to visit this Location and to hear our grievances'. It was passed unanimously.[2] When Moffat did not respond,

---

[1] L.H. Gann, *A History of Southern Rhodesia. Early Days to 1934*, Chatto and Windus, London, 1965, p. 269.
[2] Report on ICU meeting, 15 December 1928, S.138. Martha Ngano 'compared the lot of the Natives in Southern Rhodesia to that of the Israelites and advised them to follow their example'. Bowden said that it was nearly Christmas and that they should follow the Star of the ICU.

Masotsha wrote to him on both 1 and 2 February 1929 regretting that he had 'not kept your promise' to meet them and setting out 'our grievance in black and white'. He demanded a government school in the Location; an Advisory Board; a Wages Board, and representation in parliament. 'I speak as an educated man, educated by International Correspondence School in Cape Town.'[3]

Moffat was much more sympathetic to these representations than the Native Department. As we have seen, they stressed to him that the ICU was dangerous and they wanted him to ban it. He refused and ordered that no action be taken. He knew that the ICU's real target was the Bulawayo Municipality and he believed that the Location spokesmen and women had very real grievances. If these could be met by government intervention, any threat to the state by urban Africans could be dismissed. In his eyes the Native Department itself was too autocratic, always thinking of control when it should have been thinking of development.[4]

As a mining and railway man Moffat knew Bulawayo well. Before he became Prime Minister he had maintained an establishment in Hillside and had met some of the black political activists. One of these worked for him as cook and waiter. This was Mafimba Ncube, an active member of the Matabele Home Society and a colleague of Masotsha Ndlovu in the ICU:

> Masotsha came with the ardent nationalist spirit ... I was with him organising the masses ... Moffat sympathised with the Africans since he was the son of a missionary. He was not happy with what was happening. Moffat liked Africans. That is why his actions were not much liked by Europeans.[5]

In February 1929 Masotsha personally assured Moffat that Africans would stay out of the white railway workers' strike.[6] Masotsha himself remembered fifty years later that 'Moffat was far much better' than his successor, Godfrey Huggins. He was 'prepared to listen and attend to our grievances'. Masotsha recalled discussing African education with Moffat. 'The Europeans began to hate Moffat. They said "He has put a fifth wheel on the wagon".'[7]

In February 1929 Moffat actively desired to meet with African leaders in Bulawayo as soon as he had something tangible to offer them:

> I should like to deal in a reasonable way with these people [he noted on Masotsha's letters of February 1 and 2] and to show an interest in their affairs, and in particular any grievances put forward ... When we have got our Native Legislation ready I would rather like to meet them and give them an address.[8]

As Masotsha became more and more critical of the Bulawayo Council in 1929 he pressed harder and harder for a meeting. 'We fully believe that we have a just claim when we say we are entitled to some sort of interview with the Minister of Native

[3] Masotsha Ndlovu to Moffat, 1 and 2 February 1929, S.138.
[4] Moffat's desire to curb the authority of the Native Department and to work with missionaries and the Native Development Department is detailed by D.J. Murray in *The Governmental System in Southern Rhodesia*, Clarendon, Oxford, 1970. Murray remarks that 'in the late 1920s the colony's government made some effort to increase its involvement [in urban affairs] as part of the general policy of gaining control of the direction of development' (p. 315).
[5] Interview with Mafimba Ncube, 9 October 1981, National Archives, Bulawayo.
[6] Ian Phimister, *An Economic and Social History of Zimbabwe, 1980–1948*, p. 199.
[7] Interview with Masotsha Ndlovu, 8 October 1981, National Archives, Bulawayo.
[8] Moffat to Secretary, Premier, 6 February 1929, S.138.

Affairs [who was Moffat himself] which we all recognise as our guiding father', he wrote on 11 September 1929.[9]

On 7 November 1929 Moffat was at last ready to meet the Bulawayo Location associations. He had something to tell them. He had set up a Standing Native Affairs Commission to advise him on African problems – and the first item on its agenda was the Bulawayo Location. The four members of the Commission were chosen with Bulawayo particularly in mind. One of them, John McChlery, had been a liberal mayor of the city; another, F.L. Hadfield, had been a missionary in Matabeleland and was about to launch the *Native Mirror*, a paper for Christian Africans based in Bulawayo. A third, H.M.G. Jackson, was the retiring Chief Native Commissioner, who had long desired more state control over urban locations. Hadfield is described by the conservative Lewis Gann as 'an outspoken negrophile'.[10] In 1924 he had chaired the Native Education Commission out of whose recommendations the Native Development Department had emerged in 1929. CNC Jackson himself came from a missionary family and had worked with Hadfield to foster African 'welfare'.[11]

Moffat only got around to informing the Bulawayo Council that their Location was top of the new Commission's agenda when he visited the city in November 1929, a day or two before his meeting with the African associations. As the Council complained later, when Moffat met the Mayor and Town Clerk on 5 November:

> At the conclusion of business the Premier mentioned casually that he intended to appoint a Commission to assist him in the administration of Native Affairs. Among other things he stated his Commission would look into Urban Native Locations, Mine Compounds and the like, and he asked whether the Council would be prepared to afford facilities to his Commission in gathering information in regard to the administration of the Bulawayo Location, which he mentioned would be one of the first to be visited … The Council considered when the conditions of appointment were reported to them that there was no reason to think that the administration of the Bulawayo Location was singled out for individual inquiry.[12]

Two days later Moffat met representatives of Bulawayo associations, including Masotsha and Martha Ngano. He told them that the newly established Commission would immediately start investigating the Location. They were overjoyed. They were much better prepared for the Commission's hearings than the Bulawayo Council was.

At first some Bulawayo whites thought that the Commission was intended to get to the bottom of the faction fights. But as word of the membership of the Commission sank in a storm blew up even before they began their work. On 22 February 1930 a Bulawayo settler activist, F.J.R. Peel, wrote to the *Chronicle* asking whether Moffat intended 'to scrap the Native Department' by appointing this fifth-wheel standing Commission. To judge by its membership, Peel thought, 'Mr Moffat is mixing up "Teaching" and "Ruling"':

> We want more rule as far as the natives are concerned and less teaching.

On 7 March 1930, the day on which the Commission first formally visited the Location, the *Chronicle* reported 'one of the most largely attended [meetings] that has

9   Ndlovu to Prime Minister, 11 September 1929, S.183.
10 Gann, p. 242.
11 Murray, pp. 288-9.
12 'Reply of the Bulawayo Municipal Council to the Report of the Native Affairs Commission on its Inquiry into the Matter Concerning the Bulawayo Native Location', 6 May 1930, S.138.22, National Archives, Harare.

been held for a long time'. This had been summoned by the Bulawayo Farmers and Landowners Assocition which thought the Commission was needless, expensive, negrophile and 'a perfect abomination'. The Association's main spokesman, A.G. Hay, declared that 'the personnel of that Commision does not appeal to 80 per cent of the people of this country'. He had voted for Moffat but would never do so again:

> All the trouble among the natives I put down to the Mission work that is going on ... All over the country you have teachers disseminating what is almost sedition under the cloak of religion and what I don't like about the names on this Commission is that they savour too much of the missionary way of thought.

A resolution to annul the Commission was carried unanimously.

By this time too the Bulawayo Council had become alarmed. In February it discussed a draft bill in which Moffat's government proposed that all Municipal beer hall profits should be expended on 'native' welfare in the Locations under the direction of the Governor. Hitherto the Council had used the beer money to cover the costs of Location administration and had funded hardly any recreational or social activities. Councillors were furious – the proposal 'cut across the theory of local government'. Councillor Cope voiced the feelings of the majority when he said that the government's proposals 'weakened and undermined the whole responsibility of the Council for the conduct of its own affairs'.[13] When the membership and mandate of the Commission became known the Bulawayo Council protested that it appeared that 'the so-called Commission was really a *Committee of Inquiry* sent to adjudicate on the administration of the Location by the Bulawayo Municipal Council'. Had the Council known the true purpose of the Commission, it 'would have had something to say on the personnel of the Commission itself'.[14] In April 1930 the Bulawayo Labour MPs, Keller and Davies, joined with others to vote against the Commission in the Legislative Assembly, rallying seven votes against the eighteen who supported Moffat.[15]

Moffat himself intervened in the debate to deplore the attitude of Bulawayo whites and in particular the speeches made at the Bulawayo Farmers and Landowners Association:

> We are becoming more civilised. Natives in this country have learnt to organise and are organising to a very great extent. I have here a list of 18 Native Organisations [including] the ICU, the Matabeleland Home Society and ending with the Bantu Women's League. (Laughter) If there is to be a clash ... it will not be political but economic. The economic question is rising and is being directly raised by the natives. During the past year I have 50 or more representations made ... from various associations and individuals. These economic questions which are coming up require investigation.

Moffat described some of the African resolutions – one asking for a reduction in qualifications for the franchise; another for representation in the Assembly; a third for

13 *Chronicle*, 20 and 21 February 1930.
14 'Reply of the Bulawayo Municipal Council', 6 May 1930, National Archives, Harare, S.482 789/19.
15 *Chronicle*, 10 April 1930. H.W. Davies was the member for Bulawayo South, Jack Keller the member for Raylton, the white rail workers' suburb. Both men were radicals in terms of municipal politics, objecting to the complex and restrictive franchise and demanding a 'one man-one vote for all white residents'. 'It was entirely wrong that men should suffer simply because they did not own property, and big interests would always rule the country through the votes of their representatives.' But they nevertheless voted for the right of the Council to control its own Africans. *Chronicle*, 8 and 9 April 1930.

state schools. And 'yet another expresses regret that natives are not allowed to walk on the pavement'. But:

the first task of the Commission had been an Inquiry into the Bulawayo Location affairs.[16]

On the other side, African and missionary organizations hailed the appointment of the Commission and its Location mandate. In March the Commissioners met 'a gathering of all societies in the Native Location ... under the Indaba Tree'. Masotsha proclaimed: 'We are different from the natives of 20 years ago, we are leaders of the present generation and we hope we shall be heard.' Demanding 'a voice in the management of the Location', an elected Advisory Board, and African rights to own and build property, he added that 'we express our thanks to the Government for sending the Commission to hear us'. Another ICU spokesman, Solomon, protested:

against the attitude of the Land Owners and Farmers Association, who denounced the appointment of the NAC. We regard their attitude as being against the interests of the natives. We are glad that we have been given an opportunity to express our wishes to the Government's representatives ... We want a legislation to be introduced which will be drastic in its measure and unquestionable in its effects.[17]

On 12 April 'Euro-African' wrote to the *Chronicle* to proclaim that 'the Prime Minister was justified in listening to a black nation rather than a handful of farmers'. Later in the year the Missionary Conference of Christian Natives, meeting in the Bulawayo Location under the chairmanship of its Methodist minister Thompson Samkange, placed 'on record its grateful appreciation of the formation of the Native Affairs Commission and the selection of its members ... If there is anything which the Government has done for the native people of this country worthy of all praise, it is the appointment of this Commission which this conference hopes will be a standing institution.' The Conference urged Moffat to instruct the Commission 'to inquire into native wages in this country'.[18]

A great many hopes were pinned on the Commission. And it set about its business briskly. It listened intently to the African witnesses. White officials encouraged it to think in terms of government taking over the Location. 'The control of the Location is a national matter', declared Major Brundell of the CID. 'The Municipality cannot control effectively. The Government is trustee for the natives.' By contrast, municipal officials insisted that 'the Location is the property of the Council' and should contain only 'sojourners'. If the government wanted 'decent' long-term residents then it should provide a village settlement. But the Council did not take the Commission seriously and put up only a lacklustre defence.[19]

The Commission's report was devastating and fully met African expectations.[20] It

[16] *Chronicle*, 3 and 4 April 1930. Hay and Peel were unrepentant. 'Native bodies had approached the Premier on all sorts of questions, and he was taking notice of them, although apparently he was going to ignore the European farmers. I take back nothing I said. I do not think we spoke strongly enough. Mr Moffat, with his big majority, has got a bad attack of Mussolinism.'

[17] The testimony of African witnesses to the Commission is contained in file N 1/1/1 in the National Archives, Harare.

[18] The mainstream white Missionary Conference met in Bulawayo a few days later. Its President, Louw, also thanked Moffat for the appointment of the Commission. *Chronicle*, 27 June 1930.

[19] ZAN 1/1/1.

[20] The draft report can be reconstructed from two files in the National Archives, Harare: ZAN 2/1/1 and S. 235/394.

noted dryly that 'the Location Superintendent appears to have had unfettered control of the Location since its inception', adding that last year the Superintendent had been convicted of misappropriation. Yet:

> The Government has a responsibility towards the urbanised Natives of this country which has been imperfectly realised and still more imperfectly met ... We wish to say definitely that the responsibility for their future material and moral development is on the shoulders of the Government not less than on those of the Municipality. It is hard to understand how the Government or the Bulawayo Municipality could have been satisfied for so many years with the still current Location Regulations of 1895 ... Location government has apparently developed on the assumption that the Location is the private estate of the ratepayers and until recently with the minimum of responsibility from landlord to tenant. The Location is not part of the [Bulawayo] township. It is an ill-defined and unfenced part of the Commonage. It has in the past been loosely controlled by a Superintendent and a small force of 'police' who are not police at all.

The Commission blamed both the 'apathetic corporate conscience of the burgesses at large' and the 'body politic and its Government which applied no legislative stimulus or Government control over the fates and fortunes of some thousands of natives'. Something had to be done. But what? It had been suggested, noted the Commissioners, that the Location 'should be directly controlled by the State rather than by the Town Council'. But that would perhaps be too great a break with the past. The Commission recommended that 'Government control should mainly be exercised through more effiicient and thorough legislation' and by 'inspectorial means'. The Locations Ordinance of 1906 should be applied. There should be a Location Advisory Committee and a Native Advisory Board made up of 'six natives living in the Location'. Government should audit municipal accounts to prevent any further 'diversion' of Location revenue. Africans should be allowed to build their own houses 'in accordance with plans to be approved by Council'. Rents should be reduced. A clinic should be established and recreational facilities provided.

In short, the Commission endorsed almost all the recommendations made to it by African associations in the Location. The report seemed to give Moffat exactly what he needed to push through legislation which was being prepared in the Prime Minister's office. It was a remarkable moment and might even have been a turning point in Rhodesian urban history. But in fact nothing turned. Government did not act against Bulawayo. The Council continued to administer the Location under the 1895 ordinance right up until 1949. Soon after the Commission reported, the Location associations were repressed. Moffat fell from office. How is this to be explained?

In effect the Commission's report aroused a storm of white condemnation of Moffat which brought about the end of his administration. The storm began with the Bulwayo Council's ferocious response – one of the most defiant documents in the whole history of city/state relations in Rhodesia/Zimbabwe. The report was 'most misleading, incorrect in certain details and if allowed to go unchallenged might lead to harmful conequences'. Before they began proceedings, the Commissioners 'had already formed the opinion that things in the Bulawayo Location were far from what they should be'; they asked leading questions 'such as would never be tolerated in a court of law'. They 'proceeded to enter into discussions with witnesses and even to argue with them in an obvious endeavour to get them to alter the views which they had previously expressed'. And they gave the Council no opportunity to reply. 'Any accused person [should] be fully informed of the indictment and be present

112

the whole of the time the case ... is being heard and have the right to cross-examine witnesses.'

All of the 'preconceived' ideas of the Commissioners were mistaken. There was no obligation on the Council 'either legally or morally' to ensure that beer hall profits 'should have been devoted entirely for the benefit of natives. Such an idea is entirely fallacious'; Africans ought to contribute 'towards carrying on the highly necessary and essential services of the town as a whole'. The Council 'absolutely and emphatically' denied that it exercised no control over the Location Superintendent and showed no interest in African welfare. The passage in the report which praised 'the indestruct-ibility of the material of which the African is compounded' and his ability to 'adjust under unpromising circumstances to ... an atmosphere of so alien and formidable a type' was:

> an example of Claptrap which one is surprised to find in a report of a Government Commis-sion ... Its terms can only be regarded as extravagant and a stigma on the European civilisation of the Colony ... If the Commission's report is made public the statements might disturb the peaceful relaions which exist at present between the European and the native.

The Commission's recommendation that government control should be exercised through legislation and inspection 'really consitutes an impertinence'. A Location Advisory Board 'would only be a means of leading to conflict and trouble [and] might easily get into the hand of, or become influenced by, a very undesirable type of native agitator'. It was absurd to suggest that 'accommodation provided in the Municipal Location should be such as to meet the indefinite requirement of an African family and their visitors'. Africans could not be allowed to build for themselves because they only erected 'unsightly and insanitary premises'. The Commissioners seemed to think that 'the native population should never have to bear any proportion of the obligations of citizenship', and showed 'a complete lack of consideration of the interests of the European population'.

The Council's reply ended uncompromisingly:

> If the Council is to be subject to criticism and threats and restrictions of the nature recom-mended in the Commission's report there will probably be an end to all co-operation ... Many of the ill-advised statements in the report may be used by native agitators. Should the govern-ment decide to put in force all the recommendations of the Commission then they need look for no assistance from the Municipal Council and it is suggested that the best course would be for the government to expropriate and take over the whole of the Location and administer it as a government.[21]

Rumours ran around Bulawayo about this confrontation with government; the *Chronicle* published partial reports of the Commission's findings on 30 May and 3 June. Then on 7 June 1930 both the Commission's report and the Council's reply were published in full.

An editorial thought that the reply was:

> The most complete condemnation imaginable of a body which owes its existence to the desire of the Premier to have at his service a group of special investigators.

---

[21] Reply of the Bulawayo Municipal Council to the Report of the Native Affairs Commission, 6 May 1930, National Archives, Harare, S.482 789/19.

The paper remarked that the Municipal response revealed 'a loss of temper which ill becomes a Council'.[22]

There was doubt in white Bulawayo about whether it was wise to confront the government so openly. The Council's defiant reply had only been approved by five votes to three with two councillors being absent. Early in June 1930 there was a debate in Council over the very issues raised by the Commission's report. Councillor E.J. Davies, who had long argued that Council running of the Location 'had been disgraceful in the past'[23] and who had not endorsed the Council's reply, now repeated that 'I have held all along that we are not doing our fair share in administering native affairs in this town. We are repeating the injustice to the natives that has taken place in the past.' The Location building programme was too slow; too many economies were being made so that the Council's 'native budget' could be balanced. Davies was answered as the Commissioners had been, that 'there is no obligation to spend all the money derived from the native in the native interest. We would be perfectly justified in saying that the native population should be compelled to contribute something to the town, such as the upkeep of the streets.' (This was at a moment when Africans were still banned from walking on Bulawayo's pavements).[24]

The Council maintained that the interests of ratepayers were paramount. Nevertheless, its relations with the Ratepayers Association were fraught. The *Chronicle* wrote about the Association's 'monthly recreation of hauling Town Councillors over the coals'.[25] At their June AGM the Association declared that things were 'not right at Town House'. They had not been given either the Native Affairs Commission report or the Council's reply but they remembered all too vividly the eruption of December 1929. Their president, H. Issels, owner of the town's main engineering firm, said that 'we do know that location matters have been far from right for many years. We look to the Council to effect great changes.' To this Mayor W.H. Peard reacted fiercely – let the Ratepayers 'tackle the big questions and stop pin pricking'. The *Chronicle* thought that the Council's 'fierce resentment of criticim of any kind is very marked today and it cannot be said that its attitude holds out any hope for creating that atmosphere in which cooperation could be established'.[26] In July, when four Council seats came up for election, the *Chronicle* urged that the Ratepayers Association should put up their own candidates since 'otherwise there is little likelihood of a contested election for any of the vacancies'. The town's influential daily had become very critical of the municipal oligarchy.

The Bulawayo Council was divided; its ratepayers were critical; the Bulawayo press feared a clash with both government and African opinion. But Moffat decided that the time was not ripe for a confrontation with Bulawayo. His Native Affairs Commission would go on piling up the evidence. Meanwhile the Bulawayo Council elections were a non-event, three retiring councillors being returned unopposed. The oligarchy remained in place, as defiant and intolerant of criticism as ever.

---

[22] The *Chronicle* itself had editorialized on 25 February 1930 that 'there is evidence in plenty that present conditions [in the Location] are calculated to lead on to a state of widespread discontent'. No one could argue that conditions gave 'a fair chance of working out and living up to a decent standard of living'. Africans had no homes, poor sanitation, no constructive leisure pursuits. Both justice and self-interest demanded that something be done.

[23] *Chronicle*, 20 February 1930.

[24] *Chronicle*, 3 July 1930.

[25] *Chronicle*, 10 July 1930.

[26] *Chronicle*, 24 and 25 June 1930.

Moffat wrote to the Mayor of Salisbury on 6 August 1930 saying that he had directed the Commission to look into the Salisbury Location and then go on to Gatooma:

> It is unneccessary for me to mention the fact that the Government are directly responsible
> for the control and general welfare of all the Natives of this country and I feel as the minister
> directly responsible that it is essential that I should have full information in regard to the posi-
> tion of the Natives in the various Municipal Locations.[27]

The Commissioners' inquiries into Salisbury and Gatooma were much less contested
than their Bulawayo investigation. They wrote to Moffat on 14 January 1931 summing
up their findings:

> After investigating conditions at three native locations we are convinced that a persistent and
> most serious danger lies in the relation of Native finance to general Municipal finance. It seems
> as though the ethical standards applied by individuals in their own cases are departed from in
> the case of corporate bodies comprised by the same individuals. We regard it as of the utmost
> importance that it should be made impossible in the future for Native finance to merge into and
> become indistinguishable from Municipal finance. We foresee a serious source of interracial
> antagonism if the position is not safe-guarded once and for all.[28]

Moffat was now prepared to act. By early March 1931 a Native Locations Amendment
Bill had been drafted which 'intended to make it clear that Ordinance 4 of 1906 can
be applied to areas which have been previously set aside as Locations', as was the case
in Bulawayo. By the end of April 1931 the Bill was passed without amendment. Government was now empowered to intervene in the Bulawayo Location. But still it did
not. Authority was slipping away from Moffat in that general white reaction against
'negrophilia' which historians have labelled 'from civilization to segregation'. In 1932
the new Chief Native Commissioner, Colonel Carbutt, drafted a Bill in which the
clauses, mainly affecting Municipal beer halls, provided that they were to be licenced
by the Chief Native Commissioner. Regulations were to be made under this Act by the
Governor. The Municipalities bitterly opposed this Bill and it was dropped'. Moffat
then asked acting CNC, Charles Bullock, to draft another bill which 'included the
principle that local authorities could be authorized to brew and sell beer provided that
the profits from such sale were to be applied to benevolent projects for the betterment
of the Natives'. This Bill was drafted but not put before the Assembly. Moffat's urban
reforms had run out of steam. Bulawayo's bitter resistance had triumphed.[29]

Moffat might have been able to carry through his policy of placating 'reasonable'
Africans by allowing them to share in 'development' had Southern Rhodesia actually
been developing. In fact the colony was very hard hit by the depression of the early
1930s. In 1931 and 1932 the civil service was heavily reduced and its salaries cut – it was
no time to assume new government responsibilities. As Lewis Gann puts it, 'discon-
tented railwaymen and civil servants, artisans without a job and farmers in economic
distress – most of whom had voted for Responsible Government – now began to turn
against the Rhodesia Party'. The party could not afford to take on the towns. Instead
it tried to save itself by dumping a leader who had become increasingly suspect as a
'negrophile' and a friend of missionaries. In November 1932 Moffat agreed to stand

27 Premier to Mayor of Salisbury, 6 August 1930, National Archives, Harare, S.482 789/19.
28 Native Affair Commissioners to Minister, Native Affairs, 14 January 1931, S.482 789/19.
29 Acting CNC Charles Bullock to Secretary, Premier, 8 June 1934, S.482 789/19.

down after the next parliamentary session; in July 1933 George Mitchell became a very short-lived prime minister; Moffat lost his own seat in the general election which followed.[30]

With its patron a lame duck the Native Affairs Commission just withered away. Hadfield's newspaper, *The Native Mirror*, reported in April 1931 the death of John McChlery, 'a great loss to the Native Affairs Commission'. At the Native Missionary Conference in Salisbury in June 1932 complaints were made:

> that this Commission was not functioning as fully as had been hoped for. Mr F.L. Hadfield, who said he was the only living member of a dead body, stated that Mr Moffat had explained to him that it was impossible, owing to shortage of funds, for any Commission to operate.[31]

In any case, by 1933 the Location leadership whose grievances Moffat had been trying to redress had been snuffed out. Martha Ngano was dead and her Women's League did not survive her: women house-owners were steadily expropriated. And as for Masotsha Ndlovu, it was Colonel Carbutt's attitude which prevailed rather than Moffat's. Addressing the Native Missionary Conference on 5 June 1930 Carbutt warned them about 'the ICU's useless agitations'. On 7 June Masotsha addressed 800 ICU members, telling them that 'Colonel Carbutt is the man who is oppressing us ... It is the Native Commissioner who is oppressing us.' On 8 June Masotsha told another meeting that during the First World War 'Colonel Carbutt recruited us and natives followed and know he oppressed us'. On 10 July Masotsha and another ICU leader, Mtelo, were charged with defamation. 'The court was packed with natives of both sexes', reported the *Chronicle*.[32] The case continued on 24 July. 'The court was crowded with a large number of well dressed native men and women. All the benches in court were occupied from end to end and in addition a large number sat on the floor, while others crowded on the verandah near the door.' This audience was exactly that which Moffat had hoped to win over. CID detectives admitted that a lot of the ICU meeting 'was quite mild. Tributes, for instance, were paid to the Prime Minister, the Government and the attitude of the missionaries.' But the Native Department in general and Carbutt in particular had been attacked.[33] On 31 July the magistrate found the two ICU men guilty and fined them £20 and £15. He told the packed courtroom that 'incalculable injury would result to the native community unless the public representations of native organisations be restricted to fair comment and truthful criticism of the officials placed over them'.[34]

Masotsha was a marked man. He began to move out from the Bulawayo Location and to seek recruits in mining compounds and the rural areas where he 'acquired a considerable following'. He was banned from entering the Reserves; broke the ban; was prosecuted and imprisoned for three months in 1933. When he came out of prison he severed all links with the ICU which itself came to an end in Bulawayo in 1934.[35]

---

30 Gann, pp. 294-6.
31 *Native Mirror*, 15 June 1932.
32 *Chronicle*, 11 July 1930.
33 *Chronicle*, 25 July 1930. The prosecutor asserted that the white CID member, Pritchard, attended the ICU meetings 'not for the purpose of looking for illegal statements, but to take a note of the natives' complaints. By this means the natives' grievances were ventilated and, by their complaints being transmitted to the proper authorities, wrongs were often righted.'
34 *Chronicle*, 1 August 1930. On 27 August the paper remarked that 'the Native Affairs Commission has passed completely out of the limelight since its investigations in Bulawayo'.
35 See Phimister, pp. 201-2; Pathisa Nyathi, *Masotsha Ndlovu*, pp. 31-2.

In the Bulawayo Location the later 1930s became an age of 'welfare' rather than of self-reliant organization. Percy Ibbotson's Native Welfare Society began to organize boxing and football, and to provide a meeting hall and library. Masotsha deeply disapproved:

> If you competed in a bicycle race and won, you were given a new bicycle. People then began not to attend meetings. They were now fascinated by the new entertainment ... That weakened the ICU as I used to wait alone under the tree without any people coming ... I detested [football] seriously. I knew that was killing us. I then stopped the organisation.[36]

Macintyre versus Huggins

'Moffat did not last long', remembers old Mafimba Ncube. 'When Huggins became Prime Minister the spirit of hatred for Africans prevailed.'[37] Although Godfrey Huggins was welcomed by white segregationists in Bulawayo and elsewhere, his election did not end the tension between the Rhodesian state and the Bulawayo Municipality. If anything it intensified it. The tension was structural and persists today. A managerial government could not tolerate an intransigent city.

Huggins began by looking to South Africa. In January 1934 he asked for a memorandum on the South African Native (Urban Areas) Act of 1922. He must have read the memo with mingled envy and pleasure. The South African Act enabled government 'to compel the local authority to make some or all of the provisions' of locations, native villages, natives hostels, etc., and 'if the local authority does not do so then the Minister can carry out such work and charge the local authority. The local authority has to set up a Native Revenue account ... Rents are fixed by the Minister. Native Advisory Boards of not less than 3 Natives and a Chairman are to be established.'[38] Moffat's 'negrophile' Commission turned out to be ten years behind the South Africans! It took Huggins another twelve years to achieve the Rhodesian equivalent but meanwhile he kept up the pressure on Bulawayo.

In April and May 1934 Huggins told the Bulawayo Council that its Location should come under the Native Urban Location Ordinance 'rather than continuing under the present regulations'. The Town Clerk replied that the Council was 'not desirous' of such a change.[39] It was insistent that it alone could approve regulations for the Location. Bulawayo was being as irritating to the new regime as it had been to the old. In June the Acting Chief Native Commissioner, Charles Bullock, advised Huggins that:

> We shall not successfully control our natives for their own welfare and that of the Colony until locations etc. are brought back into the unified control of the Government. The situation calls not for piecemeal amendment of the Native Locations Ordinance, but for a comprehensive Act, embodying some of the features of the Native (Urban Areas) Acts 1922 and 1930 of the Union, but broader in its scope and wider in its vision. It is not proper for the Municipal Council to suggest that no rules and regulations should be made by the Governor unless ... first approved

---

36 Interview with Masotsha Ndlovu, Luveve, 8 October 1981, National Archives, Bulawayo.
37 Interview with Mafimba Ncube, 9 October 1981, Ntabazinduna, National Archives, Bulawayo.
38 Private Secretary, Premier, Memo, 17 January 1934.
39 Private Secretary, Premier, to Town Clerk, Bulawayo, 20 April 1934; Town Clerk to PS, Premier, 3 May 1934; PS, Premier to Town Clerk, 7 May 1934.

by the Municipality. His Honour the Minister may be aware that some years ago a Commission animadverted on the Bulawayo Location.[40]

As a good segregationist Huggins believed that Bulawayo was frustrating the implementation of the Land Apportionment Act. It refused to apply the Act's urban provisions and it was sabotaging its implementation in the countryside surrounding Bulawayo where so many Africans lived and commuted to work in the town. If the Act were applied there was nowhere for the occupants of Hyde Park and the other private locations to go. Great official pressure was put on the Council to build more accommodation. But, as the Superintendent of Natives. Bulawayo, wrote in February 1938: 'Natives are being continually advised in terms of the Land Apportionment Act their agreements are likely to be terminated in 1941. The Council's present rate of progress in providing accommodation for Natives employed in Bulawayo is most unsatisfactory – they are merely demolishing old buildings and rebuilding on the sites. As far as I can see it will be impossible to remove Natives off private farms by 1941 if an industrial crisis is to be avoided'.[41]

Huggins was determined to change things. Bulawayo was the setting for racism without segregation. Huggins wished to sweep away African compounds in the town and African rent-payers on the farms which bordered the Commonage and to achieve a more rational and complete system of segregation. All Africans who worked in the town should live in the Location or in new townships with facilities funded by the Council. And if whites in Bulawayo wanted black labour then they must accept a permanent black working class and African families living in these townships. The Bulawayo Council wished to change nothing. Everything should be as it had been in 1895 when the Location ordinance was drawn up: employers should make use of short-term migrant labour, and the minimal facilities such workers required should be paid for by Africans themselves out of rents and beer hall profits. The Council had remained totally unaffected by Moffat's Commission's recommendations. It carried on just as before, increasingly irritating and frustrating Huggins, until its hand was forced by a Rhodesian government which blamed its 'stone-age' attitudes for the 1948 general strike.

The tension between city and state was structural, but it was also personal. In Southern Rhodesia's tiny municipal councils and equally tiny parliament large issues easily became a joust between two rival champions. Between 1934 and 1948 the question of how Bulawayo and other towns should develop was fought out between two men: Huggins and the 'city boss' of Bulawayo, Donald Macintyre.

---

[40] Acting CNC to Secretary, Premier, 8 June 1934. In default of comprehensive legislation the Native Department kept a vigilant eye on small town locations. File S.1542 L14/1933-39 in the National Archives, Harare, deals with departmental interventions. In August 1936, for example, the Native Commissioner, Selukwe, fined the Location Superintendent for assault and ensured his dismissal and that of all the Location police. 'The record discloses a pitiful state of affairs in the Location. The [Town Management] Board is composed of illiterate and ill-educated men for the most part – quite ignorant of dealing with natives.' The Chief Native Commissioner himself met Africans in the Gwelo Location and heard their complaints in October 1936. He then urged the Municipality to dismiss its Location Superintendents. Such direct interventions were impossible in the unique case of Bulawayo.

[41] Superintendent of Natives, Bulawayo to CNC, 21 February 1938, S.1542 L14/1933-1939, National Archives, Harare. In the event the implementation of the Act around Bulawayo was postponed until after the Second World War.

Donald Macintyre as Mr Bulawayo

We have already seen Macintyre's 'master baker' entrepreneurship and his ambiguous craft socialism. He first appears in the records of the Bulawayo Council, which he came to dominate, as a successful bidder to cater for municipal entertainments.[42] He flourished as a businessman and at the end of the 1930s he took part in the establishment of Rhodesia's first iron and steel works, close to Bulawayo. He became shareholder, chairman and director of the company. But his part in the enterprise lasted only five years and ended when the industry was nationalized in 1942. It was as a baker that he continued to make his money. As we shall see, he thought about labour conditions and wages as a baker rather than as an industrialist.[43]

This business success did not dampen Macintyre's political opinions. In 1933 he was elected to parliament as a Labour member for central Bulawayo. During the Second World War when some leaders of Labour, including the Bulawayo white railwaymen's leader, Jack Keller, joined Godfrey Huggins in a coalition, Macintyre stayed out, becoming in 1940 leader of the Southern Rhodesian Labour Party and official Leader of the Opposition.

To his roles as businessman, master baker and Labour MP Macintyre added what often seemed like a full-time career as municipal councillor. He was Deputy Mayor between 1934 and 1936; he was Mayor in 1936 and 1937, again in 1938 and again for three years between 1944 and 1947. He was chairman of the finance committee, which was then responsible for the affairs of the Location, between 1938 and 1943 and again from 1947 to 1953. Between 1943 and 1947 he was chairman of the general purposes committee. In short, he was the dominant figure on the Bulawayo Council for twenty years.[44] For almost all that time he was one of Bulawayo's delegates to the Municipal Association's annual conference and usually a member of its executive. In short he became the most powerful and famous city councillor in Rhodesia.

In all these roles Macintyre outdid everyone else through sheer attention to detail. He dominated or sought to dominate every discussion he took part in, whether in the Bulawayo Council or the Municipal Association or in parliament or testifying to a commission. And always he played up his assumed Scottish characteristics. As chairman of the Bulawayo finance committee he boasted of an inherent thriftiness and gloried in being called mean. It was a joke among fellow parliamentarians that Macintyre had a special machine in his bakery. It put ham into a ham roll at one end and took it out the other.[45]

He also gloried in what he called Scottish plain speaking. To most other people this amounted to plain rudeness. The minutes of parliament and of the Municipal Association are rich with Macintyre's interjections and insults and the offended complaints

[42] Town Clerk to Osborn's Bakery, 13 June 1929, Municipal Records, B 1/10, Box 17, National Archives, Bulawayo.
[43] D.J. Murray argues in his *The Governmental System of Southern Rhodesia*, pp. 165, 346, that in the 1930s and 1940s Rhodesian industry and commerce did not need representation in national politics because their interests were catered for at Municipal level. In Murray's view the Municipalities, especially Bulawayo, represented the emerging industrial class. Macintyre, with his interests in iron and steel, is seen as an outstanding example of a councillor dedicated to industry. This chapter argues a rather different case.
[44] *City of Bulawayo: Some Facts About the Municipal Government of Bulawayo*, December 1962.
[45] I owe this ancedote to Sir Garfield Todd. Grace Todd put a more charitable gloss on Macintyre's legendary thrift, describing how throughout his career, ending as Federal Minister of Finance, he did not move from his modest house in western Bulawayo, not far from the Location.

of other delegates. 'The hon. member thinks he is licensed in this house to say rude things that anybody else would not say', complained an affronted minister of finance in May 1943.[46] McNeillie vividly recalled Macintyre's abrasiveness:

> He liked nothing better than to have a crack at whoever was Prime Minister ... He was very bitter against anybody that opposed him ... Rude, you know, he didn't mind who he was rude about ... Macintyre was always very rude to Huggins.[47]

The clashes between Macintyre, the archetypal Scot, and Huggins, the archetypal Englishman, were sometimes so loud that they woke up slumbering members. 'I do not think that this house is a shouting house', complained one such member as Macintyre and Huggins confronted each other over the Native (Urban Areas) Accommodation and Registration Act in November 1944.[48]

Contemporaries sometimes debated which of these roles – baker, employer, socialist, city councillor – predominated in Macintyre's loyalties. It was easy to mock their inconsistency. During the June 1942 debate on the nationalization of iron and steel Macintyre took the line that as a socialist he favoured total state control of planning, but that until that blessed day dawned he believed that shareholders should be given generous compensation. Huggins mocked him:

> I was horrified at the hon. Member one time when he was talking like a right-wing Tory, but he did his usual quick come-back to remind us that there was no future for this country unless we had a completely socialistic state. It was a good old Tory speech up to a point.[49]

Labour members of the ruling coalition joined in the taunting. Macintyre claimed 'to represent the workers of this Colony', said the old railway trade unionist and Bulawayo MP, Jack Keller. Yet white workers at the iron and steel factory – and Keller was concerned only with white workers – got low ages and the operation 'represents one of the most pernicious systems of sweated labour that I know of':

> The Hon. The Leader of the Opposition would not tolerate a trade union in his own establishment ... and I doubt very much that he would tolerate speaking to the leaders of his employees about the conditions of labour.[50]

And if there were serious inconsistencies in Macintyre's relation to white labour this was even more true of his position on African workers. Because Macintyre's Southern Rhodesian Labour Party was supported by genuinely left-wing people like Gladys Maasdorp and Doris Lessing, and because the Salisbury supporters had managed to set up an SRLP branch in Harare township, Macintyre was sometimes given credit by African spokesmen. Thus Lawrence Vambe included him in 'an impressive team, a brave group of people [advocating] a revolutionary school of thought'.[51] In fact Macintyre disliked the Harare branch and intervened to stop an African branch being formed in Makokoba township in Bulawayo.[52] Joshua Nkomo, the Bulawayo labour activist, could never have taken Macintyre's reputation as a political radical

---

[46] *Southern Rhodesian Hansard*, 18 May 1943, column 812.
[47] Interview with McNeillie, National Archives, Harare.
[48] *Hansard*, 30 November 1944, column 3378.
[49] *Hansard*, 28 October 1943, column 2216.
[50] *Hansard*, 23 June, 1942, column 1746.
[51] Lawrence Vambe, *From Rhodesia to Zimbabwe*, Heineman, London, 1976, p. 161.
[52] McNeillie recalls that Macintyre told him: 'I don't want them ... Some were trouble-makers.'

and 'friend of the natives' seriously. In October 1937 Nkomo qualified as a driver of public service vehicles. He got a job as driver of a half-ton delivery truck for Osborn's Bakery. His pay of £4 a month he thought 'pretty good' until he discovered that Coloured drivers were getting £12 a month. 'I went to Mr Macintyre and asked why it was … He explained that I was a native and the others were coloured; second that natives did not need beds and wheat bread and knives and forks, because they were happy with just a couple of blankets and some mealie porridge and a plate to eat off. I told him that if he would pay me £12 a month I should be very happy to sleep on a bed and eat meat with a knife and fork. So of course he sacked me.'[53]

Macintyre's master identities were those of baker and councillor. Speaking from these identities he took a very different line on African urbanization and proletarianization than did the African trade unionists and intellectuals who formed the Harare branch of the SRLP. His real views emerged clearly when he and other Bulawayo councillors gave evidence to the Howman Commission in November 1943, Macintyre doing nearly all the talking. He attacked the 'selfish view of the industrialist' who was demanding 'a steady labour force' and accommodation for wives in town. In his view, as a master baker and as the man responsible for the municipal workforce:

> The best Native today has very often got a wife in the country who looks after the mealies and the cattle. I have 10 or 12 boys who come in and work for a certain period and then they write to their opposite number and he comes and takes his place. Between them they carry on and it is no trouble to us at all. [Settled married life in the towns] will not be for the benefit of Native life in the Colony. I think the best thing for them is to live in the open spaces of the Colony, running their cattle … To suggest that you [ought to pay] a boy 3 pounds minimum now is sheer nonsense. I have 100 boys and I can get another 100. They have all the food they want. What they like is a place where they can eat. They go away at the end of twelve months as fat as butter and come back in another twelve months as thin as sticks. We have no trouble in getting boys … and we don't pay them particularly high wages, 30/- to 35/- [a month] at my place. If you establish all the Natives working in town as urban, I believe you will be creating the biggest problem that Rhodesia ever had. The best Native is the Native who comes in for twelve months and goes away and his place is taken by another Native.[54]

As a councillor, Macintyre was determined to keep costs down for the ratepayer. 'Boys' who came in and out on twelve-month rotations did not need elaborate welfare, medical, and educational provision. During the 1944 parliamentary debates on the Natives (Urban Areas) Accommodation and Registration Bill, which Macintyre opposed single-handed, one of his Bulawayo Labour opponents, Wing Commander Eastwood, delivered a stinging attack on him:

> During all the years I spent on the Bulawayo Municipality as Councillor, the attitude of the hon. member who seems to oppose the Bill was always to see how much he could get the central government to pay, how much he could shift the obligation on to the central government. During his period as Mayor and as Chairman of the Finance Committee, he seemed to think he was doing the ratepayers of Bulawayo a service if he could ensure letting those ratepayers avoid meeting their just obligation, and that he would get their favour if he was shrewd or cute enough to bamboozle the government into accepting the obligations of the Bulawayo Municipality. It is not altogether Scots blood. Usually Scots blood applies only to the individual. He is usually not prepared to shed his blood on behalf of the rest of the ratepayers.[55]

---

[53] Joshua Nkomo, *The Story of My Life*, Methuen, London, 1984, pp. 27-8.
[54] Evidence to the Howman Commission, 26 November 1943, National Archives, Harare, S.1906/1.
[55] *Hansard*, 23 November 1944, column 3137.

But to Macintyre shedding his Scottish blood on behalf of white ratepayers seemed the noblest of causes. In parliament he constantly spoke in their interests. 'It is not equitable', he declared in May 1942, 'that the government should expect ratepayers in towns to provide medical attention when the diseases are contracted in the government areas, while they, the government go off with the taxes collected in the towns'.[56] 'I am opposed', he declared in May 1943, 'to any weakening of the safeguards of the ratepayers', whether against industrialists or the state. Government, he complained, had time and again broken faith with what he called 'the Junction City', Bulawayo.[57] To Huggins's chagrin, he boasted in parliament that the Bulawayo Council, unlike Salisbury or the other towns, enjoyed 'entire control in the Location without restrictions by the government or any other body'. But in the same speech he demanded that government assume the responsibility for urban African housing rather than expecting the ratepayers to finance it.[58]

Nothing outraged Macintyre as much as a threat to Bulawayo's autonomy or a criticism of its 'native policy'. He had rejoiced in the Council's ferocious repudiation of Moffat's Commission in May 1930. He soon came to lead Bulawayo's resistance to Huggins. In Bulawayo itself Macintyre's chief irritant was the Reverend Percy Ibbotson, inspirer of the Bulawayo Native Welfare Society and a persistent critic of the Municipality – in fact Macintyre disliked and distrusted Ibbotson almost as much as Masotsha Ndlovu did. In June 1938 Ibbotson produced a report on conditions in the Location beer hall. In September 1939 he and W.C. Robertson published a report on 'Housing, Wages and Living Conditions of Africans in Bulawayo District'. It found 'serious over-crowding everywhere'; scandalous conditions in the Location; and accommodation at Macintyre's iron and steel company compound 'consisting of little more than a collection of hovels made out of odd pieces of tin and sacking'.[59]

In October 1939 Macintyre, at that point chairman of the Council's finance committee, strongly condemned the report during a Council meeting:

> It is a matter of grave concern that people of the standing of the members of this [Welfare Society] committee should lend their names to such a statement without adding that any such conditions which may be found are entirely without sanction. They are not countenanced or permitted by the Council ... The Committee of the Native Welfare Society, who visited the Location, accompanied by the Deputy Mayor and myself, were informed of this ... and their report has been deliberately made with full knowledge of these facts ... In view of this the public generally may have some difficulty in accepting the other findings of the Native Welfare Society, which deal with the living conditions of Natives generally.[60]

Thereafter Macintyre refused to attend Welfare Society meetings as a Council representative.

By the time the Howman Commission on the state of the towns arrived in Bulawayo in November 1943, however, Ibbotson had scored a major victory. Legislation had at last been passed controlling beer hall revenues. Macintyre had been superbly defiant during the parliamentary debate:

[56] *Hansard*, May 1942, column 959.
[57] *Hansard*, May 1943, column 452.
[58] *Hansard*, May 1942, column 959.
[59] Minutes of the Native Welfare Society of Bulawayo, September 1939, National Archives, Harare, S.1274.
[60] *Chronicle*, 19 October 1939. A.J. Davies, Macintyre's steady critic on the Council, said 'he was not accepting without question the statement made by Councillor Macintyre', and that the Council should pay serious attention to the report.

What I object to is any suggestion that these funds have not been properly used … The Prime Minister proves himself to be just as misguided as in many other respects. There is no reason for the song and dance the Prime Minister has made. He has suggested that we should use [beer hall profits] for borrowing money in the way laid down by the Act – the most hopeless and useless suggestion I have ever heard emanating from anyone who has a grain of intelligence.[61]

He was still defiant before the Howman Commission. He complained bitterly that 'the last Kaffir Beer Act' had made it impossible to use the surplus for housing so that 'in the future there will be only one source, the European rates of the town'. Africans could not afford economic rents but if they were given subsidized housing 'the European rates would have to be far more'. There was only one solution: 'the government should supply the money'. 'The building of houses originally with beer hall profits was helping Natives for all time … Some of the Native Welfare Society thought they knew about it and the whole thing is messed up.'

If government would not pay, the Council could do little even if it was falling behind demand. And in any case the Council would certainly not build houses for married Africans with families:

We don't accept the responsibility of a place like Luveve [the government village outside Bulawayo for married couples]. We believe that Luveve caters for an entirely different type of Native, a semi-urbanised type. We propose to provide just for the Native who works in town.

As we have seen, Huggins was putting increasing pressure on Bulawayo to increase rates, spend money, borrow more energetically, and generally to accept its responsibility to house the workers on whom the city's prosperity depended. But Macintyre remained contemptuous of Huggins. At the annual meetings of the Municipal Association he insisted that 'I do not want the government to tell me whether we are spending money correctly in accordance with the desires of the ratepayers'. Government might be 'threatening' the municipalities but 'threatened people live long, and the Municipalities will live long despite Government threats if we stand together'. When he was told that Huggins had announced that he was determined to introduce Native Urban legislation, Macintyre merely replied that the Prime Minister 'will change his mind next week if you leave him'.[62]

Huggins's Bulawayo

By 1944, however, Huggins was determined to compel Bulawayo to change *its* mind. Unlike Moffat, he had no connections with Bulawayo. He was Salisbury personified. As we have seen, he had attempted in the late 1930s to cajole Bulawayo into meeting its responsibilities. Increasingly he came to identify Macintyre as his main obstacle. Years later, in 1945, he told parliament:

When I walked round the Bulawayo Location with a town councillor [Macintyre] shortly after I had become Minister of Native Affairs, I saw a few nice houses and I saw many not too nice houses and I said to the town councillor: 'When are you going to build more of these modern houses and get rid of these filthy places?' and he said: 'When the natives drink more beer.' That was my introduction to Municipal Native housing … It was an odd remark by an odd person

61 *Hansard*, 24 June 1942, columns 1838, 1825.
62 *Proceedings of the Municipal Association*, Bulawayo, 1942.

and it should never have been made, but it illustrates the outlook of these people when they suggest that housing should be built out of beer-hall profits.[63]

In July 1936 Huggins wrote to Macintyre urging that the Council build houses 'for Native workers who are needed for the interests and convenience of its ratepayers' by drawing on 'loan provision'. No reply was received for a year, though Huggins followed up his letter by meeting Macintyre for 'a talk about this matter'.[64] In September 1937 he again wrote to Macintyre to ask for a projection of the rate of municipal building. This time Macintyre did reply, giving assurances that the Council had a building plan. But in early October he again raised the problem of finance:

> Councillors have sometimes taken the view that we should not, for the erection of native buildings, borrow money under the authority of the Municipal Act when the rateable property of the town is the security for such loans.

Government must offer especially favourable loan terms which would enable building without 'eroding our loan authority' which was 'required for other Municipal services'.[65] 'There would be no towns of any size if there were no Natives', replied Huggins. Yes, answered Macintyre: 'I agree that there would be no towns of any size were it not for the Natives but how do you square this with the policy of excluding them from towns?'[66]

Huggins was becoming so irritated by Macintyre's obduracy that he avoided meeting him whenever possible. In March 1938 he more or less wrote Macintyre off:

> You know what an obstinate fellow Macintyre is and it would appear that there is no hope for the Bulawayo Location as long as he has any influence there.[67]

But there was no hope of waiting Macintyre out. In 1938 his domination of the Bulawayo Council and his control of the Location had only just begun. It was to last until 1952. In March 1944 Huggins was still complaining that Bulawayo was not building enough accommodation for African workers:

> I have been trying to get something done for ten years [he wrote in a Memo of March 2]. Meanwhile Bulawayo have suggested that the Government buy land outside the commonage and run villages for their ratepayers' servants. [African workers] should have been given the commonage![68]

By this time Huggins had given up hope of persuading the city councils to act. In his view they, and particularly Bulawayo, were responsible for the urban crisis. They took a dangerously narrow view of the interests of white ratepayers, whose security was in fact threatened by African discontent; of the interests of white employers, who

63 *Hansard*, 1945, column 959.
64 Memorandum, Secretary of Native Affairs, July 1936; Sec/N/A to Sec/PM 224 August 1936; Huggins to Macintyre, 8 September 1937, National Archives, Harare, S.482/469/39.
65 Macintyre to Huggins, 1 October 1937, S.482/469/39.
66 Huggins to Macintyre, 15 November 1937; Macintyre to Huggins, 18 November 1937, S.482/469/39.
67 Prime Minister to Minister of Internal Affairs, 11 March 1938, S.482/469/39.
68 Huggins to Danzinger, 2 March 1944, National Archives, Harare, S.482/163/1. By 1944 a number of white suburbs had developed on the eastern Commonage but the western Commonage remained open and the Council was trying to push African housing beyond it. In the 1950s and 1960s the growth of new African townships did in fact take place on the western Commonage.

could not get efficient labour; and of the interests of white workers, whose monopoly of all building work in the Location made expansion there absurdly expensive. If the ratepayers had been made to take their proper responsibility, he thought, they would soon have abandoned such a costly policy. The old segregationist, whose appeals to the Bulawayo Council to build more houses had initially been based on the desire to carry out the Land Apportionment Act around the city, had now moved to an acceptance of the permanence of Africans in towns. As we shall see, the new bill which he was about to introduce was designed to recognize and organize this reality. By law, rate-payers would have to pay to erect housing, employers would have to pay for rents, and councils would have to accept administrative responsibility for whole clusters of town-ships. At the same time the new bill was designed to achieve segregation in and around the towns for the first time. At long last formal and adequate Native Urban Areas would be declared; all Africans would have to live in them and none could continue to reside in compounds in cities or as rent-payers on farms bordering the commonage.

Urban councils, of course, had a completely different view of where blame lay for the crisis of African housing. Government was responsible for 'prevarication and pro-crastination'. Macintyre had proposed a motion in parliament on 26 May 1943 calling for slum clearance legislation which would establish African urban housing as a state responsibility. Government did not respond. At the Municipal Conference in May 1944 a resolution was passed saying that in the absence of such legislation government must 'grant to local authorities in this country the same financial aid as is at present being given to the local authorities in the Union of South Africa'. In October 1944 Salisbury joined Bulawayo in a joint declaration that, if no financial aid was given, the councils would accept no further 'responsibility for the erection of additional houses in the Native Location'.[69] And once having blamed government for the state of the Locations, the councils felt free to describe their condition in terms which surpassed those of the Native Welfare Societies themselves. Urban Africans, said the Municipal Association in 1944, were 'living in filthy, abominable conditions which are a disgrace to civilisation'.[70] Macintyre could do little in parliament to obstruct the passage of Huggins's bill. But he still controlled the Municipal Association.

The ingredients of the bill had been around a long time. They dated back essential-ly to the Chief Native Commissioner's proposal on 8 June 1936 of 'a comprehensive Act embodying some of the features of the Native (Urban Areas) Acts 1922 and 1930 of the Union but broader in its scope and wider in its vision'. As long ago as November 1937 Huggins had proposed to Macintyre a solution which became the centrepiece of the Native (Urban Areas) Accommodation and Registration Act. 'I suggest for your consideration and reaction that we consider compelling the employer to house or hire accommodation for their Native workers or servants; this would mean that the European employer would pay the rent in Locations, not the Native as at present.'[71] Huggins got no response to his suggestion in 1937; by the early 1940s he was prepar-ing to enforce it. In October 1941 the Secretary for Native Affairs announced that 'it was the intention of the Government to introduce at an early date legislation making

[69] Town Clerk, Salisbury, to Prime Minister, 12 March 1945, S.482/163/1.

[70] The maverick mayor of Salisbury, Charles Olley, notorious for his racist attacks on Africans and his rambling addresses to the Association, even allowed himself to express some worker solidarity: 'We are perpetuating in our treatment of the natives the very treatment us from Home received, the tratment that was meted out to wage-earners in Britain.'

[71] Huggins to Macintyre, 15 November 1937, National Archives, Harare. S.482/469/39.

it compulsory for employers to provide housing'. In April 1942 Minister T.W. Beadle told the Town Clerk, Salisbury, that 'the way forward was to proclaim a Native Urban Area under the Land Apportionment Act'. When all the municipalities had done that, the government would introduce both an Urban Areas Act and a Native Housing Act. But no municipality acted under the LAA, so Huggins decided that he would combine an Urban Areas Act and a Native Housing Act into one compulsory measure whereby municipalities would be obliged by law to declare and administer Native Urban areas and employers be bound by law to pay for their workers' accommodation.

In May 1943 Huggins opened the Municipal Association conference. His mood was both jocular and ferocious. 'There is far too much bickering between central and local governments.' Some municipalities, particularly Bulawayo, 'would have to learn to accept "No" for an answer'. But in any case all smaller issues should be set aside. They must all focus on the problems of urban Africans:

> The problem of the health service and housing of Africans in the urban areas will demand considerable expansion. I know this is difficult because you cannot go faster than public opinion and until it is generally accepted that in diet, housing, etc. the African is entitled to at least the same consideration as is given to domestic pets and livestock, the whole problem bristles with difficulties.

'I have been told', he added, 'that in recent public speeches I have treated the audience as if they were enemies or potential enemies. It is possibly owing to war conditions and it is subconscious.' Macintyre, conscious of being cast in the role of enemy, reacted sourly: 'The Prime Minister made it quite clear this morning when he took the agenda not what he was going to consider but what he was going to do. I suggest to conference that the next time they ask the Prime Minister to open a Congress they ask him to open it after the Congress is over.'[72]

On 1 February 1944 Huggins broadcast to the nation, quoting Ibbotson's report on African urban conditions and deploring the terrible state of municipal locations. He was determined, he said, to do something about it. At the next Municipal Association Conference in May 1944 the more diplomatic opening speaker was the governor, Sir Evelyn Baring. He too spoke about Africans in towns:

> The historian of the future, when he comes to write the history of the present period in Southern Rhodesia, will conclude his survey by remarking that this problem of the natives in the urban areas was one of the most important problems with which Rhodesians of the forties were faced, and that the steps which were then taken to solve that problems had a profound effect on the conditions of life in the following years in Southern Rhodesia. History, of course, is an impartial judge, and the historian will make few distinctions. He will not say that this was a problem for the Government or for the Municipalities. He will say, I think, that this was a problem for the Europeans of Southern Rhodesia as a whole.[73]

The conference was not disposed to take this objective view. Speakers attacked Huggins's broadcast, claiming that they had pressed for a Housing and Slum Clearance Act and that Huggins had displayed 'masterly inactivity'. Sir Ernest Guest, the new Minister of Internal Affairs, told the delegates that before he took office 'I suspected that the relations between the local government bodies and the central government bodies, to say the least of it left a great deal to be desired, but after my appointment

[72] *Proceedings of the Municipal Association*, 1943, pp. 7, 46.
[73] *Proceedings of the Municipal Association*, 1944, p. 5.

as a Minister, I found that my worst fears were realised.' A delegate responded that government's inaction would be remembered 'when the time comes to put another government in power. I want – and I am sure this Conference wants – a government which will do something especially about housing.'[74]

In November 1944 the government at last did something. Huggins, as Minister for Native Affairs, introduced a motion for legislation making the establishment of Native Urban Areas compulsory; making employers responsible for the rents of their workers, at a fixed rate to apply to both 'single' and 'married' workers so that the former could subsidize the latter; making municipalities responsible for native administration and pass control in the towns; and making residence of Africans outside the proclaimed Native Urban Area illegal except for licensed domestic servants. 'There is nothing overbearing in this', he assured parliament on 23 November, 'because local government is merely a delegation of government in certain matters. ... Omissions by local government [have had] deplorable effects. I do not suppose any coercion [of municipalities] will be necessary. But powers will have to be taken on the lines of the Native Urban Areas Act of the Union of South Africa.'

Huggins stressed the importance of 'decent living conditions for married natives ... to get away from the unnatural life of males living together without their wives. We have to realize that a permanent urban class is arising.' The debate about whether ratepayers or taxpayers should meet the cost of African urban housing was irrelevant:

> It is not a national liability, it is not a municipal liability, but a liability of the employers and a duty of the municipalities to provide the facilities to their ratepayers at cost and in the most reasonable fashion.[75]

This was the moment Macintyre had been waiting for. He still smarted over the beer hall funds; he deeply resented the assertion that the municipalities were to blame for the urban crisis; he feared state regulation of the new Native Urban Areas; he did not favour provision for married families. He was able to summon up in opposition most of his multiple personalities – a staunch Bulawayo patriot, an employer, even a socialist radical. The proposed legislation would make 'the native a feudal serf, tied to his employer for his and his dependants' accommodation, occupying it only at the pleasure of his master ... That era has been buried without regret [together with] those responsible for such a system as the industrial age of Great Britain.' It would not stabilize marriages but break up informal urban liaisons. Municipalities would not just tamely accept new responsibilities unless they were given complete authority and adequate finance. 'There will be compulsory provision for the municipalities to provide housing, and I would like to know how the Prime Minister proposes to enforce this. If the municipalities refuse to impose a rate to meet the cost does the Government propose to impose such a rate?'[76]

Huggins replied to Macintyre on 30 November. 'I have been negotiating with these people for ten years', and still 'the hon member was meandering'. And, yes, he was certainly prepared to take powers:

> The Central Government takes power when the Local Authority will not do its duty properly ... to take over from them and carry out the necessary works and levy rates as taxes on the local

---

[74] *Proceedings of the Municipal Association.* 1944, pp. 127-9.
[75] *Hansard*, 23 November 1944, columns 2500 et seq.
[76] Ibid., columns 2562-75.

inhabitants. That is how you overcome recalcitrant Local Authorities when the Central Government is thwarted, when they will not do their duty.

Macintyre and Bulawayo had been warned.

But they still had time to waste. The draft Bill was not published for a further year, on 23 November 1945, and the actual legislation was not introduced into parliament until January 1946. Meanwhile those economic problems against which Moffat had warned were becoming intolerable. African workers were moving towards strike action, particularly in Bulawayo where black railwaymen were strongest and trade unionism most developed. Against this ominous background Macintyre mobilized all his constituencies to oppose the bill – the Bulawayo Council, the Municipal Association and the Southern Rhodesia Labour Party.

He was re-elected Mayor of Bulawayo on 8 August 1945.[77] He was re-elected leader of the SRLP on 16 September. At a party Congress in Salisbury, where nationalization of all industries was adopted as party policy, Huggins's plans were repudiated, the Harare branch taking a leading part in the debate. 'Nothing worthwhile', said Macintyre, 'could be achieved by the adoption of the Prime Minister's plan to make the native worker a serf for all time'.[78] In late December the Bulawayo Council debated Huggins's proposals behind closed doors: it elected Macintyre and four councillors as delegates to an extraordinary conference of the Municipal Association to be held on 19 and 20 December 1945. They were mandated by ten votes to one to carry with them a resolution that 'without the co-operation of local authorities ... proposals contained in the Bill would be impracticable'. The Bill should be sent to a Select Committee on which the municipalities would be well represented.[79] Nothing meanwhile was being done to meet the wage demands of Bulawayo's municipal workers or to initiate a new building programme in the Location.

But Macintyre took the Municipal Association by storm. He attacked virtually every aspect of the Bill. African urban housing was 'the Government's obligation'. 'It is immoral that the Bill should be rushed through Parliament at this stage.' He carried an amendment by 14 votes to 7 that the municipalities not be compelled to provide housing but that 'the Government should implement the Land Apportionment Act that dealt with Village Settlements, thus solving the whole urban native problem'. Unless this happened the cities themselves would be swamped and the Land Apportionment Act undermined. His chief ally, Charles Olley, protested that:

> The Bill would smash the value and protection to Europeans of the Land Apportionment Act ... It was inevitable that from eight to ten thousand black piccanins would be born yearly [from African urban marriages]. Our grandchildren will be ousted by the enormous influx of the native race. It would be suicide of the white race in Rhodesia to adopt the policy of an employed native having the right to bring his wife into town with the obligation of the white employer to accommodate the wife. It must not be.

Macintyre himself claimed that 'the Bill aimed at destroying tribal life and putting nothing in its place'.

[77] *Chronicle*, 9 August 1945. A subsequent report on 31 August documented some popular opposition to this election and demands from the Civic and Ratepayers Association that he resign either as mayor or as MP. Macintyre replied that 'he believed in fighting for his own way if he believed he was right. It was a coward's way to resign.'
[78] *Chronicle*, 17 September 1945.
[79] *Chronicle*, 18 December 1945.

Although some delegates objected to this melodrama, Macintyre and Olley's motion that a Commission of Inquiry be appointed was carried unanimously. Macintyre warned that 'the Prime Minister would appoint a commission of men who would incline to his views', but it would buy time. Surely even Huggins would now accept that 'to delay the passage of the Bill would be a wise and statesmanlike action', since 'unless he gets the co-operation of the municipalities it will be impossible to put the Bill into operation'.[80]

Huggins told the *Herald* on 21 December 1945 that he had hoped the municipalities would offer constructive amendments but clearly they did not understand the Bill. 'There is nothing to be gained by having a commission or a select committee.' The Bill would be introduced into parliament on 15 January 1946. The stage was set for a last titanic, if one-sided, battle between Huggins and Macintyre.

Huggins began by noting that 'there was considerable criticism outside the house by politicians, budding, mischievous and otherwise. This died down until the Bill was published and had a mixed reception. Some city fathers ... [received the Bill] with thumbs placed to their noses, with the forefingers extended.' Opposition was rooted in Bulawayo – 'I look forward to calm waters in Salisbury'. And in Bulawayo the root of the opposition was one man – Macintyre. Macintyre said that co-operation was needed, but he 'was speaking with his tongue in his cheek. It takes at least two to co-operate.' In the Municipal Association resolutions 'I see the hand of the Mayor of Bulawayo'. The Bulawayo Council had sent a letter of objection; the SRLP had forwarded a resolution from its African branch. But:

> Here again we see the same individual producing more noise and opposition, the Mayor of Bulawayo, the leader of the SRLP and the chief noise in the Municipal Association.[81]

Throughout the days which followed Macintyre did indeed fight a single-handed battle, moving and losing innumerable amendments, insulting Huggins and enduring innumerable insults in return. It was a 'monstrosity of a Bill' which would 'destroy many of the fundamental rights which have been built up for the native population of the country – taking away tribal life and replacing it with nothing else'. It would 'create an unwholesome increase in the number of women and children who will be living in the urban area ... There will be a large, almost unbearable burden placed on the ratepayers in the towns.'[82]

He was attacked not only by Huggins but by almost everyone else. W.M. Leggate accused him of seeking to combine in one unholy union the radical rhetoric of the SRLP and his own interests 'as an employer who wants to keep wages down'. W.H. Eastwood attacked him for seeking to forward only the interests of his ratepayers and for trying to combine advocacy of industrial development with the view 'that it was far better that these natives should go home to their reserves as frequently as possible'. He was attacked by the Labour stalwart, J.B. Lister, for representing 'town councillors, mostly men who are property owners ... more concerned with saving the rates

---

[80] *Herald*, 21 December 1945. A letter was sent from the Secretary of the Municipal Association to the Minister of Native Affairs on 20 December 1945. This noted the view that if government were determined to proceed 'it would be better for the Government to assume control over native affairs throughout the Colony, to acquire from the local authorities all moveable and immovable assets relating to their native administration'. National Archives, Harare, S.482/163/1.

[81] *Hansard*, 16 January 1946, columns 3074-92.

[82] Ibid., columns 3103-10.

on property than they are in improving the conditions of those who cannot buy their own property'.[83]

Huggins took his chance to destroy Macintyre's credibility as a radical. Indeed he embodied 'the early Victorian capitalist ... and [wanted] to wait for strikes and bloodshed. The hon. member would wait for the trouble instead of seeing that these people have better conditions now.' Meanwhile he had made trouble more likely by mischievously putting into the heads of Africans 'that we are tightening up conditions against them'. But it was untrue that employers acquired houses from which they could eject employees; workers were secure as long as they found other employment. Macintyre's allegation 'is not even good electioneering because it is palpably absurd'.[84]

Macintyre called on all his resilience and rudeness to carry a doomed fight through the committee stages of the Bill. 'There is no use the hon. Prime Minister getting shirty', he told an irritated Huggins. All his amendments were voted down. The Bill was read for a third time on 4 February 1946. Macintyre made a final oratorical effort. Government had failed in its responsibility to the 'subordinate race'. They had failed in their duty to Europeans too:

> There is an entire difference between the provisions of the Land Apportionment Act and what would take place under this Bill ... The door is left open for a large number of natives to reside in the European area. We must have a huge influx of native women and children into the urban areas and it seemed that this is the intention of Government. It has been so often said that we should build up a constant supply of native labour to develop Southern Rhodesian industry but the people of Southern Rhodesia do not desire that.[85]

With Macintyre as the only dissenter, the Bill was passed.

Still he persisted. As leader of the SRLP he contacted liberals in England and asked them to protest in Westminster about the new Act. Lord Faringdon put down a motion in the House of Lords for discussion on 19 February 1946, drawing attention to the 'severe conditions of disabilities and restrictions to which Africans will be subjected by the operation of the Bill' because of its tightening up of pass laws and its giving the Rhodesian government the power to regulate assemblies. Faringdon asked the Colonial Secretary to refuse assent. The Colonial Office asked Huggins to comment, which he did on 15 February 1946. If my narrative has suggested that Huggins had become 'liberal', his reply to the Governor makes a useful corrective:

> It must be remembered that the great majority of the Natives are uncivilized barbarians and their emergence from this condition will entail many teething difficulties. The complete lack of sense of proportion by the present leaders of urbanized Natives was well illustrated in the recent Railway strike ... In the event of firebrands gaining control the situation which would arise would be similar to that which arose in the Copperbelt of Northern Rhodesia in 1940 and 1942.[86]

This did not sound much like Moffat! But its reminder of shared difficulties, Huggins having sent troops to the Copperbelt, was enough to secure royal assent to the Native (Urban Areas) Accommodation and Registration Act. Macintyre retired to Bulawayo determined to orchestrate continued opposition in 'his' city.

---

[83] Ibid., columns 3149-53.
[84] Ibid.
[85] *Hansard*, 4 February 1946, columns 3686-88.
[86] Huggins to Governor, 15 February 1946, National Archives, Harare, S.482/163/1.

4

Mr Black Bulawayo
1930–1948

A Hero for Black Bulawayo

My narrative of the feud between Bulawayo and the Rhodesian state has brought me
to 1946. This is the year in which Yvonne Vera set *Butterfly Burning*, at a moment, she
says in its opening lines, when 'there is a pause. An expectation'.[1] Her sense of timing
was exact. The novel takes place in Makokoba just as a new urban world is struggling
to emerge from the old. Yvonne's hero, Fumbatha – who built much of Bulawayo with
his strength and sweat – personifies the old. Her heroine, Phephelaphi, personifies the
new, feminized, urban culture, with all its possibilities and frustrations. I will seek
in a later chapter to lay out Phephelaphi's world. In this one I want to look at Fumbatha's. I want to ask what Bulawayo's Africans were experiencing and doing during
those years when city and state fought over their future. And just as I personified
that struggle in the figures of Macintyre and Huggins, and just as Yvonne personifies
Makokoba in 1946, so I want to narrate the years in Makokoba between 1930 and the
late 1940s through the life of one person.

But who to choose? The Reverend Thompson Samkange, one of the heroes of the
1929 faction fights as he sallied out from the Makokoba Methodist Church to suc-
cour the wounded, left Bulawayo in the mid-1930s to serve in Mashonaland.[2] Joshua
Nkomo, who certainly became Mr Bulawayo and went on to become Father Zimbabwe, was only 29 in 1946, his extraordinary career just beginning. He was then in
South Africa and did not return to Bulawayo until early 1948.[3] Benjamin Burombo,
who figured so largely in the April 1948 general strike in Bulawayo, is a post-war
figure.[4] Burombo brought Masotsha Ndlovu back into Bulawayo politics, but again
not until after the war.[5] What is needed is a figure who personifies black Bulawayo
between 1930 and the late 1940s; ideally a figure who connects with the first Ndebele
pioneers who settled in the Location; who was born and grew up there; who came to
master the modernizing sports and musical culture of the Welfare decade, displacing

---

[1] Yvonne Vera, *Butterfly Burning*, p. 1.
[2] T.O. Ranger, *Are We Not Also Men?*, Chapter 1.
[3] Joshua Nkomo, *Nkomo: The Story of My Life*, 1984.
[4] Ngwabi Bhebe, *B.Burombo, African Politics in Zimbabwe, 1947–1958*, College Press, Harare, 1989.
[5] Pathisa Nyathi, *Masotsha Ndlovu*, 1998.

James Mambara as a youth icon; who was involved with imagining Ndebele herit-age, and who was active in the nascent trade union movement, participating with the militant black railway men after the 1945 strike and with the municipal workers in 1947 and 1948. Such a figure sounds too representative to be true. But there *was* such a man. His name was Sipambaniso Manyoba Khumalo. He has been an oddly neglected figure in Zimbabwean historiography but he is the hero of this chapter.[6]

Sipambaniso Manyoba Khumalo's Ancestry

We have seen in the Prelude how the Ndebele aristocrat Bikwapi Manyoba Khumalo established himself as a great figure in the early Location. His wife, Madhlodhlo, was prominent among the famous female stand-owners and landladies. One son among their children stood out from the rest – Arthur, or, as he became better known, Sipambaniso, the stirrer of trouble. Sipambaniso was thought of as a totally urban man, having been born in the Location, educated there, married there and lived the whole of his adult life there. He was the quintessential long-term urban resident.[7]

But urban though he was, Sipambaniso's aristocratic ancestry was well remembered in rural Matabeleland. He was accepted as a member of the royal Khumalo clan. As Gideon Joyi Khumalo told Lynette Nyathi at Old Bulawayo in January 2001:

> Sipambaniso belongs to *Inzond'ebuhlungu*, painful anger. He is the son of Matshitshi. Yes he is the son of Mpondo Zimatshtishi. Yes he is a *Nzond'ebuhlengu* but he is still of our clan because all of us are direct descendants of Ndabezitha … All these people are still the descendants of the same person who is our fore-bearer. It is like that.[8]

Sipambaniso's father, Bikwapi, had come to Bulawayo from northern Matabeleland and he retained close connections there all his life. When he died in his seventies in November 1950, the *Bantu Mirror* reported the huge crowd which attended his funer-al. 'Hundreds of Africans of all tribes in the Bulawayo African Township' came; but so also in large numbers came mourners from the Shangani Reserve, from Lupane, from the Matopos, and from Essexvale. The *Bantu Mirror* reported the funeral as that of the father of Sipambaniso Khumalo, 'the well known football player', and Sipambaniso presided over the ceremony, thanking all those who had travelled to attend it.[9]

---

[6]   He does not appear, for instance, in Richard Gray's seminal *The Two Nations*, Oxford University Press, London, 1960, which contains very illuminating sections on the Native Urban Areas Accommodation and Registration Act and on Bulawayo activism in the late 1940s. Nor does he appear, except as a figure in a group photo, in Michael West's *The Rise of an African Middle Class: Colonial Zimbabwe, 1898–1965*, Indiana University Press, Bloomington, 2002. He is not mentioned in Joshua Nkomo's autobiography. The only sub-stantial published reference to his whole career, other than in my own work, is in Tsuneo Yoshikuni, 'Notes on the influence of town–country relations on African urban history before 1957: experiences of Salisbury and Bulawayo', in Brian Raftopoulos and Tsuneo Yoshikuni (eds), *Sites of Struggle*, Weaver Press, Harare, 1999. Yoshikuni writes that the vigour of Bulawayo's social and political life 'was personified by the example of Sipambanese Manyoba, one of the most colourful figures of the 1940s' and speaks of 'his centrality to the mainstream of Bulawayo politics' (p. 119). He is drawing here, as will I, on O.W. Stuart's 1989 London doctoral thesis, 'Good Boys, Footballers and Strikers: African Social Change in Bulawayo, 1933–1953', pp. 47–9. Sipambaniso's role in the 1948 strike is extensively discussed in Ian Phimister and Brian Raftopoulos, '*Kana sora ratswa ngaritswe*: African Nationalists and Black Workers – The 1948 General Strike in Colonial Zimbabwe', *Journal of Historical Sociology*, 13, 3, April 2000.
[7]   When he died in November 1950 Bikwapi was survived by three sons and three daughters.
[8]   Interview between Lynette Nyathi and Gideon Joyi Khumalo, Old Bulawayo, January 2001.
[9]   *Bantu Mirror*, 25 November 1950.

But his aristocratic Ndebele credentials were also recognized in southern Matabeleland. The activist, Grey Bango, remembered in January 2001 a journey he made with Sipambaniso in the late 1940s when they were close associates in the African trade union movement. They travelled far south of Bulawayo to see Grey's father, who was acting chief Bango. They found the chief slaughtering cattle at a festival. When he saw Sipambaniso the old man exclaimed: 'Slaughter one for this young man here. He is a son of great men … We were with his fathers when we first came here and settled at Entumbane, when Mzilikazi came and settled behind this place called Mhlahlandlela.'[10] Sipambaniso was not just the quintessential long-term urban resident, but the quintessential *Ndebele* urban man.

Sipambaniso's Education

Bikwapi was a staunch Anglican and the family worshipped at the oldest church in the Location, St Columba's. At St Columba's school, the earliest in Makokoba, Sipambaniso added educational credentials to his aristocratic descent. In the 1920s, St Columba's was run by Reverend Sagonda, 'of the Manyika tribe, educated at St Augustine's, Penhalonga'. Sagonda ran a primary school on stern principles. 'Character building for the time being is more important than academic education', he told the Native Affairs Commission in March 1930.[11] Sipambaniso was taught by S.J. Mazwi, who had been taken to South Africa by the Anglican Father Wilson and after training had returned to teach at St Columba's school where Sipambaniso was 'one of his early scholars'.[12] I have found no evidence that Sipambaniso went on to further education after completing primary school, but in a Location where the great majority of household heads had no education at all his schooling at St Columba's in the 1920s was quite enough to qualify him as a modern man.

At the beginning of the 1930s, then, Sipambaniso was the prime candidate for the leader of Makokoba's fashionable young Ndebele men – a rival to the legendary James Mambara. And although there is no evidence that Sipambaniso was involved in the 1929 faction fights, a strand in township oral tradition casts them as part of a contest between Mambara's 'Manyika' and the Manyoba Khumalo family:

What worsened the [1929] fights (remembers Msongelwayizizwe Petro Khumalo) was that soon after they broke out James Mambara ran back to a room where he was staying with Sipambaniso's brother. When he reached the room Mambara knocked and called out for Sipambaniso's brother, saying he should open the door to that room because he was about to be attacked. Sipambaniso's brother opened the door and James Mambara, who had gone there with a group of Shona, went in and stabbed Sipambaniso's brother to death.[13]

At any rate, after the repression of the December 1929 violence and the arrest and departure of James Mambara, Sipambaniso emerged as the acceptable face of pro-

---

[10] Interview between Lynette Nyathi and Grey Bango, January 2001. Bango was 81 at the time of this interview.

[11] Evidence of Reverend Sagonda, March 1930, ZAN 1/1/1, National Archives, Harare.

[12] *Home News*, 23 August 1958. Mazwi spoke Xhosa, English, Shona, Tswana and other African languages; after St Columba's he joined the Municipal Police in the Location; became clerk-interpreter at Inyati and Matopo; and finally became chief interpreter in the High Court. He was, says the *Home News*, 'a great African … a pearl of great price'.

[13] Interview between Busani Mpofu and Khumalo, Makokoba, 26 July 2000. At the time of the interview Khumalo was 90.

gressive township youth – aristocratic, educated, elegant and Ndebele. The *Bantu Mirror* of 27 June 1936 published a studio photograph of a very young Sipambaniso, smartly but romantically dressed, with a vase of roses before him on a table and posed against a leafy glade. Looking at that photo there is no reason to doubt one of our female informants, Mrs Dlamini, who was 14 in 1936: 'Sipambaniso could never court a girl', she says, 'and be refused.'[14]

Sipambaniso as Sportsman

Like Mambara, Sipambaniso was a champion boxer and in the 1930s he devoted himself to 'civilizing' Ndebele boxing and to bringing it within Welfare Society and Queensbury Rules. But above all else, at a time when football was the speciality of school and college boys, Sipambaniso was the first great Bulawayo football star. On 1 January 1954 the editor of the *Home News*, Charlton Ngcebetsha, reflected on the history of football in Bulawayo. It began in 1929 when there was only one field in Makokoba, 'which had an ugly appearance and there was barely a blade of grass on it. There were some small stones, here and there, jotting out of the ground.' Bulawayo football in the early 1930s 'was a game associated only with the fittest ... The rule of the jungle prevailed, where when the lion roars mice and rabbits, including cunning jackals, must seek shelter in the nearest hole with lightning rapidity for dear life's sake. A player could enter the field with a hunter's knife on his belt ...Good football was found only in the schools and even here it meant shooting aimlessly – the harder and higher the better.'[15] The *Bantu Mirror* for October 1932 carried a report by Jeremiah Hlabangana of a match between the Ntabazinda Institute, north-east of Bulawayo, where he taught, and the nearby Mfengu Reserve. The villagers came on 'like a team of ostriches, running one after another in their uniform of scarlet and white' – but the school won. By the mid-1930s there were 16 teams in the Bulawayo Native Football League, many of them composed of ex-pupils from schools in Manicaland but a few representing the schools of Matabeleland.[16]

Masotsha Ndlovu of the ICU deplored the rise of a Welfare Society sporting culture in Bulawayo. Sipambaniso took a very different view. Just as with boxing Sipambaniso was associated with 'civilizing' – and Ndebelizing – football. The *Bantu Mirror* retrospect of 1955 described how 'during the late thirties and early forties' there was 'a complete revolutionary re-organisation of this game. Various schools around towns in the Colony produced polished players who in turn sought work in towns. These together with welfare officers transformed the game to something appreciable.'[17] Sipambaniso played a central role in this process, as player, referee, administrator and welfare officer.

In the early 1930s a Lions team – later to become Highlanders – was started in Bulawayo. It was initiated by Lobengula's grandsons, Albert and Rhodes. Rhodes had played for a Lions side at Lovedale College in South Africa. The two 'princes' joined with teachers and students at the Ntabazinduna Institute, including Ngce-

---

[14] Interview between Hlengiwe Mlotshwa and Mrs Dlamini, Makokoba, 26 January 2001.
[15] *Home News*, 1 January 1954; *Bantu Mirror*, 10 July 1955.
[16] *Bantu Mirror*, 18 April 1936. There were Manyika teams from Rusape, Inyanga, Mutambarara, St Triashill and Umtali.
[17] *Bantu Mirror*, 30 July 1955.

betsha himself and the Hlabangana brothers. Sipambaniso Manyoba Khumalo was recruited to play centre-half. The team at once became associated with Ndebele – and royal – identity and with superior football. Sipambaniso became captain of the Lions and his footballing feats began to appear in the *Bantu Mirror.* On 6 June 1936, for instance, he was reported as scoring two goals for a Bulawayo select side against Shabani. On 13 June 1936 he was reported as refereeing a match between the Lions team and Ntabazinduna school. Charlton Ngcebetsha, who submitted the report, noted that the Lions team was almost entirely composed of former Ntabazinduna pupils. On 28 November 1936 Sipambaniso captained a Bulawayo select team against Wankie. The *Mirror* reporter insisted that 'the Bulawayo team owes a deep debt of gratitude to its captain, Sipambaniso Khumalo, who through thick and thin of many matches has maintained, retained and inculcated the spirit of true sportsmanship'. Rough play continued, however, especially high tackling. The *Bantu Mirror* of 3 April 1937 lamented that in the previous week 'Sipambaniso, the Captain of the Bulawayo team, nearly lost his leg'. Meanwhile, Rhodes Lobengula, initiator of the 'Lions', had died and in March 1937 Sipambaniso convened a meeting in the Location to set up a fund for a 'monumental stone' to commemorate him.[18] He continued to play for and to captain Lions/Highlanders and reports of his football prowess continued up to 1945.[19] On 23 September 1944, the *Bantu Mirror* reported a match between an African team, selected from Northern Club and Matabeleland Highlanders, against a Coloured Eleven. Sipambaniso captained the African team which won four-nil. 'Masterpieces of skill were displayed and several attempted scores from either side ran amok. Scenes that can only be increased once in a life-time'.[20]

Our oral informants leave us in no doubt how great was Sipambaniso's footballing reputation. 'Sipambaniso was one of the *gurus* in football' remembers Mrs Dlamini, the woman who thought him irresistible to girls. 'This Highlander thing goes back a long way.'[21] 'Sipambaniso was a great footballer', says Grey Bango. 'He was among the first young players and people to form Matabeleland Highlanders, together with Rhodes Lobengula ... He was a young man, but he was one of the early football-ers together with Nhlebe Hlabangana, and the football ground they used was there at Stanley Square. So this is where I first got to know Sipambaniso.'[22] The Lions/ Highlanders team was supported especially by Ndebele youth. The 82-year-old Mr Ndlovu told Simon Mlothshwa in January 2001 that he saw Highlanders as a continu-ation of the December 1929 rivalry between the Ndebele and the Manyika: 'They used to play. As you know, Highlanders is the oldest team in Bulawayo. I love the game because I used to play in college. People loved Highlanders very much. All the likes of Sipambaniso, Ngcebetsha, Samuel Ndebele, Gene Thutha, were active in the team. I didn't enter it that much because of the segregation that there was in the game. As you know these people started fighting around 1930. They were still build-ing on the evil.'[23]

---

[18] *Bantu Mirror*, 20 March 1937.
[19] The *Bantu Mirror* of 3 November 1945, by which time Sipambaniso was fully engaged in Matabele Home Society, trade union and Welfare activities, reported him playing centre-half for Bulawayo against Salisbury, describing him as 'an experienced player who has captained and represented Bulawayo on numerous occa-sions'.
[20] *Bantu Mirror*, 23 September 1944.
[21] Interview between Simon Mlotshwa and Mrs Dlamini, Makokoba, 26 January 2001.
[22] Interview between Lynette Nyathi and Grey Bango, January 2001.
[23] Interview between Simon Mlotshwa and Mr Ndlovu, Mpopoma, 26 January 2001.

But, for their supporters:

Highlanders were unrebukable. Even to the extent that the supporters had their own place in the stadium. If one mistakenly sat with them and celebrated an opposition goal that person was kicked and thrown to the ground. If you spoke badly about Highlanders you were insulting Bulawayo. It was like putting a finger in the eyes of the Ndebele ... There was a Ncube who would praise Highlanders when it played, for the whole game, without sitting down. He would call 'Highlander! Highlander! Highlander! Matshobana!'. The boys were crazy ... the goal-keeper had juju. With his finger he could stop a powerful shot ... Ah! This town was beautiful. People were smart.[24]

Sipambaniso was not only a player. He was a member of the Sports Committee of the Native Welfare Society, of the Boxing Association committee, and of the Bantu Out-door Sports Club. In 1938 the Welfare Society sponsored the formation of a Bulawayo African Football Association, which controlled matches in the town, and Sipambaniso was elected to its committee. Stuart has described BAFA as 'a new form of popular mobilisation', an arena in which African ability could prove itself and an organization which proved capable of facing down the Bulawayo Municipality when the latter tried to assert control over African football in 1947. Sipambaniso, Ngcebetsha and the other officials of BAFA organized a boycott: no football was played in Bulawayo for two years; the Council gave way on 9 March 1949, BAFA resumed control and football began again.[25]

Stuart argues that the original paternalism of the Welfare era, so angrily denounced by Masotsha Ndlovu, had given way to defiant and successful African control of their own sporting activities. And certainly Sipambaniso saw the connection between foot-ball and his role as a spokesman for African urban opinion. He testified to the Native Production and Trade Commission in 1944, claiming that 'I was elected by my people ... particularly the Football Association, who knew what I had done for the Football Association. I was Captain in the First XI ever since we started the cup, which was presented by Captain Harris.'[26]

Sipambaniso as a Policeman

And what was Sipambaniso's job all this time, as he emerged as a romantic young man and a famous football player? He spent eight years in the police, specifically in the Criminal Investigation Department, of course playing for and captaining the police team. From the perspective of the twenty-first century this seems a disconcerting answer. Sipambaniso was to become a great public figure, a choreographer of Ndebele cultural nationalism, an organizer of African trade unions, an officer of the National Congress. How does all that square with his long service in the CID?

The answer is that from the perspective of the 1930s, service in the CID was not seen as a 'sell-out' or stooge activity. It was seen as a prestigious job, appropriate to an educated young man. G.A. Chaza's autobiography of his twenty-two years service in the British South Africa Police, from 1936 to 1957, makes the point. Chaza descended

[24] Interview between Simon Mlothswa and Moses Mtombeni, Njube, 4 February 2001.
[25] O.W. Stuart, 'Good Boys, Footballers and Strikers.' Stuart's account of the boycott is given on p. 109. He argues that this successful defiance of the Municipality was an event similar to the railway workers strike of 1945 and the general strike of 1948, in both of which Sipambaniso was involved, p. 148.
[26] Stuart, pp. 47-8.

from Mhlaba, who 'came from Zululand with Mzilikazi'; his father was a Methodist evangelist-teacher; he had gone through both Waddilove and Domboshawa with good grades; in 1935 he had 'a very lucrative white collar job, in which I was earning a princely salary of £3 a month,' as a cotton recorder at the Gatooma Cotton Research Station. He owned a bicycle and 'was very particular in choosing my clothes and took pride in dressing rather well'. He bought his clothes 'with the assistance and expertise of a tailor uncle in Bulawayo'. This archetypal modern young man left home in search of an esteemed job, and in February 1936 he joined the police. He worked as an interpreter and was promised eventual promotion to sergeant, a rank he attained in 1957. Through all these years he did not feel that he was being disloyal to the African cause and regarded his uniform as a mark of prestige. Then one day in 1957 he visited Mbare Location and attended a nationalist rally in Mai Musodzi Hall:

> One outspoken African nationalist, George Nyandoro, spoke about how the regime exploited the 'children of the soil'. He pointed out and gibed good-naturedly at the poor African police uniform, pointing at some African policemen in uniform, who were on duty at the rally. He drew an uproarious applause when he referred to the puttees as *mabandaji*, bandages. I could no longer feel at ease in police uniform after hearing those jeers.[27]

By this time, of course, Sipambaniso had long ago abandoned his police uniform – indeed by this time Sipambaniso was dead. But during his eight years in the CID between 1933 and 1941 Sipambaniso had a career rather different from Chaza's. Chaza was moved from rural station to rural station. Sipambaniso spent all his eight years in Bulawayo, living in Makokoba. In popular memory he is remembered as *the* policeman for Makokoba, more powerful by far than the Municipal Police. He is seen not as a repressor of African aspirations but as the representative of long-term residents in Makokoba, using his police authority to control wayward youth, loose women, gangsters and 'loungers'. Old Gideon Joyi Kumalo, who remembered Sipambaniso's ancestry so well in 2001, also remembered him as a policeman. 'Eh! Sipambaniso, eh! I saw him arresting people. He was a CID. I knew him when he was still a young man.'[28] L. Chinamora, who was 72 when he talked with Simon Mlotshwa in January 2001, remembered Sipambaniso as 'the chief policeman. People would run away when he appeared. Illegal occupants were kicked out. However, Sipambaniso did not arrest anyone. He would just chase you away.'[29] Informants remember that Sipambaniso disliked all forms of disorder. Prince Gumede recalled in June 2000 that he especially disliked the Apostolic Church members who began to move in to the Bulawayo townships from the late 1930s:

> He regarded the Apostolic Church members as *Oftsotsi*, robbers. He did not like their system of praying in languages unintelligible to other people whilst jumping around claiming to be possessed by the Holy Spirit ... If one of them spotted a beautiful woman in the congregation he could falsely prophesy that the Holy Spirit had indicated that she should become the wife of the prophet. Sipambaniso Khumalo fiercely hated them. He never wanted to see them holding their services in the township ... It was after the death of Sipambaniso that the Apostolic Churches could hold their services freely in the townships.[30]

[27] G.A. Chaza, *Bhurakuwacha: The Story of a Black Policeman in Rhodesia*, College Press, Harare. 1998, pp. 8-9; Chapter 4; p. 125.
[28] Interview between Lynette Nyathi and Gideon Joyi Kumalo, Old Bulawayo, January 2001.
[29] Interview between Simon Mlotshwa and L. Chinamora, Makokoba, 15 January 2001.
[30] Interview between Busani Mpofu and Prince Gumede, Makokoba, 14 June 2000.

His great political and trade union ally, Grey Bango, described how Sipambaniso's CID career came to an end in 1941:

> I knew Sipambaniso very well. Eh! Sipambaniso was a member of the CID. He left this job after he refused to be transferred to Harare on promotion. Sipambaniso said he could not go to stay in foreign lands so he quit his job.

But Bango thought that Sipambaniso's career in the CID, far from being detrimental to his later work as a trade unionist, was positively beneficial to it. When the Federation of Bulawayo African Trade Unions was formed in 1945, Sipambaniso 'had lots of friends in the police'. He told 'his friends in the police force' that he 'wanted to organise meetings, so that we could meet and try to solve our problems as a trade union'. In 1948, in the run-up to the general strike, 'we had our own intelligence in the likes of Sipambaniso because he was a former member of the CID'.[31]

Sipambaniso & Urban Culture

Although Sipambaniso's local reputation was not damaged by his membership of the CID it was only after he had resigned from it that he was able to make his full contribution to urban culture. This he also did as an educated man. The schools were the progenitors of the modern sport of football. They were also the progenitors of modern urban music. There had, of course, been plenty of music in the Location – 'tribal' drumming and dance, which the Council tried to control so that white residents were not uncomfortably reminded of the 'wild' Africa on their doorsteps. But the urban music which pulsates through Yvonne Vera's *Butterfly Burning* had a different origin. It came from the mission school choirs and it came from the towns of South Africa.

In February 1958 *Parade* told the story of the development of urban music in Southern Rhodesia:

> As far back as the early thirties musical entertainment among the Africans of Southern Rhodesia was provided by organised groups of singers called Makwaya (Choirs). Out in the country districts of the Colony the Makwaya sang and entertained their audiences in the moonlight. In the towns the Makwaya artists performed in halls, and in both towns and country, the Makwaya singers drew enormous crowds of primitive, semi-enlightened and enlightened music fans. By the late thirties the Makwaya had established themselves in the music business and had a big name. Most of their songs had a moral lesson, and in the country districts their songs were in reality sermons through the medium of singing ... [but in the towns they introduced] more rhythm to make things more lively and inspiring, hence the advent of Step Makwaya of the late thirties which dominated the music business until they were knocked out by the more sensational *tshaba-tshaba* dances or artists.

Tshaba-tshaba came in the early 1940s and appealed strongly to teenagers. 'Romance of a rather undignified sort was encouraged in the *tshaba-tshaba* and the corporeal shakes and twists which went with the singing were at the time almost outrageous. The *tsahab-tshaba* business gripped Matabeleland very strongly and youths, boys and girls, young men and women, went mad ... The *tshaba-tshaba* dance gripped the Locations in the towns like a highly infectious disease.' This phase of *tshaba-tshaba* fever belongs in the next chapter, where I explore the feminization of Bulawayo town-

---

[31] Interview between Lynette Nyathi and Grey Bango, January 2001.

ship culture from the late 1940s on. It is the atmosphere of *Butterfly Burning*. But Sipambaniso contributed to an earlier stage of the development of urban music.[32]

In order to do so he needed two things – a wife to lead the women singers in his choir, and a hall in which to perform. In 1941 he got both. Leaving the CID in 1941 he was at once recruited as assistant to the newly appointed African Social and Sports organizer, J. Stakesby-Lewis. This meant that he was based at Stanley Hall, Makokoba, a few minutes walk away from his house in Second Street. The importance of this one building emerges clearly from Eric Gargett's 1971 'Welfare Services in an African Urban Area'. Stanley Hall was erected in 1936:

> In the following year the Welfare Society appointed a trained African social worker as its welfare officer, his salary being paid in equal shares by the City Council and the Government. He set up office in the communal hall which was the venue (and the only one) for dances and concerts and meetings of every description. He ran a library there and played an active part in the establishment of a major sporting body, the Bulawayo African Football Association, which made its headquarters in the hall. But the Welfare Officer's main contribution lay in the personal service he provided for those in any kind of need. For twenty years he was the only professional qualified worker, during which time the African population grew from under ten thousand to over one hundred thousand ... For many years fresh arrivals in town called at the hall 'looking for the welfare', who would help them locate a friend, a sleeping place for the night, or a job or a meal.[33]

In the late 1930s this Welfare Officer was yet another educated Manyika, William Makubalo. He and Sipambaniso were friends and allies. They collaborated in the founding and management of the Bulawayo African Football Association. They sat together on the executive committee of the Native Section of the Welfare Society, whose remit was to 'arrange and hold dances, concerts, lectures, debates, theatrical performances and other social functions'.[34] It is too easy to dismiss the Native Welfare Society members as subservient 'good boys'. In the waste that was Makokoba, where only the surrounding churches offered any colour or ceremonial and only the expensive municipal Beer Hall offered legitimate recreation, men like Makubalo and Sipambaniso were responsible for developing an urban 'high' culture, musical, social, and athletic. Once Sipambaniso was appointed to Stanley Hall in 1941 they collaborated on many projects.

A government report of 5 December 1941 offers a sketch of the situation. There were 18,442 Africans employed in Bulawayo. 4,370 were male tenants in the Location; 1,050 lived on Private Locations on European-owned land; 5,571 were 'unauthorised squatters' on farms; 145 lived at the Government Native Village in Luveve; 7,304 were housed by their employers. 377 African women were employed in Bulawayo town. In Makokoba itself there were still 228 rooms owned 'privately'; 337 two-roomed cottages; 1,799 single rooms.[35] In all this scattered terrain only churches and missions

---

[32] For a fuller treatment of the origins of music in Makokoba see Joyce Jenje Makwenda, *Zimbabwe Township Music*, Storytime Promotions, Mabelreign, 2005. A photo of Stanley Hall is on p. 54.

[33] Eric Stanley Gargett, 'Welfare Services in an African Urban Area', doctoral thesis, London, 1971, p. 47.

[34] 'Native Welfare Society of Bulawayo', S 1274, National Archives, Harare. Both men were present at an executive committee meeting on 21 August 1939, at which 'it was pointed out that Councillor Macintyre, MP, the Council's representative on the Committee had not attended any meetings' as a protest against the Society's policy on beer halls.

[35] 'Native Urban Areas – Housing', S.482/163/1, National Archives, Harare. This pattern contrasted sharply with that in Salisbury where only about 500 workers were on private locations or were squatters. The other 20,004 were housed by their employers.

– and the Stanley Hall – existed for musical or dramatic performance.

Over the next few years, reports of Sipambaniso's activities as social organizer appeared in the African press. The *Bantu Mirror* reported on 26 June 1943 that he was organizing a 'Spitfire Dance', involving dancing and dressing competitions; on July 10 that he had been presented with a deckchair and tumblers by the Rhodesia Bantu Dancing Club; on July 17 that he had helped organize a 'sumptuous dinner' in Stanley Hall for delegates to the conference of the African Teachers' Association and to the annual meeting of the Bantu Congress. By this time he was being assisted by his wife. I regret that I have been unable, either from archival, press or oral sources, to discover anything substantial about Mrs Sipambaniso Khumalo. I do not even know her name. But it is clear that she was a sophisticated modern woman, a good hostess and singer. The *Bantu Mirror* recorded after the Stanley Hall dinner for the two Congresses that 'special thanks were due to Mrs A.S.B. Manyoba for making the lavish entertainment the success it was in spite of difficulties in getting out cutlery, cooking the food and serving it so well with a very small staff'.[36] Sipambaniso and his wife were the foremost couple in Bulawayo African society. They acted as host and hostess at key social occasions. On 14 August 1943, for instance, the *Mirror* reported the wedding of the year, when the taxi-cab owner and band leader, Patrick Makoni – yet another upwardly mobile Manyika – married a Coloured bride. 'The master and mistress of ceremonies were Mr and Mrs Manyoba, whose friendship for the married couple was publicly displayed ... They worked very hard.' It was inevitable that when Chief Moremi of Ngamiland visited Bulawayo in the week before Christmas 1943 he would stay with the 'Mr and Mrs A.S.B. Manyoba Khumalo at no. 29, 2nd street, African Township'.[37]

And it was at this time of hectic social activity that Simpabaniso made his contribution to township music. On 24 April 1943 the *Bantu Mirror* carried a story by 'The Eye in Music'. It declared that 'music has been known as poor in Bulawayo, but this will be untrue and a wrong conception of the real thing'. Sipambaniso Manyoba had given a concert with his new group 'The Bantu Sweet Melodians'; he proved 'a very able and keen conductor' and 'as we have seen this show we believe music is gradually paving its way into perfection'. The choir wore uniforms of 'green and red satins'; they sang a spiritual, 'You sinners break everything'; two men 'gave a fine show in tap-dancing'. It was a 'blissful evening'. In June 1943 Sipambaniso and his wife attended the wedding of his friend, the Manyika Welfare Officer, William Makubalo, at which 'fine selections were rendered by the Bantu Sweet Melodians of Mr Arthur Sipambaniso Manyoba'. The Black and White Havana Band played – 'jollification and pompous festivity were at their height when the band played *tshaba-tshaba*. An air of sanguine serenity pervaded.'[38] Mrs Sipambaniso was capable herself of taking the choir to social occasions. In April 1943, for instance, a member of the Melodians, B.B.F. Sibanda, celebrated the birthday of his daughter at his 'village in Mpopoma'. He invited the group to perform, but Sipambaniso was unable to come 'due to pressure of work'. His wife brought the choir and it was 'up to standard'.[39] On 25 September 1945 the *Mirror*

---

[36] *Bantu Mirror*, 17 July 1943.
[37] *Bantu Mirror*, 1 January 1944.
[38] *Bantu Mirror*, 5 June 1943. Other reports in 1943 reveal the musical atmosphere in which Sipambaniso was operating. On 15 May the *Mirror* recorded a competition in Makokoba between school choirs from Hope Fountain, Tegwani, Tjolotjo and Cyrene missions. 'The Hall was packed out.' Another report on the same day recorded a visit to Inyati Mission where Charles Greeley Tsiga's Blue Comedians sang a spiritual, 'Wide River', and other songs. Max Mhlanga's Royal Glee Entertainers also performed.
[39] *Bantu Mirror*, 24 April 1943.

reported that at a social reception for Miss Flora Mutasa, 'Mrs Makabulo, Mrs Man-yoba and Miss Mutasa gave greatly appreciated musical selections'.

Sipambaniso as Public Spokesman

His role as Welfare Officer gave Sipambaniso a public platform. Stakesby-Lewis erected loudspeakers at various points in Makokoba so that news of the war could be broadcast. Our oral informants recall Sipambaniso broadcasting over these. And on 15 May 1944 fifteen thousand Africans packed Stanley Hall and Square to greet the new Governor, Tait. African chiefs sat on the platform, Donald Macintyre chaired, and Sipambaniso read an address of behalf of the Location Advisory Board. This drew the new Governor's attention to low wages, and to the need for representation in parliament, for further education, for more clinics, and for aid to African ex-servicemen.[40]

This meeting marked the climax of Sipambaniso's career as an officially sponsored public spokesman. But at the end of the war he began to take initiatives outside the structures of the Bulawayo welfare system. One of these was to modernize and articulate Ndebele identity. The other was to stimulate African worker consciousness and organization.

Entumbane & the Distinguished Dead

One of the many things that Makubalo and Khumalo discussed intently was how to commemorate both Manyika and Ndebele tradition, not in rivalry but in collaboration. They decided that distinguished Africans, who had 'deserved well of their country', should be honoured by interment at special sites, ethnic heroes' acres. The model, of course, was Cecil Rhodes. They knew that every year white missionaries took part in an annual service at Rhodes's statue in Main Street in the centre of Bulawayo. Bishops and moderators led pilgrimages to Rhodes's grave in the Matopos. White ex-service organizations, like the Memorable Order of Tin Hats, planned a post-war memorial to the war dead there.[41]

When Africans venerated their ancestors they were accused of ignorant heathenism. As Joshua Nkomo wrote after his visit to London in 1953:

> I began to think about Christianity and power. At home, becoming a Christian meant giving up our own old ways to follow white clergymen and a white Christ. Our religion, in which we approached God through our ancestors, and the history of our people, was said to be primitive and backward. But here in England the ancestral tombs in the churches signified the continuity of the nation.[42]

When Nkomo returned to Bulawayo in 1953 he spoke to African audiences about

---

[40] *Bantu Mirror*, 2 June 1944.
[41] For discussion and photographs of such pilgrimages see T.O. Ranger, *Voices From the Rocks*. In the end the MOTH were refused permission to erect a monument at Rhodes's grave but allowed to create the Shrine which is still in the National Park.
[42] Joshua Nkomo, *Nkomo: The Story of My Life*, p. 52.

Westminster Abbey and the need to honour the royal African dead.[43] But he had been anticipated by Makubalo and Sipambaniso.

It was Makubalo's turn first. In April 1943 the reigning Manyika paramount chief, Mutasa, died. As we have seen, there had been many Manyika in Bulawayo since the 1920s. Their education, smartness, modernity and arrogance had provoked the backlash of December 1929. But when the fires of 1929 died down – and people like James Mambala left Bulawayo – many qualified and influential Manyika remained, as ministers of religion, teachers, entrepreneurs. Sipambaniso had interacted with many of them. Now Makubalo set up a committee in Makokoba in May 1943 to collect funds for a memorial to the late Chief Mutasa. It was chaired by another Manyika public employee, Morris Makoni, who worked in the Location Superintendent's office. But Makubalo insisted on its pan-ethnic character. Memorializing the distinguished African dead, he said, was an enterprise which could unite all progressive Africans. At the first meeting of the committee, 'several speakers belonging to different tribes paid tribute in glowing terms'; £6 18s was contributed and more was to be raised from concerts and other events. The money would be used 'to buy and erect a stone to the memory of the late Chief Mutasa'.[44]

Makubalo's was very much a modernizing project. The issue of the *Bantu Mirror* which published his appeal added a note to it:

> The sacred and long-kept custom of the Maungwe and Manyika Tribes of keeping secret the burial places of their Chieftains may cease to be observed if the stone memorial to the late Chief Mutasa is finally erected where he lays [sic] with his predecessors among the rocks. It is considered rude to ask where the place is, and supernatural forces would drive mad or afflict with disease the unfortunate who dared to find out the place.

The *Mirror* thought it most unlikely that Manyika elders would agree to the plans of the young men in the towns. 'It is wondered whether ... the memorial will have to be erected somewhere else.' And in the end it was.[45]

Sipambaniso was rather better placed than his friend to engage in the politics and choreography of interment. Most people in Bulawayo, and certainly all the Ndebele, knew where the founding king, Mzilikazi, was buried, in his cave at Entumbane in the eastern Matopos. By the late 1940s it was possible to organize pilgrimages there without giving mortal offence to the elders.

As C.S. Hlabangana, President of the Matabele Home Society, told the pilgrims at Mzilikazi's grave on 16 December 1945:

> Thirty years ago the Matabelele people spoke of Ntumbane in hushed tones, in whispers ... because the Matabele [feared] to display and advertise their deeper feelings [but now] both races have confidence in each other.[46]

---

[43] T.O. Ranger, 'Joshua Nkomo: Nationalist and Cultural Nationalist', lecture, Bulawayo, April 1999.

[44] For the interaction of the Mutasa chiefs and young Manyika urban intellectuals, see Fidelis Duri, 'The Role and Status of Mutasa Traditional Rulers during the Colonial Era, 1898–1979', MA thesis, University of Zimbabwe, March 1999. The chief Makubalo wanted to commemorate, Kadzima Chimukoko Mutasa, had been a patron of the cultural nationalist Manyika Association in the late 1930s, seeking to raise funds in his chieftancy area to support the activities of the Association in the towns of southern Africa.

[45] *Bantu Mirror*, 22 May 1943.

[46] T.O. Ranger, *Voices From the Rocks*, p. 123, citing 'Pilgrimage to Entumbane', 16 December 1945, S. 2584/4251, National Archives, Harare.

142

Moreover, unlike Makubalo, Sipambaniso was accepted as a member of the royal clan; he had played with Lobengula's sons (and Hlabangana) in the Lions/Highlanders football team, and had successfully raised funds for a memorial to Rhodes Lobengula as long ago as 1937. And *his* cultural nationalist association was older and – in Matabeleland – much more influential than Makubalo's Manyika Association.[47] In the late 1940s Sipambaniso was Organising Secretary of the Matabele Home Society, a body which had aspirations for the restoration of the Ndebele paramountcy and which sought to protect Ndebele land in the Matabeleland rural areas. But most of the 400 members recorded by Sipambaniso's ex-colleagues in the CID in July 1947 were urban men, and the CID reported that 'the Society is as much concerned as others with the economic advancement of its members'.[48] A CID report on an MHS meeting on 25 September 1947 reported that it discussed evictions of Ndebele populations from white-owned land and also issues of skilled African urban employment. 'Here are the elements of orthodox trade unionism', it commented.[49]

As we shall see, at this time Sipambaniso was himself very much concerned with 'the elements of orthodox trade unionism'. But he was also a determined and imaginative cultural nationalist, a striking speaker and an imaginative choreographer. He led the Matabele Home Society into a series of attempts to have Entumbane recognized as the place where not only Ndebele royals but all distinguished Ndebele men should be interred.[50] A year after Makubalo's appeal for a monument to Chief Mutasa, Sipambaniso got the opportunity to outdo his friend. In June 1944 Lobengula's son, Nguboyenja, died at his home at the old 'Loot Kraal' on the Commonage, where he had been leading a withdrawn and silent life since 1928. Nguboyenja had been the most highly educated of all the Ndebele but his illness had cut him off from African society and politics in Bulawayo.[51] Now his death enabled Sipambaniso to use him as a symbol of both modernity and tradition.

Nguboyenja's carer, Manja Mpondo Khumalo, combined with Sipambaniso to 'request the Native Department, which bore the funeral expenses, to agree that Chief Nguboyenja be buried at Entumbane'. In a long report entitled 'Unspeaking Mandebele Prince Honoured' the *Bantu Mirror* of 24 June 1944 described the elaborate ceremonials. Nguboyenja was interred 'at the foot of the hill where his grandfather Mzilikazi was buried on Wednesday afternoon, June 21 … As the clock struck 1.30 pm upwards of 600 Africans were drawn up along Main Street outside Crocker Brothers Funeral

[47] For the earlier history of the Matabele Home Society see T.O. Ranger, *The African Voice in Southern Rhodesia, 1898–1930*, Chapter 8.

[48] CID Report on African Organisations in Bulawayo, July 1947, ZBZ 1/2/1, volume 1, National Archives, Harare. The 400-strong membership of the MHS did not make it insignificant among Bulawayo's African organizations. In 1947 the CID thought that Benjamin Burombo's Voice Association, which played a prominent role in the 1948 strike, had only 200 members. The largest association in July 1947 was the 'African Employees Trade Union', soon to become the Federation of Bulawayo African Trade Unions, in which Sipambaniso played so important a part, with 1,200 members.

[49] CID Memorandum 8, 1 October 1947.

[50] Gender was the main issue on which Sipambaniso's modernizing efforts stumbled. In January 1946 one of Lobengula's queens, Moho, who had lived since 1893 in Makokoba, died. Sipambaniso and the Matabele Home Society asked that she be buried at Entumbane, but the Provincial Native Commissioner ruled that to bury a wife near a royal grave was counter to custom. *Bantu Mirror*, 2 February 1946.

[51] Sipambaniso's own account of Nguboyenja's life, in his address at the funeral, described how the prince had been educated at Zonnebloem College, passed his Matric there, and then went to England to begin studying medicine. He fell ill and returned to Cape Town. In 1928 Manja Mpondo and Gula Bozongwana were sent to Cape Town to bring him back home. He was given 'use of a house on the commonage near Loots Kraal' where he was cared for by Manja. *Bantu Mirror*, 24 June 1944.

Parlour to pay their last respects ... Eight buses and four half-ton vanettes formed the funeral procession out of Bulawayo.' The funeral ceremonies were a splendid combination of modernity and tradition. The Anglican rites were performed by Reverend R.H. Clarke, assisted by Reverend Peter Sekgome and Mr Oliver Somkence, all of St Columba's Mission, where Sipambaniso's father worshipped and where he had himself been to school. 'A Bulawayo Pathfinder [African Scout] patrol formed up at the foot of the grave formed a guard of honour.' 'As the coffin was lowered into the grave, three Matabele queens, Moho, Fungo and Cebili, knelt down sobbing quietly, and Sidojiwe, the only surviving son of Lobengula, stood at the head of the grave holding an assegai with head pointing down.' The Ndebele praise-singer, Gingilitshi Hlabgangana, 'repeated the attributes of the Mandebele Kings with a controlled but passionate voice' as the grave was being filled. Even nature collaborated with Sipambaniso. 'Rain clouds brought showers from the south. Rainbows, the bigger of which rose from the immediate vicinity of Mzilikazi's grave, and the smaller one from that of Nguboyenja, were the cause of comment.'

A galaxy of prominent Africans attended. Sipambaniso's old teacher, Mazwi, was there; his father was a pall-bearer, along with three chiefs. Executive members of the Matabele Home Society played prominent roles. His friend Makubalo came to see his triumph. An old colleague from the CID, Sergeant T. Mateko was present. There were leaders of African churches, though naturally only 'Ethiopian' ones – no Apostolics or Zionists. But it was Sipambaniso himself, among all these distinguished Africans, who gave the address 'on behalf of the Khumalo clan'. The still young man, ex-policeman, football star, choir leader and socialite, proclaimed that:

> The piece of ground where the Chief is being buried is associated with sacred memories of the past, and we trust that the Government will set this area aside as a burial place for the descendants of Lobengula and for other Africans who deserve well of their country.

An editorial in the *Bantu Mirror* declared that this request would 'receive the whole-hearted approval of the African people', and that Entumbane should become what Rhodes's grave was to Europeans – 'a national shrine, a hallowed spot at which those Africans who deserve well of their country may be laid to rest ... with ceremony, due respect and honour'. In a shrewd comment on the values of white Bulawayo and the dominance of Donald Macintyre, the *Mirror* noted that Africans were only too aware that few things were named after distinguished Africans and that there was discontent when the Girls Hostel in Makokoba was named after Mrs Macintyre 'because she had never been connected with Africans in a public way, or shown any interest in their welfare'. The whole affair was a triumph for Sipambaniso, bringing together all his roles and constituencies.[52]

In the next few years, even though Sipambaniso was developing his last and most conspicuous public role as a trade unionist, he persisted with his interment politics. It looked as though they might be successful. In December 1944 the National Monuments Commission agreed to erect walls to protect Mzilikazi's tomb and wagon. A committee to raise funds for a King of the Matabele Memorial Fund was set up, including the chairman of the MHS and one of Sipambaniso's brothers.[53] A year later, in December 1945, the MHS held a chiefs' conference in Bulawayo, followed

52 *Bantu Mirror*, 24 June 1944.
53 *Bantu Mirror*, 30 December 1944.

by a pilgrimage to Entumbane. The chiefs complained that they still had to enforce the conscript labour regulations even though the war had ended. 'The position is so bad', said one, 'that I do not go out after dark without an escort because of the feeling created by my trying to carry out the instructions of the Government in forcing my subjects to go to conscripted labour farms.' The conference determined that the system was 'simple slavery'.[54]

The pilgrimage to Entumbane on Sunday 16 December 1945, on the other hand, was a great statement of the continuing prestige of modernized Ndebele tradition. This time the MHS President, C.S. Hlabangana, made the main speech – which was carried in full in the *Bulawayo Chronicle* of 17 December. Hlabangana drew a direct comparison between 'two champions of freedom' for whom 'the Matopos has provided a resting place':

> C.J. Rhodes, who believed that the greatest amount of freedom was possible only under the British rule, and King Mzilikazi who sought that freedom which was denied him under the rule of Chaka … We settled [here] to be free.

But Sipambaniso also spoke. Looking out over the great concourse of pilgrims, which included hundreds of townspeople as well as chiefs, he admitted that 'this place is a sacred place … According to Native custom we should not be here, but we are here to do work which is very important.' That work was to rededicate themselves to the memory of the founder king. Sipambaniso quoted the words of Cecil Rhodes: 'in these hills is a great King and Founder of the Matabele Nation. This should be the burial place for heroes.' And at a moment when the African inhabitants of the Matopos, facing eviction, were claiming that Rhodes had given them the land, Sipambaniso proclaimed that 'we are aware that Rhodes bought land to be used by African chiefs'.[55]

The pilgrimage contained one of those symbolic moments, fusing royal tradition and the promises of modernity, at which Sipambaniso was so good. This one involved a sword which the missionary Moffat had given to Mzilikazi but which had long been in white possession. Now it was presented to chief Ntando Mhlatuzana by a Native Department official and given by him in turn to old Nyanda, the 103-year-old son of Mzilikazi. The ancient prince went out to Entumbane, 'communed with the spirits of the departed', sang an 'old war song', and placed the sword 'with the King's other possessions'.[56] In May 1946 Nyanda Mzilikazi himself died at Mtshabezi Mission. At his funeral on 18 May Sipambaniso gave the oration and it was announced that the MHS planned a memorial.[57]

By this time Sipambaniso was actively engaged in the Federation of Bulawayo African Trade Unions. In April 1948 he was at the centre of the Bulawayo general strike. But his commitment to the MHS, to Ndebele land rights and to memorialization did not falter. He took up the case of the Matopo National Park and at a special executive meeting of the MHS in Stanley Hall on 22 April 1948, attended by delegates from

---

[54] *Bantu Mirror*, 12 January 1947.

[55] Sipambaniso's speech is given in his own account, 'Pilgrimage to Ntumbane, King Mzilikazi's Grave, 16 December 1945', S.2584/4251. For the controversy over the promises of Rhodes and evictions from the Matopos see T.O. Ranger, *Voices From the Rocks*.

[56] *Bantu Mirror*, 5 January 1946. The *Mirror* has an excellent photograph of the sword. For Nyanda's role in Wenlock, south of the Matopos, see T.O. Ranger *Voices from the Rocks*, pp. 113-15.

[57] *Bantu Mirror*, 25 May 1946.

the Park, he gave a long history of the promises of Rhodes. The MHS executive decided that the case should be taken to court and that an Aid Fund should be set up in Bulawayo so that 'all Africans who have national love at heart' could contribute.[58] On 12 December 1948 Sipambaniso addressed a huge meeting in the Matopos which demanded a Commission of Inquiry into the National Park.[59]

But he was busy as ever with funeral orations. On 27 June 1948 old Chief Ndaniso, 'the only Chief living who attended Rhodes's meeting', died in Wenlock. Sipambaniso had earlier guided lawyers out among the rocks to take Ndaniso's testimony about the promises of Rhodes. Now he acted as master of ceremonies at the funeral. It was attended by the Chief's own *nqameni* people and by members and officers of the MHS from Bulawayo.[60] Almost the last mention of Sipambaniso in the *Bantu Mirror*, on 17 March 1951, returned to his favourite theme. At Queen Mafungo's burial he declared once again that 'the authorities should set aside a special burial ground for the Matabele royal family and other distinguished Matabele'.

These burials and pilgrimages had drawn Sipambaniso out of Bulawayo into southern Matabeleland and his interment politics had interacted there with issues of land, forced labour, chiefly authority and the nature of African Christianity. He did not have burials or pilgrimages to occupy him in northern Matabeleland. No one knew where Lobengula's grave was. But as we have seen, Sipambaniso was even better known and more influential among the chiefs of Lupane and the Shangani. In those areas in 1949 and 1950 the prestige of the Matabele Home Society and especially Sipambaniso was very high.[61] In June 1959 the chiefs of the Shangani Reserve rebelled against the existence of the Reserve Council saying 'they could see no need for it'. 'We have never seen the constitution of the Native Council', said the chiefs, 'but the Matabeleland Home Society had a constitution which is being taken to the High Court in Bulawayo and the Government will be forced to recognise the MHS as the "Voice of the People".'[62] The outraged Native Commissioner discovered that several of his chiefs were members of the MHS and that Sipambaniso had held several meetings in the Reserve to discuss land alienation, destocking, compulsory labour, the need for further education, etc. In November 1950 'a meeting of all Chiefs, Headmen and followers insisted that they did not want a Council. The majority are members of the MHS and they have asked that the Society be recognised as their medium of expression.'[63] The Native Commissioner was scornful. 'The MHS no more represent the bulk of the people than does the Queens Club or the Sons of England represent the majority of the people of Southern Rhodesia.'[64] But the support of the chiefs was nevertheless a remarkable achievement for the essentially urban Sipambaniso.

[58] *Bantu Mirror*, 8 May 1948. The paper's issue of 24 April 1948 had carried a statement by Sipambaniso about the 'despair' of African urban workers.
[59] Quarterly Intelligence Report, 12 March 1949, S.482/517; *Bantu Mirror*, 1 January 1949; *Chronicle*, 13 December 1948; T.O. Ranger *Voices from the Rocks*, p. 160.
[60] *Bantu Mirror*, 17 July 1948; T.O. Ranger *Voices from the Rocks*, p. 123.
[61] For the Matabele Home Society and the Shangani Reserve see Jocelyn Alexander, JoAnn MacGregor and Terence Ranger, *Violence and Memory*. James Currey, Oxford, 2000, p. 89.
[62] Quarterly Report, Nkayi, June 1949, S.1618.
[63] ANC Nkayi to NC Lupane, 28 November 1950, S.2797/1453.
[64] NC Lupane to PNC, 5 December 1950, ibid.

Sipambaniso as Trade Unionist

Sipambaniso was representative of black Bulawayo in the 1930s and 1940s precisely because he was atypical. But I am aware that in trying to illuminate the background to Yvonne Vera's Fumbatha, the clenched fist, I have so far not come very close to his own experience. Sipambaniso was, after all, the very opposite of an introspective man. As Yvonne portrays him, Fumbatha would have left very little impact in the archival, press or oral record on which I have to rely as a historian. It is the privilege of the novelist to be able to invent and embody the reticent 'ordinary' man. (It is also the privilege of the novelist to be able to invent and embody an aspiring young woman, while I have been unable to discover the personal name of Sipambaniso's wife, even though she *did* break through some of the barriers which so frustrated Phephelaphi.) But as Sipambaniso made contact with the workers of Bulawayo in the late 1940s, so he became closer to men like Fumbatha, the layer of bricks. The builders' union was, after all, one of the first to join the Federation of Bulawayo African Trade Unions of which Sipambaniso was the energizing force. And through the Federation men like Fumbatha *did* find their voice.

Yvonne writes of Fumbatha that 'for almost twenty years Fumbatha has done nothing but build, and through this contact, Bulawayo is a city he understands close-ly, which he has held, brick by brick in his palm ... He has built. When he is dead, his hands will remain everywhere'.[65] One of the builders' union representatives mar-shalled by Sipambaniso to give evidence to the Bulwayo Native Labour Board in June 1948 anticipated this image:

> The factories started from nothing in Bulawayo and had been built up entirely by African hands. Now they had 'So and So Ltd' written up over their doors. "The 'limited' are these hands", he declared, holding up his own hands. "Who caused the 'limited' to be written up over the works? We did. But because we ask for a little more money they come and tell you we can't work."[66]

In the context of the emergence of African unions in Bulawayo in the late 1940s, indeed, one can see that Fumbatha and Sipambaniso both stood on the same side of the great divide in Makokoba. Both were Ndebele long-term residents rather than short-term migrants. Sipambaniso had lived all his life there; Fumbatha, a man of about the same age, had 'done nothing but build' for almost 20 years. He had lived in Makokoba since the later 1920s. He was typical of the men represented by the Federa-tion of Bulawayo African Trade Unions. In September 1947 the Federation circulated a 'plea to all employers, including Government and Municipalities'. It condemned the sort of labour system endorsed by Macintyre:

> Too often we are regarded as a necessary menace, to be accepted temporarily as workers ... We feel that we must have a stable society. The Government and the Municipalities, nay, all Europeans, must accept the fact of a permanent urban African population ... Migrant labour lowers the level of our efficiency and, by interfering with the institution of the family, under-mines the moral integrity of our society. Equally depressing and unsettling is the demoralising sense of insecurity that the present system of migrant labour engenders. Civil responsibility is

---

[65] *Butterfly Burning*, p. 20.
[66] *Chronicle*, 23 June 1948. Sipambaniso had given evidence on the previous day.

impossible so long as we are made to feel strangers in urban areas ... In spite of the foregoing restrictions, some Africans have managed to remain in towns for long periods during which they have given loyal service to their masters [but] long loyal service is not sufficiently recognised and rewarded.

The Federation ended its plea with a demand for a minimum wage of 35 shillings a week for unskilled male workers, 25 shillings for women. But 'all skilled labourers – carpenters, builders, tailors, salesmen, fitters, upholsterers, teachers, social workers, orderlies, nurses, drivers, messengers' etc. should receive a minimum wage of £2 10s per week, with £1 7s 6d for women. This demand included Sipambaniso as a 'social worker' and would have included Fumbatha as a builder and, indeed, Phephelaphi as a nurse.[67]

It can be seen that the Federation of Bulawayo African Trade Unions was concerned mainly with the industrious long-term residents of Makokoba for whom Sipambaniso had always been a symbol and a spokesman.[68] But why and how did he come to move from athletic and social and cultural nationalist expressions of African urban culture to emerge as a trade union, and hence as a political, leader?

The reason that Sipambaniso took action was that the very future of the men and women he represented seemed imperilled in 1945. As the Federation's plea put it: 'Men who have remained in the same employment for five, ten or fifteen years are not exempt from economic depression ... [many] who master their work through continued employment remain in the same class in which they began, namely, unskilled labourers ... Most of us have received no cost of living allowances to enable us to meet the rising cost of living ... Through contact with western civilisation, we have wants and needs which can only be satisfied by possession of money ... Our economic, educational and religious relations with the rest of the world have at once increased our necessities.'[69]

Makokoba, which Sipambaniso had struggled so hard to police, modernize and improve had been transformed during the Second World War. In 1941 Bulawayo had 18,500 African workers; by 1945 it had 30,000 and by 1948 it had 60,000. The population of Makokoba itself had more than doubled, without any increase in welfare facilities. In 1941 thousands of Africans had lived as tenants or 'squatters' on the white-owned farms bordering the Commonage. By 1945 it had become obvious that this land was soon to be cleared of its black occupants. In Bulawayo itself Huggins's Native Urban Areas bill would mean that all Africans except those employed by the Railways or as domestic servants, would have to live in the special 'Native' area still to be proclaimed by the Bulawayo Municipality.[70] And yet the old Location, Makokoba, remained almost the only place for them to go. One of our informants, Edward Phikelila Mhlanga, remembered the still surviving Ndebele villages on white-owned land, in one of which he was born, in which until the late 1940s chiefs still lived and from

---

[67] Patrick Makoni, President of the Federation of Bulawayo African Workers, 'A Plea', 23 September 1947, CID reports, Memo 8/81, ZBZ 1/2/1, National Archives, Harare.

[68] Ian Phimister, drawing on V. Gregson's BA thesis on the leadership of the general strike, cites Sipambaniso's own testimony: 'The majority of people who join [the Federation] are people who have been in Bulawayo for a long time and are acquainted with the conditions. Migrants do join us but they are in the minority.' Phimister, *An Economic and Social History of Zimbabwe, 1890–1948*, 1988, p. 267.

[69] Makoni, 'A Plea'.

[70] The Mayor of Bulawayo, H.A. Holmes, announced in October 1947 that 'the Council was at present setting aside areas under the Land Apportionment Act', *Chronicle*, 16 October 1947.

which people cycled to Bulawayo to work. These villages retained a connection with pre-colonial times. One was 'a village called Esizindeni where there is now Cold Storage. It was Lobengula's place'. Their inhabitants also thought of themselves as people of the city. 'I am not a son of Makokoba', says Mhlanga. 'but a son of Bulawayo.' But from the late 1940s onwards 'the government overthrew all the existing villages. In this way Ndebeles were scattered to Wankie, Lupane etc., places which people could not reach by cycling'. If one wanted to be a son of Bulawayo one had to become a son of Makokoba.[71]

The push factor of eviction was exceeded by the pull factor of labour demand. During the war years Bulawayo industrialized rapidly and there was continuous demand for labour.[72] Between 1944 and 1948 the average annual rate of growth was estimated at 24.4 per cent, the building, furniture and joinery industries growing the most rapidly. Our informants recall the impersonality and servility of industrial relations. 'We used to be very much afraid of our white bosses', recalls Mhambi Ncube. 'Old Africans were expected to show some form of respect even to the young whites. Most of us at work were known through numbers. My number at work was 106.'[73] Makokoba residents still remember industrial dangers and disasters. Yvonne Vera finishes her introductory account of the children of Sidojiwe road in Makokoba in 1946 by describing industrial Bulawayo burning:

> The older children walk as far as the border which encloses the factory and touch the barbed wire fence. They place their fingers within the diamond mesh and gaze at the men working underneath the large tank which is raised from the ground. The men are under the tank.
>
> Then they vanish. They vanish in a cloud of violent and impeccable flame.
>
> Sidojiwe E2 sees the fire blaze the sky as the oil tank bursts at the factory site and the men working underneath are swallowed by the blistering flames ... the flames lick the sky like a liquid, a giant flower blossoming in the sky ... A solid flame.[74]

As industry grew, wrote the *Chronicle*, 'the City of Bulawayo finds itself in a period of rapid expansion and, caught on the wrong foot, is scarcely competent to keep pace with it'. Manufacturers themselves were in no hurry to assist. At least one industrialist quoted in the *Chronicle*, the recently arrived Dr V.E. Haas, 'an authority of native affairs in the Union', told the Chamber of Industries in October 1947 that he deplored 'unnecessary urgency' about native housing conditions. 'I'm not worried about natives sleeping in the open air', he said. 'They've done so since they came to this country and multiplied very nicely under such conditions.'[75]

Meanwhile the Bulawayo Muncipality had made little attempt to respond to the need for more accommodation. Its own Medical Officer of Health protested on 6 August 1947 that 'if the natives are to take a contented place in the system which we

---

71 Interview between Simon Mlotshwa and Edward Phikelila Mhlanga, Mjube, 23 January 2001. Another informant, Gile Ndlovu, told Mlotshwa how she was born 20 miles from Bulawayo in Siphongweni village and 'we usually walked coming to town and back home'.

72 Ian Phimister, 'Industrialization and Class Struggle, 1939–1948', Chapter 5, in *An Economic and Social History of Zimbabwe*; A.S. Mlambo, E.S. Pangeti and I. Phimister, *Zimbabwe: A History of Manufacturing*, University of Zimbabwe Publications, Harare, 2000.

73 Interview between Busani Mpofu and Mhambi Ncube, January 2000. Mhambi had worked in a textile mill.

74 *Butterfly Burning*, pp. 16-17.

75 *Chronicle*, 3 October and 13 October 1947. The President of the Chamber of Industries, C.M. Harries, replied, however, that 'we are giving more food, clothing and wages and getting results ... We feel the time is now opportune to give every facility we can to improve conditions of natives.'

have substituted for their tribal existence they must be allowed to live together with their wives and families ... but there are few signs that the responsible authorities feel the urgency of the matter ... new industries are springing up ... and an ever-changing and uncontrolled mixed native population continues to live and increase in an area which has no services for them.' He went so far as to suggest that Africans be allowed to build their own homes. But as he attended the Council meeting in 'its hall of sardonyx and chrysophase' and heard its deliberations, 'I saw that the line which separates the improbable from the impossible had been crossed and knew that it was only a dream.'[76]

A new location, Mzilikazi (whose name was perhaps a tribute to Sipambaniso's politics of interment and pilgrimage) had been begun adjacent to Makokoba; further out was the government village of Luveve. But Makokoba remained the receptacle for most people being shifted from nearby rural areas and most people were attracted to work in the new factories. The inhabitants of the township responded to the demands. 'No one living in Makokoba could ignore a friend or relative with nowhere to sleep and stay', says Maxwell Mhlanga. 'You know patriotism was very much at work there. As a result you could find some people sleeping outside the rooms.'[77] And this was indeed a period of gross overcrowding in Makokoba, its slum-like state reported in inquiry after inquiry. As prices soared, wages remained the same and there were regular food shortages, climaxing in the drought of 1947. Prostitution, illegal brewing and gangsterism grew beyond the power of any policeman or social worker to restrain.

Our oral informants recall the terrible living conditions vividly:

You could find people crowded as if they were goats in a kraal. You could find four male workers sharing a room. Worse still, some of them were married or could smuggle their girl friends into these very crowded rooms divided only by curtains inside. For us who came to stay with our sisters married to such workers we had an unforgettable experience. There was almost no secrecy in those rooms. That was terrible, I tell you.[78]

Another young female migrant ran away from home to Makokoba when she was 14 and already pregnant. Her married sister took her in:

Living conditions were pathetic. Just imagine a situation where one has to sleep under the bed of married people. Those other males who shared the room with sister's husband could sometimes also bring in their wives or girlfriends and I had a terrible experience there.

She gave birth to her child in this room.[79] Another female informant added detail. 'Beds were made of grass, so some slept under a bed and they would remove the grass from their heads every morning. We slept with our clothes on.'[80] 'The bedbugs did what they know best in these rooms', says Clever Mpofu, 'feeding and feasting on us. Sometimes you would prefer sleeping outside the room to run away from these very

---

[76] Annual Report of the Medical Officer of Health, 6 August 1947. This was Dr A.H. Shennan, who died soon after. His successor, E.F. Watson, returned to the issue in his report of 11 August 1948. 'A large and illegal population is daily increasing in number, under highly insanitary and unhygienic conditions.' On 10 August 1949 he reported 'conditions of well-nigh indescribable squalor'.

[77] Interview between Busani Mpofu and Maxwell Mhlanga, Makokoba, 16 June 2000.

[78] Interview between Busani Mpofu and Mrs N. Ndlovu, Nguboyenja, 16 June 2000. This informant worked 'for some factories', one making plywood, another sweets, at a wage of £1 a month.

[79] Interview between Busani Mpofu and Mrs S. Nkomo, Mzilikazi, 19 June 2000.

[80] Interview between Simon Mlotshwa and Gogo Mamathe, Makokoba, 18 December 2000.

determined bugs which really gave us a torrid time.'[81] Everywhere smelled – 'sanitation was terrible. There were literally no toilets':

> Makokoba was dirty. Human waste was a common sight in the untarred, dusty streets. People used buckets in their houses which were carried away by people who did not wish to be seen. They took it around 12 a.m. If they met someone during the operation they would throw some waste on him for they feared identification.[82]

In these filthy and pullulating conditions the efforts being made by the social workers to encourage good housekeeping and to award prizes for tidy township bedrooms were in vain. So were efforts to outlaw 'illegal' drinking and to control prostitution. Informants remember with much amusement the tricks used to frustrate police searching for *skokiyana* hooch:

> People would be arrested for brewing *skokiyana* … At Epampurekari if they saw a police car approaching … they would rush and bury their *skokiyana* underground and pretend to be selling chickens. People had learnt techniques of survival in that environment. I remember the party I attended where people buried their *skokiyana* underground. When the police came they started singing church songs declaring that they were praying.[83]

Others took more radical measures – 'they would bury *skokiyana* in the ground and defecate on top'.[84]

Prostitution became more open. One of our informants, who worked at Macintyre's Osborn Bakery, shared a room in Makokoba with three other men, none of them married. They smuggled in prostitutes. 'I also did that you know, I couldn't afford to ignore that system.' They paid differential rates for prostitutes 'previously impregnated' and with children, who got 1s 6d; and for 'night ladies' without a child, *intombi esagewele*, who got 2s 6d per night. 'I will never forget that life. At night I had to put my bicycle on top of the roof because there was no space in the room.'[85]

Plainly Sipambaniso needed to try to save Makokoba from total degeneration. More housing was needed, as were vastly improved services, sewerage and electrification. Above all, higher wages were needed at a rate which would allow a married man to support his wife and family in town. Government cost of living statistics had shown the rate of inflation. From football and choirs and cultural nationalism, Sipambaniso needed to turn to the basics. But how was he to make that transition?

Vera provides a hint in her only reference in *Butterfly Burning* to organized African action. She writes of the return of African soldiers from the Second World War – men with whom, as we shall see, Sipambaniso was particularly concerned in the last months of his life:

> From 1945 they could be seen walking down any road in Makokoba, glazed and perplexed by the events of the war. Not at all proper citizens of Southern Rhodesia. With no power to choose

---

[81] Interview between Busani Mpofu and Clever Mpofu, Nguboyenja, 25 July 2000.
[82] Interview between Simon Mlotshwa and Mr Dube, Makokoba, 8 January 2001.
[83] Interview between Hloniphani Ndlovu and MaNdlela, Entumbane, 14 June 2000.
[84] Interview between Simon Mlotshwa and Mr Ndlovu, Makokoba, 25 January 2001.
[85] Interview between Busani Mpofu and Kembo Ncube, Thorngrove, 18 July 2000. For a brilliant and disturbing study of rape and prostitution in Bulawayo between 1946 and 1956 see Koni Benson and Joyce Chadya, '*Ujubinya*: Gender and Sexual Violence in Bulawayo, Colonial Zimbabwe, 1946–1956', *Journal of Southern African Studies*, 31, 3, September 2005.

151

who would govern they witness the first Railway Strike wondering how swiftly to trust their own stirring of pride; better wages, and perhaps, the possibility of reversal ... Not only did they wonder, they made suitable plans of their own which they pursued with ambition. Through this ... they strove to be heard. After all, they were a majority. If each man was listened to, each man could be heard. The question they needed answered was much more urgent and vexed, not about numbers, that was simple, but about being human.[86]

And it was indeed the railway strike of late October 1945 which brought Sipambaniso and many others into action.[87] Grey Bango, who became President of the Federation of Bulawayo African Trade Unions, with Sipambaniso as General Secretary, remembered in January 2002:

> When we began to form the trade union that's when he worked very hard ... Most specifically Sipambaniso emerged when there was a General Railway Strike which was led by Mr Sigeca. During this strike Sipambaniso came in with another gentleman, that is Jasper Savanhu ... They more or less had a lot of friends in the police. These people tried to get favours from their friends who were in the police force and told them they wanted to organize meetings, so that we could meet and try to solve our problems as a trade union for those who were working in the railways ... Then when we saw that the railway people had organized themselves and staged a strike we also decided to organize ourselves and hold meetings prior to staging a strike. And then a meeting was held, a constitution was drawn up, and we proposed to form a Federation of Bulawayo Workers Unions, including all industries and Bulawayo workers together. Having done that, those who were in the engineering industries were grouped together, those in the commercial sector on their own, those in the carpentry sector on their own, those in the grinding/milling industries on their own, the drivers on their own, but forming that federation. Having done that a strike was planned that was purely motivated by the fact that the railways had organized themselves and were earning better wages ... Sipambaniso was a great man, brave and very daring .... He contributed quite a lot to the development of the Bulawayo townships. I must say he was very vocal.[88]

It was Jasper Savanhu who led Sipambaniso into trade unionism. After completing his Standard 7 Savanhu had been trained as a carpenter and industrial instructor at Domboshawa. He went to Bulawayo, where 'he made his mark in all circles, social and otherwise'. He made money as a successful carpenter but was 'impatient and hot-headed', testing the colour bar whenever he could. He 'refused point blank to join the African Welfare Society', arguing that 'Africans wanted greater things than football grounds and other social amenities.' He was the author of a cogent pamphlet, *The Native Problem in Southern Rhodesia*, which focused on the urban crisis. Perhaps oddly, he became editor of the *Bantu Mirror*, which became much bolder under him – 'the editorials he wrote were full of fire'. The paper's management censored him and he resigned.[89] Savanhu knew Sipambaniso well and saw in him leadership potential beyond the limitations of the Welfare era.

By mid-1945 Savanhu was looking for an opportunity to act. He was overjoyed when on 29 June 1945 Reverend Thompson Samkange, President of Congress, wrote

---

[86] *Butterfly Burning*, p. 77.
[87] I do not propose to give an account of the railway strike here. It has been very thoroughly narrated and analyzed in two excellent articles by Ken Vickery in the *Journal of Southern African Studies*, 24, 3, September 1898 and 25, 1, March 1999.
[88] Interview between Lynette Nyathi and Grey Bango, January 2001. Bango said that he used to hold a great deal of written material about the Federation but that during his detention in Gonakudzwinga he ordered that all his 'books' be destroyed.
[89] *Parade*, November 1956.

to ask him to take office as its Acting Secretary. Writing from Mzilikazi Village on 3 July Savanhu accepted. 'I have been waiting for such an opportunity to do my bit to help our people in the dire conflict for the Four Freedoms of the World.' He asked that his pamphlet on urban policy be placed on the agenda for Congress's annual conference in September. He became Secretary on 9 July 1945 and at the September Congress in Gwelo:

> the suggested native urban policy of the Government was criticised from all sides, some describing it as a further step to restrict the Africans' economic expansion, freedom of movement and as tending to introduce semi-slavery conditions through the suggested Native Labour Bureaux.

A committee was set up to draft a Congress policy on the basis of Savanhu's pamphlet.[90] Savanhu drew Sipambaniso into Congress.

A month later the railway strike took place. Savanhu and Sipambaniso visited the strike committee to advise it during the negotiations and continued to work with it in the difficult months after the strike. They were inspired by what they saw. As a CID retrospective on labour unrest recorded in June 1948, before the railway strike there had been 'tribal committees, associations and organisations but certainly not one collective body unanimous in opinion'. The Railway African Employees Association had no more than 200 members, held no regular meetings and had no constitution. But 'during the course of the strike spokesmen were born overnight'.[91]

Inspired by this new labour militancy, Savanhu and Sipambaniso launched a new movement in early November 1945 and on 13 November 1945 'a well represented' general meeting of African trade unions in Bulawayo agreed to come together in a federation, initially named the Bulawayo African Workers Trade Union. Savanhu was elected President of the new body; Sipambaniso became its Secretary. It was at this meeting that Savanhu made his now famous speech:

> The Railway strike had proved that Africans have been born. The old African of tribalism and selfishness has died away … We have found ourselves faced by a ruthless foe – exploitation and legalised oppression by the white man for his and his children's luxury. The days when a white man could exploit us at will are gone and gone forever. The employer who ill treats one of the least of African workers does it to all of us. We must not fail in our duty to suffer with him. [Cheers] We have called you here tonight not only to explain the strike situation and to appeal for funds but also to start what might be called the AFRICAN TRADE UNION OF BULAWAYO. These ATUs will take the place of the ICU which failed because we were then less informed.[92]

Savanhu had given notice to Thompson Samkange as early as 1 November 1945 that 'as a result of the Railway Strike, Trade Unions of Africans are being started in Bulawayo under the supervision of the Federation of African Trade Unions of Bulawayo. I have been elected President of this organisation and I should like to know whether it is not a wise thing for the Southern Rhodesian Bantu Congress to form or spon-

---

[90] T.D. Samkange to J. Savanhu, 29 June 1945; J. Savanhu to T.D. Samkange, 3 July 1945; Annual Report of the Southern Rhodesian Bantu Congress, 1944–1945, file 'Congress', the Samkange Papers, The Castle, Harare.

[91] Report by Officer Commanding, CID, June 1948, enclosed in Memo 21, 11 June 1948, ZBZ 1/2/1, vol. 2.

[92] This version of Savanhu's speech appears in Timothy Scarnecchia, *The Urban Roots of Democracy and Political Violence in Zimbabwe*, University of Rochester Press, Rochester, NY, 2008, pp. 30-1. Scarnecchia explains that the *Chronicle* refused to publish the speech. Another version, ending with an assurance that workers could trust Congress, appeared in the *Bantu Mirror* on 2 March 1946.

sor similar organisations in other towns'.[93] And indeed in January 1946 Sipambaniso – who had been busy in December with Congress and the Matabele Home Society pilgrimage to Entumbane as well as with the Federation – invited workers' associations in Salisbury to attend an inaugural meeting of a new workers' organization to be addressed by Savanhu. This took place on 10 February but attracted only 60 workers in stark contrast to the 5,000 who had attended the 13 November meeting in Bulawayo. Henceforth the Federation focused on Bulawayo.[94]

Tim Scarnecchia has recently shown that the main Salisbury political and trade union activist, Charles Mzingeli, who took advantage of the February Salisbury meeting to launch his Reformed ICU,[95] was privately denouncing Savanhu to officials of Macintyre's Southern Rhodesian Labour Party. Savanhu, he said, represented both Congress and the Bulawayo Native Welfare Society and his rhetoric was 'more deserving of suspicion than otherwise'.[96] He was right about Congress but wrong about the Native Welfare Society. Indeed the late 1940s saw a breach between Bulawayo's African leaders and Percy Ibbotson, the iconic figurehead of the Welfare Society. Sipambaniso, who had been the very epitome of the Welfare era, now moved in what Ibbotson thought to be 'communistic' directions.

In September 1945 – the same month in which Congress was endorsing Savanhu's criticism of government urban policy – Thompson Samkange had declared that 'the refusal of the Native Welfare Federation to admit Africans on the Federation is a revelation of the attitude of the white skins in the Colony. People we looked on as our friends and believed that they were going to create good race relations, but we see how they have come out in their true colours.'[97] A year later Percy Ibbotson attended the first meeting of the Native Labour Advisory Board. The Board's proceedings began by noting that the Federation of Bulawayo African Trade Unions, through Sipambaniso, had approached the Bulawayo City Council for recognition. 'Officials of the Native Department had to say they knew the Federation existed but they knew very little else about it.' Ibbotson, though, certainly did know about the Federation and he did not like what he knew. Citing a British Home Office circular on 'Labour Supervision in the Colonial Empire', he endorsed its view 'of the irresponsible and often political character of some of the newly formed trade unions, the almost complete ignorance which prevails of the true aims, functions and responsibilities of trade unions, and the lack of competent leaders':

> Here there is an attempt on the part of Africans to organize. What we have to decide – and it is a fundamental principle – is whether we are going to encourage that organization and attempt to develop and guide it, or whether we are going to do what I possibly feel in the present circumstances is the most warranted – to attempt to slow down the process. I am speaking very frankly. There are some of us who are directly concerned with African welfare but who view with some concern this attempt to force this organization among the Africans.

Mzingeli – 'what work does he do?' – was primarily a politician. The Bulawayo leaders had 'some education' but 'the rank and file is to some extent illiterate and in the hands of these tub-thumpers'. Rather than recognizing African trade unions it would be

---

[93]   J. Savanhu to T. Samkange, 1 November 1945, file 'Congress', Samkange papers.
[94]   Report by OC, CID, June 1948.
[95]   Scarnecchia, pp. 32-3, describes the 10 February meeting in detail. Savanhu spoke in English but translated Mzingeli's own speech from English into Shona.
[96]   Scarnecchia, p. 31.
[97]   Thompson Samkange to Gideon Mhlanga, 5 September 1945, file 'Congress', Samkange papers.

better to set up Wage Boards which would make 'a proper examination of the African's position'. Ibbotson read out without attribution the closing passages of Savanhu's speech of 13 November 1945, agreed that 'you cannot repress or kill' African workers' bodies, but urged that their representations be channelled into 'specially selected boards'. When one of the other members, A.T. North, said that 'it is rather amazing to me that there has not been a general strike throughout the country', Ibbotson agreed that 'there is terrific unrest throughout the country'. Nevertheless, he insisted that any 'sharp' rise in pay would be disastrous and would 'go through the country like veld fire'; that 'one thing will have to be guarded against, that is the infiltration of skilled Native artisans in an industry like the building industry'; and that if wages went up 'too suddenly you are increasing the amount available for gambling, beer and women'.[98]

By November 1946, when he described the leaders of the Federation as 'tub-thumpers', Ibbotson's ire was mainly directed at Sipambaniso, whom he had known very well in the past, both in the Bulawayo Native Welfare Society and in his role at Stanley Hall. At the end of April 1946 Savanhu was 'in hospital critically ill'. He could no longer act as Secretary of Congress but his radical influence there continued. In May 1946 Congress cabled the British Government demanding that they disallow Huggins's Native (Urban Areas) Accommodation and Registration Act.[99] In the Federation Savanhu's leadership was effectively replaced by Sipambaniso as General Secretary. And throughout 1946 Sipambaniso was a very busy tub-thumper indeed.

He represented Bulawayo African milling employees when they threatened to strike early in 1946. In May 1946 'came the first rumblings of dissatisfaction among Bulawayo Municipal African employees who formed their own union and in June 1946 affiliated with the Federation'. Sipambaniso became their foremost adviser and advocate. He also took up the grievances of dairy roundsmen and chemist employees. In June 1946 there were strikes at Bulawayo brick works, textile factories and general construction companies (in which Fumbatha might have been involved).[100] By August 1946 Sipambaniso was able to claim that the Federation now included bakery employees (presumably including Macintyre's), garage employees, store workers, drivers, messengers, foundry workers, butchery workers and tailors, as well as the new Municipal Employees Association.[101]

But throughout 1946 Sipambaniso's main concern was with the aftermath of the railway strike. As Dr E.M.B. West, the Native Affairs director for the Railways, told the Native Labour Advisory Board on 20 November 1946:

> The Railway African employees generally were never satisfied with the awards of the Strike Commission, and over the last year it has been a very tricky business to prevent another strike … If such a thing happened again they would not be back to work in a week and you can visualise what would be the effect of a paralysis of the transport system of this country.

In order to avoid this the Railway authorities tried hard to marginalize the Rhodesia Railways African Employees Association by forming compound committees with a

98 Minutes of the first meeting of the Native Labour Advisory Board, 20 and 21 November 1946, S.2824/5/1, National Archives, Harare.
99 Dhliwayo to T.D. Samkange, 12 May 1946. On 24 May 1946 P.M. Ndebele wrote to Thompson Samkange urging him to 'oppose, cause to fail and make of no effect the notorious Natives Registration and Accommodation Bill'. The executive's cable was revealed in Samkange's presidential address on 6 July 1946. All in 'Congress', Samkange papers.
100 Report by Officer Commanding, CID, June 1948.
101 *Chronicle*, 2 August 1946.

mixture of 'tribal' and departmental representatives. These committees made monthly representations to the compound managers. It was Sipambaniso's task to support
and advise the RRAEA how they could maintain relevance in this situation.[102]

His answer turned out to be an appeal to the National Native Labour Board. The
creation of such a body had been recommended by the Tredgold Commission of
Inquiry into the railway strike. It was also recommended by the Native Labour Advisory Board in November 1946.[103] Parliament passed a Native Labour Boards Act in
August 1947.[104] The idea of a Board mediating after negotiations between workers and
employers had failed was consciously intended to avert strikes and to undercut trade
unions. A Board was appointed for the railways in September and the CID report
for October 1947 noted that railway workers were 'quietly' waiting for its award.
Meanwhile Sipambaniso and the Federation were preparing the case for a Board to
determine wage rates for all workers in Bulawayo. But in October 1947 the Boards
were savagely repudiated at a Congress meeting in Bulawayo attended by Benjamin
Burombo and Masotsha Ndlovu, though not by Sipambaniso:

> The National Labour Board was a Lewis gun, to be directed against the economic progress
> of Africans ... Africans should form themselves into one unified entity. If they did this, their
> influence would be similar to that of an atomic bomb.[105]

Henceforth, debate raged among African organizations in Bulawayo over whether to
prepare for a Board or a strike, with Sipambaniso consistently opting for the former
until his hand was forced in 1948.

Appearing before a Board was no soft option, costing a great deal of time and
money, in appointing lawyers and working with them to produce effective witnesses.
Nevertheless when the first National Labour Board, for the railways, was appointed in
September 1947 after 'threatened unrest by the Railway African employees', Sipam-

---

[102] West added that 'one is not committed to the recognition of any particular Association of Africans. If they
put their members on these committees, it is all right. If they don't, it is still alright.' Nevertheless, 'this
organisation has very definitely brought to our notice complaints which don't brook delay'. Joshua Nkomo,
who was appointed as chief social worker for the railways in early 1948 and who was elected President of the
African Railway Employees Association later in that year, writes in his autobiography that the AREA 'had
not managed to do much' since the 1945 strike. 'Its members and committee were all fairly simple working
people and they did not know how to run a union organisation'. *Nkomo: The Story of My Life*. p. 44. Before
Nkomo's appointment the union relied on guidance from the Federation and from Sipambaniso. The Federation's close links with the union continued after Nkomo became its paid General Secretary. There were
six delegates from the Federation at the annual congress of the Union on 25/26 October 1952. Rhodesia
Railways Employees Association, General Secretary's Report and Annual Congress proceedings, Register of
African Organisations, Bulawayo, file S.O.8, vol. 1, T Box 100, now held in the office of the Housing Department, Bulawayo Municipality.

[103] Report of the Native Labour Advisory Board, 14 January 1947, S.2824/5/1, National Archives, Harare. The
report was sent to government as a 'matter of extreme national urgency' and urging that there be no delay.
If it took as long as ten months to set up Boards 'it would be too late to prevent a very serious situation ...
Certain Africans were holding their hand in the expectation of some early action.'

[104] The Act, however, did not follow the recommendations of the Advisory Board which had wanted standing
regional boards which could deal 'speedily with suspected or existing unrest'. Instead it provided for the creation of a Labour Board only in an emergency, with 'a clumsy and slow' procedure. Commissioner of Native
Labour to Secretary, Native Affairs, 3 June 1947, S.2793/7, vol. 2.

[105] CID Memo 9, 30 October 1947, ZBZ 1/2/1, vol. 2. This was a moment when Congress as a whole was once
again reaching out to workers. Tennyson Hlabangana told Thompson Samkange on 18 July 1947 that he was
due to address the railway workers to urge them to affiliate with Congress, and on 1 September 1947 that the
railway workers were in favour of affiliation but were debating whether to do this through the Federation or
directly. 'Congress'; Samkange papers.

baniso believed that it was proving itself a success. In Bulawayo in October 1947 the RRAEA's lawyer, Shaknovis, was aggressive in his cross-examination of the General Manager of Rhodesia Railways, Sir Arthur Griffin. 'What could be more important than the pigsty conditions – plague conditions – in which your native employees are living in that No. 2 compound?' he asked. 'Our primary consideration is to keep the Railway running efficiently', replied Griffin. 'At the expense of human life and health?' asked Shaknovis.[106] The Association chairman, Simon Mayeza, gave evidence that he had ten children and he thought he should receive an allowance for each, and when one of the commissioners said that the railways would sack men like him if they had to support every dependant, responded: 'Surely the Government would not suggest that I should live out in the veld by myself like an old Kudu bull.'[107]

Meanwhile, the Municipal workers, whom Sipambaniso had worked hard to organize, began to revolt, bringing him into direct confrontation with Donald Macintyre, who was determined to keep Council wage bills down. In late October 1947 employees in the Municipal Compound refused the reduced meat rations provided for them. On 24 October their spokesmen went to the Acting Native Commissioner, Bulawayo, demanding:

> Payment in lieu of rations, increase in wages, recognition of marriages and provision of married quarters, or an allowance for such quarters, rations for wives or payment in lieu.

He told them he would report at once to the Council and urge a quick response.[108] At first there was an immediate reaction. A special committee of Council, of which Macintyre was a member, met worker representatives on 27 October and told them 'that as matters must be fully investigated it will take a little while before a final decision'.[109] Silence then fell for three months.

The recommendations of the Railway Board were published in January 1948 – the *Chronicle* reporting them under a banner headline: NEW DEAL FOR NATIVES STARTS NOW. In 'commendably plain and forceful language' the members of the Board condemned the railway compounds as 'a lasting disgrace to the Railway Administration and the Government of this country'; condemned the Railway's African Affairs Department for trying to replace the RRAEA with compound committees; recommended higher wages (though less than the £3 10s minimum claimed by the RRAEA), pensions as well as medical services. There was immediate consternation. On 5 January the Railways General Manager, Griffin, estimated that the Board's recommendations would add 50 per cent to the wage bill. Ibbotson, who had been one of the Board members, defended the award: 'Conditions towards the end of last year were more serious than people imagined and we were virtually sitting on the edge of a volcano. Discontent has been voiced by Africans steeped in Communism, while others have been more reasonable and have aroused the sympathy of those who have their welfare at heart.'[110] Municipalities showed no such sympathy. The Mayor of Bulawayo quickly declared that 'the Bulawayo City Council was not directly bound by the regulations, which referred to the railways specifically'. The Council would find

---

[106] *Chronicle*, 1 October 1947.
[107] *Chronicle*, 4 October 1947.
[108] Acting Native Commissioner, Bulawayo to Town Clerk, 25 October 1947, S.2793/5, National Archives, Harare.
[109] Town Clerk to Native Commissioner, 28 October 1947, ibid.
[110] *Chronicle*, 10 January 1948.

'a balance between the municipality, native employees and ratepayers'. It continued to do so very slowly.[111]

On 13 February 1948 the Town Clerk told the Acting Native Commissioner that a schedule was being drawn up of the various types of labour the Council employed – 'this means a very extensive report and a special meeting of the Council'. On the same day the Municipal Workers' Committee told the ANC that they could no longer tolerate the delay. They demanded an answer before their next meeting on 27 February. The ANC urged Council to meet this deadline. Since October, he wrote, 'I have had the unenviable task of maintaining a spirit of patience. I have brought this about by attending fortnightly meetings of the African Committee ... I feel that should the Council be unable to satisfy the request of the Committee by the 27th, your employees will ask for a Labour Board. There should be no need for this if the conditions of service of your employees be given priority over all other business of your Council.' And indeed the Council did come up with an offer within the deadline, offering an all-round wage increase of 10 per cent but making no promise of improved housing. On 2 March the African Municipal Workers Association rejected the offer. They demanded something close to the Railway settlement. They would wait until the Council meeting of 4 March and if they then did not receive an acceptable offer they would call for a Labour Board.[112]

Sipambaniso, who had been in close contact with the Municipal Workers throughout, had not in fact waited so long. On 11 February 1948 he wrote to the Commissioner of Labour, telling him that the Federation's executive had determined:

> to request the Minister of Natives Affairs to call upon the Matabeleland Native Board members to sit and hear evidence in connection with (a) the scale of wages (b) conditions of employment (c) holidays/annual leave (d) sick pay and sick leave, in various industries and the Municipality of Bulawayo. Last year we sent out circular letters to various employers in Bulawayo requesting them to consider the scale of wages. We have not had any reply. The cost of living in Bulawayo has gone up and the African employee cannot meet his way. We appeal to you, sir, to appoint the Board as early as you can.

On 25 February Sipambaniso addressed a Federation meeting in Stanley Square – it was 'extremely well organised and orderly'. He contrasted the new rates of railway pay with the wages of municipal employees, 'the worst paid of the lot'. He urged that money be collected towards a Labour Board hearing into wages and conditions in all Bulawayo industries: it had cost the rail workers £1,200. He had invited the Acting Native Commissioner and Ibbotson to explain Labour Board procedures to a meeting on 19 February.[113] Writing again on 28 February, Sipambaniso warned that there was 'intense dissatisfaction among African workers about the low wages and bad working conditions that they have to endure ... The matter is of extreme urgency ... It is becoming increasingly difficult to persuade the workers to wait for the Board to sit and investigate their conditions, so hopeless do they feel about their ability to make ends meet.'[114]

[111] *Chronicle*, 14 January 1947.
[112] Town Clerk to ANC, 13 February; ANC to Town Clerk, 16 February; Town Clerk to ANC, 24 February; ANC to Town Clerk, 2 March 1948, S.2793/5.
[113] CID memo 18, 25 February 1948. ZBZ 1/2/1, vol. 1.
[114] A.S.B. Manyoba, General Secretary, Federation of Bulawayo African Workers Unions, to Commission of Labour, Salisbury, 11 February and 28 February 1948, S.2793/5, 'Matabeleland Native Labour Board'. Sipambaniso specified in particular milling, baking, tailoring, engineering, brewing, Municipal workers, lorry drivers, garage workers and shop workers. 'Applications for others will come later.'

This was exactly the situation envisaged when the Native Labour Advisory Board has recommended that Labour Boards be set up. But amendments in parliament had required that a Board only be appointed if employers agreed that an emergency had arisen. So Sipambaniso was fobbed off. He was officially told that Boards could be convened for one industry or employer and not for a whole city. Workers could be represented by their own association and not by a Federation. The Commissioner of Native Labour, recommending this reply, realized that it would throw the emphasis again on the municipal dispute. 'Owing to the delay, I expect an application from the Municipal employees at any moment. I may say I warned the City Council of the position several months ago and if a Board is asked for the Council will have itself to blame.'[115]

During March the pace became hectic. The Bulawayo Municipality took offence at what they held to be bullying by the Acting Native Commissioner and impertinence by the workers. Only the Minister could decide on a Labour Board and the Council believed that it had a promise from government not to appoint one. Government officials were becoming increasingly desperate, fearing the outbreak of a general strike. On 5 March Moses Mapasa, Secretary of the Municipal African Employees Association, wrote to ask for the appointment of a Labour Board. The Commissioner for Native Labour recommended that there be no delay in appointing a Board. A strike had been narrowly averted on 4 March and there were rumours of one for 8 March. The situation was 'somewhat grave'. By now government was even more irritated by the Bulawayo Council than usual. 'I hope the Chief Native Commissioner will point out to the Council what a bad lead they are giving to all employers', wrote Huggins. 'I note that if this is not settled out of court, we shall have to set up a Board for every industry. I note that the City Council did not agree about wives. Now they have an Urban Area they will have to.'[116]

Sipambaniso intensified the pressure on the Council. The *Herald* on 20 March 1948 reported that the municipal workers were not prepared to wait for the 6 April round-table conference of Chambers of Commerce and Municipalities convened to reach a decision on wages. The Federation 'had obtained the services of a legal firm to represent' Municipal workers before a Board. It planned to ask for Boards for all other industries in Bulawayo.[117] The Commissioner for Native Labour on 30 March expressed his anger with the Municipality:

There is no doubt that the City Council committed a grave blunder in not meeting the reasonable demands of their employees submitted in October last year. The Council has put itself in a most difficult position and has consequently caused the Government considerable embarrassment. It is difficult to understand the attitude of some of the Councillors who show an extraordinary lack of vision and foresight in dealing with their African employees. I was astounded at their views. The Council was unanimous ... that Government should not appoint a Labour Board at any rate until after the meeting on the 6th. Certain Councillors went so far as to say that the threat of a strike amongst their employees should not be allowed to influence their attitude ... I warned the City Government that if the Government withheld a Board there was

[115] Commissioner of Native Labour to Secretary, Native Affairs, 16 February 1948, ibid.
[116] Town Clerk to ANC, 4 March 1948; Moses Mapasa to Commisioner of Labour, 5 March 1948; Commissioner for Native Labour to Secretary, Native Affairs, 8 March 1948; handwritten memorandum by Huggins on Secretary, Native Affairs to Secretary, Prime Minister, 13 March 1948, ibid.
[117] *Herald*, 20 March 1948. The *Chronicle* of the same day reported Sipambaniso as saying that he had warned the authorities that 'there is intense dissatisfaction' and threat of 'industrial unrest'. 'The Federation had approached employers for discussion about wages and working conditions but their letters had been ignored.'

every possibility of a strike, and that I feared the repercussions of such a movement would be felt in every industry in the Colony. The Council, however, has a parochial outlook and was more interested in domestic affairs.

He had met with the municipal workers and urged them to wait still further; he talked with Ibbotson and the CID. And he interviewed Sipambaniso, 'the power behind the scene', who assured him that 'a strike would result if a Board were not granted and that Africans in other industries would follow suit'. He came to the conclusion that 'a Board should be appointed at once'.[118]

There was further governmental delay, the acting Prime Minister saying that 'I would prefer not to make a decision in the absence of the PM.' But he would cable Huggins to say that a 'board will have to be appointed if stalling does not work'. It did not work. At last, on 5 April, the very eve of the Salisbury conference of Municipalities and Chambers of Commerce, Sipambaniso and the municipal workers were told that a Labour Board would be appointed. On 8 April the Secretary of the Matabeleland Native Labour Board asked the Bulawayo Town Clerk to provide full information on wages, rations, overtime, leave, pensions, uniform, accommodation, welfare, 'recognition of native employees' association', and the machinery for settlement of grievances. All this was required by 17 April because 'it is imperative to start hearing evidence on Wednesday, April 21st'.[119]

In fact the Municipal Labour Board never sat. By 21 April events had overtaken it. Up to this point I too have been treating Sipambaniso as 'the power behind the scene'. But he was very far from unchallenged, even in the heart of Makokoba. At the increasingly huge meetings held in Stanley Hall and Stanley Square, he was attacked by rival leaders and struggled to maintain control over the crowd.

Sipambaniso's great adversary was the Shona orator, Benjamin Burombo.[120] Burombo had founded the African Workers' Voice Association in 1947. He was a populist who appealed directly to the crowd rather than working with and through existing trade unions. Burombo had none of Sipambaniso's connections with Makokoba and he spoke not so much to its established residents as to people recently displaced from the countryside or drawn to the city by the new industrial demand for labour. He was a much more charismatic speaker than Sipambaniso and could arouse audiences to fervour. At meetings of the Voice or the Federation in late 1947 and early 1948 Burombo consistently attacked Sipambaniso. On 20 November 1947, for example, he condemned the Federation's restriction to long-time skilled workers – no union could be accepted by the Federation unless it had at least fifty members and a constitution. Appeals for action should rather be directed to 'all natives in Southern Rhodesia in any employment whatsoever' since, if all Africans united, employers would be compelled to give way. Sipambaniso was 'all talk and no action'.[121] On 9 March 1948 fifteen hundred people attended a Federation meeting where Burombo denounced Federa-

---

118 Commissioner for Native Labour to Secrertary, Native Affairs, 30 March 1948, S.2793/5. Interestingly, the Commissioner noted that Burombo's Voice organization had promised to wait for the results of the 6 April Salisbury meeting. It was the Federation which was pressing for an immediate Board and it was this threat which proved effective. 'If it was possible to confine a strike to the Bulawayo Municipal employees only I would think otherwise.'

119 Secretary, Matabeleland Native Labour Board, to Town Clerk, Bulawayo, 8 April 1948, ibid.

120 For a full biography of Burombo see Ngwabi Bhebe, *Burombo: African Politics in Zimbabwe, 1947–1958*. Bhebe ascribes to Sipambaniso a very much less significant role than I have done.

121 CID memo 13, 20 November 1947, ZBZ 1/2/1, vol. 2.

tion leaders as 'traitors to the people', provoking Sipambaniso to threaten a strike unless government acted.[122]

Sipambaniso was caught in a trap. Government had failed to take the opportunity he had offered them in his appeal for a general wages Board. Its negative reply to the appeal exposed him to ridicule at public meetings. (And yet, of course, a general wages Board *was* conceded soon after the general strike began.) He had to threaten a strike both to outflank Burombo and to keep up the pressure on government and the Bulawayo Council. And yet he knew that there were inadequate funds to support a strike and no commitments by workers in other towns to take simultaneous action. On 8 April at a stormy meeting of 6,000 workers in Makokoba, Burombo warned them that 'they must be sensible and not behave like children. He asked the meeting who would take the blame in the event of trouble. Sipambaniso replied that the Federation would take it. Burombo then stated that they had a noose round their neck and were hanging themselves. He was not allowed to carry on. Sipambaniso then asked those in the audience who were not in favour of a strike to raise their hands. No one did so. He then asked those in favour. All those present raised their hands ... He said that in view of the fact that everybody wanted a strike they must begin at once to raise money.'[123]

By this time opinion in black Bulawayo had shifted decisively away from Macintyre and towards Huggins. As we have seen, Congress had joined with Macintyre in asking the British Government to disallow the Native (Urban Areas) Accommodation and Registration Act. The newly formed African Voters League had gone so far as to urge its members to vote for Macintyre's party as a protest against the Act. But by April 1948 the Bulawayo Council, and Macintyre in particular, had become the villains. They had obstructed the municipal workers' pay claim for months. And when government belatedly stepped in with a Municipal Labour Board, Macintyre protested violently. On 7 April the *Chronicle* reported the determinations of the round-table conference in Salisbury. African readers were scandalized at the decision that urban basic pay should be 30 shillings a month. But they were equally outraged that the first action of the Salisbury meeting was to condemn the appointment of the Bulawayo Municipal Labour Board. Macintyre moved that motion – 'this action affected every municipality and every employer', he said, 'for it showed the Government attitude to be that if employers did not behave they would get Boards ... the expense in the case of Bulawayo Municipality would be borne by the ratepayers of Bulawayo.'

African reactions were very strong. The Federation decided to call its mass meeting on 8 April to discuss the *Chronicle* report. The authorities attempted to pacify Sipambaniso. On the afternoon of the 8th he was interviewed by Lt Col. Seward who assured him that 'the recommendations of the conference were not binding and that the Government had the last say in the matter. Sipambaniso replied that the natives had every confidence in the Government but none whatsoever in the round table conference.'[124] At the heated mass meeting later that day Sipambaniso lambasted Macintyre for obstructing government policy and assured his audience that the round table was 'not a national affair but an organisation merely to help the municipalities'. An official of the Federation 'called for an instant strike in support of Government

---

[122] CID memo 19, 9 March 1948.
[123] J.E.Ross, CID, 'Secret Memorandum'; Bulawayo CID to Officer Commanding, CID, Bulawayo, 9 April 1948, ZBZ 1/2/1, vol. 2.
[124] Ibid.

against the municipalities'. There was 'a roar of affirmation'.[125]

Sipambaniso still wished to avert or at least postpone a strike. He asked his audience to wait for the Congress meeting in Gwelo on 10 April. But at that meeting he was given little but good advice. Tennyson Hlabangana said that 'proper organization was needed'; there was 'no point in allowing the people to go on strike spontaneously ... It should be a colony-wide affair.' Charles Mzingeli of the Salisbury RICU said that workers in Bulawayo should wait 'until Salisbury people were better organised'. Thompson and Stanlake Samkange urged that no strike 'be simply a local or hasty affair'.

To all of this Sipambaniso replied that:

The workers in Bulawayo had become impatient because of broken promises by employers of African labour ... They had become out of hand and stubborn. He thought there might be a strike against the advice of the leaders. This the leaders could not obviate. [The Salisbury round-table] showed that the Europeans did not consider the African to be a human being. He did not personally feel that a strike at the moment was the best course of action, but the people were not in a mood consistent with any talk of procrastination and negotiation.

It was all very well for those present to instruct him 'to try to settle the trouble in Bulawayo by asking the African employees to first see their employers' and 'then approach the Labour Board if no satisfaction were received', but that had already been tried to no effect.[126]

On 12 April the *Chronicle* carried a report on the Gwelo meeting, commending those present for their 'wiser words'. It argued that the government had surely done enough in appointing a Municipal Labour Board and that strike action now would show that Africans feel 'they can hold a community to ransom'. But it quoted Sipambaniso: 'The final day is Tuesday', he said, 'when I am afraid the balloon will burst in Bulawayo.'[127] There followed on Tuesday 13 April the famous meeting in Stanley Square, 'attended by practically every Native in Bulawayo'. The balloon did burst. According to the CID report there was 'complete pandemonia'. Bango and Sipambaniso tried to address the crowd. So too did leaders of the Congress. But 'the mob became extremely vociferous, refused to listen to the leaders and finally broke up in disorder, everybody shouting "Strike! Strike!"'.[128] The leaders went off to tell the authorities that immediate action was needed. They called in the name of the Federation for a general Labour Board for all 'local commercial and industrial spheres' in Bulawayo. Next day Sipambaniso sent a follow-up telegram. But by then the strike was on.[129]

Until recently it was assumed, on the basis of the CID report, that an outraged pro-

[125] Ibid.
[126] Phone call by DSI MacCormack to DCIO, Salisbury, 10 April 1948; A.J. Frost, S/O to Commissioner of Police and Chief Native Commissioner, 10 April 1948, ibid.
[127] Enoch Dumbutshena's account of these words reveals the layers of condescension among Africans. As Stephen Thornton cited Sipambaniso himself talking about the Municipal workers: 'You must take the class of people you are dealing with ... they [are] chiefly Mtongas and with them it takes some sinking in.' Dumbutshena reveals a similar assessment of Bango and Sipambaniso themselves. 'They knew their limitations, so when it came to sending representatives to negotiate with the Chambers of Industry and Commerce, they invited Hlabangana, Rubitika and the writer to be their spokesmen. It was agreed that [Sipambaniso] Khumalo would read a one-sentence statement before the full discussions began. The magistrates' courtroom was full to capacity when Khumalo stood up, paper in hand, and read "If nothing happens before Wednesday the balloon will burst." The newspaper printed the sentence and the message was received by all the workers.' Enoch Dumbutshena, *Zimbabwe Tragedy*, East African Publishing House, Nairobi, 1975, p. 26.
[128] CID Memo, 28 May 1948, ZBZ 1/2/1, vol. 2.
[129] 'Report by the OC, CID on the African Strike', June 1948, ZBZ 1/2/1, vol. 2.

letariat had thrown off its elitist leaders. Grey Bango's account in the *Bantu Mirror* of 2 July 1960 seems to confirm this:

> It was when Mr Bango was explaining to the people at a mass meeting in Stanley Hall the results of negotiations for higher wages that the inevitable explosion which shook the whole country and brought troops to Bulawayo flared up. The people demanded immediate strike action. Before the meeting was half way through leaders had to flee for their lives from a missile of stones hurled at them. Bulawayo was tense. Police were too small for the situation. Troops were called in the following morning. Gangs of workers and township people carried out ruthless pickets on those Africans who were going to work. Hell was let loose and no leader would dare to walk the streets.

More recently, however, a rather different picture has been painted of the role of the leaders, and especially of Sipambaniso. Bango's own oral account to Lynette Nyathi in January 2001 says that he, Sipambaniso, J.Z. Moyo and others 'decided that tomorrow (14 April) all the people had to stay away from their work places. So we went to sleep and when we woke up in the morning we discovered that young men had gone to the Eastern Suburbs where the whites lived, getting all the black people who were working there and taking them to the Location ... The situation got so confused that it was up to the masses. When this strike was taking place, the fourth state of emergency was declared and Lobengula Street became the boundary.' At this point, Bango says, 'Burombo came in and joined these young men who by now were scattered all over.'

But the Federation leaders were faced with two immediate responsibilities. One was to negotiate with the authorities to try to avoid the use of firearms. 'We went to the Native Commissioner and said: "What are we going to do now that the government is threatening to use guns on us?"' 'Burombo went about door to door mobilizing people but the negotiations were done purely by us – me, Sipambaniso Khumalo and the whole executive of the trade union.' The other was how to deal with the crisis in Makokoba. 'These young men collected all these people who were working in the eastern suburbs and brought them to the Old Location – that place which is called Renkini. When they dumped all these people in the township we had no access to food, we had no access to housing.' The dangers of a 'spontaneous' strike were immediately apparent. After the drought, food was in short supply and expensive everywhere. 'The situation was bad and we had to ask the government to subsidize.' Bango added with relish that 'Macintyre who had said that black people had to get £1 10s as a salary had his bakery vandalized. Young men broke into his bakery and took everything they could lay their hands on.'[130]

I will not seek to narrate here the confused developments of the strike. I have already written about them from the perspective of the leaders of Congress – Samkange, Hlabangana and Rubatika – who remained involved in negotiations until the strike ended.[131] Moreover Brian Raftopoulos and Ian Phimister have recently published an authoritative account which puts the scattered evidence together. In their

---

[130] Interview between Lynette Nyathi and Grey Bango, January 2001. In an earlier interview Grey Bango linked his rival Burombo to the hated Macintyre. 'Burombo took advantage of the fact that people were starving. He went to buy bread from Osborn's Bakery, owned by the very man we were angry with, and sold it to the workers from his kiosk [in Makokoba].' This interview is cited in Brian Ratopoulos and Ian Phimister, *Keep on Knocking. A History of the Labour Movement in Zimbabwe, 1900–97*, Baobab Books, Harare, 1997, pp. 70-1. Enoch Dumbutshena recalls that 'the strikers roamed the streets of Bulawayo, ate food in all the hotels and helped themselves to newly baked bread in the bakeries all over town.' *Zimbabwe Tragedy*, p. 28.

[131] T.O. Ranger, *Are We Not Also Men?*, pp. 118-19.

account, Sipambaniso emerges as central and very much in control. After the Gwelo meeting, they say, Sipambaniso and Grey Bango knew that there would be a strike and they prepared 'a fall-back position'. They decided that it was vital that 'the lead in calling for a strike' should come from the unions which constituted the Federation, 'and they chose the obscure Aaron Mageti, a textile worker, to do it'. They did not inform Burombo or Hlabangana of this plan. As for the famous disorderly meeting of 13 April, six members of the platform delegation spoke – 'the crowd's patience may have been stretched to breaking point but it never actually snapped. Manyoba [Sipambaniso] rose to his feet some 90 minutes into the meeting.' He was interrupted with catcalls but even then 'a semblance of order prevailed'. When all the speakers had left, Mageti – called Maghato in the CID reports – took over. While the leaders were negotiating with government Mageti was organizing strike action.

On 14 April, as pickets brought African domestics into Makokoba, 'the leaders of the Federation and the Voice displayed a quite remarkable degree of control over the gathering'. The CID reported that 'the crowd was split up ... by section leaders ... into their various categories of employment and addressed by Patrick Makoni, Sipambaniso and Burombo'. The sections determined that the strike should continue until the Prime Minister gave a satisfactory answer; collections were made for a strike fund; there was very tight discipline. Meanwhile government lined Lobengula Street with police and soldiers and ordered marches around the Location perimeter, though no ammunition was issued. On Thursday 15 April, Hugh Beadle, the cabinet minister sent to deal with the crisis, having first talked with Sipambaniso, Hlabangana and Burombo, spoke to a crowd of 25,000 men in Makokoba. He warned that no food would be supplied until they went back to work. But Beadle had already promised the leaders that a general Labour Board would be rapidly appointed to deal with every industry in Bulawayo. They were anxious to bring the strike to an end. A huge crowd reassembled in Makokoba on Thursday afternoon. 'From the start it was apparent that this was very much the leaders' show. The police and army were nowhere to be seen.' The leaders combined to end the strike by claiming large wage increases which had not in fact been granted. Burombo spoke, interpreted into Sindebele by Sipambaniso. He announced a £5 per month award to single men and £7 10s for married, claiming a 'legal and binding document'. Thompson Samkange, President of Congress, congratulated the leaders and the strikers. He and the leaders 'had all worked very hard'. The meeting broke up rejoicing. Subsequently Beadle insisted that Sipambaniso, Hlabangana and Samkange should issue a statement 'regretting that some of the leaders must have misrepresented the position ... and that many had returned to work under a misconception'. But the strike was over. Phimister and Raftopoulos conclude by finding that 'migrant labourers did not take the initiative in Bulawayo after all ... The city's established African leadership exerted considerable if occasionally shaky control over the entire course of events between Monday 12 and Thursday 15 April.'[132]

But who 'won' the general strike? Ngwabi Bhebe, who credits Burombo with organizing the strike, claims that he also won it. According to him, 'the Federation was not strongly in favour of the Labour Board' whereas 'Burombo had striven for the setting up of a National Labour Board'.[133] My narrative makes this hard to accept. Sipambaniso had, after all, applied for a general Labour Board in February 1948 and consistently demanded it at mass rallies. I think the CID summary at the end of its

[132] Ian Phimister and Brian Raftopoulos, '*Kana sora ratswa ngaritswe*'.
[133] Ngwabi Bhebe, *B.Burombo*, p. 71.

report on the strike sums up the situation well: 'The concept of the Bulawayo Federation [and Sipambaniso] of a National Labour Board was eventually acceded to. [But] Burombo claimed all the credit for having sent the Bulawayo natives back to work and for having achieved a Labour Board.'[134]

The 1948 strike, then, was not the betrayed moment of proletarian uprising of some historians' imaginations. But it was a turning point in the history of Bulawayo, nevertheless. It marked a high point in Sipambaniso's career and a low point in Donald Macintyre's. Strike leaders had singled out Macintyre as the main enemy of the workers. And in his evidence to the Board in late April Acting Native Commissioner Fitzpatrick put the blame for the strike squarely on the Bulawayo Municipality. It had refused the reasonable demands of its employees; a couple of councillors had even said, 'let them have a strike'.[135]

Bulawayo's whites reacted to life without servants. Husbands went to get milk and bread and meat – 'there was an element of novelty and I heard a score of women remark "We're not so dependent on them after all".'[136] One correspondent even returned to the old problem of the pavement:

> I wonder how many people appreciated on Wednesday, as I did, what a lovely town we have when there are no noisy natives cluttering up the streets and getting in the way generally ... At the Post Office boxes, where natives are always in evidence, there was an air of quiet efficiency and despatch where only ourselves moved easily past each other.[137]

But there was fear, too. White women had been intimidated by pickets coming to take their servants. Africans had shown themselves capable of disciplined action. For both white and black the strike portended change. It fatally weakened Macintyre's ability to resist the imposition of the Native (Urban Areas) Accommodation and Registration Act, and through the operation of the Act would emerge a transformed Bulawayo.

Conclusion

In 1952 the Federation of African Welfare Societies in Southern Rhodesia published B.W. Gussman's two-volume *African Life in an Urban Area. A Study of the African Population of Bulawayo*. Gussman raised the interpretative problem of the number of different roles taken by 'all the more advanced Africans' in Bulawayo. He cited the example of a man who was chairman of the Bulawayo African Welfare Society,

---

[134] Report by the OC, CID, June 1948, ZBZ 1/2/1, vol. 2. Also in June, however, the CID's Memorandum 21 asserted that 'the stated policy of the Federation is to carry on negotiating with employers of labour whilst the Voice will only deal through the National Native Labour Board'. This merely meant that through its constituent unions the Federation had the means for collective bargaining, as well as representations at the Board, while the Voice did not. Both were 'active in preparing their cases' to the Board. The CID report recorded that all the Federation representatives appearing before the Board were in employment, while none of the Voice representatives were. Memo 21, 11 June 1948. In his own submission to the Board on 28 April Sipambaniso 'said that his organisation was willing to co-operate with the African Workers Voice Assocation and to continue to negotiate with all employers who were willing to do so for the improvement of working conditions without the intervention of the Board. This would ease the Board's work and save their organisation expense.'
[135] Ibid.; *Chronicle*, 23 April 1948.
[136] *Chronicle*, 15 April 1948.
[137] *Chronicle*, 19 April 1948.

(African Section); chairman of the Matabeleland Home Society; chairman of the Nta-basinduna Burial Society; director of the Bantu Co-operative Trading Society; secretary and clerk to the Ntabasinduna Presbytery; and assistant secretary of the Kings of Matabeleland Memorial Society. Gussman commented that:

> Europeans would question the intention, even the honesty, of a man who actively worked for the interests of workers (Trade Unions and Co-operatives), the royal family (Kings of Matabeleland Memorial Society), and the Church (Ntabasinduna Presbytery). Such interests are too devious to have a common purpose if sublimation is not accepted as the main motif.

This man worked as a book-keeper 'answering the call of "boy" from his immediate European superior'. He found an outlet for his self-esteem and 'surplus mental energy' in his work with his numerous and, Gussman thought, incompatible associations.[138]

I don't think Sipambaniso's even greater diversity can be explained in this way. It is, after all, highly unlikely that Stakesby-Lewis ever summoned him as 'boy'. Moreover, Sipambaniso would certainly not have seen his many activities as incompatible or dishonest. He believed that in everything he did he was working in the interests of the long-term residents of Makokoba, even if especially the Ndebele ones. He used his evidence to the Labour Board on 21 June 1948 to make the point:

> He had been in the CID for eight years and had an honourable discharge. From his detective experience he considered there was more theft among the lower paid natives. There was also a loafer class of natives in Bulawayo, which was of equal nuisance to both European and native. He advocated action by the police to rid the towns of this type of native ... The Federation admitted that there was considerable gambling, drinking and prostitution.[139]

From CID man to trade unionist, Sipambaniso saw himself as all of one piece.

---

[138] Gussman, p. 248.
[139] *Chronicle*, 22 June 1948. Grey Bango told the Board that 'the number of native loafers would be reduced if better wages were paid'. 'We suggest', he added, 'that a carpenter who can make a complete article, a tailor who can make a complete suit, to be worn by a European, and a man who can drive a car are among skilled men.' Yet 'even among the well dressed natives listening to the proceedings before the Board there were some who were hungry'.

5

The Feminization of Black Bulawayo
1948–1960

Transition, 1948–1953

The 1948 strike changed everything in Bulawayo but it did not change it all at once. Donald Macintyre continued to dominate the City Council. Sipambaniso continued to be the big man in Makokoba. But by 1953 both had gone from the political life of Bulawayo. Sipambaniso died in 1952 and in 1953 Macintyre became Federal Minister of Finance, continuing to live in west Bulawayo but no longer controlling municipal policy. They were replaced, as we shall see, by other black and white leaders, who played out the drama of the 1950s. But first we must narrate the humbling of Macintyre and the waning of Sipambaniso.

The Humbling of Macintyre

When the black Bulawayo workers went on strike in favour of the government and against Macintyre he could no longer maintain his stance as a socialist. In mid-1948 he resigned as leader of the Southern Rhodesia Labour Party and joined Huggins's United Party. He retained his seat in parliament at the next election as a government candidate. In parliament he had to abandon his feud with Huggins and his opposition to the Native (Urban Areas) Accommodation and Registration Act, but in Bulawayo he did what he could to delay and impede its implementation.

It was clear that Huggins blamed the Bulawayo Municipality, and Macintyre in particular, for precipitating the general strike. On 10 May 1948 he wrote frankly to the manager of the Wankie Colliery workforce:

> I sent you police when you asked for them, but we do not use troops at an early stage. We have no standing army here ... The Government were forced to intervene in the Native labour disputes owing to the reactionary attitude of certain employers. The Railway Strike, when this concern was directed by the Company, was the last straw .... The Labour Boards are for [dealing] with employers ... requiring compulsion to ensure equitable conditions for their employees ... I do not think these public enquiries do any harm: the European and the Native have to be educated. I am afraid that the time has passed when there was no need to consult the Native. The recent outbreak was the black proletariat putting out its head ... The immediate cause of

the strike was the employers' meeting and my delay in appointing a Board for the Bulawayo muncipal employees, whose conditions are just about as bad as the Railways – in other words, are scandalous. I told Bulawayo that I had to appoint a Board to stop a general strike, but at their request waited too long.

As I told the Mayor of Bulawayo and Mr Macintyre before the strike, I was not interested in their dispute and the clever arrangements they had made to meet it, but as I knew it was a signal for a general strike I could not let them sit pretty while the rest of the country went up in flames.

Huggins added that the Municipality used 'a type of white man who could not make his living with either his head or his hands, the worst type to boss up Natives.'[1]

Meanwhile T.F.W. Beadle, Minister of Internal Affairs, was authorized to tell correspondents from Bulawayo that 'the big Municipalities will have to have what amounts to small Native Departments to administer the Act. ... Central Government will have to watch the situation very closely, and if, after a reasonable period of time, it is quite clear that the Municipalities are not capable of administering their own Native affairs, so far as urban Native accommodation is concerned, the Central Government will have to step in and undertake the task itself which will of course mean that they will have to take over from the Municipalities the right to levy urban rates to pay for the administration.'[2] No prospect could have alarmed Macintyre more.

The Bulawayo Council had no alternative but to be seen to be reviewing their whole 'native urban administration'. They called in an experienced urban administrator from South Africa – J.P. McNamee from Port Elizabeth – to write a report. This document, submitted in December 1948, made all the criticisms expressed in the Native Affairs Commission report of 1930. But this time they could not be angrily denounced and dismissed.

McNamee expressed his 'fervent hope that you will realise the need – the real and urgent need – of improving the conditions under which natives are living in Bulawayo at the present time'. He found that 'Native Administration in Bulawayo is being performed – or perhaps one should say, not performed – under impossible conditions.' 'With all due respect to the Town Clerk, I suspect that his knowledge of the practical side of native administration amounts to just about nothing. He is inexperienced and probably has never come into contact with the native section of the community as a group. To the natives, no doubt, he is but a legend.'

Of the 50,000 Africans in Bulawayo, 15,000 lived in 'overcrowded' Location accommodation; 'in the compounds provided by the City Council for its native employees [where 1,784 people lived] ... the habitations and sanitary arrangements were primitve in the extreme'. There were appalling black spots. Lamb and Stuart's property, near Mzilikazi, was 'nothing short of a menace to the health, orderliness and welfare of the inhabitants of the location ... disgustingly filthy and [reeking] of liquor'; there were no sanitary facilities at the Municipal Quarry; at the Government Steel Corporation there was 'a lot of filthy water lying about'; and at Schur's Hide and Skin stores 'the conditions under which natives are here accommodated were among the worst seen and are indescribable'. McNamee thought that these places might qualify as 'the worst slum in the world'. They must all be swept away. In general much more and much better accommodation was needed.

[1] Huggins to Major Darby, 10 May 1948, S.482/49/40, file 1, National Archives.
[2] Beadle to B. Estcourt, Bulawayo, 4 May 1948. S.482/49/40, file 1, National Archives.

'For maintaining good order in the Bulawayo Locations there is an establishment of seventeen municipal police boys. Judging by the appearance of these men, their physique, carriage, dress and general deportment, I should imagine that, as far as controlling a location is concerned they are a dead loss. They must be replaced by government police.' McNamee thought 'that the relations between the native people and the local authority here were just a little bit strained'. The answer lay in a functioning and recognized Advisory Board. Other African organizations 'must be made to understand in no uncertain terms that the Advisory Board is the *only voice of the people* recognized by the local authority.' The existing Advisory Board was powerless and inadequate.

The remedy for all these deficiencies was 'to be found in the Natives (Urban Areas) Accommodation and Registration Act', and in the rest of his report McNamee carefully explained what this involved and how it should be implemented.[3] The Bulawayo Council had no alternative but to accept these scathing criticisms. In 1949 they advertised for a Director of Native Affairs – a job which McNamee thought would be almost impossibly dfficult, with the appointee caught between the ignorance of the the Council and the suspicion of the Africans.

There were no applications from inside Southern Rhodesia but two from South Africa. One of these fell away and the Council was left with a single – and very unusual – applicant. Hugh Ashton was 38 years old; he had done Politics, Philosophy and Economics at Oxford and postgraduate work in Anthropology in London; he had been district administrator in Mafeking, private secretary to the High Commissioner in Pretoria and Cape Town, and most recently had worked as Senior Welfare Officer in Johannesburg, 'dealing with the African townships and doing welfare service'. 'Many people said it was a terrible place', Ashton remembered, 'but I used to enjoy it and enjoyed the work very much, very varied, and I used to lecture in African administration and I had three very eminent students.' One was Joshua Nkomo; another was Eduardo Mondlane. Ashton decided to leave South Africa because 'I did not like the nationalist government at all'.

The Bulawayo councillors were unhappy with so academically well qualified a candidate and one with close African associates. 'There was no contest', recalled Ashton, 'but they were very reluctant to take me. They thought I was a liberal. Anyway, they had to get on with this and they had no choice.' Ashton reviewed his tasks and his municipal colleagues. His first task was to recruit good men to set up 'a proper organisation'. The next thing was 'to get on with housing. The housing was unbelievable, it was horrible. I went into the Municipal Compound. It was so disgusting there that I felt sick ... Makokoba was grossly overcrowded ... you would see people sleeping outside the houses ... There was a great big quarry in the middle of where Barbourfields comes round and I had never seen people living in such conditions ... there was one firm, a skinning factory where people were living on the skins in the sheds ... You've never seen anything like it. Terrible. I'm not surprised that people struck.'

Ashton at once urged not only that Mzilikazi be completed but that many more townships be built in a determined attempt to house all those displaced by the implementation of segregation and all those required by industry. He had a very difficult time at first. He was closely watched and rebuked by Council for making public state-

---

3   J.P. McNamee. *Report on Native Urban Administration in the City of Bulawayo and the Implementation of the Native (Urban Areas) Accommodation and Registration Act, 1946,* 2 December 1948.

169

ments without authority. Many councillors feared that they would build houses and find no one to occupy them. And then there was Macintyre:

> The City Council was then under the influence of a very prominent councillor called Macintyre. He was very negative; he was reactionary; and did his best to prevent the Council taking over .... We had a few [other] white councillors who were not at all helpful .. Some of the councillors were unbelievable. There was one there who refused to shake hands with an African; another one [the trade unionist, McNeillie] a very fine man but his whole approach was so negative. He told me that when he went home he felt he had to wash his hands.

Despite Ashton's appointment things were moving too slowly, so Huggins intervened. 'He waved a big stick and said "Look, if you don't get on with the housing the Government will not approve of the transfer of any industrial stands." Now the Council was very keen to bring industry to Bulawayo and the thought of not being able to have any industry was the sort of pressure that was needed. I give great tribute to Sir Godfrey Huggins. He was very far-sighted.'[4] But the real breakthrough came when 'Councillor Macintyre was made the Minister of Finance in the Federal Government and he had to resign his position as councillor. Up to that time he had been the big city boss.' But now 'we got a new chairman in his position', Councillor Newman. The committee was discussing building 1,400 houses in Njube; Newman suggested that the number be doubled – 'and from then on the Council began to realise that housing was necessary'. The age of Macintyre was over.[5]

The Last Days of Sipambaniso

Sipambaniso and the Federation of Bulawayo African Workers Trade Unions were adjusting to the new situation. As Huggins told Major Darby: 'There is one bright spot. The Native leaders had such a fright that they did all they could in the end to stop the strike, but the mob threw them over and they will be chary of doing anything again for a time.'[6] And although, as we have seen, the leaders never completely lost control, it was certainly true that they did not want another major strike. Deeply involved in the Labour Board, the Federation determined to become more and more like a trade union congress and less and less like a political movement. On 31 October 1951 Charles Mzingeli came from Salisbury to hold a meeting of his Reformed ICU in Stanley Square. Only eleven people turned up and half of them were members of the Federation executive, including Sipambaniso, who at that point was still organizing secretary. They told Mzingeli that the Federation was 'already well established'; that it was organizing as a trade union; and that they wanted nothing to do with a 'quasi-political' body like the RICU.[7]

---

4   Ashton's first Annual Native Administration Report for the year ending 31 July 1951 noted that 'on the 3 January 1950 the Government imposed a ban on the sale of industrial sites. One of the grounds for this was that the influx of Natives to Bulawayo attracted by industry was too greatly outstripping the provision of accommodation by the Municipality. After considerable negotiation the Government finally recognised the magnitude of the Council's effort and in December 1950 the Minister for Native Affairs formally announced that the ban had been withdrawn'.

5   Interview by Mark Ncube with Hugh Ashton, 1 June 1994, National Archives, Bulawayo. Ashton's upper-class accent defeated the transcriber so that the typed text is very unreliable. I quote from my own transcription of the tape.

6   Huggins to Darby, 10 May 1948, S.482/49/40 file 1, National Archives.

7   CID, Native Affairs Memorandum 59, 31 October 1951.

Indeed in their overall responses the Federation took a very different line from Mzingeli. He despised the National Congress. Sipambaniso belonged to it and believed in it; for him, Congress was the political body and the Federation the trade union body. In February 1949 he had written to Stanlake Samkange urging him to accept the Secretaryship of Congress: 'Mr Samkange, let us put a new blood in the Congress.'[8] Sipambaniso also differed from Mzingeli in his attitude to the Native (Urban Areas) Accommodation and Registration Act. Mzingeli had led fierce opposition to the Act in Salisbury. The Federation decided to place itself in an advantageous position within the operation of the Act in Bulawayo.

Advisory Boards had hitherto not been of interest to the Federation. Most of the men elected to them had been Nyasa hotel workers. But now that MacNamee was recommending that the Boards be accepted as the only legitimate voice of the people, Sipambaniso decided to focus on township affairs by means of the Advisory Board. In December 1948 he was elected to the Bulawayo Townships Advisory Board. He issued a bold statement:

> Today is D Day. I believe there is much to be done, very little has been done. My first move is to press for a Commission of Inquiry to investigate the conditions in the Location.[9]

In fact his first move was to call a meeting 'regarding the formation of a Rent Payers' Asssociation' in Makokoba and Mzilikazi. The proposal came before the Municipal Native Affairs Committee on 13 July 1949 where it had a chilly reception.[10]

A division of labour then began to develop: Sipambaniso would focus on Makokoba; others would focus on making the Federation more efficient. These arrangements were ratified at the Federation's AGM on 27 October 1951. One hundred and twenty members attended. Sipambaniso was among them, but no longer as organizing secretary; Grey Bango was chairman, and Philip Nkohozana was secretary. Bango spoke of 'the recent increase of efficiency of the Federated Bulawayo African Workers Unions and stated that it was now the duty of the Federation to negotiate with the Government for full recognition'. (Bango was soon to emerge as the full-time, paid organizing secretary of the Federation.) Yet Sipambaniso was still playing a central role. He was elected to almost every one of the committees set up to reshape the Federation and to carry on its work – the deputation appointed to see the Ministers of Native and Internal Affairs about desired amendments to the Industrial Conciliation Act; the 'anti-Federation' committee 'which would consist of registered Bulawayo African workers' and which would call a meeting of the chiefs of the two Rhodesias and Nyasaland to discuss Federation at the Victoria Falls; a committee to protest against the eviction of township dwellers convicted of liquor offences; a committee to amend the constitution of what would in future be called the Southern Rhodesia African Trade Workers Union. Above all he was elected to a committee to 'form a Rent Payers Association in the Old location and Mzilikazi Village, the Association to meet once a month to hear the results of the Location Advisory Board's efforts on housing'.[11]

[8] Sipambaniso Manyoba to Stanlake Samkange, 16 February 1949, file 'Congress', Samkange papers.
[9] *Bantu Mirror*, 4 December 1948.
[10] Minutes of the meeting of the Municipal Native Affairs Committee, 13 July 1949. Sipambaniso's application to lease an offal shop was also turned down. Hugh Ashton's first attendance at the Committee was a month later on 18 August 1949; his first monthtly report was for September. Once Ashton was in place the idea of an extension of democracy from Advisory Board voters to all rent payers was more favourably received.
[11] CID, Native Affairs Memorandum 59, 31 October 1951.

The time was now ripe to accomplish this idea. In the Advisory Board elections in August 1951 eight of the 12 members elected were candidates sponsored by the Federation, three by Burombo's Voice Association, with one other.[12] Working with this Advisory Board Sipambaniso's committee established the Rent Payers Association. In mid-1953 Sipambaniso's long-standing friend and supporter, Charlton Ngcebetsha, lost his job as a clerk when the firm he worked for closed its Bulawayo branch. Charlton moved to live in Mzilikazi, opened a bookshop in Makokoba and began to publish news-sheets on behalf of the Rent Payers Association, i.e., the community of Makokoba and Mzilikazi. The CID reported on 8 August 1953 that he aimed to publish a Rent-payers Association Bulletin; a social weekly, the *Weekly News*; and a political weekly, *Southern Rhodesia Bantu Opinion*. Three publications were too much even for Ngcebetsha's energies and by October 1953 he had settled on one title, the *Bulawayo Home News*, published weekly on behalf of the Rent Payers Association. 'Stronger language is now more commonplace', reported the CID.[13]

Alas, Sipambaniso did not live to see the emergence of this remarkable Makokoba journal, though Ngcebetsha did everything he could to keep his memory green. In November 1950 Sipambaniso's father, Bikwapi, died and was given a huge Anglican funeral, attended by 'hundreds of African from all tribes in Bulawayo African Townships together with people from the Shangani, Lupane and Matopo'.[14] Sipambaniso featured as the standard-bearer of the next generation. But in fact he had less than two years to live himself. At the end of 1951 he fell ill. He did not stand for the Advisory Board elections in August 1951 and thereafter spent several months in hospital, where he died on 4 April 1952. His colleagues ensured an appropriately elaborate political funeral. Though Sipambaniso was still formally an Anglican, 'some African leaders of Bulawayo approached Reverend Lesabe of the African Methodist Episcopal Church' – the favoured 'Ethiopian' church of Bulawayo radicals – 'to conduct the funeral service at the graveside'. Reassured that the Anglicans had no objection, Lesabe did so.[15] On 12 April 1952 the *Bantu Mirror* reported that thousands attended. 'Every African organisation and race in Bulawayo was represented at the burial of Mr Arthur Sipambaniso Manyoba Kumalo, who was described as a "man among men".' There were 7 buses, 21 cars, the Bulawayo brass band, representatives of the Matabele Home Society, Congress, the Advisory Board, the Federation and the Highlanders Football Club. Highlanders chairman, Charlton Ngcebetsha, declared that the African Football Association 'owed its existence to Sipambaniso'.[16]

Charlton had not yet begun his own weekly so he published his eulogy in the *Bantu Mirror* on 26 April 1952: Sipambaniso had died 'in the prime of life ... a young man of great promise, who in a variety of ways was extremely useful. Here in Bulawayo there was hardly a movement which aimed at benefitting the African people which Sipambaniso did not actively associate himself with and because of his executive ability some of these movements grew in numbers and influence.' He died while carrying out yet another service, collecting information on African ex-servicemen:

who, though most of them are in reduced circumstances, have never received any financial assistance from the Southern Rhodesia National War Fund which, in large measure through

[12] CID, Native Affairs Memorandum 57, 27 August 1951.
[13] CID, Native Affairs Memorandum 80, 8 August 1953 and 82, 3 October 1953.
[14] *Bantu Mirror*, 25 November 1950.
[15] *Home News*, 8 January 1955.
[16] *Bantu Mirror*, 12 April 1952.

our people's contributions in money and cattle, rose to astronomical figures. [He] was very anxious to see all the ex-servicemen, one by one, but God Almighty decided otherwise. As he lay on his deathbed, he, not unlike the illustrious British imperialist, Cecil John Rhodes, must have muttered to himself 'so little done, so much to do'.[17]

Charlton organized a series of fund-raising football matches and almost as soon as he did have his own weekly he was able to announce that:

there is a beautiful tombstone laid on the grave of the late Sipambaniso Manyoba by the Matabeleland Highlanders Football Club … It was originally hoped that there would be a Mbuyiso ceremony on the eve of the unveiling but the African Administration Department has refused permissions to brew in the traditional manner.[18]

Thereafter, Charlton carried constant reminders of Sipambaniso in the *Home News* and paid particular attention to his old mother. In December 1954 he stressed that the old lady had 'absolutely no visible means of earning a living' and depended on the charity of 'those Africans who are still remembering the good work her son did for Location Africans'. Yet she had been the owner of a house, still standing, for which the Council now received £4 a month rent. On 30 April 1960 he wrote that 'it hurts to the quick the pride of the decent Africans of Bulawayo when the old mother of the late Sipambaniso has to line up with her grand-daughters at the Mzilikazi clinic for medical examination and yet it is well known that she is no longer interested in sex'. On 1 September 1962 he reported that the mother of the 'famous Sipambaniso' had died.[19]

And Sipambaniso did remain famous. The African Townships Advisory Board put both his name and his father's on the list of illustrious men after whom streets might be named. In September 1956 the Western Commonage Advisory Board agreed to name its Youth Centre after Sipambaniso. He had been a 'footballer who brought much fame to Bulawayo' and 'one of the most untiring organisers of African political and workers' organisations'.[20] But the most remarkable tribute to Sipambaniso came more than 40 years later. In 1999 Joshua Nkomo, 'Father Zimbabwe', died. The war veterans' magazine *Demob* described how his cortege 'went walk about' on Saturday 3 July, passing through 'the legendary western suburbs of Makokoba and Mzilikazi … One felt as if the history of political development was looking on. [Nkomo] began his political career in Bulawayo and supported the likes of Mazibisa, Siphambaniso, John Kumalo, Burombo and others in their fight against social injustice.'[21]

The Feminization of Township Culture

The story of black Bulawayo between 1953 and 1960 can be told through the lives of archetypal men. Sipambaniso's role was split. His footballing, welfare and social activities came to be embodied in Yvonne Vera's uncle, Jerry, the Mr Bulawayo of the 1950s. His trade union and political activities came to be embodied in Jerry Vera's great

---

17 *Bantu Mirror*, 26 April 1952. Ngcebetsha added that Sipambaniso 'was not a tribalist nor did he have time for mortals who insisted on practising class distinctions'.
18 *Home News*, 29 August 1953.
19 *Home News*, 25 December 1954, 30 April 1960, 1 September 1962.
20 *Bantu Mirror*, 29 September 1956.
21 *Demob*, vol. 1, 1999, 'The Giant Hero Has Fallen'. Siphambaniso is the correct Ndebele spelling. I have used Sipambaniso in my text because all my sources, including the African press, do so.

friend, Joshua Nkomo. White Bulawayo and its City Council, so long represented by Macintyre, came to be thought of internationally as the employer of Hugh Ashton. But first I must fulfill the promise in the previous chapter to match my account of Bulawayo's Fumbathas – as embodied in the figure of Sipambaniso – with an account of Bulawayo's Phephelaphis, the tragic heroine of Yvonne Vera's *Butterfly Burning*. However, the women of the 1950s townships cannot be represented by any single archetypal figure, even if, as we shall see, numbers of strong women emerge by name.

The 1950s was undoubtedly a time when women of all sorts became much more important than they had recently been in the culture and politics of black Bulawayo. This feminization took many different forms. Makokoba filled up with girls in the 1950s. It was the chosen destination of young women running away from rural families in search of the exciting life of town. Some of these young women, seizing upon new urban female fashions, became the 'swinging chicks' of the shebeens. Others, increasingly employed for wages as nannies and even in factories, were able to spend money on clothes and bicycles just as the young men had done before the war. The 'nannies of Khumalo', a new European suburb, were a famous sight as they cycled into the township wearing the latest fashions. Fashion became a female rather than a male domain. On the other hand, the implementation of the Native Urban Areas Act and of full residential segregation meant that for the first time women of every age and class came to live in the townships. Formidable Christian matrons, leaders of uniformed church guilds, now moved into Mzilikazi and the increasing number of new townships. These women formed female rent-payers associations to match and soon to outgrow the male ones which Sipambaniso and Ngcebtsha had fostered. In this way they entered black urban politics, not until 1960 as supporters of nationalist parties, but as participants in the politics of the Advisory Boards. The women's associations lobbied the Boards on issues of divorce, custody, and house ownership. They appealed to Board members to support them in their disputes with township traders. They canvassed for their favoured candidates in Advisory Board elections – and a few women were elected themselves. They reinvigorated township Christianity. Of course, there was no single female political, social or moral interest. The matriarchs of the associations and the guilds denounced good-time girls, prostitutes and mistresses as much as they did greedy male traders.

Women in Makokoba

In Salisbury the rapid and clumsy implementation of the Native Urban Areas Act had meant widespread police raids and expulsions of 'unmarried' women. Charles Mzingeli's Reformed ICU was able to attract very many women to support its protests against the Act.[22] Ashton had the advantage of starting later in Bulawayo and of learning from Salisbury's mistakes. Early in his administration there were raids and expulsions in the Bulawayo townships too. But fairly soon Ashton and the Bulawayo African Townships Advisory Board agreed that, in Makokoba, they caused more trouble than they were worth. Ashton decided to leave Makokoba alone and to concentrate on enforcing the Act in the new townships which were being created and designed either for properly married couples or for properly 'single' men.

---

[22] Timothy Scarnecchia, *The Urban Roots of Democracy and Political Violence in Zimbabwe*, Chapter 3.

Charlton Ngcebetsha in his *Home News* was literally in two minds about this:

> The Bulawayo Municipality [he wrote in December 1953] is, to some extent, responsible for the morality of the African people being in a low state, because it allows Africans in the Old Location to sleep cheek by jowl under most shameful conditions … married people with their children and bachelors as well as unattached women sleep together in disgustingly over-crowded small houses. It seems nice to some Europeans to see Africans living like animals that are strangers to shame.

On the other hand, he added, for the average African urban man:

> Bulawayo is the best place to live in because there is plenty of native beer, plenty of skokiaan … And, of course, plenty of women.[23]

In urban oral memory official tolerance of women in Makokoba was attributed to Ashton's benevolence. In January 2000 Lynette Nyathi interviewed Gogo Madamu in Mzilikazi. Madamu triumphantly personalized the whole issue; the end of police raids was due to her – and to Hugh Ashton:

> When I came here to Bulawayo my husband was living in shared quarters. We used to divide the room with curtains. So when I came I was pregnant. Then it happened that the council policemen were conducting their nightly raids for women. It was then I was arrested … I was some months pregnant. They were arresting us under the instructions of Taylor. This Taylor used to regard all women who lived in Makokoba with their husbands or otherwise as prostitutes. What was I doing in a house with beds for four bachelors? I was then labelled a prostitute because only prostitutes could stay with four men. Mmm! It was four o'clock in the morning when we heard the police-man knocking. I was arrested. I was then force-marched to the offices. At 8 a.m. the white man [Hugh Ashton] came in. Then he started inspecting the people, assessing us. Then he said 'What is this woman doing here? How did you classify her as a prostitute when you can actually see that she is pregnant? That alone proves that she is married.' Then they said 'Ah! We were doing our duty since it is the law that says we have to arrest all the unmarried women we find in the male quarters in Makokoba.'

In Madamu's narrative, Ashton told the police sergeant that he could himself be arrested 'together with this Taylor of yours. What would you have done if this lady had given birth on the way from Makokoba?' He then phoned Taylor and told him: 'From this day forward I do not want to see you coming here with female ladies assuming that they are prostitutes. You hear me!' And Gogo Madamu ends triumphantly: 'The raids were stopped on that day … From there life began to be normal, we were living peacefully. Dr Hugh was a very good man.' He got her a house. She went on to become a leading figure in successive nationalist parties' women's leagues.[24]

The Bulawayo African Townships Advisory Board endorsed this policy but knew that it contributed to the gross overcrowding in Makokoba. So it urged that women be allowed to stay in the new townships in Western Commonage 'exactly as they are staying in the Old Location'.[25] Ngcebetsha, himself a member of the Board, wrote on

---

[23] *Home News*, 5 December 1953. The first issue of the paper was dated 17 October 1953. At this point Ngcebetsha was very critical both of Prime Minister Garfield Todd and of Ashton.

[24] I tell the story of Gogo Madamu in my article, 'Myth and Legend in urban oral memory: Bulawayo, 1930–60', in *Journal of Postcolonial Writing*, vol. 44, No. 1, March 2008, pp. 77-8. I include it in a section on 'Legends of Resilience'.

[25] Amos Mazibisa was Chair and Jerry Vera Secretary of the BAT Advisory Board which in February 1954 discussed 'the ban on women entering and staying at Western Commonage'. *Home News*, 6 February 1954.

27 March 1954 that the problem of overcrowding in Makokoba 'is still easy to allevi-
ate by allowing women who wish to go and stay at Western Commonage with their
husbands to do so. At present no women are allowed to stay at Western Commonage. We have never been persuaded by the argument brought forward by the African
Administration that it would be unwise and foolish to permit the slum conditions
which obtain in the Old Location to exist in the Western Commonage by allowing
women and children to stay there.'[26] In his turn, however, Ashton was not persuaded
by the case of the Advisory Board. Makokoba remained the one township in which
women could come and go and stay as they pleased.

Indeed for some men there were too many women in Makokoba, and they were too
independent. In December, E. Madziwa, a resident of the township, complained that
'there were too many widows residing in Bulawayo'. When men died their widows
were allocated the houses:

> The township most predominated by these widows was the old Location ... This township was
> a horrible spot. Widows are now on the increase because they are allowed to occupy a room
> or a cottage after the death of their husbands. This has resulted in bringing about a certain
> amount of freedom and self-control in these women and the freedom so easily demonstrated
> by these widows may tempt faithful neighbour women to commit a crime on their husbands so
> that they may also be 'free' ... There were too many hooligans in the Location ... because due
> to the shortage of accommodation young men often attached themselves to these widows with
> houses.[27]

In February 1958 a correspondent to the *Bantu Mirror* complained that 'one cannot
find so many wicked women in other towns as can be counted in Bulawayo. They
should send their policemen to arrest any women found harbouring in rooms which
are supposed to be for "men only". The factories should also be blamed for employing
women in place of men. This will surely encourage young girls of school-leaving age
to run away from the reserves into town in order to make money from factories and
from men.' Another correspondent complained again about the 'acts of immorality'
committed by widows. 'The number of such unwanted, self-styled young ladies is on
the increase every year. Such dangerous women are allowed to pay the rentals when
good and hard-working men with families and bachelors have lost their dingy rooms
through no payment or late payment of rentals.'[28]

Towards the end of the 1950s the Municipality again began to threaten police raids
and to broadcast warnings to 'illegal' women, but both the Advisory Board and Bulawayo leaders of the African National Congress opposed raids and nothing was done.[29]
Partly as a result of its female population, Makokoba remained 'crowded to suffoca-
tion', as the *Home News* complained in March 1957: 'Young children are still made

[26] *Home News*, 27 March 1954.
[27] *Bantu Mirror*, 28 December 1957.
[28] *Bantu Mirror*, 8 February 1958. On 13 November 1958 the *Mirror* carried a letter saying that 'frequent
divorces have made African townships like Mzilikazi become a "widows" home ... The unhealthy position
prevailing in this township, like any other African township these days, has been caused by women obtaining
jobs in the factories and industrial concerns. These employments have made women independent and in
some cases women have private lovers at work who give them some money ... Today at Mzilikazi unmarried
women are occupying almost a quarter of the houses in the township.'
[29] On 20 September 1958 J.M. Tabulinga from Makokoba wrote to the *Bantu Mirror* congratulating J.Z. Moyo,
who was both a Congress leader and a Board member, for condemning night raids. 'Mr Moyo still remembers the people who nominated him to the Board – the tenants. He is not like other people who when they
are elected to the Board just forget the people who elected them.'

to sleep under beds. Rooms in block buildings which are as old as the hills are chock a block with tenants ... the kitchen places are housing tenants as well ... [there is] sickening over-crowding.'[30] And things were still the same in 1960. On 2 February of that year Ngcebetsha wrote an open letter to Hugh Ashton congratulating him on the great expansion of African housing in Bulawayo. But Makokoba remained a slum. 'A large group of Africans are packed like sardines, living like wild animals with no sense of decency at all.'[31] Three months later the *Bantu Mirror* complained that:

> Even single men live here with their 'take and sit' girl friends ... There are now 8,000 people living in Makokoba. I went around the township in the early hours of the morning and what I saw was appalling. Everywhere from Fourth Street to Eighth Street were bundles of human beings wrapped up in flimsy blankets sleeping outside in the biting weather. Most of these outside sleepers are unemployed youths but in some places I saw families with small children spending their nights this way. This is usually near the place of a relative or an acquaintance so that the few earthly possessions are put inside a room during the day.[32]

The *Bantu Mirror* reported in June 1960 that Makokoba had a total of 5,578 'single' men with official rent cards and 554 married men with their families. The 'single' men had friends and relatives and unofficial wives 'who share with them the small rooms'. The total population was over 8,000. But the *Mirror* was unsympathetic:

> Any overcrowding there is in Makokoba Township is not official. It is the fault of the tenants themselves ... The problem is a moral one. It is contrary to religious or ethical principles for men to live with women years on end outside legal or customary marriage rites and raising families. Some people will blame the authorities for not having made it impossible for women to be in the township by authorizing night or early morning police raids. In other towns in the country the authorities have been heavily criticized for carrying out these raids.

A letter from Makokoba in the same issue complained that 'this township has become a den for all runaway girls who could never be traced by their parents'.[33]

Some of our informants were themselves such 'runaway girls' who were seeking the fabled glamour of Bulawayo. 'I was from the rural areas', said Zelitha Malaphahla, 'where life was sort of quiet. I was therefore curious to find out more about town life ... I was carried away ... I became one of the chief dancers. These days people don't know how to dance compared to the olden days.'[34] MaNcube ran away to Makokoba much to her father's fury. She became 'one of the best dancers' and at parties would dance until she came down to her knees, 'dancing with her knees'. Spectators threw money at her feet. It was good to be young and in the swing even if you had to live in crowded Makokoba.[35]

30 *Home News*, 9 March 1957.
31 *Home News*, 27 February 1960.
32 *Bantu Mirror*, 14 May 1960.
33 *Bantu Mirror*, 9 July 1960. These press accounts of Makokoba's population were much too low. In 1963 Patricia Batty and Mrs M. Mabena made a 'Children's Survey, Makokoba'. They noted that the census of 17 July 1962 had found 17,000 residents of Makokoba together with 2,000 in hostels. There were some 1,200 pre-school children living in the township. 'Life and vitality there is in abundance but what course will it take in the years from now?' Ashton Papers, Historical Reference Library, City Hall.
34 Interview by Hloniphani Ndlovu with Zelitha Malaphahla, Makokoba, February 2000.
35 Interview by Hloniphani Ndlovu with MaNcube, New Magwegwe, February 2000. I have a section on 'Legends of Youth' in my 'Myth and Legend in Urban Oral Memory: Bulawayo, 1930–60'.

Dance in the 1950s

Dance was indeed a major part of the feminization of Bulawayo urban culture. In the old days the 'tribal' dances which had been a feature of Makokoba life – and of life in the labour compounds – had been all-male, a mixture of war dances and mine dances. By Sipambaniso's time as a band leader women had become dance partners in the first versions of urban jazz. But it was in the 1950s that popular music developed into an all-consuming enthusiasm and young men and women went wild for *tshaba–tshaba*. In the new dance forms young women could jive and twist almost solo, as well as follow an elegant partner's lead in the elite recreation of ballroom dancing. It is striking that our by now elderly female informants in particular remember their achievements as dancers – and the old men recall how smartly they were dressed.

In some ways this is odd, because the 1950s were a time of the feminization of fashion as well as the feminization of dance. In the 1930s township girls wore no shoes and went about dowdily. It was the young men who were the peacocks before whose glory urban girls could hardly be seen. But in the late 1940s and 1950s all that changed. Lawrence Vambe recalls that after 1946 there emerged in the towns of Rhodesia 'an altogether new class of African woman: young, vital, emancipated and fashion-conscious'. He remembers a friend asking him, 'Where were all these wonderful girls before?' Vambe's answer was that 'they had, of course, been kept in the reserves'.[36]

The emergence of these 'white butterflies', their waists 'a tight loop',[37] had an immediate impact on African urban photography. Ritah Ndlovu remembers the 'parties' of 1960, 'twisting and jiving there seriously'. She wore *amajelimana*, 'long, colourful, flowery dresses, starched petticoats' and shoes known as *Boom* which 'were high and made one feel very special'. Dressed for the dance like this she would go to be photographed at Stanley Square:

> We used to go and queue at the studios. Photos were special things for special people so if one was seen by one's neighbours at the studio in the queue one would feel proud and civilized.[38]

African newspapers, which had once carried only photos of smart young men, now packed their pages with photos of beautiful young women. The 1950s were the decade of the Beauty Contest. The first contest for Miss Bulawayo was set up in October 1951 by the Townships Social Organiser 'solely for the African ladies of the city'. It was to be judged by the Bulawayo African Townships Advisory Board and Ashton's Native Administration Department. It was to be judged not in the flesh but by pictures. 'Photographs, some dating back as far as the early thirties, are being reviewed by the ladies wishing to join the competition. Those without photos have hurriedly gone to the studios to ensure that they have a snap for the competition.'[39] Soon the contest became more fleshly, as beauties paraded in the Stanley Hall to the applause of packed audiences. On 29 May 1954, for instance, Miss Mzilikazi was chosen there; the winner was one of Mzilikazi's modern girls, 19-year-old Lizzie Maseko, 'a Bulawayo

---

[36] Lawrence Vambe, *From Rhodesia to Zimbabwe*, Heinemann, London, 1976, p. 190.
[37] Yvonne Vera, *Butterfly Burning*, p. 54.
[38] Terence Ranger, 'Pictures Must Prevail: Sex and the Social History of African Photography in Bulawayo, 1930–1960', *Kronos*, 27, November 2001, p. 266.
[39] *Bantu Mirror*, 27 October 1951.

factory worker'. 'As they took their steps to line up for the judges, there was deafening applause ... the judges looked at them from all angles.'[40] Beauties, once stocky, became slimmer and taller – Yvonne Vera says that the young men began to call them 'portables', like the cameras which snapped them. The great singer Dorothy Masuka, whom the *Mirror* christened 'Bulawayo's Judy Garland', was voted 'Miss Makokoba'. The *Mirror* ended the decade with a photo of a young township woman, 'too beautiful to be true. Undoubtedly she is beautiful, charming and certainly gorgeous. Every young man's dream girl ... popular 22-year-old Miss Josephine Mvundla, a cracking beauty in Makokoba township, where such earth-treading stars are in abundance.'[41]

Some of these 'earth-treading stars' were 'runaway' girls from the reserves who could be smartly dressed too if they managed to find a paying job and have some disposable income. MaNcube – the fugitive from her rural father's wrath – was employed as a nannie at the new European suburb of Khumalo and used to cycle from there to the townships for weekend dances. She 'attracted a lot of attention' as she cycled with her 'flared Stiffs [starched white petticoats] flying all over':

> With your 'Stiff' petticoat on, and flared there just like a peacock what more could you want? One would walk confidently with one's head high, proud and confident. Those were good old days, I tell you, so wonderful that if one was getting on a bus wearing a 'Stiff' one was really seen!! I mean seen!!

The old obscure days for urban young women were over. Being seen was everything. MaNcube was waiting for a bus when her husband-to-be 'saw' her: 'He saw! Ah! A beautiful, young, attractive girl wearing a "Stiff" and he was immediately attracted, taken or bowled over.'[42]

But MaNcube remembers with greatest joy her dancing days before her marriage:

> *Wasira!! Wasira!!*[43] Spokes Mashiyane would be playing there as we showed them what dancing means – me and my partner there with the rest of the people watching and throwing money to encourage and congratulate us ... *KwaKarengo!*[44] We would shake our bodies to the *tshaba-tshaba* dance, jive dance , having fun never experienced before ... If I stand up now and dance it for you, you would be amazed that a granny like me is still able to shake her body because I will bend and kneel on the ground. I was taken up with parties, the need to really feel town life.[45]

Dancing took place in many different locations and at all levels of black Bulawayo society. Dances were held in Stanley Hall and other townships' halls where professional bands played kwela and jazz.[46] Some of the incoming young women and their

---

[40] *Parade*, July 1954.

[41] *Bantu Mirror*, 25 June 1960.

[42] Ritah Ndlovu says that when she was approached by her present husband, 'he started confessing that he had "seen" me for a long time'. Ranger, 'Pictures Must Prevail'. For a profound treatment of the role advertising played in the development of African urban standards of beauty and fashion, see Timothy Burke, *Lifebuoy Men, Lux Women, Commodification, Consumption and Cleanliness in Modern Zimbabwe*, Leicester University Press, London, 1996.

[43] An Ndebele idiomatic expression meaning 'Don't get left behind'.

[44] 'At Karengo's shebeen'. Spokes Mashiyane's Kwela records would be played on the gramophone at Karengo's and other shebeens.

[45] Interview by Hloniphani Ndlovu with MaNcube, New Magwegwe, February 2000.

[46] A file marked 'for Dr Gargett, African Welfare and Recreation' among the Ashton papers in the Historical Reference library at the Bulawayo City Hall contains a number of reports on township dance. One by Zamani Homela, Clerk Interpreter to the Social Organiser, written on 18 April 1955, discusses why attendance at 'dance halls' has fallen. 'The poor standard of music provided by the Municipal Dance Band is the main reason ... Many of them were sick and tired of listening to the few poor and same dance tunes.' And people

partners became almost professional dancers. The township elite felt outdone by their proficiency. In February 1956 the Welfare Officer based at Stanley Hall, Jerry Vera, proposed that a Cultural Club be formed for this elite:

> Mr Vera said that for some time now there had been a need for a Club for more advanced Africans where they could meet and play games, practise dancing and jiving and also arrange for special shows, concerts and dances. Mr Vera said that there was a feeling among the more advanced Africans that the present dancing and jiving shows that are held in the Stanley Hall are always competitive dances. This, he said, cut away many people from taking part, as they were not experts to take part in competition.[47]

When Jerry Vera ceased to be Welfare Officer and became the manager of black Bulawayo's first hotel, the Happy Valley, ballroom dances were staged there by Jerry and his beautiful nurse wife. Ashton himself would sometimes take part.

Great efforts were made by those who had little claim to be 'advanced' to organize popular dancing and make it respectable. The very first association registered on Ashton's files was the African Jiving Society, formed in Mabutweni in 1957. 'The aim of this Society is to create mutual understanding and to advance a high standard of jiving among the African people in Southern Rhodesia, both in having lectures, practices and travelling to compete in other towns in and out of the Colony.' Members of the Society 'shall be asked to help the Police to maintain discipline in the Hall and to see to it that gangs of law-breaking Africans are punished. The Society shall encourage every member to come to the dance smartly dressed and if possible competitors should look respectable.'[48]

But dances were not by any means always respectable. They were held at 'parties' in the townships, where urban jazz was played on gramophones, and where gambling and drinking took place. And they were staged in shebeens. Shebeens, where African urban men could drink *skokiaan*, had long existed in Makokoba. They had always been controlled by the formidable shebeen queens.[49] But now with the development of a vibrant musical culture, of sophisticated female fashions and eager young dancers, they reached a new high. They were especially celebrated in the illustrated monthly *Parade*, which combined photographs of respectable rural weddings with pictures of urban beauty queens. Influenced by South Africa's *Drum* magazine, *Parade* carried columns of hard-talking reports by young African bachelors about Bulawayo's township culture. Daniel Dlamanzi contributed a regular 'Makokoba Party Talk' feature. In the February 1960 issue, for instance, he wrote of:

[46 ctnd] wanted to have drink at dances. As a result, 'private dances controlled by clubs' flourished and took place almost daily. He added that Seventh Day Adventists and Jehovah's Witnesses 'do not attend dances because dancing is satanic'. Two girls criticized the cost and gender imbalance of dances in Stanley Hall but both went to the dances because 'it is their form of recreation, i.e., they like to jive, dance, meet their friends, to chat and see dress fashions worn by other girls.' A 'well known jiver', Lovemore, said that 'speaking candidly his interest in dances is centred on girls. He and the rest of his mates are convinced that the beer halls and dances are the places to make love to women for either immoral or moral purposes .... He is a character who delights in immoral dealings with girls.'

[47] *Bantu Mirror*, 25 February 1956.

[48] Application from Mabutweni, 10 January 1957, file S.O.8, vol. 1, T Box 100, now in the Municipal Housing Department, Bulawayo.

[49] The African Welfare Society report on 'African conditions in Bulawayo', written by Percy Ibbotson and Jerry Vera and published on 31 May 1954, found that *skokiaan* brewing and sale was not due to poverty. 'The majority of Africans convicted for skokiaan brewing are those in receipt of satisfactory wages; their homes are well furnished and there are few signs of poverty.'

Hooch Maningi and his battalion of two score thick-lipped dolls making this little spot in the suburbs stink as though it was the devil's den ... the perfume scent everywhere and of the worst type too.

Hooch imported it from the Congo just as he imported Pata Pata and Kwela dance music from South Africa. 'It is rocking dolls everywhere', wrote Dlamanzi. In the April 1960 issue he moved on to the new leasehold township of Mpopoma. He found it 'full of booze dumps'. At Ma Msindo's 'Falling Leaves' one could catch 'the latest jazz craze, *sinjonjo*', and the hottest dancing girls. 'Mpopoma is a dump that makes Makokoba look like the original Garden of Eden.'

Dumps they might be, but the shebeens and house parties helped to make over-crowded, impoverished – yet feminized – Makokoba 'the cradle of good music in the 50s'.[50] And it was the shebeens and their liquor which provided the name for Makokoba's greatest hit, August Musarurgwa's *Skokiaan*. Musarurgwa played saxophone with his Bulawayo Sweet Rhythm Band in the Stanley Hall 'as the germ of music was biting hard'.[51] And as Joyce Jenje Makwenda tells us, 'when *Skokiaan* was played on the loudspeakers [in the townships] people would take to the street in crazy dances'.[52]

Crazy music and crazy dances resonate through the tragedy of Vera's heroine, Phephelaphi. Phephelaphi's visit to Deliwe's shebeen is like a scene from this chapter – or this chapter is like a footnote to the visit. Phephelaphi goes by night along 'the longest and darkest street in Makokoba'. She is wearing her Stiffs – 'a flaring white skirt underneath which is a stiff petticoat which she has dipped in a bowl of warm water thickened with sugar and then ironed it hot till it dried'. She enters the shebeen to find it full of sharply-dressed men. One man rises to play 'a shining instrument':

> She is thoroughly unprepared. When the music tears into the room she almost falls to the floor with agony. It hits her like a hammer, a felled tree.

Some days later Phephelaphi is in Makokoba with Fumbatha and they are drawn by the sound of singing into 'these small rooms which have no light at all, and sing past midnight about how deep the river is ... They dance with a joy that is free, that has no other urgency but the sheer truth of living, the-not-being-here of this here-place. Fumbatha and Phepehelaphi dance together in perfect harmony, they swing sideways and up and let all their hurt expand ... The room explodes ... Two agile female dancers pull their white cotton skirts with blue dots high up and hold them way over their swinging waists then collide with the music ... One room. The number of people large to bursting.'[53] One little room in Makokoba was where one *really* felt town life.

Charlton Ngcebetsha & the Varieties of Bulawayo Women

Charlton did not carry photos of beauties in the *Home News*. But he was famous as a ladies' man, or more accurately as a man for women. His paper – and the Advisory Board while he was on it – supported the interests of all sorts of township women. Although he detested and denounced Apostolic churches, he defended the right of

50 Joyce Jenje Makwenda, *Zimbabwe Township Music*, Storytime, Harare, 2005, p. 152.
51 *Parade*, March 1958, 'The World is Agog. Smoky Skokiaan'. An ex-CID man, Musarurgwa lived in Mzilikazi. His band recorded his hit 'in a fierce crashing crescendo'.
52 Makwenda, p. 103.
53 Yvonne Vera, *Butterfly Burning*, pp. 54–6; 72–5.

Apostolic young girls to hawk in the townships, just as he defended the right of old widows to sell cooked food at the beer hall. Although he often expressed his commitment to 'traditional' male supremacy in marriage, he stoutly defended the Advisory Board's decision to allocate houses to divorced women with children, or to widows. Some men, he said, changed their wives as others their shirts; most women could not now return to the rural areas; the interests of the children must be paramount. He obtained from Ashton the use of several acres of land on the Western Commonage for cultivation by women and himself measured and allocated the plots.

He gallantly defended the young women of Makokoba and Mzilikazi against the charge of prostitution. The common European use of the word prostitute was 'a calculated and uncalled for insult to our women-folk':

> We cannot suppose that the European gentlemen who speak of prostitutes know such prostitutes carnally. Where then did they collect this information?[54]

At the other social extreme he lavished praise on modern professional young women. On 17 August 1957 he deplored the fact that African nurses – those symbols of Phephelaphi's frustrated aspirations – were obliged to queue up to buy European liquor, 'in their smart white uniforms', with ordinary township women:

> We cannot afford to see our much loved, much respected and dignified Florence Nightingales … being tossed about in these queues by irresponsible nobodies.

And he defended an African girl, expelled by the white matron of the Gertrude Macintyre Hostel for 'communist leanings', as 'one of the best African ladies who constitute the pride of the African today'.[55]

In March 1958 he described the scene at the beer halls and beer gardens in terms of the conflicting interests of different sorts of women:

> There are many decent African women in Bulawayo who curse the beer hall and the beer gardens today because they say it is there that the fathers of their children, their husbands, are attracted and stolen by women of easy virtue, who flirt with them. The women who lose their husbands are, for the most part, church women who generally spend several hours on Sundays in God's House of Worship whilst a large proportion of their husbands … spend practically all their free time on Sundays in the beer hall … Some of these men, strange to say, never even return home for lunch … They buy and eat food from women who sit together at one place selling cooked food … most of whom are widows with large numbers of orphans … The women are always there in all kinds of weather. In the burning heat of the sun they are there. On a windy and dusty day they are there … They make some good profit. No-one envies these women.

Men bought food for themselves and for 'those they flirt with'. 'We hate to describe such women as prostitutes', wrote Charlton, 'but they are regarded by many people as prostitutes. They get everything, food and drinks, free, gratis and for nothing. What lucky people these "darlings" are.' And so the church women complained against their husbands and divorces resulted.[56]

---

[54] *Home News*, 26 June 1954. Koni Benson and Joyce. M. Chadya, in their 'Ukubhinya: Gender and Sexual Violence in Bulawayo, Colonial Zimbabwe, 1946–1956', *Journal of Southern African Studies*, 31, 3, September 2005, draw on over 500 criminal cases of rape and sexual assault in Bulawayo between 1946 and 1956. They remark that 'Europeans were not the only people to assume that African women in town were prostitutes. In over 90 per cent of the court cases African men had offered African women money before or after raping them', p. 602.
[55] *Home News*, 8 March 1958.
[56] *Home News*, 29 March 1958.

Charlton was interested, too, in the Christian devotion of the church women. At Easter 1958 he described how 'some enlightened African leaders' went to the Mhlahlanhela Memorial Tree to pay homage to Mzilikazi. 'One of them spoke to the King in words of great reverence.' On the way back into Bulawayo they picked up five red-bloused Methodist women going to church. The women told them that they too were 'going to a place of mourning. We have suffered a serious bereavement.' The leaders asked who had died, and the women answered 'almost in unison "Jesus Christ is dead".'[57]

Urban Women's Associations

But Charlton was most interested in women's entry into Advisory Board politics. By the late 1950s the male rent-payers' associations which Sipambaniso had set up with such great expectations had withered away. The *Home News* was no longer published on behalf of the Bulawayo African Townships Rent-payers' Association. But now the church women moved in. Charlton, always a political eccentric, had moved during the late 1950s from passionate support for the revived African National Congress to membership of the United Federal Party, even going so far as to chair a meeting in Makokoba addressed by Donald Macintyre.[58]

Not surprisingly, Congress put up very strong candidates for the December 1958 Advisory Board elections in Mzilikazi, hoping to defeat Charlton. But Advisory Board politics were not yet national politics. Charlton headed the poll, gaining 157 votes to Joseph Msika's 87. 'The last effective power', he wrote complacently, 'is still with the common people.'[59] And particularly, he thought, with the uncommon woman. On 3 January 1959 he ran an interview between himself and old Beaton Longwe, the Nyasa head waiter who had once topped Board polls himself. 'How could you lose your Mzilikazi seat,' asked Beaton, 'when some women from Makokoba township and some from Nguboyena and Barbourfields spent days before the election canvassing for you among their fellow women of Mzilikazi?' And moreover, Charlton enjoyed the support of Mrs Reuben Moeketsi, 'one of the most influential women in Bulawayo'. 'She is my maternal aunt', confirmed Charlton.[60]

Mrs Moeketsi certainly was a formidable woman. She was the daughter of the Fingo Chief Mkotamo Kona and married to the carpenter Reuben Moeketsi. She had several children living with her and her husband in Mzilikazi, and was a passionate member of the African Methodist Episcopal church. In the early 1950s she organized a spectacular boycott by women of Mzilikazi stores. By August 1959 she could claim 500 members of her Bulawayo African Townships Women's Association. She represented the respectable married women who had moved into Mzilikazi after the implementation of the Native Urban Areas Act. These women were much concerned with the Advisory Boards because Board members were involved in determining divorce and custody cases and in allocating accommodation. Respectable women

---

[57] *Home News*, 12 April 1958.
[58] *Home News*, 8 November 1958. Macintyre remarked that it was the first time he had been chaired by an African. On 22 December 1958 Charlton printed an imagined dialogue between him and a Congress member. 'I changed my mind from hating European political parties which I bitterly criticised for years', he recorded himself as saying. 'I all of a sudden changed my attitude and supported very actively the UFP.'
[59] *Home News*, 20 December 1958.
[60] *Home News*, 3 January 1959.

wanted the right to attend Board meetings and express their own opinions on such issues. On 11 April 1959 Charlton declared that there were:

> Very healthy signs especially at Mzilikazi and Barbourfields of African women taking great interest in matters which affect their townships. In recent years two Women's Associations, one at Mzilikazi and the other at Barbourfields, have come into existence under the leadership of educated women. They belong to ... various churches, Methodists, Anglicans, SDAs, AMEC, Catholic, as well as members of various separatist African churches.

In May 1959 Violet Moeketsi drew up a constitution for the Mzilikazi association. A meeting condemned mixed bathing – 'How on earth can a mouse be put together with a cat?' The women were 'determined to make themselves a force to be reckoned with ... the moral backbone of the womenfolk of Bulawayo.' They aimed 'to set a good standard of respect and good behaviour towards our husbands' though 'naturally we cannot be expected to co-operate with "nonsense husbands" who are ill-treating some women for nothing'.[61] Violet and Charlton were close allies against African traders – so close that one of Charlton's trader enemies spread the rumour that they were secret lovers.[62] Violet hit back by calling a meeting of women to condemn African traders who were neglecting their wives and even buying houses for their girlfriends in Mpopoma. BATWA 'will see to it that the right people are chosen' for the Advisory Boards, she said. 'No Advisory Board member whose marital life is unsatisfactory can be the right sort of person to discuss and settle quarrels between married people.'[63]

In December 1959 Charlton was again elected to the Bulawayo African Townships Advisory Board, as were three women. Despite rising challenges to Advisory Board politics,[64] Charlton and Violet Moeketsi could still celebrate their alliance in June 1960. In that month the BAT Women's Association held a big party in 'a fairly beautiful large hall'. There was a 'splendid turn-out of women' and a 'much appreciated sprinkling of men', mostly husbands of Association members. 'The women entered the hall singing Matabele traditional songs and clapping their hands in a way reminiscent of olden days. They were headed by two well known Matabele witch-doctors ... dancing, more or less, like Shangaan dancers.' Charlton was there. So was Ashton, who 'as usual made a fine, fatherly speech'.[65]

---

[61] *Home News*, 16 May 1959.

[62] *Home News*, 20 February 1960. Charlton sued David Kwidi, a member of the African Chamber of Traders, for defamation and won. Many women and many traders were in court to hear the case. Charlton was constantly suing and being sued. In August 1959, for instance, he was fined £30 for defaming Chigumira of the Chamber of Traders. The Bulawayo African Townships Women's Association donated £10 9s towards the payment of the fine. *Home News*, 15 August 1959.

[63] *Home News*, 15 August and 24 October 1959.

[64] In December 1959 the Mpopoma Tenants' Association voted to abolish their Advisory Board. They wanted direct representation on the Council. Charlton, who had begun the 1950s complaining that the Boards were powerless, now protested that the Board 'system has magnificently stood the test of time'. In July 1960 a new tenants' association emerged in Makokoba which attacked the Advisory Board for not assisting the poor and unemployed. Charlton told them that the Board was 'the legitimate spokesman for the people' and that when associations did good work, like the Women's Association, 'they work hand in hand with Advisory Board members'. The best study of Advisory Board politics in the first half of the 1950s is Ngwabi Bhebe, *Simon Vengayi Muzenda*, Mambo Press, Gweru, 2004. Chapter 4 concerns Muzenda's political career in Bulawayo between 1950 and 1955, making very effective use of Advisory Board minutes.

[65] *Home News*, 25 June 1960.

6
Black Bulawayo Transformed

Ashton's Bulawayo

Ashton's fine, fatherly qualities had not always been appreciated. In fact he made a disastrous start in Makokoba. In February 1950 he called a meeting in the township to discuss an increase in rents. A thousand people turned up. Sipambaniso, still at that point on the Advisory Board, was there. So was Burombo. According to the CID report, the audience introduced 'irrelevant subjects'. Ashton lost control of the meeting, so Burombo took it over and 'at one stroke, achieved the pedestal of popularity and gave a fillip to the Voice Association'. The main demand of the crowd was for tenancy – they should themselves be the tenants and be reimbursed by their employers. If such a change did not place, thought the CID, 'Burombo will have another issue to contest for his "people's good", and one that would affect many in the location'.[1]

Nor were Burombo's African opponents more helpful or sympathetic to Ashton. Charlton Ngcebetsha's *Home News* began in 1953 by glorying in Burombo's humiliation at an attempted mass meeting of the British Voice Association in Stanley Square, 'thanks to the educated "boys" of the Southern Rhodesia Federation of African Workers Unions'. In December 1953 it gleefully reported Burombo's expulsion from the Advisory Board for absenteeism.[2] But in the same issue Ngcebetsha complained that Ashton and the Council treated the Advisory Board like a rubber stamp. 'Location rents were raised in the teeth of opposition by all the members of the Advisory Board'. He demanded direct representation in the African Affairs Department. These were Ngcebetsha's radical years. He excoriated Prime Minister Garfield Todd.[3] And he continuously criticized Ashton himself.[4]

---

[1] CID Memorandum 44, 24 February 1950. This issue was still being discussed by the Bulawayo African Townships Advisory Board in January 1952 when Ashton told it that 'the Government was putting pressure on the Bulawayo Council to bill the employer' so that 'the employer would pay the rents for all its employees directly to the Council'. BATAB minutes, 17 January 1952.

[2] *Home News*, 5 and 19 December 1953. Burombo's seat was declared vacant at the Board meeting on 20 August 1953.

[3] *Home News*, 30 January and 13 February 1954.

[4] CID reports in 1953 and 1954 paid a lot of attention to the *Home News*. Memorandum 82 on 3 October 1953 said that in Charlton's paper 'stronger language was now more commonplace'. Memorandum 83 of 2 November 1953 said that Charlton 'continues to pour abuse on his enemies in the *African Home News*'. Memo 85 of 5 January 1954 said that the *Home News* had carried many irresponsible reports. The CID had

185

Things used to be much better in Makokoba and Mzilikazi, he proclaimed. As Municipal Police rounded up and expelled 'loafers' in June 1954, Charlton lamented: 'For many years the Africans of Bulawayo were very happy. They liked to stay here and there were no worries or pinpricks as there are now ... Bulawayo, Bulawayo thou art indeed heartless and cruel to poor Africans! What does God Almighty think of all this humiliation of the Africans?' The Bulawayo African Township Advisory Boards refused to sit in protest against the eviction, as well as the fining, of *skokiaan* offenders – 'double jeopardy'. In July 1954 Charlton threatened: 'even if the Advisory Boards have the patience of Job they may be compelled in the long run to kick out like a donkey driven to desperation ... Bulawayo was not like this before. It has now completely changed. African leaders who speak for their people are told by some of the African Administration that they are inciting the people against the Council. This mental attitude reminds one of the late Adolf Hitler.'[5] In an open letter to Ashton in August 1954 he maintained that 'Bulawayo was never like what it is now since we have been here for twenty-five years.' 'Must we break the law? Must we defy the authorities?' The Advisory Board began to hold mass protest meetings, attended by many women with babies on their backs.[6]

Gradually, though, this indictment of Ashton began to slacken and then to cease. The main reason for this was that Ashton's new townships were rising up. In October 1956 Charlton confessed that though 'the Africans of Bulawayo [are not] very pleased with everything Ashton did ... compared to the magnificent work he has done in reducing the chronic problem of African housing, destructive criticism dwindles into nothingness'.[7] Moreover, three of these new townships offered leasehold tenure – houses in Mpopoma on a 99-year lease; in Pelendaba on a 30-year lease and in Hyde Park on a 10-year lease. All these schemes, wrote Charlton, were Ashton's idea.[8] By January 1958, although Charlton was still an ardent supporter of the revived Southern African National Congress, he could write:

> In Bulawayo relations between the City Council through its African Administration Department and the Africans as represented through the combined Advisory Boards left little or nothing to be desired mainly because of the right man at the head of this Department. Last year was notable for very splendid collaboration.[9]

How did Ashton bring about this transformation?

When he was interviewed by Mark Ncube on 1 June 1994 Ashton was in no doubt about the answer. Gradually he had converted city councillors to the idea of building adequate housing, to family housing and the ideal of secure tenure:

[4 cntd] warned Charlton. Ashton had rebuked him on 12 December 1953 after the paper had said that Europeans like Africans to live like animals and that township superintendents were bullies.

[5] No elected members attended the Advisory Board Meetings on 30 July, 27 August or 30 September 1954. Charlton attended a meeting on 23 November but only 'to make the adjournment official'. He declined an offer of talks with the African Affairs Committee because 'it was part and parcel of the Council'. A compromise was reached at a meeting on 16 December 1954.

[6] *Home News*, 12 June, 24 July, 28 August 1954. 'The Bulawayo Council is cruel, bad and heartless', Charlton wrote on 13 November after the eviction of a husband and children. 'What heartlessness on the part of Dr Ashton.'

[7] *Home News*, 27 October 1956.

[8] In fact the Mpopoma scheme was initiated by the Southern Rhodesian government. Michael. O. West, *The Rise of an African Middle Class*, pp. 113-15.

[9] *Home News*, 1 January 1958. 'The voice of the SRANC will be heard louder and louder than was the case last year', wrote Charlton.

The Council had bought Hyde Park and thought of building housing right out there. It was too far out and fortunately the first plan for that was submitted to the Government who turned them down saying it was far too far. You've got all the Western Commonage. Why don't you just start building on the Western Commonage, which was what we did, that was sensible. So that was how we started with Mabutweni and Iminyela [which] were the first built for single men ... The first major improvement was at Barbourfields with the same houses that were being built elsewhere but on bigger stands.[10] We finished Mzilikazi, got on with Nguboyenja.[11]

But 'the big breakthrough' came when Macintyre resigned on 12 September 1953:

We got a new chairman in his position, Councillor Newman, and we were just considering the tenders for Njube which were 1,400 houses. That was pretty big, 1,400 houses on one contract. And he called me and he said 'Do we really need more houses?' I said 'We really need more houses'. He said 'Well what would you say if we doubled it.' I said it would be a really good idea. He immediately doubled the contract so we had suddenly 2,800 houses in Njube. And from then on Council began to realize that housing was necessary. One of the major things was that we got across to the Council and then the Government to accept home ownership.[12]

The new mayor, J.M. Macdonald, reported with pride on 31 July 1954 that 'the Council has now embarked upon a programme of 2,800 additional cottages which will be built in under two years. It is the largest single contract ever to be placed in the Colony for native housing.' Government had warmly congratulated them. Macdonald added that the Western Commonage could accommodate a further 1,500 plots. 'No other centre is as well placed in respect of land and future native development as Bulawayo.' And Ashton was able to report that progress was being made on a leasehold home-ownership scheme at Pelendaba, Western Commonage 6 – a 'considerable step forward in the meeting of the genuine need for security of tenure'.[13]

Bulawayo was being transformed. For many decades the Old Location was not even shown on the annual town map; then it was the only thing shown outside the European city and suburbs. Now the map was dotted with new townships all over the Western Commonage. Ashton recalled in June 1994 that he insisted that the new housing must be accompanied by new amenities:

There used to be some criticism from members of the [Advisory] Board and others when we developed a new township because one of the first things we developed was a beer garden. They would say 'Why not schools?' In those days the school was not our responsibility. We produced offices, and beer halls and libraries and things. Of course one can say people should have been allowed ordinary pubs. That's fine but my job was not to be concerned with the should have hads. I quite agreed with the should have hads but that wasn't the way the Government worked ... I wasn't here as a reformer, I wasn't a politician. We wanted people to be happy and develop,

---

10 On 31 July 1950 Mayor J.H. Butcher's annual report recorded that 300 houses were being added to Barbour-fields 'for the better type of native'. On 31 July 1951 Butcher reported a futher 600 semi-detached cottages were being built there. Only men earning £9 a month or more were eligible. The first Native Administration Report by Ashton in July 1951 reported the success of Barbourfields. 'The great majority of tenants are appreciative of what has been done for them by the Council. Many are taking a great deal of trouble with their gardens and making improvements in their houses, such as putting in doors, painting the walls and gauzing-in the verandahs.' Ashton reported in July 1952 that Barbourfields now had a shopping centre with two general dealers, a milk depot, a butchery, five general shops, two wood shops and 15 hawkers' shops. All these traders were, of course, Africans.

11 Mayor Newman reported on 31 July 1952 that 554 'married' houses had been completed in Nguboyenja, making 'an attractive village'. Ashton reported a shoemaker, a hairdresser and a book seller.

12 Interview by Mark Ncube with Hugh Ashton, 1 June 1994, National Archives, Bulawayo.

13 Advisory Board minutes show that the leasehold schemes were discussed in detail at Board meetings.

encouraging the new places to be happy, comfortable, beautiful … for the townships to be places people were happy to be in.

In South Africa and elsewhere in Zimbabwe, said Ashton, 'the townships are terrible places'. He and his colleagues tried to avoid that. The Bulawayo Council, used to being thought of as reactionary,[14] was now delighted to be hailed as progressive. There were still some Council critics of Ashton and his colleagues. In October 1958 Councillor J.G. Pain labeled Ashton and his department as 'negrophiles' for giving commensurate salaries to four African graduate employees, and described the graduates themselves as 'agitators'.[15] But generally the Council was proud of its well-qualified African administrators and the Bulawayo African townships became places to show off to visiting dignatories, stray royals, and big men from Salisbury and South Africa. (Ashton was careful not to take them to Makokoba.) African businessmen opened shops. New Advisory Boards were created.

It still took some time for Charlton to be convinced. In August 1954 he warned the people who had bought houses in Pelendaba on 30-year leases that they would 'get a rude awakening'. If they were convicted of liquor offences they would be evicted just like people in Makokoba, Mzilikazi, Nguboyena and Barbourfields and their leases would do them no good. Moreover he invoked Makokoba's historical memory: once, men and women had owned houses there 'on free-hold property' but 'all these people had lost their houses'.[16] It was the development of the Southern Rhodesian government's Mpopoma 99-year lease scheme which finally won Charlton over. Mpopoma was officially opened on 27 October 1956. 2,580 houses were planned. Anglican, Assemblies of God, Brethren in Christ, Salvation Army, DRC and Baptist churches were built there by the end of that year. By June 1957 the first 708 houses completed had been bought and occupied. By June 1958 all 2,580 houses had been built and occupied, not only by their new owners but by the tenants whose rents enabled them to pay their purchase instalments.[17] Soon Mpopoma had an Advisory Board and a very lively leaseholders' association.

Charlton was impressed. 'Those who own houses in Mpopoma will be there for ever and ever', he wrote in April 1957. 'There is no unless about it at all. That is a fact. They will be there for all time.'[18] Nor was it only Charlton and the *Home News* who were impressed by Mpopoma.[19] The other African periodicals gloried in it too. *Parade*, indeed, had been ecstatic about Bulawayo's leasehold schemes even before Mpopoma, while Charlton was still expressing skepticism. In its August 1954 issue

[14] Ashton recalls that most councillors were 'insular and racist … There was one … who told me that when he went home he felt he had to wash his hands.' This was Councillor, later Mayor, McNeillie, an old railway trade unionist. But 'thanks to his meeting people on the Board and his work on the African side he switched from being really a very negative person … he became a very fine person and did a tremendous amount.'

[15] *Home News*, 25 October 1958.

[16] *Home News*, 21 August 1954.

[17] Annual Report, African Administration Department, 30 June 1958. At this point there were 3,306 lodgers in Mpopoma.

[18] *Home News*, 6 April 1957.

[19] In fact Charlton allowed letters to appear in the *Home News* in late 1956 which criticized him for being too impressed with Mpopoma and for praising Ashton too highly. Others wrote to criticize the effect of so many young, single male lodgers. On 17 November 1956 Ngidenoiyana wrote of Mpopoma: 'The lease is long enough … The area is big enough but the houses are built too close together … there is not even a little room for one's car … Even the very element of human life is entirely forgotten, that is the air which human beings inhale and exhale. Mpopoma is fast becoming a slum and when it is fully settled it will be a frightful place to live.'

it reported glowingly on the Western Commonage 6 and Hyde Park schemes, which 'heralded a great turning point in the history of Southern Rhodesia':

> The English have a saying that a man's home is his castle. Almost every man's basic need in life is a home he can call his own, some secluded edifice where he is the master.

Already in Bulawayo 'whole townships have sprung up almost overnight'. But hitherto the aim has been to provide basic accommodation. Now 'the country has reached the next stage and the most important in its history ... the acceptance of the principle of home ownership and security of tenure for Africans [who can now] plant their roots in the urban areas'. Visiting the schemes 'was one of my greatest experiences ... a noble act that is going to transform and shape human relationships in this country towards a good end'.[20] The *Bantu Mirror* joined the chorus of praise, reporting on 12 March 1955 that the Mpopoma scheme had been 'received with more approval in the African community than any other scheme in recent years'. It quoted P. Rubatika of the Sons of Mashonaland Cultural Society saying that 'it would make true African citizens in the country out of a race that had appeared aliens'.[21]

In the 1950s, therefore, there not only arose around Bulawayo many more African townships but also much more variegated African townships. Makokoba continued to contain 'single' men and 'married' families living cheek by jowl, but elsewhere there were strictly policed 'bachelor' hostels, schemes where 'single' lodgers lived with lease-holding families, leasehold family cottages and site and service schemes where wealthy Africans built some large and costly houses. Charlton noted in July 1957 that many modern houses were being built in Pelendaba at a cost of £1,000 each. As Michael West writes, 'Pelendaba ... quickly became the address of choice for Bulawayo's black entrepreneurs and higher income professionals ... In 1958 one couple built a ten room house, a far cry indeed from the way Africans were accommodated in the old municipal townships.'[22] Enthusiasm for leasehold schemes and a longing for freehold, shared by editors of all African publications including the maverick Charlton, was very much a mark of their middle class aspirations. In Chapter 4, 'The Best of all Homes: Housing and Security of Tenure', West's *The Rise of an African Middle Class* shows that these elite preoccupations stretch back to the 1930s. In the late 1950s they could begin to be realized. But they still meant little to the great majority of township dwellers. Letters to the *Home News* accused Charlton of overvaluing education and tenurial security and not caring enough about unemployment and poverty.[23]

Ashton certainly allied himself to the aspirant black middle class. But he explored

---

[20] *Parade*, August 1954. In his annual report in July 1955 Ashton declared that 'there can be no doubt that the two home ownership schemes in Bulawayo paved the way for, and encouraged, the Government to embark upon more eleborate schemes with their greater security of tenure'. The Mayor, J.M. Mcdonald, reported that the 99-year lease scheme in Salisbury would be 'administered entirely by the government on government land but in Bulawayo, as the government has no land nearer than about six miles from the cloest industrial areas it offered the scheme to the Municipality ... This was a handsome offer. Its acceptance was vital to Bulawayo's prosperity.'

[21] The *Mirror* recorded on 2 April that Joseph Msika was a 'die-hard supporter of this society' and that he had become its chairman.

[22] Michael West, *The Rise of an African Middle Class*, pp. 115-16.

[23] These allegations were a little unfair. On 23 October 1954 Charlton contrasted in the *Home News* the well-dressed Africans from comfortable homes and driving luxurious cars with 'real poverty, real suffering' in Makokoba. The car owners dumped refuse in the old quarry where 'old women are soon busy looking for bones which they collect and sell to rag and bone dealers. They are so dirty that they are hardly recognisable.'

yet other sorts of residential differentiation. In October 1954 he spoke to the elite Gamma Sigma Club in the Stanley Hall library where, according to Charlton, he explored 'allocation of accommodation to urban Africans on an ethnic basis'. Charlton was appalled. 'Tribal meetings, tribal churches, tribal football matches, and so on. Emphatically no. Again, no, no, no.'[24] Indeed, there were no voices raised for ethnic separation, though the operation of family networks and allocation of trading licences could combine to produce ethnic colourations; Mpopoma, for instance, became known as a Kalanga stronghold. Ashton was ready to give this process a helping hand. As he wrote in his African Administration annual report for 1954/5:

> In Western Commonage 3 a suggestion was made that there be compatible grouping of the tenants. This was confused with specifically tribal grouping and rejected by the tenants who preferred to live wherever the Superintendent allocated them houses. However, they accepted that there should be some attempt at grouping according to friendship, church membership and such like ties, and the Superintendent allocated houses accordingly, placing friends, co-religionists and people from the same districts together in groups of varying sizes.[25]

Ashton, with his team of 'doctors' in anthropology and sociology, was running the new African Bulawayo on 'scientific' lines. His old student and friend, Joshua Nkomo, approved, announcing that anthropology was the new queen of the disciplines and ought to be taught in every African school.[26]

Jerry Vera, Joshua Nkomo & the Rise of Nationalism

In the Bulawayo of the 1950s no one man could combine all the roles Sipambaniso had played – welfare officer, sports hero, social leader, cultural nationalist, trade unionist, Advisory Board member and Congress politician. These roles had become too specialist and demanding, and by the end of the 1950s some of them were becoming contradictory. In the later 1950s they were partly shared by and partly divided between two friends, Jerry Vera and Joshua Nkomo.[27] They had a good deal in common. Both were graduates of the Jan Hofmeyr School of Social Work in Johannesburg; both were keenly interested in 'reviving' African history and culture and worked together to achieve it; for a few months in 1957 they worked together in the surviving Bulawayo branch of the old Bantu Congress. But there were many differences. Jerry Vera was a sports star, excelling at football, cricket and golf. Nkomo could claim no athletic distinction. Jerry Vera was a glamorous figure, an icon of the adverts, his love-life a constant topic of press speculation. Nkomo kept a low social profile. Jerry Vera played a full part in Advisory Board politics, working with Charlton Ngcebetsha, for many years being Secretary to the Bulawayo African Townships Advisory Board and the main advocate of a national Association of Advisory Boards which might confront the Municipal Association. Nkomo never stood for an Advisory Board seat. On the

24 *Home News*, 23 October 1954.
25 African Administration Report, 31 July 1955. Ashton added that 'a policy was pursued of persuading self-employed Africans to take advantage of the home ownership scheme at Pelendaba'.
26 *Bantu Mirror*, 30 June 1956. Nkomo was addressing the Shona Cultural Society and telling them that 'African tradition, custom and culture' were unknown to schoolchildren. They needed anthropology.
27 In his *Nkomo: The Story of My life*, Joshua Nkomo refers to 'my social worker colleague, Jerry Vera [who] was then and long remained a very close friend of mine', p. 62.

other hand, Vera took no part in trade union activities, whereas Nkomo was the first leader of the Railway Trade Union and then President of the African TUC, which replaced Sipambaniso's Federation of African Workers Trade Unions. And when the new, more militant, Southern Rhodesia African National Congress was founded in September 1957, Vera left nationalist politics while Joshua Nkomo became President of the new body. In other words, Jerry Vera was the undisputed 'Mr Bulawayo' in the later 1950s while Joshua Nkomo was in waiting to become 'Father Zimbabwe'.

Jerry Vera[28]

Jerry Wilson Vera was yet another of Bulawayo's glittering Manyika, his friendship with Joshua Nkomo echoing Sipambaniso's friendship with William Makubalo. He was the son of a prosperous, if cantankerous, master-farmer – a man who hated paying taxes and who spent at least two periods in prison for refusing to do so. He named the sons born to him while he was prison *mujeli*. The eldest made the name respectable and modern by calling himself Jerry. The younger Jerry Vera, Yvonne's father, who also came to Bulawayo, did the same. The Veras were a family of educational aspiration and achievement.[29]

Jerry himself attended St Augustine's school in Umtali, at that time regarded as the best in the country. He was the school soccer hero and played for the Umtali African representative eleven in regional cup games. He then went down to South Africa to the Jan Hofmeyer School of Social Work (where Joshua Nkomo was also a student). He played for the Johannesburg African Football Association first team, becoming vice-captain. He was being trained as a social welfare worker, completing his academic courses in 1948.[30] In 1949 he came to Bulawayo to carry out his 'field work' assignment. Another brother, Robson, followed Jerry to St Augustine's and to the Jan Hofmeyer School; also became a soccer star; and also ended up in Bulawayo. The *Bantu Mirror* reported on 18 March 1950 that Robson was in the city on 'school holidays', describing him as 'a first-class athlete' who in 1948 'broke a South African record in athletics'. During his holidays he played football in Bulawayo, excelling 'himself as a centre-forward for the United Africans against the Matabeleland Highlanders. His accurate passes and ball-control were delightful to watch, he was all in a class by himself.' When he had qualified, Robson returned to Bulawayo, played many times for the city's Red Army football team, and later became its manager. A photo of him – 'Robson Vera on the Move' – showed him, foot on ball, as 'a dex-

---

28 Jerry Wilson Vera was Yvonne Vera's uncle. As a schoolgirl she was proud that Mzilikazi secondary school was sited in Jerry Vera Road, and she used to eat her lunch in his Happy Valley hotel. Later they fell out. But when Jerry died in 1999 she was outraged that the death of this once so famous man received no mention in the Bulawayo press. She asked me to write something about his glory years which she could give to his family. So in April 1999 I wrote 'A Bulawayo Hero: Jerry Vera, 1950 to 1960', on which I have drawn for what follows.

29 The *Bantu Mirror* paid detailed attention to African educational attainment. In March 1951, under the heading 'Another Mushona Passes BA by Private Studies', it told the story of Jerry's relative, Adam Vera, 'born in the backveld of Seke Reserve' in 1923. Adam studied for his primary education at Chishawasha and Kutama Catholic missions and then at St Augustine's and St Faith's Anglican ones. He taught in these Anglican schools while studying Junior Certificate privately. He gained six distinctions; went to to Grace Dieu College in Pietersberg; and back to teach at Bonda Mission in Nyanga. In June 1947 he passed six matriculation subjects and finally in 1951 achieved his BA in History and Psychology. Adam – 'a man suffering from an acute case of changing-schools fever' – did not come to Bulawayo.

30 *Bantu Mirror*, 11 February 1951.

terous sure-footed foot-ball player'.[31] The old combination of higher education and higher football skills persisted. As Charlton Ngcbetsha wrote: 'Jerry Vera seems to have studied soccer exactly as he studied arithmetic at school for he has a special knowledge of it.'[32]

The two Vera brothers made an instant impact on Bulawayo, but it was Jerry who was to become much the more famous. This was largely because in 1950, when he had completed his field work in Bulawayo and qualified for his social work degree, he was immediately appointed by Percy Ibbotson and the African Welfare Society to succeed Makubalo as Welfare Officer in Makokoba, based at Stanley Hall.[33] Under Jerry, indeed, the Welfare culture reached its highest level.

He controlled funds for relief and was in regular contact with the very poorest. 'The African Welfare Society's Office, managed by a singularly gifted officer, J.W. Vera', wrote Patrick Rubatika in June 1960 when the Council took over Stanley Hall and Jerry resigned, 'has endeared itself not only among the literate but also among the illiterate Africans. Those who were in distress and needed advice, those who could not make ends meet because of family difficulties, flocked to the Office for help. It covered all social problems in the interests of the community it served.' *Parade* for February 1956 ran a feature on Jerry Vera, 'an extremely busy man, who must know every nook and house in Bulawayo'. He was 'a credit to Bulawayo, where, to me, he is about the most popular man'. Charlton Ngcebetsha joined the chorus:

> Jerry Vera's versatility is remarkable in the extreme. As a well trained social worker ... he has no peer. Through the accident of birth, Jerry is a Mashona, but it would perhaps be appropriate to describe him as a non-tribalist – an African pure and simple – for Jerry gives the impression that his general outlook is completely divorced from tribalism ... J can keep his company roaring with laughter cracking most entertaining jokes ... He is human to the core and his humanity finds practical expression in the excellent way in which he treats justly and impartially Africans of various tribes who demand his attention, off and on, at the Stanley Hall where both in season and out, he is as busy as a bee. Yet, strange to say, even some notorious *tsotsis* like and respect old J. J is a great linguist. He speaks Chishona, Chinyanja, Sindebele, Chibemba (a bit), Sisutu, Sitshwana, a bit of Xosa, English, Afrikaans.[34]

Jerry Vera was therefore in touch with multi-lingual, multi-cultural Bulawayo in a way that Sipambaniso had not been. He did not descend from a township family nor, indeed, live in a township since his rooms were in Stanley Hall. Although, as we shall see, he was elected as member of the Bulawayo African Townships Advisory Board, inevitably becoming its Secretary, he did not represent the interests of the long-term residents in the way Sipambaniso had done. But he certainly was at least as much in touch with Bulawayo's high society. He controlled functions at Stanley Hall; he was master of ceremonies at elite weddings, receptions and concerts. Indeed, he was spokesman for the most 'advanced'. He became Secretary to the Bulawayo African Football Association, the Bulawayo Cricket Association, the Bulawayo Committee for the University of Rhodesia and Nyasaland, and the Ibbotson Memorial Fund. He was patron and adviser to the Athletics Society, the Choral Society, the Bulawayo and District African Pioneers Society. He was on the executive committees of the Inter-

---

[31] *Bantu Mirror*, 5 July 1952.
[32] *Home News*, 10 April 1954.
[33] *Bantu Mirror*, 14 March 1959. Makubalo left to work in Northern Rhodesia.
[34] *Home News*, 12 May 1956.

racial Club, the Social and Cultural Club and the Sons of Mashonaland Society. In all of these he was, as the *Bantu Mirror* declared a 'fountain of suggestions'.[35] He worked closely with Ibbotson, the pair of them researching and writing influential papers on urban conditions in Bulawayo, on Native Courts, and on black female industrial employment.

In touch as he was with black Bulawayo's poverty, and representative as he was of its social and cultural aspirations, it was no surprise that in January 1957 Vera became the first African to be appointed to a Labour Board 'which will enquire into matters relating to African labour in the urban areas of Southern Rhodesia'. 'A wise choice has been made indeed', wrote Charlton Ngcebetsha. African trade union leaders were much less happy and met together to complain that they should have been consulted. Charlton asked rhetorically whether any of them had 'made a comprehensive survey of African living conditions in any urban area? We think African labourers are extremely fortunate to have on the Labour Board an African who will know precisely what he is talking about on behalf of them.'[36]

But Jerry's popularity transcended all this. Handsome, well-dressed, debonair, he featured in dozens of advertisements carried in the African press. His love life – and he was very much a ladies' man – was the source of endless speculation. Having listed all his accomplishments in May 1956 – ending with 'he can dance a tap dance' – Charlton wondered that 'with all these fine qualities Jerry still remains a bachelor. Come on, Jerry ma'an. Get married soon. Don't be so naughty.'[37] By August the *Home News* was able to announce that 'a most popular celibate of Bulawayo, Jerry Wilson Vera, is busy making preparations for the purpose of quitting the state of celibacy … It is understood Jerry has already made his choice among thousands of African beauties.' On 25 August the paper celebrated Vera's wedding to a beautiful Manyika nurse at Bulawayo Memorial Hospital, Abigail Mutambanengwe.[38] The wedding took place at Dowa Native Purchase Area, the bride's home in Manicaland. The reception took place, of course, at Stanley Hall, presided over by Charlton, and attended by Joshua Nkomo.[39]

What gave Jerry this extra aura, above all, was his fame as a footballer. It is impossible now to tell whether Jerry was a better footballer than Sipambaniso. But he certainly got much greater press acclamation – a feature of the larger number of outlets, with *Parade* and the *Home News* added to the *Bantu Mirror*, of the growth of advertising aimed at the African market and of improved action photography. Jerry played as a forward for Highlanders; for the Bulawayo select team, the Red Army, which had its most intense struggles with another globally named team, Salisbury's Yellow Peril; and was chosen as captain of a Southern Rhodesian African team to tour South Africa. He played as right wing, left wing and centre-forward, from each of which positions he scored many goals. Press reports often stressed public reaction to him and the nicknames they gave him.

The *Bantu Mirror* tells us that by July 1954 he had been nicknamed 'Atomic Bomb'; in September he rejoiced in the name *Ayigugi Intsehebe*. In April 1955, playing for the Red Army, he made 'no mistake by pulling a hot shot that settled at the corner

---

35 *Bantu Mirror*, 2 April 1955

36 *Home News*, 12 and 19 January 1957.

37 *Home News*, 12 May 1956.

38 By contrast with Sipambaniso's wife, whose surname was never given in the African press, Abigail was at once acknowledged as a personality in her own right. Very many years later, after her marriage with Jerry had broken down, she became nurse, companion and carer to Sally Mugabe.

39 *Home News*, 18 and 25 August 1956.

of the nets'; in December, playing for Highlanders, 'he made determined drives. At one time playing for a short while in defence, he collected a pass from an opponent outside the eighteen-area and pulled a long bullet-like shot that beat Mfanyana completely. A short while later, working out an individual move he lifted to the nets with a grass-mower. He was undoubtedly the best player for Highlanders.'[40] In April 1956 he played for the national team against the Congo, the crowd roaring 'Come on Jerry'; in June 1958 he scored three goals for Highlanders and 'sensation ran high'.

The *Home News* gave less space to sport but it always had room for Jerry's exploits. Charlton constantly marvelled that though Jerry was too busy to train he always performed superbly. 'Jerry played exceedingly well', reported the *Home News* on 24 April 1954 when the Red Army played the Transvaal. 'It was shots that came from him which in most cases found the net. Fleet of foot and a clever dribbler, who would ever [think] Jerry did not have a full football practice since the football season commenced this year?' In a eulogy to Jerry on 12 May 1956 Charlton wrote that 'his football shots, especially in close proximity to a penalty are like a bullet sound'. 'Chapson, the popular Bulawayo African football commentator, lovingly calls him *intshebi – intshebi ayigui*, as soon as Jerry receives the ball and starts racing to the opposite goal with it. And if he is not intercepted he, more often that not, sends in a pistol-like shot.'[41] As late as February 1959, at the sunset of Jerry's football career, a report on a Highlanders game described how Jerry received a corner kick 'alone, unmarked. As the ball sailed in the air towards Jerry a fellow player tried to meet it whereupon Jerry shouted *bassop*, a shout which reverberated through Barbourfields to the great amusement of many spectators who answered him then and there, saying *intshebe*, Jerry's former football nickname given him by his football admirers because of a long beard he used to grow in those days. He kicked the ball hard first time. The shot was so terrific that off like a bullet the ball went into Mashonaland's goal ... What a classic goal that was!'[42]

When the makers of OK cigarettes wanted a local hero to advertise his devotion to their brand, the 'famous all-round sportsman'[43] Jerry Vera was the obvious choice, though they did conscientiously add that he was also a social worker. From 1957 photos of Jerry Vera, without his beard, appeared regularly in the African press.[44] Jerry was instantly recognizable wherever he went in Bulawayo.

Jerry Vera & Joshua Nkomo: Ethnicity, Culture & History

Charlton Ngcebetsha thought that Jerry Vera was only Shona by accident of birth and that he was really an essential African. Yet Jerry was in fact very much concerned with trying to create a larger Shona identity in Bulawayo. In 1950 there were no 'Shona' football teams or burial societies or boxing clubs in Bulawayo – there were Zezuru, Karanga, and Manyika clubs and societies which competed with and often

[40] *Bantu Mirror*, 10 December 1955.

[41] *Home News*, 25 August 1956.

[42] *Home News*, 14 February 1959. Converting to play centre-forward and 'terribly fleet-footed', Jerry scored again in the match.

[43] On 11 February 1956 the *Bantu Mirror* commented that Jerry was 'one of the two best tennis champions in Bulawayo, a top ranking player in cricket, and an interested golfer'.

[44] The advertisement first appeared in the *Mirror* on 30 March 1957, showing Jerry smoking with the slogan, 'It's OK for me says J. Wilson Vera'. For the development of commercial advertising to Southern Rhodesian Africans, see Timothy Burke, *Lifebuoy Men, Lux Women*.

fought with each other. In May 1952 Jerry combined with Simon Muzenda, Joseph Msika and Patrick Rubatika to convene 'an all-Shona meeting' in order to create 'a common platform for all Mashona-speaking people [and] learn to appreciate all that is noble in all that is Shona'.[45] In mid-June 1952 Vera and the others formed the Sons of Mashonaland Society with the aim of showing all Shona-speakers in Bulawayo that 'they are brothers'.[46] Later, in April 1955, he proposed a sub-committee of the Sons of Mashonaland Society in order to study 'all Shona articles appearing in the *Bantu Mirror* in the interests of the Shona reading public'. He was seeking to reinforce a common Mashona identity with a standard Shona language. Paradoxically, a man might come to feel more Shona in Bulawayo than in Mashonaland.

Some critics deplored what they thought was Shona tribalism. Ngcebetsha and Nkomo were not among them. They supported Jerry Vera's endeavour as part of a process of creating a series of nesting identities – one might be Manyika at the level of home and clan, Shona at the level of language and culture, and African at the level of history and aspiration. Nkomo followed this trajectory. He was himself a member of the Kalanga Cultural Promotion Society; he praised people who built traditional Kalanga houses; in July 1955, a year after his father's death, he took one of the Matabele Home Society's activists, Mazibisa, down to Bida to take part in a Kalanga Umbuyiso ceremony.[47]

For Nkomo, being Kalanga was a matter of family and household. But he also put a lot of effort into being Ndebele. He was a leading member of the Matabele Home Society, went on pilgrimage to Mzilikazi's grave at Entumbane, and spent hours at the feet of Ndebele bards, learning the royal praise-songs. All this prepared him to become more rather than less ready to collaborate with Jerry Vera in taking the next step beyond both a Shona and an Ndebele identity.[48] In August 1952 Nkomo and Vera got together to form a society 'whose duty it will be to preserve all the African culture and heroes of Africa ... to encourage and collect all African folk stories and dances; the erection of a monument to great Africans; the preservation and collection of African national costumes'.[49]

Thereafter, Nkomo was more consistently active in the Africanist cultural cause than Vera. He addressed teachers in Matobo district, stressing the need 'to preserve customs, language, folklore and traditional song', and called for an annual gathering to praise 'African heroes of long ago who had done wonderful work for the African races before the Europeans came to this country'.[50] In August 1956 he told six hundred people at a cultural gathering in Bulawayo that a day should be set aside annually to remember 'the past heroes of Africa in general and Central Africa in particular'. Without such a commemorative day 'present-day heroes cannot base their work on the history of past heroes'.[51]

---

[45] *Bantu Mirror*, 29 May 1952.

[46] *Bantu Mirror*, 21 June 1952.

[47] *Home News*, 16 July 1955. Ngcebetsha, a Fingo supporter of the Matabele Home Movement, delighted in this performance of a traditional Kalanga death ritual.

[48] In March 1956 S.J. Dzwittie congratulated the Sons of Mashonaland for coming together and no longer being ashamed of the name Mashona. He urged them to collaborate with the Matabele Home Society 'which is filling an important gap among the Sindebele people'. *Bantu Mirror*, 10 March 1956.

[49] *Bantu Mirror*, 30 August 1952.

[50] *Bantu Mirror*, 17 April 1954.

[51] *Bantu Mirror*, 18 August 1956. Nkomo appealed to both Shona and Ndebele heroes, including Monomotapa and Mutasa along with Mzilikazi and Lobengula.

Joshua Nkomo

By 1956 Joshua Nkomo was already thinking of becoming a 'present-day hero'. But here there arises a problem. For most of the 1950s Nkomo was far less recognizable than his friend Jerry Vera; received far less publicity; was less of a star. There is a tension between the evidence of African oral informants, the African press, and municipal and government documents and Joshua Nkomo's own account in his auto-biography. As we shall see, by 1960 he undoubtedly had become a hero. But what about the years before?

In *Nkomo: The Story of My Life*, Joshua describes 'the return of the native son' to Bulawayo in 1948. He became Welfare Officer for the Railways, president of the African Railway Employees' Association, and in March 1952 was elected Chairman of the old National Congress, Bulawayo branch.[52] He admits and even emphasizes that 'there was a tremendous amount of apathy'; that the railway union was ineffective; and that the ANC was very weak. Things changed for him, though, in 1952. A conference was to be held in London on the idea of a Federation for Central Africa; the Rhodesian government had been told that they must make at least a show of African representation. So, as Nkomo tells the story:

> One day, sitting with my wife in my little house at Number 3 Railway Compound, I saw a car pull up outside the door. I recognized it as belonging to the Reverend Percy Ibbotson ... He seemed a bit tense, and after a while he asked if I would mind taking a walk. Once outside, he revealed that he had a message for me from no less a person than Sir Godfrey Huggins ... inviting me to join the Southern Rhodesian delegation to the forthcoming London conference ... But what, I asked, was he inviting me as? As a prominent person, said Mr Ibbotson. I replied that I was not a prominent person, just a young man.[53]

On further inquiry Nkomo discovered that Huggins 'had nothing specific in mind for me. All he wanted was for me to be a member of the Southern Rhodesian delegation.' The Bulawayo Congress branch agreed that he should 'go to London and oppose the Federation'.[54] So off he flew in late April, on the same plane as his old employer, Macintyre, and the other 'black face', Jasper Savanhu. Nkomo is not, of course, claiming that this strange invitation transformed him from a young man into a leader. In fact it put him in a very awkward position.[55] There was plenty of protest from other Southern Rhodesian African spokesmen, and Salisbury leaders, including Aaron Jacha, President of Congress, sent a telegram denouncing Nkomo;[56] Nyasa and Northern

---

[52] *Bantu Mirror*, 22 March 1952.

[53] *Nkomo: The Story of My Life*, pp. 48-9.

[54] *Bantu Mirror*, 22 March 1952. On 26 April 1952 the *Mirror* reported that 17 different African organizations in Bulawayo had voted confidence in Nkomo and Savanhu. It was deplored that Africans had not been consulted but blame for disunity was accepted. The associations represented included the Bulawayo Congress branch; the MHS; the Federation of African Trade Unions; several burial societies; the Football Association; the Bulawayo African Townships Advisory Board and the Chamber of Bulawayo African Traders.

[55] For a trenchant account of Nkomo's predicament and performance in London see Michael West, *The Rise of an African Middle Class*, pp. 185-6.

[56] George Nyandoro scornfully repudiated the Bulawayo organizations which had backed Nkomo. They were mere 'social organisations, such as football clubs and burial associations and thus incompetent on political questions'. *Bantu Mirror*, 3 May 1952. Charlton Ngcebetsha's backing for Nkomo was dismissed by the Salisbury 'Joint African Organisations' as the view of 'an alien African not representative of major African organisations'. West, p. 282, note 33.

Rhodesian African leaders boycotted the conference; the Labour Party described Nkomo and Savanhu as stooges. They rescued their reputations a little by walking out of the first session of the conference and Nkomo even got to meet Dr Banda, 'a stern figure, very reserved, like most Malawians'. But it was when he returned to Bulawayo that 'Sir Godfrey Huggins and his government gave me an importance that was more than I personally felt I deserved – although I was delighted to take advantage of it.' Nkomo's passport was taken away. 'I was becoming a bit of a celebrity.' He became even more of a celebrity when he returned from his second visit to London in January 1953, this time funded by public subscription in Bulawayo:

> In England, as usual at the end of public meetings, there had been all sorts of people handing out leaflets. I had accepted them more or less at random, and stuffed them into my brief case with my other disorganized papers. When I arrived in Bulawayo the customs took away those papers, and among them they found a couple of copies of a pamphlet that I had not even read, emphasizing the contrast between black and white people's housing in Southern Rhodesia. This gave the government the chance to put me on trial for importing subversive literature. I was summoned to answer the charge at Bulawayo magistrates' court.[57]

It was this, Nkomo writes, which began to make him a hero. There was 'an amazing show of public support for my defence. From all over Southern Rhodesia people came to stand in the street and cheer when I went in and out of court. Bulawayo was blocked solid.' Nkomo was cautioned and discharged. But his 'own triumph was in the street with these thousands and thousands of people from all over the country. Factories closed because so many of their workers had taken time off to go to court … There had never been anything like it before.'[58]

I find this account a little puzzling. Of course, I don't doubt that Nkomo was charged and cautioned. But there is no reflection of his triumph in the African press. The *Bantu Mirror*, which reported black Bulawayo political events so assiduously, makes no mention of closed factories or blocked streets. There is no report of Nkomo's trial or its repercussions in the CID memoranda. Most of all, though, it seems clear that Nkomo, after a brief spasm in 1953 of anti-Federal emotion, could not command large-scale public support in the years that followed.

In mid-February 1953 Nkomo chaired a meeting of the Bulawayo Supreme Council, which unanimously deplored Federation and elected a committee to fight it.[59] Nkomo himself declared that 'before any form of federation the rights of the Africans and the power of the chiefs should be restored, the land should be re-divided in consultation with Africans, wages raised to a living wage and franchise laws amended.' [60] In mid-March Nkomo chaired a huge public rally, numbering some ten thousand, which passed a unanimous resolution against Federation and empowered Nkomo and Ngcebetsha to go to Fort Jameson to liaise with northern African leaders. In mid-April the two men reported back to a mass meeting of the Supreme Council which endorsed the 'non-cooperation' policy agreed at Fort Jameson. 'The first move in non-cooperation will be that no African will stand for the Federal parliamentary election.'[61]

57 *Nkomo*, p. 59.
58 Ibid., p. 60.
59 The CID Memorandum 73 for 2 January 1953 revealed the tensions inside the Supreme Council. It reported 'a somewhat violent meeting' at which Charlton Ngcebetsha had 'made himself unpopular by criticism of other African leaders present. Only Philip Nkomazana prevented Ngazimbi from assaulting him.'
60 *Bantu Mirror*, 21 February 1953.
61 *Bantu Mirror*, 21 March and 18 April 1953.

So far so good for Nkomo mobilizing his mass support. But things rapidly changed once Federation was established. Despite the April resolution, Nkomo had decided by October 1953 that he would contest one of the African seats in the Federal parliament.[62] In his book he says that his motive 'was to show [federal politics] up as a farce .... As the demonstrations at my trial had shown, I had massive African support, but the rigged electorate excluded the vast majority of the people from voting. The electoral system was absurd and my defeat proved it.'[63] But very many members of the enthusiastic crowds of April were disconcerted by Nkomo standing. A meeting of the Bulawayo African Voters in October 1953 ended in fisticuffs when 'strong exception was taken against leaders of the Supreme Council who a few months ago were hard against Federation and supported a policy of non-cooperation but who had suddenly decided to stand for Federal election without notifying the people they told to oppose Federation'.[64]

In 1954 African politics in Bulawayo went into paralysis. On 17 July a correspondent to the *Mirror* could decry 'the utter silence' of Bulawayo political leaders, including Nkomo. 'The Southern Rhodesian National Congress ... has gone to a big sleep ... The Supreme Council made a noisy opposition to Federation and then died a natural death.' On 25 December the *Mirror* reported the rumour that Congress was dead. Nkomo retorted that it was not dead but resting. It was the same story in 1955. In March a *Mirror* editorial declared that the idea of partnership had 'submerged the Congress and other racially conceived bodies. Congress itself never met in the whole of 1954.' A Congress meeting called for 11 September 1955 in order to approve a revival plan had to be postponed because of low attendance. 'Congress is in a really deep sleep and it will take men to wake it up.'[65]

Nkomo as Trade Unionist

Whatever reservations might be harboured about the consistency of Nkomo's political leadership, there was little doubt about his effectiveness as a trade union organizer. Among Hugh Ashton's files on Bulawayo African associations is Nkomo's report to the Annual Congress of the Rhodesia Railways African Employees Association, 25 and 26 October 1952. It is an impressive document. Nkomo paid tribute to the founders of the Association, who first applied for recognition in March 1943 and who persisted in making unacknowledged representations to the management throughout 1944 and 1945. 'Things came to a head when in October 1945 a strike was called in Bulawayo and finally spread to all centres throughout the system. This was described as the most orderly strike in the world. All this was due to the commendable organization by this Association.' The end result was the Labour Board whose findings, published on 27 February 1948, were 'quite satisfactory'. And the Association was recognized.

But in this success lay danger. 'Many members of the Association, especially in the rural centres, thought the publication of the awards meant the end of the activities of the Association. The result was that a number of branches became inactive' and even

---

[62] In fact Nkomo was chosen as a candidate on 1 November by the Supreme Council which chose him by 60 votes to 24 for Grey Bango. Charlton Ngcebetsha declined to stand.

[63] *Nkomo*, p. 65. Nkomo received 2,124 votes, Mike Hove 9,090.

[64] *Bantu Mirror*, 24 October 1953.

[65] *Bantu Mirror*, 11 March and 17 September 1955.

in Bulawayo and Salisbury 'the enthusiasm was not as great as during previous years'. Moreover, in June 1950 Northern Rhodesian rail-workers broke away to form their new Union. 'There was from the start until now no wholesome relationship between the Association and the Union. The Union has and still is organizing membership in Southern Rhodesia and has completely disregarded the rights of this Association.' When William Sigeca, who had led the Association since 1943, retired in 1951, Nkomo was employed as full-time organizing secretary. But he was immediately faced with another crisis. The Umtali branch of the Association demanded a Special Central Council Conference; one was called in Bulawayo in March 1952 (the month before Nkomo flew to London) but the Umtali branch did not send a delegate; the Conference then went to Umtali 'to settle matters there'; their reception 'was a disgrace'. So the Conference decided to close down the Umtali branch and take over all property and funds. As Nkomo spoke in October 1952 the branch was still refusing to comply.

So the Railways Association was suffering in 1952 the same confusion and lack of momentum which characterized Bulawayo African politics generally. But Nkomo was actively recovering the situation. Knight Maripe was appointed as Assistant General Secretary; the executive held nine ordinary and 15 Special meetings in the first nine months of 1952; a joint industrial committee for African Railway Workers was set up in September 1952, bringing together the Association, the Union and the management. Nkomo was able to report 22 branches of the Association and a membership of 2,684 (600 paid-up members residing in the Bulawayo Railway African Township). But he was very far from satisfied. There were over 12,000 railway workers employed in Southern Rhodesa. But:

> A large number of this 12,000 is comprised of labour supplied by the Native Labour Supply Commission and most of these people are so ignorant that they have no conception of what collective bargaining means. We have found it most difficult and at times impossible to organize this type of labour. Apart from these people there is a certain religious sect [Jehovah's Witnesses] that has abstained from any other form of organization but their own.

Moreover, 'in most cases today the African is an employee of another employee', a white worker, and this has created 'a situation unparalleled in the history of labour organizations'. European Unions are hostile; African organizations have to struggle against both them and the employers. Yet:

> No rest is possible. If the little rights and liberties handed down to us by our predecessors are to be preserved and expanded; if our standard of life and conditions of employment are to be improved; we must strengthen our Association until it is 100% strong.[66]

Six delegates of the Federation of African Workers Unions attended as observers and witnessed the railway workers urge 'the formation of a Trade Union Congress ... as soon as possible'.[67]

In fact it took a further two years for a TUC to emerge. In May 1953 Nkomo chaired

---

[66] Nkomo's Report to Congress, 25 October 1952, Bulawayo Associations File, S.O.8, Vol.1., T Box 100.

[67] Together with this report in Ashton's file is a list of all African organizations active in the Bulawayo Railway Township, which gives a glimpse into that closed world. There was a football club with 200 members; a baseball club; a boxing club which 'has a large following'; 120 scouts, cubs and sunbeams; a women's club of 100 members; a debating society; the Fort Jameson Burial Society, 'largely an Angoni Tribal Society', with 40 members; the Barotse Tribal Society which tried cases under tribal law; some 15 different religious sects with a total following of 1,150. There was a Railway Township Advisory Committee of 18 members on which sat Daisy Peters, Female Social Worker.

a meeting of trade unions in Gwelo. He gained the support of a strong Salisbury union, Reuben Jamela's African Artisans Union, and they agreed to set up the SRTUC.[68] Grey Bango of the Bulawayo Federation was desperately anxious to hand over responsibility for an increasingly dangerous industrial situation but Charles Mzingeli was bitterly hostile. It was not until 1954 that the SRTUC was founded and the Federation was able to dissolve.[69] When it did, Joshua Nkomo was elected as President. Knight Maripe took over the Railway Workers Union.[70]

Industrial Strife in Bulawayo

As CID reports make clear, Bulawayo workers and their leaders had been waiting impatiently for the formation of a TUC which would bring railway workers together with everyone else, as they had not been in 1948, and enable any strike action to be co-ordinated between Bulawayo and Salisbury as it had not been in 1948. Sipambaniso's Federation of Southern Rhodesia African Workers Unions was booming, borne aloft on the waves of worker discontent, and Stanley Square in Makokoba was once again the site of huge and militant rallies. On 5 January 1954 CID Memorandum 85 reported that the Federation had expanded greatly, compelling Grey Bango to elect new officers to help him administer it, who were 'not always as moderate and responsible' as himself. If he were to be undermined 'the consequence might be dangerous'. If Bango retained control, however, he would not call a strike until the formation of an African TUC.

Memo 86 of 15 February 1954 reported that Bango himself had violently opposed the provisional wage award and that the Federation had rejected it. On 17 January a thousand workers attended a Federation meeting in Makokoba, several shouting for a strike. It was agreed instead that the Provincial Native Commissioner be petitioned on 19 January and a reply demanded by the 24th. On the 24th, 800 card-bearing members of the Federation agreed to wait until a mass meeting on 7 February. There were 'universal rumours' of strike action. Bango himself 'became apprehensive of the consequences of his meeting and intimated to an African detective that he did not think he would be able to control it'. On 5 April Todd's government acted. All meetings were banned. Bango asked permission to go to Wankie, where troops were deployed, to mediate in the strike there. He was refused.

Memo 87 of 10 March 1954 reported mass meetings in Stanley Square, Makokoba,

---

[68] Scarnecchia, *The Urban Roots of Democracy and Political Violence*, p. 73; *Bantu Mirror*, 16 May 1953.

[69] There is some uncertainty about the date of the SRTUC foundation. Brian Raftopoulos says that it was launched in January 1954, consisting only of Bulawayo trade unions. Raftopoulos and Phimister, *Keep on Knocking*, p. 75. Raftopoulos's date is confirmed by the *Home News* of 13 February 1954 which reported that the TUC had been formed in Gwelo, that Grey Bango and the Federation had been thanked for blazing the trail and that Nkomo's Presidency represented a new beginning. But this is almost certainly some months too early for the emergence of an effective TUC. CID Memorandum 87 for 10 March 1954 makes it clear that in March 1954 the Federation still very much existed but that there was 'movement' towards a SRTUC. Then at last CID Memorandum 92 reports that on 7 August 1954 Grey Bango had declared the dissolution of the Federation and the formation of a regional council of the TUC. Bango was 'relieved of the responsibility of the Federation'. Memorandum 94 reported a TUC meeting in November. Charlton Ngcebetsha's *Home News* reported the dissolution of the Federation and the emergence of the SRTUC as early as 12 June 1954. It was clearly a process rather than an event.

[70] The *Home News* hailed Nkomo's leadership. The new TUC, wrote Charlton, was supported by all 'experienced Trade Union leaders'. But Burombo's Voice Association was 'now courting workers of Bulawayo to join it. This is merely playing football with workers.'

on 28 February and 1 March at which there was 'much strike talk … heated verbal exchanges, out of control':

> The confusion and danger aroused by the irresponsible leadership of Bango, who having stirred up the fire on Sunday and Monday tried to put it out on Tuesday by advocating support for the Weaving Industry Industrial Labour Board, exactly the opposite course of action previously urged by him. After the meeting on Tuesday Bango got thoroughly frightened at the temper of the meeting and voluntarily asked to see the Police authorities in order to cover himself for the consequence of any strike action by recommending that preventative police action should be carried out the following morning, in case of picketing.

Trapped in this thoroughly unheroic role, Bango told the authorities that he would dissolve the Federation as soon as a TUC was established.

Charlton Ngcebetsha's *Home News* was born at this time of industrial crisis, when the Federation of African Workers Unions, once led by his much admired Sipambaniso, found itself once again at the centre of the storm. The *Home News* provides an impassioned accompaniment to the CID reports. In January 1954 Charlton reported that workers were angry at the inadequacy of wage awards and were clamouring for strike action at mass meetings in Stanley Square. Only the 'responsible leaders' of the Federation, particularly its President Ngazimbi, kept them in check.[71] On 30 January 1954 Charlton angrily refuted Todd's claim that the Federation's leaders were 'agitators'. In fact they were trying to restrain workers who were 'in a state of ferment', offered wage increases which were 'a drop in the ocean', and demanding that their leaders tell the government that they wanted more. 'The workers are straining at the leash to put their tools down'. Charlton finished with a characteristic footballing metaphor:

> Instead of the Government kicking the ball back hard to the leaders as a sign of its adamantine attitude we feel that the proper thing is for the Government to dribble the ball nicely towards the centre and try and bring about a compromise.

When in February 1954 Garfield Todd banned all meetings in Bulawayo, because of strike rumours, and troops and police patrolled the townships, Charlton mocked the Prime Minister. 'Africans stood, looked at the police and laughed because they realized that these myrmidons of law and order had been deceived by groundless rumours.' He also carried a premature report that a TUC had been formed in Gwelo and Bango – thanked for having borne the heat of the day.[72] On 20 February, as the Wankie strike was declared illegal, Charlton asked rhetorically 'What then is the illegality of strikes staged by Africans in this country? Why is the so-called democratic Government of Southern Rhodesia behaving seemingly in an undemocratic manner?'

On 27 February 1954 Charlton described two mass meetings in Stanley Square at which the Federation's leaders had narrated the negotiations since 1952, when 'the workers were literally starving', but nevertheless rejected the inadequate recommendations of the Labour Board. And now the Labour Board heard evidence from boss-boys and foremen and refused to hear trade union leaders and officers of the Federation:

> This information was too much for the workers to stomach. They cried 'Let's all die; no work tomorrow; tomorrow strike.' The people were so electrified that it took some minutes before they were calmed down.

---

71 *Home News*, 23 January 1954.
72 *Home News*, 13 February 1954.

In May Charlton reported that Grey Bango had been warned by police, as General Secretary of the Federation, not to convene any meetings 'unless he is confident that such meetings will be orderly and not lead to unlawful action'. Yet, Charlton commented, Bango was 'no extremist. If anything he is too cautious.'[73] Charlton's relief was as palpable as Bango's when on 12 June 1954 he was able to report that the Federation had dissolved itself and the TUC taken over.

After Nkomo's ascension to the Presidency of the TUC things calmed down, but it is far from clear what role the new body played in this. He does not mention the TUC at all in his book He does, however, speak of a 'justified strike' by railwaymen in 1956, when 'the Todd government sent in the police with dogs to put the strikers in their place'.[74] And, indeed, Nkomo's successor, Knight Maripe, endured a terrible time. He was detained in September 1956 under emergency regulations proclaimed at the beginning of a chaotic railway strike:

> Tuesday morning the Police had to disperse with tear gas a crowd of Africans estimated at about two thousand [wrote the *Bantu Mirror*]. One African was injured … They were given ten minutes in which to disperse and when the warning was ignored by the crowd, a force of African and European police, armed with tear gas, steel helmets, truncheons and shields, advanced on the crowd and used tear gas. There followed a general stampede.

The entire executive of the union was detained. Six were charged in October under the Public Order Act. The strikers were dismissed and then re-employed at the beginners' rate of pay.[75] The strike was barely organized – 'most centres plainly defied the call to strike'. Ngcebetsha called the strike 'a fiasco'. Nkomo made no public statement.[76] It took a younger and more radical trade unionist to complain that the repression of the strike and 'the tragic mass dismissal and re-employment of many railway-men … was the worst act of injustice in the industrial history of this country'.[77] That unionist was J.Z. Moyo.

J.Z. Moyo deserves a prominent place in this story. In many ways he was like a much more self-confident and articulate version of Yvonne Vera's hero, Fumbatha. He first appeared in the African press on 10 March 1951 as 'one of the most outstanding members of the Bulawayo Builders Association'. He told the *Bantu Mirror* that 'he will never give up building unless he gets someone to prove to him that building makes people grow older.' And as he did grow older so he became more and more active in defending the interests of builders. In January 1956, as President of the Southern Rhodesia African Artisans Union, still 'so young and yet so high up the scale of responsibility',[78] he found himself contesting with aggressive white building artisans. The white union had petitioned the Governor for equal pay for equal work as a way of preventing themselves from being undercut by African builders. A Labour Board was appointed to look into the question and Moyo complained that officials of the National Industrial Council were 'busy at work raiding African artisans in and

---

[73] *Home News*, 1 May 1954.

[74] *Nkomo*, p. 66.

[75] *Bantu Mirror*, 29 September and 13 October 1956.

[76] Nkomo was at this moment calling on every African to donate a shilling towards an African Heroes Day 'to remember their past heroes like Mambo, Lobengula, Monomatapa, Chaminuka, Mtasa and so on'. *Home News*, 18 August 1956. He was also reported as attending a meeting of the Bulawayo branch of Congress chaired by Jerry Vera. *Bantu Mirror*, 22 September 1956.

[77] *Bantu Mirror*, 13 October 1956.

[78] *Parade*, January 1956.

around Bulawayo, ordering them to appear before the Labour Board, likely to hear evidence at the end of this month and look at the question with blinkers'.[79]

In early February 1956 Moyo himself appeared before the Labour Board in Bulawayo along with Joshua Nkomo. They argued that it was not exploitation for employers to pay African artisans at one-third of European rates because Europeans had training as apprentices and gained skills and experience which Africans were denied.[80] In May Moyo reacted with fury to the Labour Board's finding that African builders in skilled work had to be paid at European rates:

> It is a way to strengthen the rigid apartheid which has hitherto been a feature of the building industry in Southern Rhodesia. All the talk about African advancement in this country is mere contemplated humbug.[81]

In June the young militant met Prime Minister Garfield Todd, who told him that 'African artisans were a threat to the European artisan in the building industry. In Bulawayo the number of European artisans had dwindled to about 700, whereas on the other hand the number of African artisans had risen to about 600 ... Africans were not trained to work in European areas but were in actual fact trained in order to go and improve their huts in the reserves.'[82] Moyo, whose 'hut' was in Makokoba (and who was a key ally of Ngcebetsha and Vera on the Advisory Board), was outraged by Todd's reply and was very ready to denounce his handling of the abortive railway strike.

But as Moyo became active in the TUC it was not only white builders, the municipality and the government which he criticized. In March 1957 Moyo and the TUC were 'at daggers drawn' with the Bulawayo Chamber of African Traders. 'The interests of the workers and the interests of the Chamber clash', wrote Charlton. J.Z. Moyo accused African shopkeepers in the townships of exploiting both their customers and their staff. 'Shop-keepers are seen to charge extravagantly and to suck the blood of their African customers until they are bone-white.' At a meeting between the Chamber and the TUC there were 'heated exchanges' between Z.T. Chigumira, spokesman of the Chamber, and J.Z. Moyo. There were 'angry words' and 'uproar' and the meeting spilt out of Stanley Hall into the square.[83]

But while J.Z. Moyo was becoming more militant, Nkomo was moving his attention away from trade unionism in two other directions. One was the process of establishing himself in Bulawayo's black middle class. He moved out of his cottage in the railway compound, first to rent in Barbourfields and then to build his 'hut' in Pelendaba. In 1956 he became President of the Bantu Co-operative Trading Society, the object of which was to carry on wholesale and retail business and to run shops, butcheries and eating houses under a co-operative system.[84] In November 1957 he opened a £3,000 building 'in the heart of the African area ... and thus became the first African in Matabeleland to set himself up as an auctioneer, one of the few instances as yet

---

[79] *Bantu Mirror*, 14 January 1956.
[80] *Bantu Mirror*, 4 February 1956.
[81] *Bantu Mirror*, 5 May 1956.
[82] *Bantu Mirror*, 9 June 1956.
[83] *Home News*, 2 and 23 March 1957.
[84] A file on the Society exists in Ashton's records of Bulawayo African associations, S.O.8., Vol.1, T Box 100. The advisers of the Society were Prag Vaghmaria and F.Tarham; Nkomo was joined on the Board of Managers by Amos Mazibisa, I.J. Mtimukulu, W.T. Ngwenya and four other committee members. 'The Society gives clear proof that Africans are capable of conducting business on sound lines.' It planned 'to expand its activities to the newly opened townships in the Western Commonage'.

which mark the arrival of the Colony's Africans on the commercial plane as property owners, employers and commercial magnates ... An astute businessman ... he has already sold a few cars at his auction floor ... On auction days his employees and himself work from sunrise to sunset.'[85]

The Rise of African Nationalism in Bulawayo

Nkomo's second, apparently contradictory, concern was to revive Congress in Bulawayo. In this enterprise all of the 'characters' discussed in this chapter – Charlton Ngcebetsha, Jerry Vera, J.Z. Moyo and Nkomo himself – were involved. Their joint efforts were certainly needed. As we have seen, at the end of 1955 Congress had been declared dead by the African press. And in 1956 although there was plenty of Congress activity in Bulawayo, it was the work of the Northern Rhodesian and Nyasaland African Congresses.

In January 1956 the Northern Rhodesian National Congress sought permission from Ashton to hold meetings in Mpopoma and Mabutweni in order to tell 'the wealthy members that it is their duty to send their money home and not keep it in Southern Rhodesia'. In March 1956 the secretary of the Bulawayo branch sent Ashton a copy of the Congress constitution and Ashton approved a request from K. Lungu, Makokoba branch secretary of the NRC, to take collections 'at regular branch meetings' there.[86] Thereafter Ashton received copies of the regular Congress newsletters sent from Northern Rhodesia for distribution at their Bulawayo branches. They were militant stuff. The July newsletter exhorted: 'Let us sound the drum of African Freedom in our beautiful mountains and valleys to all our people ... preach to the next person about African Salvation.' The October newsletter included Labouchere's parody, 'Onward Christian Soldiers', 'about the seizure of thousands of Matabele arable lands and cattle'. The December newsletter, written by Kenneth Kaunda, proclaimed a Marxist message:

> The means of production should not be the property of any privileged person or class but should be owned and controlled by the whole community; a person who is dependent on the will or consent of another for the privilege of earning a livelihood by labour is verily a slave. A nation whose workers are dependent on a small fraction of non-producers for access to the instruments of wealth is a nation of slaves and tyrants.

Ashton, unperturbed by the thought of these ideas being disseminated in Makokoba, wrote to ensure a more regular supply.[87]

---

[85] *Parade*, December 1957, 'Great Matabele Businessman'. Ashton's African Administration annual report in June 1957 recorded that Nkomo had been given permission to set up 'as an Estate Agent and Auctioneer. A start was made on premises for him in Mzilikazi.' Ngcebetsha, who had fallen out with Nkomo politically, criticized his auction business in the *Home News*. On 14 February 1959 he accused Nkomo of exploiting African women hawkers, who had to 'pay double money for things which they buy' because they had both to buy the goods and then pay the car driver to transport them to the retail market. 'There is absolutely no excuse for grinding innocent women to most degrading powder'. See also 12 April 1959.

[86] Superintendent, Mabutweni to Ashton, 5 January 1956; Branch Secretary, NRANC, to Ashton, 6 March 1956; Superintendent, Makokoba to Ashton, 8 March 1956; Ashton to Superintendent, 26 March 1956, file 'African National Congress of Northern Rhodesia', S.0.8, Vol. 1, Box 100.

[87] NRANC newsletters, 31 July, 31 October and 31 December 1956. Ashton did, however, ask township Superintendents to ensure that Congress meetings were attended and reported on. Ashton's files contain newsletters for 1957 and 1958. S.0.8, Vol. 2, Box 101.

The Nyasaland African National Congress was yet more visible. In July 1956 its Secretary General, T.D.T. Banda, spoke in Makokoba. On 13 August Wellington Chirwa, MP, spoke to a rally in the Vashee Hall. He came from Barbourfields through Makokoba, 'in a procession led by the M'ganda soldiers and Angoni soldiers'. Some 800 people attended the meeting. Chirwa was greeted by 'a roll of drums and thunderous shouts of Afrika! Afrika!' 'When we have succeeded', he said, 'we will help you too to become free.' There were 'prolonged cheers and applause'. Chirwa appealed to local leaders. 'Have we no Nkrumah here? Have we no Gandhi? Have we no Moses? Come forward and lead your people.' On 10 January 1957 the Nyasaland ANC held a meeting in Stanley Hall. A choir 'sang very wonderful melodies'. The provincial president of Congress, Mr Jele, 'told us that people in Nyasaland are doing famously while those in Southern Rhodesia are doing nothing except eating sugar and drinking beer and they think they are Lords and Masters'.[88]

The leaders of Bulawayo strove to respond to these provocations. At the end of 1956 there were some signs of the Southern Rhodesian African Nation Congress coming back to life in Bulawayo. In September Jerry Vera, Treasurer of the 'mother body' and vice-chair of the Bulawayo branch, presided over a meeting of Congress in Stanley Hall; Nkomo was present; there was discussion of whether to combine with the Youth League to form a dynamic new body. (J.Z. Moyo was the leading figure in the Bulawayo Youth League.)[89] On 6 October the *Bantu Mirror* published a letter from Edson Sithole in Mount Silinda, taking off his hat to Moyo, Nehwati and Vera. 'Their efforts to make Congress once more an active and strong political body will meet the ends of a hungry flock of Africans. I wish you success and luck, you good old guys.'[90] In March 1957 Jerry proposed to a meeting which brought together the Northern Rhodesian, Nyasaland and Southern Rhodesian Congress branches in Bulawayo 'that there should be birth to one African national organization which will recognize a black man as an African no matter his tribe and place of origin'.[91]

The meeting passed Vera's resolution unanimously, but there was little chance of its realization. The Northern Rhodesian and Nyasaland Congresses were forging ahead to transform themselves into monolithic bodies with a sole claim on the loyalty of their members. The Bulawayo Congress branch found it difficult to abandon Thompson Samkange's vision of Congress as the umbrella organization over innumerable affili-

---

88 File 'Nyasaland African National Congress', S.O.8, Vol. 1, Box 100. In May 1957 a Congress meeting in Stanley Hall heard letters written by Dr Banda from 'Gold Coast' addressed to the 'leaders' of Bulawayo. He had been invited back by the people of Nyasaland but would not return until there were strong branches of Congress everywhere. The Bulawayo branch resolved to inform the ATUC 'to hear what Dr Banda has written. In May 1958 Secretary-General Kuchunjulu came from Nyasaland to address an Annual Conference in Stanley Hall. He said that the Southern Rhodesia ANC doesn't fight for freedom because Southern Rhodesia is not a Protectorate. They have no power to force independence here. They are bound by the blood of Starr Jameson ... In Nyasaland we have no grave for settlers who struggled to win it.'

89 For the Salisbury Youth League see Timothy Scarnecchia, *The Urban Roots of Democracy and Political Violence in Zimbabwe*. On 1 January 1954 Ngcebetsha wrote in the *Home News* that 'the Youth League must be supported by African leaders of various experience because it is from this organization that we shall raise suitable leaders to take the place of the "old guard". Please note this. It is very, very important.' But there was no way in Bulawayo that the Youth League could dominate the Advisory Board elections and sweep away the old leaders as it did in Salisbury.

90 Meanwhile, though, Bulawayo branch meetings remained very small, and addressed 'welfare' issues. Jerry Vera chaired a meeting on 20 January 1957 in the library of Stanley Hall. Thirty attended. Issues discussed were discrimination on the railways and the availability of European liquor to Africans. A meeting on 5 May 1957 was also devoted to the question of liquor. Joshua Nkomo 'had some difficult in making himself heard because a section of the crowd kept shouting him down, telling him to sit down', S.O.8, Vol. 1, T Box 100.

91 *Bantu Mirror*, 30 March 1957.

ated associations and societies.[92] In particular, Joshua Nkomo, with his idea of layered identities found the new totalitarianism hard to swallow. In April 1957 the Bulawayo Congress branch, under Jerry Vera's chairmanship, resolved that no member of Congress could join any other party. Nkomo condemned this resolution. The Bulawayo branch met again under Vera's chairmanship and expressed its disappointment in Nkomo. 'Mr Nkomo, as a Bulawayo man, should first of all have consulted Congress leaders.'[93] Nkomo was finding it difficult to establish dominance over a mere branch of Congress, let alone a whole newly dynamic organization.

In fact the bickering among men who had been around for too long made it impossible to regenerate even the Bulawayo branch. On 3 May 1958 the *Bantu Mirror* published a sardonic backwards look at the old Congress and its Bulawayo branch, emphasizing the cleavages within it:

> The Bulawayo branch, which kept the nucleus alive, was nurtured (among others) by such conservative figures as A. Mazibisa, W.T. Ngwenya – such moderate but forceful personalities as J.Z. Moyo and J.M.N. Nkomo. Mr Charlton Ngcebetsha (the political chameleon) and Mr J.W. Vera, who could be neatly described as having coming into the Congress for ulterior motives soon fell out when the Congress storm was gathering momentum. R.M. Bango left the branch … following hard boxing with two of Bulawayo's African tardy boys – Messrs K.T.T. Maripe, Edward Ndlovu and J.W. Vera. The latter appeared to have been acting for the Congress old guard, whose rusty power Bango set out to dismantle.

A brand-new set up was needed. Jerry Vera stayed around long enough to draw up a Memo demanding universal adult suffrage.[94] But in June both he and Nkomo resigned their offices in the redundant and defunct 'mother body' of Congress so as to allow the Bulawayo branch 'to forge ahead with re-organising Congress'.[95] In July Joseph Msika, now Chair of the Bulawayo branch, announced that it had agreed with the Youth League in Salisbury to inaugurate a new Congress on 12 September. On 31 August Msika, J.Z. Moyo, and Nehwati reported back to the Bulawayo branch on the final details of the re-launch.[96]

When the Congress was launched in Salisbury on 12 September – Occupation Day for white Rhodesians – these men featured on its executive. Msika was treasurer, J.Z. Moyo vice-secretary, Nehwati a committee member. Youth Leaguers George Nyandoro and James Chikerema were general secretary and vice-president. But who was to be president over this radical grouping? In his book Joshua Nkomo gives an oddly accidental account of his elevation. He had 'been hi-jacked into the Presidency'.[97] A few days later a Bulawayo branch of the new body was constituted with Nehwati as chair and J.Z. Moyo as secretary.

The New Southern Rhodesian Congress in Bulawayo.

Nkomo writes that this new Congress was very different from the old. To mark the difference J.Z. Moyo applied both on 29 November 1957 and on 2 April 1958 for per-

---

[92] For Thompson Samkange and Congress see T.O. Ranger, *Are We Not Also Men?*
[93] *Bantu Mirror*, 13 April 1957.
[94] *Bantu Mirror*, 1 June 1957.
[95] *Bantu Mirror*, 11 May 1957.
[96] *Bantu Mirror*, 6 July and 31 August 1957.
[97] *Nkomo*, p. 71.

mission to hold a march 'led by banners' through Makokoba and other townships. He reported the refusal of permission and displayed the banners in a meeting in Stanley Hall on 13 April 1958 which was 'filled to capacity'.[98] The main speaker was George Nyandoro, who certainly struck a different note from any heard before. He said he would not speak in English because 'we cannot put a white guinea fowl among us'. He spoke in Shona and Moyo translated into Sindebele. He described his visit to Ghana:

> It was then that I saw the owl had no horns … It was then that I breathed the air of freedom. I was like an Ambassador going for UN Summit talks. When in Rome do as Rome does. I danced when they danced and drank when they drank. I was served by a white waitress … Everybody in Ghana has great confidence in the ANC of Southern Rhodesia. They want to see it grow. There are no bosses in Ghana as we have here.

At a football match, 'a primitive man in shorts' shouted his love for Nkrumah who 'shook hands with the primitive man because he voted him to power. Do you love Whitehead or Todd?' 'I have come back with a sound experience of how to fight for freedom.' Nyandoro denounced Charlton Ngcebetsha, who had by now moved into multiracial politics. 'Lobengula had no degree or any bit of training but he was wise. He never learned like Ngcebetshta but he was wise.' Moyo brought the meeting back home. He talked of rising unemployment in Bulawayo and of the crowding brought about by the Land Husbandry Act.[99]

This new outspoken Congress rapidly made its mark. There were branches in many of the townships.[100] The two notable areas of Congress support were Makokoba/ Mzilikazi and Mpopoma, though the reasons were very different. In Makokoba/ Mzilikazi support was linked to increasing immiseration and unemployment[101] and with the emergence of a new rent-payers' association headed by J.Z. Moyo. It savagely criticized the Advisory Board, rather than, as with Sipambaniso's original Associa- tion, supporting it. The Board was told that it was interested only in property and not in poverty. In Mpopoma, that leasehold jewel in the municipality's crown, it was the leaseholders themselves – who were *very* interested in property – who backed Con- gress and elected an Advisory Board almost entirely consisting of Congressmen. As Michael West has commented, African leaseholders were natural allies of Congress.[102] They were bitter about harassment over arrears and frustrated by delays in extend- ing their 99-year leases. The Mpopoma Leaseholders Association, headed by Frank

---

[98] The banners bore sloganas which were both indusrial and political – 'Congress demands apprenticeship for all'; 'Congress deplores apartheid in industry'; 'Congress demands adult suffrage'.

[99] S.O.8, Vol. 1, T Box 100. Moyo said that 'even a soldier from Malaya was told there was no place to stay, yet he had gone to Malaya to fight for land which it is prohibited for him to stay'. In March 1958 Ngcebetsha had announced his support for the United Federal Party. On 22 March 1958 Charlton described Nkomo's criticisms of him as 'puerile, parochial and unconvincing' On 29 March he asked whether Nkomo would have called Saul of Tarsus or Winston Churchill 'sell-outs'. On 28 February 1959 the *Home News* complained that speakers at ANC meetings were 'denouncing and cursing all those who do not generally agree with the politics of this organization … Speeches were highly inflammatory'.

[100] The *Home News* reported on 23 November 1957 that Fraser Gibson had set up an Njube branch of Congress and that many women were joining.

[101] Ashton's African Administration report for June 1958 spoke of 'the growth of African unemployment in Bulawayo in the first few months of 1958. The abundance of labour usual in the first two months of the year was augmented by retrenchment due to the National Wage Award.' The press had reported 8,000 unem- ployed; Ashton thought it was more likely 4,000.

[102] Michael West, *The Rise of an African Middle Class*, p. 115.

Ziyambe, demanded the privileges of property. They aimed for freehold, which must involve, they declared, citizenship in Bulawayo. The Makokoba/Mzilikazi nationalists focused on one man, one vote; the Mpopoma nationalists demanded their right to vote for city councillors as qualified property owners.[103] As West has pointed out, Joshua Nkomo also belonged to a leaseholders association – the one in Pelendaba, with shorter leases but much larger houses.[104] The range of the new Congress support ran from the poorest to the richest and it was to prove very difficult to hold them together.

Then on 26 February 1959 Garfield Todd's successor, Sir Edgar Whitehead, declared a national state of emergency. In police swoops 307 members of the Southern Rhodesian ANC, 105 members of the Nyasaland ANC and 83 of the Northern Rhodesian ANC were detained.[105] Whitehead's emergency had very little to do with conditions inside Southern Rhodesia – it was declared in order to free white troops and police to be sent to Nyasaland. It had even less to do with conditions in Bulawayo, where Congress was perceived as moderate. Nevertheless, the leaders of SRANC and of the two northern Congresses were all detained and most of them taken to the fort-like Khami prison outside Bulawayo. The three Congresses were banned and it became a criminal offence to possess a membership card of any of them.

These events fell like a thunderbolt on black Bulawayo. Advisory Board members were picked up. Three members of the Bulawayo African Townships Board – J.Z. Moyo, Lazarus Nkala and Mutuma – were detained. Four members of the Mpopoma Board – Amos Mazibisa, Grey Bango, Frank Ziyambi and Francis Nehwati – were picked up. Fraser Gibson was detained in Njube. Joseph Msika was detained. The Bulawayo Municipality, which had been working well enough with these men, was shaken. McNeillie, now Mayor, publicly declared that he was sorry that there were some Board members, especially those of Mpopoma, who were detained 'in large numbers'.[106] Ashton was outraged that his politics of collaboration had been senselessly disrupted. In his annual report in June 1959 he reported that the emergency had picked up 76 local residents, including 11 Board members and three employees of his African Administration Department. 'The Bulawayo detainees were generally responsible people who did not fall into the category of "rabble-rousers" described by the Secretary for Native Affairs as "having little or no education ... who could not even manage a business".' These Bulawayo people, wrote Ashton, were 'generally believed to be very different from the extremists in other parts of the country'.

Several of those detained were storekeepers. Joshua Nkomo, that 'Great Matabele Businessman', was out of the country when the emergency was declared and did not return to Bulawayo for 18 months.

Black businessmen, Advisory Boards and the African Administration Department showed significant solidarity with the detainees. W.T. Ngwenya, a store-owner

---

[103] In September 1958 the Bulawayo branch of Congress sent a resolution to the mother body 'that Africans should be directly represented on Municipal Councils'. *Bantu Mirror*, 6 September 1958. On 1 November 1958 the *Home News* reported that Joshua Nkomo and the ANC had offered to combine with the Advisory Boards to obtain direct representation on the Council. In Charlton's view 'this is none of Congress' business'.

[104] R.M. Bango was chair of the Pelendaba Residents' Association. In November 1959 the Association described leading Congressmen, many of whom had been detained in February, as 'some of the best leaders' in Bulawayo. *Bantu Mirror*, 28 November 1959.

[105] I discuss the detentions in T.O. Ranger, 'Memories of an Emergency', Zomba, July 2009.

[106] *Home News*, 14 March 1959.

in Mpopoma, kept Grey Bango's and Amos Mazibisa's stores there going. The BAT Advisory Board set up a committee of three to manage Nkomo's auction business. A group of African traders organized transport to Khami prison for families of the detained.[107] When some of the detainees were released in May the Council re-employed its workers. For the remainder of 1959 a sullen peace was maintained in Bulawayo. It remained to be seen what would happen when the detainees, radicalized by their interaction with leading Nyasaland ANC men in Khami prison, returned to the townships; when a successor to Congress emerged; and when unemployment intensified. All of these things happened in 1960.

[107] *Bantu Mirror*, 18 July 1959. The three were Jerry Vera, Charlton Ngcebetsha and J.B. Patsika.

1. 'Dad, Uncle and Mum', 1959 (Source: Roger Sibanda)

Photographs 1-4 were part of 'Thatha Camera', an exhibition held at the National Gallery in Bulawayo in 1999 while Yvonne Vera was Director of the gallery, and which Yvonne Vera gave me permission to reproduce in this book.

The photographs illustrate the pride of possession of township residents in the 1950s as they came to possess radiograms, and even cars, and posed with them in their smartest clothes. In the comments books at the 'Thatha Camera' exhibition people expressed their astonishemnt at how modern and swinging their grandmothers had been – hence 'My grandma' in her wig and jeans. By contrast, the Municipal policemen and the beer-laden herbalist are presented as figures of traditional absurdity.

2. 'Lady in a car', 1952 (Source: Nkosilathi Ngulube)

3. 'My grandma', 1950s
(Source: Japhet Funwayo)

4. 'Byo Municipal Police', 1962
(Source: Edson Marwizi)

5. The back streets of Makokoba, c. 1960 (© Patricia Battye)
6. Old Location life outside the market, c. 1960 (© Patricia Battye)

7. An Ndebele model for textile design, c. 1960 (© Patricia Battye)

8. Ericah Gwetai, 1972.
Yvonne Vera's mother
as a township belle
(© Ericah Gwetai)

9. Yvonne Vera, 2002.
Berlin conference
(© Mai Palmberg)

216

7

Black Bulawayo Burns
1960

The Emergence of the National Democratic Party

On 1 January 1960 a new mass party – the National Democratic Party – was formed in Salisbury. Much of the literature connects or attributes this to Joshua Nkomo. In his autobiography Nkomo himself writes:

> At the beginning of 1960 a group of people from the banned African National Congress met to form the new National Democratic Party. Its provisional constitution was almost identical with its predecessor's, and to underline the continuity I was elected president in absentia, while I pursued my work abroad.[1]

Obituaries of Nkomo in leading newspapers gave Nkomo a more active role. The *Times* on 2 July 1999 asserted that Nkomo 'responded immediately' to the ban on Congress 'with the creation of the NDP, with the same executive and constitution as the ANC, while he campaigned abroad'. Also on 2 July the *Guardian* obituary affirmed that 'when the ANC was banned he [Nkomo] formed the NDP – and became its President'. But all these statements are in error.

Nkomo did *not* form the NDP or stimulate its formation. Indeed, for some time after its emergence he did not know what it was or whether he should throw in his lot with other parties which were seeking to establish themselves at the same time.[2] He was *not* elected as President *in absentia* on 1 January nor mentioned as the new party's overseas representative. The last thing that the leaders of the NDP wanted was to underline its continuity with the banned ANC, which would have been fatal under the Unlawful Organisations Act. It certainly did not have 'the same executive' as the ANC. Indeed none of its leading officers had held positions on the ANC executive. (Most of these were still in detention.) The formation of the new party was stimulated by senior detainees from inside prison but they desperately sought an ucompromised figure to lead it. Both Herbert Chitepo and Stanlake Samkange were approached, until eventually, Michael Mawema, provincial organizing secretary of the Railway African

---

1   *Nkomo: The Story of My life*, p. 90.
2   Other organizations struggling to be born at this time were the Non-Violent African Voice, the Freedom Party and the United Peoples Party. I have among my papers a letter from Joshua Nkomo asking me what the NDP was and whether it was the true successor of the ANC.

Workers Union, agreed to accept the presidency. The rest of the executive was made up of younger men, who had been members of Congress but not leading figures in it.[3]

Partly because Nkomo was not associated with it and partly because its executive contained no other well-known Bulawayo figure, the NDP was not an immediate success in Matabeleland. In May 1960, indeed, the *Home News* carried a letter from E.H.P. Hlangabaza:

> The NDP is not supported in Matabeleland by the Matabeles. Matabeles are quite away from support [for] the NDP ... Matabeles are looking forward for the better advancement of their children .... Those who say the NDP is supported in this province are not saying the truth. What I know is that it is being supported by immigrants, Shona ... for their own selfrule. Does it mean that Matabeles [are] still going to claim their rights [from] Mashonas after when the government has given the Shonas selfrule?[4]

But this letter was already out of date. A turning point for the NDP in Bulawayo came in April 1960 with the release from detention of J.Z. Moyo, Francis Nehwati and Fraser Gibson. Even Charlton Ngcebetsha reported 'scenes of great rejoicing throughout Bulawayo when African detainees arrived being freed from the clutches of the law'.[5] The Shona Cultural Society took the initiative to organize a meeting at Iminyela Hall on the Western Commonage to welcome them back. But the meeting was 'attended by all Africans irrespective of tribal origin'.[6]

The return of the leading detainees sparked off a wave of NDP activity. In July an NDP branch was set up in Mpopoma with Francis Nehwati as chairman. J.Z. Moyo was immediately active in Makokoba. He chaired a meeting in the Stanley Hall on 21 July, condemning the arrests of NDP leaders in Salisbury and calling for the withdrawal of troops from Harare and Highfields townships. Only 300 people attended but it was the sign of a much more active NDP presence. Moyo announced that another, and much larger, meeting would be called for the following weekend.

The Atmosphere of 1960

This resurgence of organized nationalism took place in a newly tense atmosphere. Hugh Ashton put it a wide context when he wrote his annual report for the year ended 31 July 1960. 1960, he pointed out, was 'Africa Year'; there had been Sharpeville and the Congo, and:

> On top of it all, Matabeleland experienced one of the worst droughts on record. To anguish caused by natural disaster was added the despair caused by unprecedented degree of unemployment in Bulawayo. This was caused by ever-growing population, application of the Land Husbandry Act, the recession caused by political uncertainty and the drought itself. All these things created a most uneasy situation.

The discontents of unemployment came to a head in early June 1960 when there were demonstrations by jobless at factories in Bulawayo and outside the Labour Exchange.

---

3   I have described how the NDP was formed in my *Are We Not Also Men? The Samkange Family and African Politics in Zimbabwe*, pp. 176-8. I drew upon my own memoranda in the Ranger Archives in Rhodes House, Oxford, and on Maurice Nyagumbo, *With the People*, Alison and Busby, London, 1980, p. 134.
4   *Home News*, 14 May 1960.
5   *Home News*, 30 April 1960.
6   *Home News*, 2 July 1960.

'Women seeking jobs were greeted with howls and jeers.' Hugh Ashton himself told the *Chronicle* on 4 June that there were at least 6,000 unemployed men in Bulawayo and asked 'Why won't the State act on the African jobless? It just does not realize how serious the position is becoming. Why do people always wait for trouble before they take action?' Councillor Jack Paine, Chairman of the City's African Affairs Committee said that 'the whole position is alarming … we shall just have to grin and bear it for the next three months'.[7] A *Bantu Mirror* reporter, in the issue of the same date, said that he had 'been out with large numbers of unemployed, some married and others not … The plight of hundreds of hungry, jobless Africans in and around Bulawayo is simply pathetic, sickening and unnerving. They have roamed to and from the factories and unemployment exchanges during the past six months in daily despair and frustration. Some of them have spent the night in football grounds and deserted places. A good many were seen putting up for the night at the dumping pit near the Luveve Road Bridge.' The *Mirror* declared that the 'building industry [has] virtually come to a standstill'.[8]

In the association-rich Bulawayo of 1960 there was a Southern Rhodesia Unemployed Africans Association, led by R.S.M. Mpande. 'We live in constant fear of starvation', he declared, 'and [have] no place where we can lay our heads.' The *Home News* of 4 June 1960 reported that Mpande had led a delegation of unemployed to meet the Provincial Native Commissioner. They asked that 'foreign Africans in employment in Bulawayo as well as African women in employment should all be dismissed'. True to his Advisory Board stance, Ngcebetsha thought this would be 'a most stupid way of solving an acute problem'. Many foreign men were married to local women and had children by them 'whose uncles and aunts are locals'. As for employed women, many of them were widows and paid their children's school fees from their wages. To sack them would merely 'swell the ranks of street-goers'. But Ngcebetsha was worried. 'Already in some places in the townships it is not safe to travel at night because of wandering Africans of no fixed abode.' Because of crop failure 'there is the prospect of large numbers of Africans from the country districts flooding Bulawayo'.[9]

And if Ngcebetsha and the BAT Advisory Board were at odds with the Unemployed Africans Association they also found themselves attacked by the rent-payers of Makokoba. As we have already seen, Ashton decided in the end not to clear 'single' men and their unregistered 'wives' out of Makokoba. But in mid-1960 he made gestures towards slum clearance. New 'single' hostels were being erected in Nguboyena and the Council, with the concurrence of the Advisory Board, determined to move 400 'bachelors' from Makokoba into them and to rent their rooms to legally married families. On 2 July 1960 the *Bantu Mirror* warned that this policy 'might create grave social problems with far reaching consequences … When the Hostels are ready for occupation, these "bachelors" with their their families will be faced with serious problems of finding alternative accommodation where they will live with their families as women will not be allowed to live with men in the hostels.'[10] According to the *Daily News* of 15 July 'fear and uncertainty grip illegally married Makokoba Africans'. Women were openly expressing their resentment. 'Many women could suffer as

---

7 *Chronicle*, 4 June 1960.
8 *Bantu Mirror*, 4 June 1960.
9 *Home News*, 28 May and 4 June 1960.
10 *Bantu Mirror*, 2 July 1960. The paper said that there were 5,578 single men with official rent cards and 554 married men with their families. At least 5,000 friends, relatives and girlfriends shared 'the small rooms'.

most of them could be sent to their homes. If all of us get married where shall we get married accommodation?' Some women were planning to leave their 'husbands' and to seek industrial employment; others planned to move in with legitimate 'married' men, whose wives were back in the rural areas.

Early in July 1960 'single' men gathered in Makokoba to form a new Tenants' Association. There were bitter complaints of bugs, rats, double-bunking and threats of eviction. Superintendent R.S. Woods was shouted down with cries of 'We are being pestered with bugs and rats.'[11] Charlton Ngcebetsha, who used to attend all the meetings of the original Tenants' Association, and who had published the *Home News* in its name, now wrote that 'it seems as if a Tenants' Association has been formed at Makokoba … It has had a meeting recently where a number of complaints were made against some Advisory Board members of the area, for, so it was alleged, not doing anything for Makokoba residents.'[12] There was resentment because the Bulawayo African Townships Advisory Board had agreed with the proposed evictions and there was tension between the threatened women and the respectable wives of the Women's Associations. J.Z. Moyo put himself at the head of this new rebellious Tenants' Association.

And there was tension between 'married' and 'single' in Mpopoma. Leaseholders there were virtual property owners. But few could afford the payments and it had been arranged that each house could accommodate up to two 'single' lodgers, whose rents would make the leases economically possible. In Mpopoma, then, families and lodgers lived in the closest proximity. Neither group liked the arrangement. The *Home News* reported 'a widespread feeling among the owners of Mpopoma houses that the system of keeping African lodgers in their houses is very unsatisfactory'. Householders could not get 'the respect to which they are entitled' from the lodgers. If the lodgers were poor, then they were thought to be likely to add to Mpopoma's high rate of street crime; if they were well-paid they were 'a source of great danger to women of easy virtue who are married and own houses in Mpopoma while their poorly paid husbands are away from their homes'. Lodgers had 'grievances against the owners of the houses in which they live, more or less on sufferance'.[13] In Mpopoma, too, the old Advisory Board politics was under pressure, but here it was not the impoverished 'single' men who led the attack but the leaseholders who threatened to suspend the Advisory Board and demanded direct representation on Council.

Both Makokoba and Mpopoma, those two bastions of nationalism, were divided among themselves. All this, together with the hostility of customers towards township traders, contributed to Ashton's 'uneasy' situation. Some people at least feared a revival of ethnic bitterness as well. Just before Christmas 1959 the *Home News* reported that the authorities were having 'sleepless nights' over the 'recrudescence of tribalism' and expecting a clash between Ndebele and Shona. Large numbers of police had been sent to Barbourfields football stadium because of rumours of a planned tribal fight.[14] In January 1960 Ngcebetsha reported 'complaints by the Matabele people of Bulawayo that they were not getting a square deal in the matter of businesses. The last straw was the giving of a number of African shops in various parts of the townships to Mashonas and the Matabeles only got one. Like a prairie fire that kind of talk spread

---

[11] *Daily News*, 6 July 1960.
[12] *Home News*, 9 July 1960.
[13] *Home News*, 10 September 1960.
[14] *Home News*, 2 January 1960.

to many Matabeles of Bulawayo. They then decided that the time had come for them to assert their rights.'[15]

In the coming months Charlton's own rhetoric grew more extreme. The Shona were conspiring to take over all the Advisory Boards as they had already taken over the Bulawayo Football Association. They were 'power hungry', 'sly foxes' seeking to provoke the Ndebele into conflict:

> We write mainly on this subject because we were here in Bulawayo in 1929 when there was a tribal flare-up between the Matabeles and the Mashonas, fomented, so it was believed, by some few irresponsibles among the Bulawayo Mashonas. They did then what the present Mashonas are doing in Bulawayo which is definitely to the annoyance of the Matabeles concerned. They wanted to take charge of practically all important things in Bulawayo. Naturally, the Matabele people of those days, as now, opposed and resented that until time came when they could no longer put up with it.

Ngcebetsha warned that 1929 might soon come again.[16]

And there was another source of ethnic tension. The unemployed had made up a delegation in early June 1960 to meet the PNC and demand the dismissal of all foreign African workers. The *Bantu Mirror* thought that 'the presence of non-indigenous labour employed in industries when indigenous Africans roam about the streets hungry and looking for work makes it imperative for the Government to reconsider its labour policy'. On 6 June P. Ndhlovu wrote to the *Chronicle* from the Western Commonage:

> Africans from the neighbouring territories ... have thrown the indigenous Africans out of everything, especially employment ... The Government does not dream of the trouble caused. It is prepared to see the indigenous African a tramp.[17]

Black Bulawayo Burns: The Zhii *Riots of July 1960*

On Tuesday 19 July 1960 police in Salisbury arrested the three main leaders of the National Democratic Party, Michael Mawema, Sketchley Samkange and Leopold Takawira. There were no arrests in Bulawayo but the houses of the NDP chairman, Z.K. Sihwa, a Pelendaba carpenter, of the Secretary, J.R. Mzimela, a cycle repairman, and of the leading committee member, J.Z. Moyo, a Makokoba builder, were searched and papers taken. In Salisbury the arrests provoked the famous protest march from Highfields to Harare; police use of teargas; a withdrawal of African labour; and widespread riots. Troops were moved into the Salisbury African townships.

Bulawayo, meanwhile, was quiet and Ashton was convinced that he could keep it that way. As we have seen, there was a peaceful NDP meeting on Thursday 21 July. It called for another, much larger, meeting in Stanley Hall on Sunday 24 July. During Saturday 23 July 'rumour [was] rife in the city as to the outcome of [Sunday's] mass meeting and the main question being asked was: "Is this city in for a repeat of Salis-

---

[15] Ibid.
[16] *Home News*, 6 February 1960.
[17] *Bantu Mirror*, 11 June 1960. In fact official action was taken. In 1960 Migrancy agreements with Northern Rhodesia and Nyasalands were terminated and 'the employment of foreign Africans was prohibited in all local authority areas'.

bury's labour stay-away?'"[18] At this moment of emergency two of the characters with whom I have been concerned were out of Bulawayo. Joshua Nkomo was still in exile in London. Jerry Vera was in Lusaka, training to become Bulawayo's first African hotelier. Charlton Ngcebetsha was gloomily awaiting an ethnic clash between Ndebele and Shona. J.Z. Moyo and Hugh Ashton were seeking to avert an explosion. Moyo was preparing to chair the Sunday meeting. Ashton was planning to defuse it.

Ashton met police commanders on Saturday morning and they decided not to ban the next day's meeting. Arrangements were made that it should be discreetly policed. Ashton contacted the NDP leaders who promised that the meeting would be non-violent and would not call for demonstrations or strikes.[19] Edgar Whitehead's Southern Rhodesian Government, however, had other ideas. During the day it contacted the Civil Commissioner and Chief Magistrate of Bulawayo, Farewell Roberts, and told him that 'it had information of its own' which made it necessary to ban the meeting. Roberts passed this on to the police and as late as 10.45 p.m. it was announced by the Officer Commanding, BSAP, that all meetings within a 20-mile radius were prohibited for a month. 'There was to be a big meeting tomorrow', said the OC. 'It has now been banned as we do not want anything happening which might start trouble.'[20] Ashton only learnt of the ban five minutes before it was publicly announced. He was able to pass the news on to the NDP leadership, but not of course to the people preparing to attend the meeting.

As Francis Nehwati, Bulawayo NDP leader turned Ruskin College graduate student, wrote in his thesis, 'political rallies were popular occasions among the Bulawayo Africans. All the roads leading to Stanley Square were thronged as early as 6 o'clock [on the morning of Sunday 24 July] and some had to walk several miles to the Square.'[21] By 8 a.m. some 500 Africans were waiting outside the locked Stanley Hall and 'yet more people from all the African townships continued to fill the ground in front of the square'.[22] Soon there were over 1,000 people there. The NDP leaders – Sihwa, J.Z. Moyo, Nehwati and the rest – were absent 'for fear of being arrested', *Parade* reported later. 'The crowd decided to choose new leaders.' Four men took on the responsibility of channeling the crowd's anger at the ban. Three of them were ordinary members of the NDP – Jafta Nhliziyo, Charles Pasipanodya and Aaron Ndhlovu. The other, Willie Ncube, was not even a member of the party.[23]

The four 'leaders' formed the crowd into a procession which marched through 'Makokoba Township, that squalid township, where complaints against living conditions would make one dumb'.[24] The crowd sang 'the national anthem, God Bless Africa', as they marched, and hundreds of men came out of their houses to join them. By the time the march turned out of the township towards Lobengula Street its number had swollen to over 5,000.

Police evidence when the four leaders were put on trial later, revealed the efforts they made to control their followers:

They all wanted to know why the meeting had been banned. They were waiting for someone to

[18] *Sunday News*, 24 July 1960.
[19] *Bulawayo Chronicle*, 5 August 1960.
[20] *Sunday News*, 24 July 1960.
[21] Francis Nehwati, 'The Social and Communal Background to Zhii', *African Affairs*, 59, 276, July 1970, p. 251.
[22] *Parade*, September 1960.
[23] *Daily News*, 7 October 1960, reporting the sentencing of the four men for Unlawful Asembly.
[24] *Parade*, September 1960.

give them a lead ... Ndhlovu suggested that they march to the City Hall and the crowd followed him and the other three accused. The procession first marched towards Mzilikazi township, urging people to join them ... The procession stopped on a number of occasions while the four accused stood on dustbins and urged the crowd not to be violent.

An African detective, Godi, testified that Pasipanodya was so moved by his appeals that he saw 'tears streaming down his face'. When the procession turned towards the city it was still orderly and the two detectives joined it.

When the crowd reached the junction of Lobengula Street and Second Avenue their way was blocked by 90 steel-helmeted police and police reservists, armed with tear gas. Superintendent Tuke ordered the crowd to withdraw:

Two of the accused, Ndhlovu and Nhliziyo, asked permission to address the crowd. Permission was granted and they urged the people to disperse. The two men showed responsibility throughout [testified Tuke] and there was a genuine desire on their part to prevent any trouble with the police. If they had not controlled the crowd it could have got out of hand.[25]

The still orderly procession turned back to Stanley Square, followed by the police. But at this point order broke down. A fresh crowd joined with the marchers; they played 'hide and seek with the police'; and by 1 p.m. the police 'who had moved to the Stanley Square Area were under a heavy hail of stones ... The police started using tear gas to disperse the crowd.'[26] The *Chronicle* of 25 July reported what happened next:

Sullenly [the crowd] waited. Then, in four lines of 20 men each, followed by a stretcher party, the police advanced. The Africans stood firm and only as the smoke-carrying canisters burst among them, did the mob scatter. But it re-formed as soon as the smoke cleared. Two more advances and smoke bomb attacks were made. All afternoon police made repeated attacks. By now there were two main groups of Africans, numbering several hundred each ... By 5 pm the road from Lobengula Street along Sixth Avenue was lined by hundreds of Africans watching the attacks.

By this time people in other townships had learnt about what was happening. 'The Western Commonage hooligans got wind of the news that the police had failed to control the crowds in Makokoba. They rushed into Makokoba armed with sticks and iron bars. In an hour of wanton destruction the attention of the rioters was drawn to the beer halls. They roamed about the pubs, getting people off their beer mugs and looting the beer gardens and bottle stores.'[27] By this time, though, the police were much too busy to be able to defend property in the townships. Some of the Africans confronting the police cordon managed to dodge the smoke-bombs and to break through it. 'They ran towards the city centre and started stoning cars in Lobengula Street, Fort Street and Jameson Street.' The nightmare of white Bulawayo of an armed invasion from the townships seemed to be taking place. 'Troops were then sent for', reported the *Chronicle*, but 'in the next hour, before they took up their positions with fixed bayonets in Lobengula Street, gangs – several dozen strong – roamed the streets attacking cars. From as far afield as the Old Falls Road cars were being stoned. Indian stores in Lobengula Road had their windows broken as gangs ... ran amok among the helpless store-keepers.'[28]

[25] *Chronicle*, 10 September 1960.
[26] *Parade*, September 1960.
[27] Ibid.
[28] *Chronicle*, 25 July 1960.

From this point on police and troops concentrated first on removing rioters from the white city and the on establishing a ring around it. They made no attempt to enter the townships. On Sunday night these were left to the rioters. *Parade*'s reporter, a township resident, later described this 'first taste of terror ... We moved with our hearts in our hands. Anything could happen.' What happened was fire. Shops in Makokoba, Mzilikazi, Barbourfields and Nguboyena were set alight and looted. The war-cry *Zhii* was heard everywhere; 'that ominous Zulu howl', wrote the *Daily News*, 'a relic of the terrible days of Chaka's reign'.[29]

Oral testimony presents a varied picture of the day's events. A few people remember them with pleasure. 'To me *Zhii* was one of the most interesting scenes I ever witnessed in my life', recalls G. Dube, who in 1960 was a rather mature member of NDP youth. 'You know, we really enjoyed'. He remembers:

> That confrontation we had with the policemen near Lobengula Street in an open space – the encounter there was terrible. The policemen fired tear gas at us and we retaliated with stones. They wanted to block us from going into the city centre but that time they had found their match. They couldn't disperse us with tear gas [and] we demonstrators managed to get into the city centre and smashed shop windows. We then proceeded to the white suburbs ... We wreaked havoc in the city, there was rampant looting.

Dube thinks of this attack on the city as rationally and politically motivated. But even he admits that the violence became random and inward-turning. 'Our aim was to destroy anything that belonged to Europeans. But during the violence the situation just deteriorated into a very much uncontrolled activity. Many stores in the townships were destroyed and goods looted; meat was looted from township butchers; some youth members attacked some houses in the townships, especially in Makokoba, where they suspected that some men who didn't want to participate in the violence were hiding.'[30]

Many other informants remember the whole series of events as anarchic and confusing. A man who was a schoolboy in 1960 remembers the evening of Sunday 24 July as the worst night of his life. He had never before drunk beer, either African or European. But he was caught up in the crowds and marched from beer hall to beer hall, drinking his fill at each, ending up sick and sorry on Monday morning. As he recalls, 'we paid for beer with stones', the terrified cashiers hastening to serve beer when a stone was laid before them.[31] Ritah Ndlovu of Entumbane township, who was fifteen in 1960, recalls of *Zhii*:

> Every old person who was there during that period will no doubt never forget it, as I will not. I remember people running everywhere, crying *Zhii*! *Zhii*! *Bulala*! *Bulala*!, meaning Kill! Kill! It was as if people were possessed by demons. Food was being looted from stores and beer in the beer-gardens. Everyone was being forced to join the violent crowds. I was very afraid during those days, I tell you, because I thought a war had started.[32]

---

[29] *Daily News*, 8 August 1960. Nehwati says that *Zhii*'s nearest meaning in English is 'devastating action', 'destroy completely', 'reduce to rubble'. 'It takes its origin from the sound caused by the fall of a huge rock.' Nehwati, p. 251. During the trials of the rioters African police said that they did not think the slogan, 'brought to Matabeleland by Mzilikazi', had been used since 'the Matabele Rebellion'. *Chronicle*, 11 August 1960.

[30] Interview between Busani Mpofu and G. Dube, February 2000.

[31] Interview beteen Hloniphani Ndlovu and Major Ndlovu, Entumbane, January 2000.

[32] Interview between Hloniphani Ndlovu and Ritah Ndlovu, Entumbane, February 2000.

Zelita Maluphahla, who was 28 in 1960, recalls the shouts of 'Kill! Kill!':

> I do not know who they wanted to kill. I was scared because some people were being beaten.
> As for us women the only safe thing we thought of doing was closing the doors of our houses,
> closing the curtains and keeping quiet.[33]

MaMhlanga, who was also 28, remembers that 'black people were fighting each other'.
She was looking after her two nephews. 'They were outside when the violence started.
I tried to look for them but in vain. They were teenagers. When they came back they
had bloody faces and legs. They told me that they had been beaten as everyone was
beating everyone. I was so shocked and scared that I did not know what to do. We just
had to sit inside the house, close the door and all the windows.'[34]

Monday 25 July dawned on a scene of devastation. A four-mile-long line of police
and troops, numbering over 2,000 men, stretched from Khami Road along Lobengula Street up to the Victoria Falls road. As the *Daily News* of 26 July put it: 'For
the whole day troops and police lined up and marched along Lobengula Street whilst
in the African areas rioters looted practically every shop and business premises.' No
African was allowed to leave the townships. 'All day', reported the *Chronicle* of 26 July
'Africans approached the military cordon and asked to be allowed through. They were
turned back and many sat, huddled and frightened in the no-man's land of 300 yards,
between the troops and the Old Location – too scared to go back to their homes, for-
bidden to cross to the safety of the city.' The only police penetration into the townships
was an operation to rescue the Paramount Chieftainess of Bechuanaland, who had
been staying in a new flat in Mpopoma and was 'brought to safety by a police detach-
ment which fought its way in to save her'. 'In Makokoba, reported the *Daily News*,
'there were huge stretches where there was neither policemen nor soldiers in sight'.

There were, however, some Africans who were allowed out of the townships early
on the Monday morning. These were workers who had reported to their factories.
They did not stay there long. Pickets came to 'pull them out' and they streamed into
the townships. Some of them spread out to attack factories on the way. The Mayor of
Bulawayo, Councillor Millar, 'was a prisoner in his dry cleaning works on the Khami
Road for nearly an hour … while Africans massed in the roadway, stormed the building, smashed windows, and yelled at him in Sindebele … When the stoning and
yelling was at its height he bobbed down behind the counter.' He was able to phone his
wife who sent police reservists to rescue him from this undignified situation. Other
workers spread out into the southern suburbs and tried to bring domestic workers
out on strike. 'The effect was patchy. Some servants left hurriedly. Others refused
… Some intimidators came face to face with the house-wives and were threatened in
turn. House-wives locked their servants in the lavatory; one went into her garden with
a pistol and chased the pickets off.'[35]

The *Chronicle* admitted that 'what was happening in the townships nobody knows'.
But it is possible to reconstruct the events of Monday 25 July from reports in the African press. It was a picture of chaos, though the *Daily News* found that 'in the heart of
the Location [Makokoba] there is complete calm, with women going about their daily
household chores'. Elsewhere, however, 'gangs were in full swing'. At 1 p.m. unnamed

33 Interview between Hloniphani Ndlovu and Zelita Maluphahla, Njube, February 2000.
34 Interview between Hloniphani Ndlovu and MaMhlanga, Entumbane, February 2000.
35 *Chronicle*, 26 July 1960; *Sunday News*, 31 July 1960.

leaders, 'not NDP men', called a meeting on the open land between Makokoba and Mzilikazi. 'People were pulled from their houses to attend.' Some 8,000 people came; the leaders appealed that all looting and violence should stop; the crowd appeared to be ready to listen to them, but police suddenly appeared and tear-gassed the meeting. The police were stoned and 'they rushed out of the townships as fast as they came in'. The crowd then formed up for another march into town but they were bombed with tear gas by a spotter plane:

> With tear gas smarting in its eyes, the crowd became uncontrollable. It charged towards the main beer hall [in Makokoba] and set it on fire.[36]

With the flames now blazing again, 'police were taking no chances. Shots were heard. In every corner there was some noise.' Men were shot dead and others wounded. A group of youths, 'armed with sticks, hatchets and axes', used stolen cars to ferry the wounded to Mpilo Hospital, which lay in a sort of no-man's-land between the rioters and the soldiers. To avoid the cars being stoned they tied bandages soaked in the blood of the wounded on their bonnets.

At night, however, the police again withdrew. There was another night of terror. More shops were set afire and looted. 'People, including women, could be seen rushing from their houses to the damaged shops and helping themselves to whatever food they could find.' 'Africans', found the *Daily News* of 26 July, 'feel that Government has betrayed them by sparking off a fire and then failing to protect the loyal citizens.' Nobody felt this more strongly than African supporters of the government party, the UFP, whose shops and houses had been left to the mercy of the mob. Charlton Ngcebetsha was at this point a UFP member. But on 6 August he strongly disputed Sir Edgar Whitehead's claim that the riots had been masterminded by the NDP. 'This is simply not true', wrote Charlton. The authorities were themselves to blame.[37] 'They held inadequate forces in hand to put the riot down before any serious damage was done … Practically all the African trading stores were destroyed and looted and in some cases set on fire.' Troops and police had concentrated on protecting Europeans. 'The authorities must take the lion's share of the blame for the complete destruction and looting of African trading stores, criminal negligence by the authorities in their dire hour of need of protection.'[38]

We have seen that Charlton had strongly criticized African storekeepers for 'wickedly' exploiting their women customers and even for planning a Shona takeover. But now he published an eloquent threnody for the downfall of a whole class, of which after all he was himself one:

> Except for Foster Mnapi's store in the Old Location, all the other stores in 2nd Street – Alfred's, Lameck's, James's, Kahlu's and so on – were completely destroyed, as well as the old co-op stores situated behind Kanda's hair-dressing shop. And they were looted … Some were set on fire. The Old Location Butchery, which belongs to Lewis Mapfumo, was broken into … and a lot of meat stolen. The new block of flats situated next to the office of the Superintendent,

---

[36] *Parade*, September 1960; *Daily News*, 26 July 2000.
[37] The same attitude was taken by the *Bantu Mirror*. 'The Government bears the lion's share of the blame for the lamentable Bulawayo riots', it wrote on 6 August 1960. 'After causing the muddle by banning the NDP meeting, the Government did not use all the forces at its disposal and command to protect innocent and law-abiding people in the African community'.
[38] *Home News*, 6 August 1960.

Old Location, was also invaded with the same results, that is the smashing up of the shops and looting. The same is true of Lizzi Skosana's grocery shop.

And so the list went on, roaming through all the other townships – Mzilikazi, Nguboy-ena, Njube, Mpopoma, Pumula, even Luveve. Everywhere the same story of destruction, with the single exception of Brown Luza's store in Njube, where Luza's 'boys and friends and relatives defended the store as one man and threw back the attackers'.[39]

On Tuesday 26 July no one went to work. Police opened fire on crowds for the fourth time. Food was running short. The *Daily News* of that day reported that:

> By late morning it was estimated that half the women population of Makokoba African township had fled across the river to seek shelter with friends and relatives in Mzilikazi. Many have been seen streaming across carrying their babies on their backs and whatever belongings they could on their heads.

Yet another meeting was held, this time on a football field in the Western Common-age. It was addressed by the Provincial Commissioner and by Industrial Officers who urged the men to return to work. 'In reply they said they would only return to work if the three leaders of the NDP were unconditionally released.' The crowd broke up and the police opened fire on what had become a 'threatening mob'.

But the energy was running out of *Zhii*. By the afternoon troops had entered the townships and were in control. The *Chronicle* of 27 July reported that 'a full scale military police sweep was organized for 2 p.m.' It met with no resistance. Major Ndlovu, the schoolboy who was swept up by the mob on the first day, recalls:

> Then came the Federal army. That was no joke. They came. Guns were fired! They went Po! Po! Bho! Bho! It then became tough and worse. The aeroplane shouted from above that the government would take serious action against anyone seen carrying a stone or throwing a stone. People went to their houses. We went to our houses, with tails cut down, very ashamed. It became quiet as if nothing had occurred. People got into their house and closed their doors, switching off their radios.

Soon police and soldiers began to search houses for loot. The *Daily News* of 27 July recorded that its reporter followed men and women he had seen looting and found them 'seated outside their houses reading their Bibles'. But this display of innocence did nothing to stop the searches. The *Chronicle* reported that at one house troops 'uncovered rolls of cloth, packets of tea, bottles of drink, bags of cigarettes … The man of the house was forced at gunpoint to carry it out in front of the watching by-standers before being arrested.' A *Chronicle* photo showed shield-bearing police searching a house in Makokoba, with husband and wife sitting glumly on the stool outside (see cover photo). Major Ndlovu remembers that 'police started going house by house. The police would find meat covered by blankets. A person would declare that under the blanket was his wife or child not feeling well in order to survive the torture from the police.'[40]

The searching of houses and arrest of looters went on for several days. It was a brutal business, well remembered in oral narratives. A Northern Rhodesian migrant to Bulawayo, Mr Zulu, recalls:

[39] Ibid.
[40] Interview of Hloniphani Ndlovu with Major Ndlovu, Entumbane, January 2000.

The army came armed with guns. Facing guns people had no alternative but to stop, because if one was found rioting it had been established that they would be shot. There was a helicopter flying and someone with a loudspeaker inside was appealing to the people to stop the violence or they were going to be shot. He-He! Who wanted to die at that moment without first seeing the country liberated? Who could try anything stupid, who indeed could try anything with a gun facing him or her?

People, however, had seen nothing yet. The consequences were yet to come. Others had run away to their rural places, walking all the way to places as far away as Kezi and Lupane in fear of the brutality they were seeing [from the rioters]. When they came back a week later after hearing that the violence had stopped they were faced with another violence, though of a different nature. The owners of stores where people had looted had reported to the police. The police then came house by house armed with baton sticks, ready to brutalise and torture all those who had taken part in the looting.

I think this was the worst part of the *Zhii* period. The police would turn one's house upside down in search of looted mealie-meal and meat. Some people in fear of being tortured buried sacks of mealie meal underground … Neighbours turned out to be spies who told the police that their neighbour had been leading others in looting. You could not trust anyone during that time. You could not even trust yourself because after being asked a lot of questions by the police one could lie to save oneself from the torture.[41]

MaMhlanga's two nephews tried to take refuge from the police. 'I remember the police coming to my house, my sister's boys hid under the bed in fear, but the police discovered them anyway in their search for the stolen mealie meal and meat. They would ask me *Salukazi ulani, uphleni wena?*, old woman, what are you hiding?'[42]

After the troops went in, the townships were 'deadly quiet'. Men went back to work. The *Daily News* reporter found that moving about in the townships was 'like walking in a ghost town [where] everyone had either died or fled'. There were many arrests, the police being guided both by unfriendly neighbours and by plainclothes detectives. Trials began on 8 August, 'the tense atmosphere of the riots re-lived in all four of the city courts, as Africans appeared still wearing their soiled, torn and blood-stained clothing'.[43] There was a wide range of men brought before the courts. The oldest was Gilbert, aged 70, who was jailed for two months but without hard labour. The youngest was Promise, 'who had been on the court roll for the two opening days' but who turned out to be only 8. He was 'sent home by the police after a suitable warning'.[44] In all, 515 men appeared in court; 131 were convicted, 90 were acquitted and charges were withdrawn against 277.

There were funerals to arrange. The official death-toll in *Zhii* was twelve. Nehwati tells us, however, that 'it is generally known that many more people were killed and injured, but as these were picked up by colleagues and relatives and the former taken for burial in the rural areas the exact figures are to this day unknown'.[45] Still, the inquests on some of the twelve deaths give a vivid impression of the atmosphere of *Zhii*.

Some of the dead had been shot by police. One such affray took place in the Mzi-

---

41 Interview between Hloniphani Ndlovu and Mr Zulu, Mzilikazi, February 2000. The *Daily News* of 28 July reported that 'one of the people arrested was heard to shout at a policeman: "Hey! What's the idea of arresting me alone? The chap next door also has some loot buried in his yard." The chap next door was arrested too.'
42 Interview between Hloniphani Ndlovu and MaMhlanga, Entumbane, February 2000.
43 *Chronicle*, 9 August 1960.
44 *Chronicle*, 11 August 1960.
45 Nehwati, op.cit., p. 253.

likazi Post Office where a crowd was trying to break down the main strongroom door. The men were drinking from bottles of beer and one witness testified that 'he had seen an African open a bottle of beer with his teeth. They were opening up all the bottles with their teeth.' As he added, 'You don't expect them to carry a tin-opener around with them when they had just smashed the beer halls up.' A ten-strong police patrol arrived and in the fight that ensued three men were arrested and one was shot dead.[46] Others were shot by police reservists. One such reservist, Dennis Scott, had been taking 'official films' with a ciné camera from the back of a police Land Rover. But the vehicle 'had been separated from a convoy trying to disperse mobs in the Old Location'. It was surrounded by stone-throwers and slowed down by roadblocks. 'The situation was extremely grave … The trucks in front had dropped tear gas which did not help us very much and they had no idea where we were.' Scott fired at one of the three Africans running towards a roadblock and a man, Elias, fell dead.

Two men were shot and killed by a 'Coloured' small-holder and storekeeper, Julius Van Beek, who lived close to Luveve. Van Beek's wife had warned him the day before that passing Africans had threatened to burn the store down. He sent her and the children away, 'rushed to a neighbourhood home, borrowed a rifle and prepared to defend his property'. A crowd of 700 surrounded the store. The leaders called to them: 'The police will not shoot us so why are you afraid of Van Beek?' The crowd began to stone the store and house; Van Beek fired in the air and at the feet of the men in the front row. Two of them were shot and killed. A police riot-squad coming to Van Beek's rescue was heavily stoned. It used tear gas to no effect. Sergeant Tomlinson 'fired a shot-gun but the mob still advanced … I fired directly at the ones in front of me. After this shot they dispersed very rapidly.' Stories like this reminded the white population of Bulawayo all too vividly of the 1896 rising.[47]

Finally, black storekeepers and householders also defended their property. Togara, a leaseholder in Mpopoma, told the inquest 'how he hit out at two young Africans with a knobkerrie when they forced their way into his house after he refused to join a mob … He was sitting outside his quarters with his children on the Monday night while his wife was preparing the evening meal. A mob of Africans said "Come and join us." He refused and went inside with his children, bolting the door.' The crowd stoned the house, breaking the windows and hammering on his door. 'When all the windows were broken his wife opened the door and escaped with the children. As she did so, two young men pushed their way into the room. "I remained inside armed with a knobkerrie. I was determined to defend myself and my property."' He struck and killed Mfanya.[48]

At Iminyela a butcher, Charles Gumu, tried to phone the police when his store was broken into. No help came. He was seen by the crowd, who threatened him. He retreated outside the butchery, filled beer bottles with water, and lobbed them inside. One of the looters, Patrick, was hit and killed. His body lay inside the store unrecovered for the next two days.[49]

It is important to record that no policeman, soldier, reservist, store-owner, house-

[46] *Chronicle*, 28 August 1960.
[47] *Chronicle*, 30 and 31 August 1960. Strangely the *Sunday News* of 24 July, on the very day the riots began, carried a story by an old-timer, P.L. Poole, who recalled that 'within a week [in 1896] no Europeans were left alive in Matabeleland outside the laager'.
[48] *Chronicle*, 1 September 1960.
[49] *Chronicle*, 2 September 1960.

holder or, indeed, *anyone* – white, coloured or black – was killed by the rioters themselves.[50]

Zhii: *An Analysis*

After the violence was over officials expressed themselves as baffled. Hugh Ashton merely said, 'It shouldn't have happened – but it did.'[51] The *Sunday News* of 7 August found that 'officials are stumped'. 'Until more facts are accumulated, until inquiries are complete', said the paper, 'no official or security man is going to say anything. Security men are expected to be able to come up with a reasonable answer in future.' So far as I know, they never did. There was no commission of inquiry into *Zhii* and no report. The Mayor, S.H. Millar, who had been so humiliatingly trapped in his factory, made an immediate comment in his report for the year ending 31 July 1960:

> I now regretfully refer to the recent riots. I say regretfully because of the tragedy of suffering they have brought to so many innocent people and because of the interruption of the fine record of peaceful achievement that they represent ... It is too early fully to assess the cause of the riots. Many explanations are being aired – that they were anti-European, anti-African middle class; that they were the struggle of the have-nots against the haves; that they were politically inspired; that they were a revolt against authority and the present regime. Possibly there is some truth in them all for commotion is a complex thing and is unlikely to stem from any single cause ... It is not difficult to point to the negative side of the troubles ... but we would be stupid if we did not learn from them as well ... for these disturbances are symptomatic of the winds of change. If such things can happen under our present policies, should we not rethink these policies immediately and be prepared to reverse them in fundamentals?

As we shall see, there was a good deal of municipal re-thinking in the coming months and years. More immediately, both black and white in Bulawayo struggled to come to terms with what had happened. There were two explanations available when the riots came to an end. One was Charlton Ngcebetsha's prediction of renewed ethnic conflict. The other was Sir Edgar Whitehead's assertion that the violence had been planned and directed by the NDP. Both were rapidly abandoned or discredited.

Ethnicity

After the riots were over not even Ngcebetsha argued that they had been in any way 'tribal'. Stores owned by Kalanga and Ndebele were burnt and looted as well as stores owned by Shona. The men arrested included Kalanga, Ndebele, Shona, Northerners, Mozambicans. None of our informants believed that ethnicity was important in *Zhii*. Neither Shona informants nor Northern informants felt that they were in special danger. Francis Nehwati insists that except for the women, 'everybody came out to fight. Everybody carried a stick ... as a passport for movement or transit in the African townships. No distinctions were made as to tribe or country of origin. All

---

[50] Yet some informants recall a bloody African triumph over whites. As the octogenarian Ndlovu told Simon Mlotshwa on 28 January 2001: 'It was a war that the white men saw that a black man can really fight with a stone ... Many whites were killed. White women would sometimes be heard pleading for mercy, saying "Don't kill me, I'm your wife."'

[51] Report of the Director of African Administration for year ending June 1961.

were united as Bulawayans.'[52]

In the 1960s, after the riots, one of Ashton's assistants, Eric Stanley Gargett, gathered material for a London University doctoral thesis. He cited research by the Department of Housing and Amenities to the effect that 50 per cent of Bulawayo's African population regarded itself as Ndebele and only 25 per cent as Shona. So much for Charlton's fears of a Shona takeover. Gargett found, moreover, that the only tribal organizations in Bulawayo were those 'maintained by expatriate Zambians and Malawians who used to receive visits from their chiefs'. 'Among Rhodesians there was no strong indication of preferential association by tribes.' Half the men who shared double flats roomed with someone of a different tribe. The 33 burial societies in Bula-wayo were 'not based on tribe' but either on shared employment or on 'local kinship and residential ties'.[53]

Sir Edgar Whitehead's ban of the Nyasaland and Northern Rhodesian Congresses in 1959 had turned the supporters of those two radical movements into followers of the NDP. The Northern Rhodesianer Zulu insists that:

> At these political rallies I did not look at myself as a Zambian but as part of the Southern Rho-desian people … I considered myself part of the Southern Rhodesia *povo* who supported the political leaders.[54]

Other informants, while clearly remembering ethnic job differentiation, insisted on a Bulawayo 'patriotism' which brought people together. Black Bulawayo had come a long way since 1929.

Nationalism

As for the idea that *Zhii* was planned and carried out by the NDP, Sir Edgar White-head's allegations were oddly seconded in the early 1980s by Edison Zvogbo. In a brief history of the national struggle, largely aimed at discrediting Nkomo, Zvogbo hailed Michael Mawema and Sketchley Samkange as the most radical and effective lead-ers of open mass nationalism. In his version they planned ahead by organizing and preparing youth cadres who played the major role in *Zhii*. And obviously there *were* NDP connections with *Zhii*. The riots began because of the ban on an NDP meet-ing; an NDP vehicle was seen in the midst of rioters in Stanley Square; some of those involved in the attempt to break through the police cordon and get into the town now say that they were NDP Youth; the mass meeting addressed by the Provincial Native Commissioner on Tuesday 26 July broke up when men refused to return to work until the three arrested NDP leaders, who included Mawema and Samkange, had been unconditionally released.

Nevertheless hardly anyone in black Bulawayo believed that the NDP co-ordinated *Zhii*. Our oral informants, even the self-professed NDP Youth, unanimously say that no one led or controlled *Zhii*. It arose out of 'restlessness'. The *Chronicle* reported on 27 July that 'there is no political pattern in the violence, and tragic-comedy stories

[52] Nehwati, op. cit., pp. 254-5. Nehwati admits that there had been previous ethnic tensions. But he insists that by 1960 tribal associations had been replaced by trade unions, political parties and civil associations. 'Conglomeration in diversity in time leads to conglomeration in unity.'

[53] Eric Gargett, 'Welfare Services in an African Urban Area', PhD thesis, University of London, 1971, p. 30.

[54] Interview between Hloniphani Ndlovu and Mr Zulu, Mzilikazi, February 2000.

are emerging from the townships of the confusion'. Houses of some leading NDP men had been attacked. Hugh Ashton told the Bulawayo Council early in August that 'the present weight of evidence is that the leaders had little intention to start violence' and that there was 'little evidence to suggest any organisation'.[55] The *Sunday News*, reporting on 7 August the bewilderment of officials about the riots, said that at least one thing was clear – 'it was not deliberately planned'.

Charlton Ngcebetsha, now supporting the UFP, roundly disagreed with his party leader:

> The disturbances in Salisbury and in Bulawayo took totally different courses and were not in any way similar. The Salisbury riots were clearly sparked off by the apprehension by the Salisbury police of some top-ranking leaders of the NDP. On the contrary, the disturbances in Bulawayo were caused by irresponsible hooligans … It is said that the riots in Bulawayo were engineered by the NDP. This is simply not true. The hooliganic elements of Bulawayo who kindled the riots belonged to no political party.[56]

Ngcebetsha remarked that a 'leading African member of the NDP was stoned near the Stanley Hall on the evening of the riots'.[57] As for the NDP Land Rover, it had been driven into the midst of the crowd by Sketchley Samkange – one of the three NDP leaders arrested by Whitehead, but virtually unknown in Bulawayo. Out on bail and visiting Gwelo, Samkange heard that riots had broken out in Bulawayo. He drove straight there – in an echo of his father, Thompson Samkange's, drive in 1948 – to try to take control and restore order. His Land Rover was heavily stoned, amidst cries of 'To Hell with the NDP. We don't know the NDP'. Samkange discreetly (and hastily) withdrew.[58]

Those who were soon to take the lead in the NDP Youth Council were significant only at the very beginning of the riots, before the violence began. One was Dumiso Dabengwa, who has given his own account in which he describes how the controlled demonstration was broken up by the police and became uncontrollable violence, leaving him frustrated and furious on the sidelines. His subsequent conviction under the Law and Order Maintenance Act was not for either organizing, participating in, or justifying the riots but for saying that the police were to blame for them.[59]

In so far as *Zhii* was structured by youth – and it partly was – it was not NDP youth, Whitehead's imagined 'NDP hooligan branch', who were involved. On 26 July the *Chronicle* reported that 'the pattern of rioters and looters is now revealed as mobs of 100 to 500 moving from public centre to public centre' and led by 'hooligans who were not without organization and [their] own brand of cleverness'. These came from the long-standing youth gang tradition in the Bulawayo townships. Back in 1929 youth gangs had played a leading role in the faction fighting. In the early months of 1960 there were plenty of references to gangs. In December 1959, for instance, an Mpopoma gang posted notices on trees and fences in the township warning people not to go out after 7 p.m. If they were caught after that hour they would escape with their lives only by paying a fine – £5 if they were Ndebele and £15 if they were not![60]

55 *Chronicle*, 5 August 1960.
56 *Home News*, 6 August 1960.
57 Ibid.
58 T.O. Ranger, *Are We Not Also Men?*, p. 188.
59 Temba Moyo and Ole Gjerstad, *The Organiser, Story of Temba Moyo*, LSM Press, Richmond, 1974.
60 *Home News*, 12 December 1959.

In the immediate aftermath of the riots, the *Daily News* reported that some co-ordination had been provided – the organization of stolen cars as ambulances, for instance – by 'a gang of youths who call themselves Section 17'. This was 'an all-African unit composed of young gangsters, all 17 years or below'. It had first emerged during the 1948 strike and had constantly renewed itself ever since. A leader told the *Daily News* reporter: 'Ours is gangsterism. We shall continue looting, stoning and burning.' The *News* commented that 'Bulawayo had a very weak branch of the NDP [but] a huge population of the *tsotsi* element'.[61] Many of our female informants told us how terrified they had been of these young gangsters during *Zhii*.

In these circumstances what the NDP needed to do in Bulawayo was to bring youth into a disciplined party organization and to involve more women in nationalist politics. So after *Zhii* the Bulawayo leaders of the NDP went out of their way to make it clear that the party did not support random violence. At the end of July a Defence Committee was set up in Bulawayo to raise funds for the defence of men charged as rioters. The Bulawayo executive of the NDP condemned the fund 'since looting is not party policy'.[62] At the end of August the NDP held its first public meeting since the ban, 5,000 people gathering in Stanley Square for the launch of the party's Youth Council. Four speakers, including Dumiso Dabengwa, condemned 'in the strongest terms all forms of hooliganism'. The police present congratulated them on their excellent speeches and good discipline.[63] On 4 September 10,000 met in Stanley Square to hear NDP leaders attack 'the law of the jungle'. It was at this meeting that Jane Ngwenya, 'the only female speaker', made her debut. To great cheers she urged men to bring their wives to political meetings so as to civilize them.[64]

Gender

Iain Edwards' account of the Cato Manor riots in Durban in June 1959, just a year before *Zhii*, emphasizes the leading role of women. Women armed themselves; attacked beer halls; claimed to be Zulu warriors and taunted cowardly men. 'The 1959 riot was considered an enormously important event because it involved women as the central actors. The politics of gender actually constituted the event itself.'[65]

We have already seen that there was a politics of gender in Bulawayo in the 1950s. But how did it manifest itself in *Zhii*? In Bulawayo, too, the beer halls were attacked; in Bulawayo, too, women suffered from many of the same pressures and insecurities which Edwards describes for Durban. One might have expected women to be major participants in *Zhii*.

They were not. Nehwati says that 'except for women' everyone came out to fight. Ashton made a special point that 'there is no evidence that women took any part in the troubles'.[66] All oral informants, especially women themselves, agree that the women's

---

61 *Daily News*, 26 and 27 July, 3 August 1960.
62 *Daily News*, 29 July 1960.
63 *Daily News*, 29 August 1960.
64 *Daily News*, 6 September 1960.
65 Iain Edwards, 'Cato Manor, June 1959. Men, Women, Crowds, Violence, Politics and History', in P. Maylam and I. Edwards (eds), *The People's City: African Life in Twentieth-Century Durban*, University of Natal Press, Durban, 1996, pp. 102-3.
66 *Chronicle*, 5 August 1960.

role was to lock themselves in their houses, venture out only to loot, to look after the children, and if necessary to flee across the stream from Makokoba to Mzilikazi, or to move off into the countryside. (Some male informants gleefully described how fashionable young women had to take their high heels and mini-skirts off in order to run away.) Again, one might have expected women and girls to have been major victims of 'nights of terror'. During the Youth League bus boycott in Harare women were raped in the Carter Hostel. During *Zhii* there were no allegations of rape or of assault on women.

All this was part of a Bulawayo 'tradition' of township activism. In 1929 women were prohibited from speaking at the meeting which ended the violence; in 1948 they were told to stay at home; they were clearly expected to take no part in *Zhii*. Peter Mackay writes, in the first published account of the famous protest march from High-field to Harare in July 1960 that it was 'a man's march in a man's world'.[67] Urban violence in Rhodesia *was* a man's world.

And yet in other ways *Zhii* arose profoundly out of gender relations. The chief issue in Bulawayo township housing policy in 1960 was the changing ratio between 'married' and 'single' men. After the riots many commentators, both black and white, blamed the violence on 'bachelors', some of whom were taunted by 'wives' as the troops entered the township. After *Zhii*, just as before it, there was plenty of female participation in township politics; women in the townships were deeply divided on issues of morality and status.[68]

In 1940 the ratio of 'single' to 'married' men in Bulawayo was 19.3 to 1. During the 1940s spokesmen of the Bulawayo Council constantly asserted that the city did not need married labour and had no need to pay wages or provide housing for a man to support a wife. This was the position taken by Bulawayo's 'big city boss' and Labour MP, Donald Macintyre. By the late 1940s, however, the ratio had come down to 7.2 'single' to 1 'married'. When, against Macintyre's opposition, the Council decided in 1949 to implement the Native (Urban Areas) Accommodation and Registration Act, to accept full responsibility for married accommodation and to set up an Afri-can Affairs Administration, things changed rapidly. Ashton set out to increase the number of family homes. By 1950 the ratio was down to 4.9 to 1. By 1955 it was down to 3.9 to 1. By 1960 it had fallen to 2.6 to 1. Five years later it was 1 to 1.[69]

These changes ranked high among the reasons why Ashton had not expected vio-lence. In the jargon of the time, Bulawayo's African population was being 'stabilized'. In 1959 one-fifth of the African population had been born in Bulawayo; by 1969 almost a third. Eric Gargett declared that 'the Bulawayo African population is overwhelm-ingly local and increasingly born there'.[70] But, as we have seen, in 1960 these processes were creating their own tensions. With Ashton's policy of clearing 'single' men out of Makokoba into newly-built hostels and evicting their 'illegal' wives there was great tension in the township. Mpopoma married leaseholders feared and disliked their 'single' lodgers. *Zhii* could be seen as the last throw of the 'bachelors'.

It was generally alleged after *Zhii* that 'single men' had been 'spearheads of the

---

[67] Peter Mackay, *We Have Tomorrow. Stirrings in Africa, 1959-1967*, Michael Russell, Wilby, 2008, p. 78.

[68] For a thorough discussion of these points in relation to Salisbury see Teresa A. Barnes, *We Women Worked So Hard. Gender, Urbanisation, and Social Reproduction in Colonial Harare, Zimbabwe, 1930–56*, James Currey, Oxford, 1999.

[69] Gargett, p. 22a; Hugh Ashton, 'The Economics of African Housing', *Rhodesian Journal of Economics*, 1969.

[70] Gargett, p. 27.

rioters'. In the exclusively 'bachelor' townships of Mabutweni and Iminyela, 'savage acts of vandalism were performed'.[71] Donald Macintyre, who had done more than anyone to stop Africans living in married accommodation, now visited the devastated townships in his capacity as Federal Minister of Finance. A photograph in the *Chronicle* of 30 July 1960 showed him outside a wrecked general store, 'looking grim'. He described the losses of 'decent, hard-working' married men as a real tragedy. Nearly all the 'loafers and hooligans', he added, were 'apparently single men'.

After the troops had entered the townships and humbled the rioters, married African women openly mocked 'bachelors' and blamed them for the upheavals:

> Married women in the townships [wrote M.S .Malebengwa Ndlovu from Mabutweni] have even gone so far as insulting us by calling us such names as 'bulls'. [Yet] the trouble started in the Old Location. We at Mabutweni were forced out of our houses by people from the Old Location who came shouting 'Zhii' … There are good and polite people in Mabutweni and Iminyela. We have our wives in the reserves. As far as the recent rioting is concerned, I find it most unfair that we Africans should start blaming each other. If there is any blame at all then it is the Government to blame.[72]

In fact, as many married men as 'bachelors' were prosecuted after *Zhii*. Ngcebetsha's allies, the respectable Women's Associations, restricted their demands to pleading that married Africans who had looted should not be evicted from their houses because of the suffering that this would cause to children.[73]

Poverty

On 5 August 1960 the *Chronicle* carried a letter from A.T.M. Mehlis, a police reservist. 'The good old days came to a fiery end on July 24', he wrote. The reason was destitution. 'Searching the township houses for stolen goods, I found little but vast numbers of children and also everywhere poverty. The grass is dry: we have had one serious fire: agitators are ready to light more matches.' Mehlis had been searching in Makokoba and, as Ashton himself had admitted in 1957, 'the Old Location is still a slum, even though it is the only slum'.[74] It was into this township that the procession marched on 24 July. It was no wonder, then, that the *Parade* reporter recorded:

> as the procession progressed in Makokoba and still attracting more people, the complaints were no longer political. They centred on low wages, poor living conditions and unemployment.[75]

After *Zhii* it was natural to blame the very poor and especially the unemployed for the violence. The *Bantu Mirror* claimed on 6 August that it was 'unemployed Africans who roam the city streets' who did the damage. The chair of the Unemployed Association, Mpande, called for a Commission of Inquiry into the riots. 'The Association being aware of the danger to come told the Government of the grave social problems

---

71 *Daily News*, 27 July 1960.
72 *Bantu Mirror*, 27 August 1960.
73 *Home News*, 6 August 1960. Many store-owners took a different view.
74 H. Ashton, 'African Administration in Bulawayo'. City of Bulawayo, 4 September 1957. The *Bantu Mirror* of 16 July added that there were other slums. Living conditions in Mshasa where 'single' men were accommodated, were disgraceful. 'Its immediate abolition is not just a mere necessity but a MUST.'
75 *Parade*, September 1960.

followed by crimes which would be a result of unemployment in Bulawayo.' Now the riots had happened 'it would be better if the Government did something to deal with and solve the problem of starving people instead of calling in people to join the African Special Police Reserve'.[76]

And yet the *Sunday News* of 7 August revealed that it was certainly not only the unemployed who had been involved in the violence. 'Police, who first believed that the unemployed element played a large part are changing their tune. Most arrested for riot activities were in employment. They also figured strongly among the looters.' Urban poverty was pervasive. It was after all in the houses of married families that Mehlis had been searching for loot and finding poverty.

Class

The *Sunday News* on 7 August 1960 proposed a final element in the riddle of *Zhii*:

> What were the causes of Bulawayo's riots? Government officials and Security agents say they do not know. But as investigators probe point by point there emerges a possibility that a class consciousness is developing among the labouring type of African and, if this is true, it might offer a completely new line of thought.

We have seen the growth of differentiated townships on the Western Commonage during the 1950s. Eric Gargett, writing about the 1960s, found that 'the ordering of social relationships in town ... is beginning to occur on class lines. In Bulawayo, prestige differentiation has occurred in the development of associations such as tennis and golf clubs and in the leadership of voluntary groups, as well as by educational, occupational and economic standing. Home ownership schemes have encouraged the greater cohesion associated with class consciousness.'[77] Two townships in particular had developed by 1960 as communities of a self-satisfied elite. One was Pelendaba, meaning 'the matter is concluded' – Joshua Nkomo's home – whose very name came from 'the successful conclusion of the struggle for security of tenure'. In 1959 leases there were extended from 30 years to 99 years. The other was Pumula, meaning 'a resting place', named by its inhabitants because 'many have built homes to retire to'.[78]

Although the NDP demanded yet further privileges for these townships, in particular the grant of freehold tenure, there were a number of their residents who belonged to the United Federal Party, the Central Africa Party and in one case even the Dominion Party. This was Jeremiah Hlomane Sobantu, who died in March 1960. The *Home News* hailed him as 'a most enterprising businessman'. He had been the first to set up 'a sound business as a photographer'; he had a hairdressing shop in Makokoba and a grinding mill in Ntabazinduna. He gave all his businesses the name *Maliyavuza*, 'money leaks through', or a superabundance of money. He was one of the first to move from Makokoba to Pelendaba, 'whose grandeur in magnificent houses of modern design beggars description'. He was chairman of the Residents Association there when it was called merely No. 6 African township, but under his leadership long leases were obtained and it was renamed 'in memory of the happy settlement of the

[76] *Bantu Mirror*, 13 August 1960.
[77] Gargett, p. 32.
[78] City of Bulawayo, *Some Facts About the Municipal Government of Bulawayo*, December 1962.

troubles'. He sought the support of the right-wing Dominion Party, openly declaring that 'he was interested in riches even if it was entirely against the interests of the African people as a whole'.[79]

Sobantu died before *Zhii*. But there were other wealthy men with big houses for the rioters to target.

It was true, of course, that the process of class formation and class consciousness was incomplete. There was very little separation of poor space and rich space. Ngcebetsha might claim that 'most Africans are jolly proud of Mpopoma for it is one of the best places within the Bulawayo Municipal Boundary which is, for all intents and purposes, owned by Africans themselves'.[80] But Mpopoma, as we have seen, was full of lodgers, shebeens and gangsters. African stores were situated in the very heart of Makokoba and other poor areas. Gargett recorded that Bulawayo's housing projects had been criticized by elite Africans for allowing too little scope for the development of class consciousness. 'Bulawayo's high-class owner-builder scheme, Pelendaba, was considered unsatisfactory because it was sited among housing of a poorer standard.' And if 'the emergence of a property-owning middle class is accompanied by resistance to traditional kinship demands', at the same time 'a feature of the household budget was exchange of gifts between one urban household and another. The upper income groups gave far more than they received.'[81] Nehwati argued in 1970 that the townships of Bulawayo formed a total community. Prosperous Africans did not 'live in isolation from the total society, but are part of it. Outside their narrower groups they are also fathers, brothers, uncles – real or classificatory – of someone else.' Together with trade union leaders, Advisory Board members, and civic association leaders they were accorded the status of 'fathers' and patrons.[82]

Nevertheless, the very incompleteness of social separation meant that the African middle class suffered badly in *Zhii*. The *Sunday News* reported that when police and troops moved in they found that 'well kept and trim houses and gardens had been damaged and looted. Hovels and badly kept houses were not damaged and many contained loot.' It asked: 'Did the element of jealousy and envy come into it?'[83] Charlton Ngcebetsha was in no doubt of the answer:

> The wanton destruction in the African shops stemmed merely from jealousy for it is well known that Africans are jealous of the success of any of their people and will do anything to torpedo and destroy them. It is true that a leading African businessman who is also a leading member of the Western Commonage Advisory Board – to prove the jealousy of Africans – suffered the complete loss of his shop at Western Commonage, and that before they went to Luveve to destroy his shop they first went to his house at Pelendaba and ransacked it, looking for him, but without success.[84]

---

[79] *Home News*, 5 March 1960. On 16 March the paper recorded a case of the opposite trajectory. Richard Makoni 'was once a very rich African in money' and patron of both the Voice and the Federation. He had run more than five buses. But now 'he has no money and earns his living by selling bones and old steel pieces'. Punished for selling European alcohol illegally, 'he is a physical wreck and a burden to himself'. He was allocated a small place in Mzilikazi intead of being able to settle in Pumula and would 'suffer the humiliation of being packed like a sardine in a small house'. Bulawayo's nascent African capitalist economy was a jungle in which there were spectacular winners and spectacular losers.

[80] *Home News*, 18 June 1960.

[81] Gargett, pp. 35 and 40.

[82] Nehwati, pp. 264-5.

[83] *Sunday News*, 7 August 1960.

[84] *Home News*, 6 August 1960.

R.M. Bango, General Secretary of the Transport Workers Union and chair of the Pelendaba Residents Association, described how rioters had broken into his and other houses at Pelendaba, and how 'rather than have their houses wrecked and their families attacked, the men pretended to join, taking up sticks and bars and shouting the slogans of the rioters'.[85] On 18 August an article appeared in the *Chronicle* entitled 'The Dilemma of the Moderates'. Ngcebetsha was one of those interviewed, together with trade union leaders. They told the reporter that 'part of the feeling was directed by African "have-nots" against the African "haves". At night during the height of the riots, peaceful Africans were pulled out of their beds and homes by demonstrators crying "You must suffer with us."'

As the Mayor said, commotion is a complex thing. Anti-white feelings, anti-municipal feelings, gender tensions and class tensions were all inter-twined in *Zhii*. Like many violent outbursts it revealed a great deal, much of it perturbing, about Bulawayo black society.

Aftermaths

Above all, *Zhii* shook things up. As Ashton wrote, 'the riots profoundly shocked everyone, European and African alike, and shattered the complacency of the "it can't happen here" attitude. This has led to heart searching and appraisal.'[86] The Mayor was true to his promise that municipal policies would be reviewed, and in the next 18 months the Bulawayo Council assented to African freehold and voted for direct African representation as elected councillors. In doing so, it once again stood in opposition to government policy which favoured autonomous African local government.[87] Ashton added a year later that 'the riots can be said to have disturbed the national conscience'.[88] Bulawayo industrialists came together in a Reform Movement which asked the Federal Government for road building schemes and for tariffs which would allow Rhodesian industry to grow and hence to do away with unemployment. When Donald Macintyre as Federal Minister of Finance objected to the £250,000 cost of a road building scheme which would employ a thousand Africans, the Reform Movement replied that 'perhaps Mr McIntyre should be reminded that this was precisely the cost of the rioting in Bulawayo over three days'.[89] Sir Edgar Whitehead announced a 'crash programme' for African housing and declared that it was government policy to separate the African classes in distinct townships.[90] But nothing much came of any of these ameliorative plans. Unemployment continued to grow. Middle-class townships were not built in Bulawayo remote from any other. Finance was not found for a crash programme of house building or for a major road construction project. The

---

[85] *Chronicle*, 28 July 1960.

[86] Report of the Director of African Affairs for year ending June 1960, p. 5.

[87] Ashton's annual report of July 1961 recorded that 'another important piece of legislation was the Local Government Act which though opposed in principle by Council at least had the virtue of placing the issue of African progress in Local Government squarely before the public'. The Bulawayo Council voted unanimously on 4 January 1961 that 'there should be direct African representation on the City Council and that African Townships should be incorporated into the Municipality as a single ward which would return four councillors'.

[88] Report of the Director of African Affairs for year ending June 1961, pp. 1-2.

[89] *Chronicle*, 24 August 1960.

[90] *Chronicle*, 29 July 1960.

unemployed 'loafers' were rather to be dealt with under a new Vagrancy Act which provided for them to be arrested and removed to rehabilitation camps. Mpande, chairman of the Unemployed Association, wrote bitterly to the Minister of Labour. They had asked for bread and been given the stone of the Vagrancy Act:

> I delivered to these hungry men what I thought was your concrete promise. But now I am embarrassed to see the pain of the men and the cry of the women and children at what has happened [to] those lost Sons of God who are today called unemployable but who are unemployed.[91]

Bulawayo remained restless.

The effects of *Zhii* on Bulawayo African politics were complex and contradictory. All our informants agreed that the NDP did not organize *Zhii* but many of them declared that it was 'the beginning of the freedom struggle'. Hugh Ashton's report for the year ended July 1961 spoke of the 'unprecedented prominence of African politics, especially on the local scene ... innumerable local meetings. Those called by the NDP mustered crowds of up to 15,000 ... By the end of June [1961] scarcely a township was without its weekend political meetings or local branch of the NDP.' *Zhii* certainly stimulated this intense activity. At the same time, though, it exacerbated the cleavages and tensions within Bulawayo nationalism.

When African 'moderates', including trade union leaders, spoke to the *Chonicle* on 18 August 1960 they deplored the behaviour of the 'have-nots', but they added:

> We are told economic is better than political advancement but we do not see any economic advancement anyway and begin to think we shall never have freedom until we have a black government.

After *Zhii* such 'moderate' nationalists demanded firm action against 'single'men. R.M. Bango, whose house had been attacked in Pelendaba, demanded that Makokoba should be demolished and that 'all single men be put in an area of their own'.[92]

The more radical tenurial nationalists of the Mpopoma Leaseholders Association, who were pressing for the abolition of Advisory Boards and proportionate African representation on the Council, demanded in September 1960 that householders be given firearms to defend themselves, and that all single men should be removed from Iminyela and Mabutweni, which lay between Mpopoma and Pelendaba.[93] At the Western Commonage Advisory Board it was said that 'the recent riots have shown that some of the tenants in Pelendaba had been singled out for punishment by rioters' and that it was necessary to set up a Pelendaba Home Guard. It was left to 'Singleman' to write from Mabutweni:

> These Board members are comfortable in their own houses and would like some of us to walk the streets without any place to put our head ... They say we are a danger ... They are a greater danger because they seem to have no feelings for others. They seem to regard us as animals.[94]

---

[91] *Daily News*, 29 October 1960.

[92] *Chronicle*, 28 July 1960. Jasper Savanhu, who in 1945 had hailed the 'reborn' African worker, now declared that 'the present situation is a struggle between the haves and have-nots'. He demanded that African businessmen, teachers, and professionals be given a suburb of their own: then 'people with a stake in the country and something to defend' could form a Home Guard to protect themselves against the mob. *Chronicle*, 2 August 1960.

[93] *Bantu Mirror*, 10 September 1960.

[94] *Bantu Mirror*, 17 September 1960.

'Singleman' expressed the feelings of many proletarian nationalists. On 16 September a meeting of the Mpopoma Leaseholders Association attracted an audience of 300. The leaseholders asked that an armed Home Guard be formed. But this was shouted down by more than half the audience 'who appeared to be a mixture of lodgers and young people from other townships who had come to the meeting thinking it was being held by a political party'.[95] NDP leaders in Mpopoma came from the Leasehold-ers Association. In Makokoba, though, J.Z. Moyo appealed to another constituency. On 27 November 1960 some 600 tenants in Makokoba crammed into the Stanley Hall to hear Moyo. He told them that as an ex-detainee he was barred from standing in the Advisory Board elections, though he was the obvious choice. Moyo spoke up for all 'singlemen in Makokoba who lived with women outside wedlock who had children with them that they should not be sent to the hostel'. Moyo recommended two NDP men – Mutuma and Madlela – as candidates for the Board. The audience expressed their overwhelming support.

From R.M. Bango, who wanted Makokoba demolished, to J.Z. Moyo, who wanted it preserved, was a wide stretch. Ashton remarked on the varied character of NDP leadership after *Zhii* in his annual report ending July 1961:

> The quality of the Party leadership in Bulawayo was far more varied than before. Some was as good as it had ever been but much was younger, wilder, ignorant and emotional. Many were unemployed – building artisans were the worst hit by the recession.

He also remarked that by the end of 1960 'people were getting jittery from rumours of strikes and threats of reprisals'. It was feared that *Zhii* might come again.

The Return of Joshua Nkomo as Hero

What was needed was a Pelendaba man who could inspire the loyalty of J.Z. Moyo, attract moderates by his trade union and business reputation, and inspire a mass fol-lowing through heroic myth. By November 1960 Joshua Nkomo was ready to return.

Nkomo had had a difficult time in London during 1960. For months he was no closer to becoming President of the NDP. At the end of August a document entitled 'Who will be elected National President of the NDP?' was distributed in Salisbury. The document suggested Ndabaningi Sithole as the most likely candidate and specu-lated about his cabinet should an NDP government be elected. Nkomo was tipped as Minister of External Affairs.[96] Then on 22 September an NDP executive meeting deposed Michael Mawema. Three votes were taken for a successor but ballots were cast equally for Moton Malianga and Leopold Takawira. There was 'talk of calling in Moyo from Bulawayo or making Nkomo the President'.[97] But it was not until 30 October that an NDP Congress in Salisbury elected Nkomo. It was three weeks later, on Sunday 20 November, that he at last returned home. His response to *Zhii* and to the shootings in Bulawayo had a good deal to do with the reception he received. As Nkomo writes in his autobiography, 'Garfield Todd joined me in London to ask the

---

[95] Ibid.
[96] Diary of John Oliver Reed, 31 August 1960. Mawema was to be Minister of Labour, Chitepo Minister of Justice. T.G. Silundika would become Minister of European Affairs!
[97] Reed Diary, 23 September 1960.

British Government to suspend the constitution of Southern Rhodesia and take back power from the men who were abusing it.' This statement created a sensation in both Salisbury and Bulawayo.[98]

But Nkomo's return had obvious dangers. Michael Mawema had just been convicted under the Unlawful Organisations Act of running the NDP as direct successor to the banned ANC. Surely, many people thought, Nkomo would be arrested as soon as he landed at Salisbury airport. This time Nkomo's account of what happened did not need to strain for effect:

> As I emerged into the sunlight on the steps at Salisbury airport, I looked down into an ocean of faces, all turned towards me, all shouting and laughing. It was the largest crowd ever seen up to that time in Southern Rhodesia, orderly, happy, confident that I embodied their future. The official police estimate was that 50,000 people were present at the airport that day. Some observers thought it many more.[99]

One observer describes how 'Nkomo appears, surrounded by the NDP leaders. He is embracing one after another. I see him hugging Sketchley. They are really excited, moved to see each other and not embarrassed by their feelings as Europeans would be.'[100] Police made no move to arrest Nkomo and he moved off into the huge crowd.

Nkomo's return to Bulawayo on 23 November was even more emotional. Here he faced other, more local, dangers arising from the collapse of his auction house. 'Nkomo, prior to his exile, had accumulated unpaid business debts to Jewish wholesalers in Bulawayo. These wholesalers wanted Nkomo to be arrested as he alighted from the aeroplane'. His past, as a Matabele Business Man, now threatened to derail his future as leader of the people. With the help of his close Indian friend, Ramanbhai Naik, this threat was averted.[101]

The return was extremely well organized. J.Z. Moyo formed a team, consisting of Dumiso Dabengwa, Ethan Dube, Pilani Ndebele, Ramanbhai and Don Naik, to orchestrate a triumph. Survivors of that committee claim that as many as 150,000 people watched Nkomo's progress from Bulawayo airport in the NDP Land Rover with Robert Mugabe at his side. They stood ten to fifteeen deep along the roads. Nkomo stopped first at Vashee Hall at the junction of Lobengula Street and 6th Avenue where he spoke from the balcony to a crowd of 2,500. Then he progressed to his house in Pelendaba. The *Daily News* of 24 November 1960 reported that the crowds were 'drunk with excitement' and that by the time he reached Pelendaba 'the crowd had grown to a mighty 20,000'. This was a crowd come to celebrate rather than a mob come to intimidate.

Our oral informants remember the day vividly, some indeed thinking of it as the founding of the NDP. Major Ndlovu told Hloniphani Ndlovu in January 2000:

> Joshua Nkomo came from London after *Zhii*. The NDP was then formed. When Joshua Nkomo came people went to meet him shouting praises for him. Welcome! Welcome! *Baba Wethu*! It

---

[98] Nkomo. *The Story of My Life*, p. 91. T.O. Ranger, *Are We Not Also Men?*, p. 189. The urban shootings in Southern Rhodesia made the British Government, for the first and last time, consider an intervention. On 9 November 1960 Harold Macmillan told a meeting at Admiralty House that Britain 'might have to take control' and send in 'a strong man to take charge, rather as in Malaya'. Philip Murphy (ed.), *British Documents on the End of Empire. Series B Volume 9. Central Africa. Part II. Crisis and Dissolution, 1959–1965*, p. 175.

[99] *Nkomo*, p. 91.

[100] Reed Diary, 20 November 1960.

[101] Marieke Clark, 'Ramanbhai Naik', ms. Oxford, 2002.

was indeed a welcome. People even lifted the car he was in. Those were indeed some years, I tell you! Which I will always find hard to forget because they revealed how people had become aware of their difficulties.

Now was a moment for Joshua Nkomo to be celebrated in myth. One of our informants, the septuagenarian Mrs Timothy Moyo, told Simon Mlotsha in Makokoba on 15 January 2001 a myth of how a revived Ndebele king had brought *Zhii* to an end:

> *Zhii* ended after a three-legged leopard appeared at Vundu and later strolled into town via MaDlodlo Beer Hall, It was shot when it got to town but it woke up and disappeared. This leopard resembled Mzilikazi, who is said to have been injured in one arm. So when people saw the mysterious leopard they stopped fighting. Even today the leopard is there at Mzilikazi's grave site.

In 1960 people were ready to see Nkomo as an incarnation of the Ndebele monarchs. One of our informants could still recite a traditional praise poem composed in 1960 to Nkomo as Ndebele ruler. Others recalled the stories of Nkomo's visit to the High God shrine at Dula in the Matopos in 1953; the Voice's promise that he would come safely through a great war; and Nkomo's cult name of 'little slippery rock'.[102] 'Nkomo had magic', said Gogo Mamathe, interviewed in Makokoba on 18 December 2000. 'People would follow him and he would disappear into thin air. One day he is an adult and the next he would come as a schoolboy.' And if Nkomo could be connected to those great Matabeleland symbols of the Ndebele monarchy and the Matopos Mwali cult, he could also be connected to the twentieth-century Ndebele myth of the promises of Cecil Rhodes. It had long been believed that Rhodes promised an Ndebele national home but that his promises were oral and were hence dishonoured after his death. Gogo Madamu, interviewed by Lynette Nyathi in Mzilikazi in January 2000, explained Nkomo's long absence in England in terms of this myth. She insisted that in Britain Nkomo had searched high and low for 'Rhodes's letter which promised the people of Matobo some land … Rhodes said that Britain should rule us and give us back our land after 30 years.' Nkomo made a vow that 'no matter what, he was going to find it'. He searched all the British archives. 'He finally retraced it. He then used it to prove the authenticity of the nationalist cause: he proved that it was time that the British gave us back our land.'

The Close of 1960

Nkomo's return as hero rooted the NDP in Bulawayo. At the end of 1960 Nkomo and Jason Moyo were riding high. Nkomo's old friend, Jerry Vera, had opened his Happy Valley Hotel. No longer in contact with every sort of African in Bulawayo, he was now limited to elite activities – tennis and golf instead of football; ball-room dancing instead of kwela.[103] Charlton Ngcebetsha persisted with Advisory Board politics. But as 1960 ended turbulently the NDP scored an electoral triumph. Hugh Ashton had to learn how to live with the NDP in township power.

In October Charlton Ngcebetsha still spoke for the BAT Advisory Board. Together

---

[102] T.O. Ranger, *Voices From the Rocks*.
[103] In the week of Nkomo's return to Bulawayo the *Daily News* carried photographs of dancing at the Happy Valley on no fewer than three days.

with his colleagues on the other Boards he was busily engaged in discussing the issue of rifles to store-owners and 'property owners'; it was proposed by the Mpopoma Board that 'all other responsible people in Bulawayo, teachers, ministers and so on should also be armed'. Then they could defend themselves if the government once again failed to do so. Charlton thought 'it would be a most dangerous precedent'.[104] But he still issued a warning to NDP youth. Rumours were spreading that they planned more riots. If they did so, wrote Charlton, 'they will have themselves to thank for the shedding of blood on a large scale since the decent, quiet and law-abiding citizens of Bulawayo will certainly not be silent spectators'.[105]

By the end of October there were troops deployed in the townships, welcomed, said Charlton, 'with open arms'. There was surely no need, he thought, to issue arms to the African middle class now that government was doing its job. Implementing the new Vagrancy Act, police began to pick up 'hooligans, spivs and loafers'. 'This is grand', wrote Charlton.[106] In many ways, of course, he was being consistent. Sipambaniso had railed against 'loafers' and always spoken in the name of the long-term residents. But things had changed. The very Tenants Association which Sipambaniso had championed would now ensure Charlton's defeat. On 3 December he deplored that the NDP was sponsoring candidates for the Advisory Boards. The *Daily News* reported that 'election fever' gripped Bulawayo's townships, little attention was being paid to ethnicity, and women were showing 'increasing interest'. As candidates campaigned, women asked them whether they were sponsored by residents' associations. Then on 12 December the *Daily News* reported *SHOCKS GALORE IN BULAWAYO ADVISORY BOARD ELECTIONS: OLD MEMBERS OUSTED*. Charlton lost, as did Mazibisa, Masunda, Chigumira and others of the old guard. Young NDP men won. 'Supporters of the winning candidates burst out in song and dance outside the halls with women ululating while the winners were being carried shoulder high. The defeated candidates stood in absolute dejection.'[107]

---

[104] On 12 October the Joint Advisory Boards met. The minutes show that the Mpopoma Board urged 'the great need' for firearms to be issued. Some of those present stated that 'they were in favour of this but that this should include all the Africans in general and pointed out that members of the other community were already in possession of firearms.' The Council was alarmed at the idea of rifles in African hands. On 14 November Councillor Pain told the Joint Boards that 'Africans would never again be left unprotected as had been done during the July riots'. Ashton said that the government 'had been caught completely unaware. It had to ask for additional forces from the Federal Government.' But now it had put 'precautionary measures' in place and created a Police Reserve. Charlton said that 'the Government was to blame for failing to protect the Africans'.

[105] *Home News*, 8 and 15 October 1960.

[106] *Home News*, 22 October 1960.

[107] Charlton complained that he had been overthrown by 'the shebeen vote'. The victorious NDP men were 'absolutely green'. *Home News*, 17 December 1960. Ashton reported in July 1961 that 'at first [the newly elected NDP men] adopted an intransigent party line but with experience and participation they gradually mellowed to a more constructive and practical approach'.

Postlude
Bulawayo after 1960

I hope that readers who have followed my narrative and its characters thus far will want to know what happened next. To do that properly they will have to wait, I fear, for another book by another author.[1] But I should indicate briefly here how the history of Bulawayo between 1893 and 1960 relates to the history of the city between 1960 and 2010. There have been both disjunctions and continuities.

Although so many people feared – and a few hoped for – a repetition of the *Zhii* riots they turned out in fact to be the last great upheaval of colonial Bulawayo. Nkomo, Moyo and the other nationalist leaders managed to hold together their fractured movement. When the NDP was banned in 1961 there was a smooth transition in Bulawayo to the Zimbabwe African People's Union (ZAPU). When ZAPU was challenged in 1963 and 1964 by the Zimbabwe African National Union there was savage inter-party fighting in the African townships of Salisbury. But Bulawayo remained solid for ZAPU and Nkomo's leadership. When the ZAPU leadership was removed Bulawayo remained quiescent. Historians have not yet explored the interactions between the cities and the guerrilla war and there will doubtless be a hidden story to tell.[2] But on the face of it black Bulawayo was in many ways subdued in the 1960s and 1970s. Not only the nationalist movement but also the trade union movement was effectively repressed.[3] The vibrant musical and cultural life of black Bulawayo was dampened, as singers like Dorothy Masuka left the country. The great era of township jazz was over.[4] The *African Daily News*, which had replaced the *Bantu Mirror* and which had carried so much African political and cultural news, was banned. Even the Bulawayo *Home News* ended in 1965.

[1] Busani Mpofu, who helped me research this book, is completing a doctoral thesis on Bulawayo after 1960 at Edinburgh University. He is focusing on the poor. Jane Parpart and Miriam Grant have been working for some years on the black middle class in Bulawayo, with particular reference to Pelendaba. Jane Parpart and Miriam Grant, 'Constructing Difference and Managing Development: Material and Discursive Visions of "Progress" among African Elites, Bulawayo, Zimbabwe, 1953-1980'. *Labour, Capital and Society*, 37, 2004, pp. 289-95.

[2] The story of rural southern and northern Matabeleland *has* been carried through to the 1990s in Terence Ranger, *Voices From the Rocks*, and Jocelyn Alexander, JoAnn McGregor and Terence Ranger, *Violence and Memory*. There are references in both these books to developments in Bulawayo.

[3] E.M. Sibanda, *The Zimbabwean African Peoples Union. A Political History of Insurgency in Southern Rhodesia, 1961–1987*, Africa World Press, Trenton, NJ, 2005.

[4] Joyce Jenje Makwenda, *Zimbabwe Township Music*, p. 28.

The characters whom I have been following fared variously in the 1960s and 1970s. Jerry Vera became a famous golfer and his hotel continued to flourish. He became secretary of the new Joint African Advisory Board in 1968 and had he continued in that role he might well have emerged as the first black mayor of Bulawayo after 1980. But for reasons I have been unable to determine he lasted only a year, to be succeeded by Nicholas Mabodoko, who became the first African chairman of the Joint Board in 1975 and who *did* later become mayor. By the 1980s Jerry had passed into obscurity; his marriage had broken up, and he was to die unremarked in a care home. Today he is recalled mainly as a footballer. In August 2008 the Highlanders Football Club carried on its website an article about Paul Tsumba Dzowa, Jerry's successor in the 1960s, as 'goal scorer supreme'. It noted that 'Paul was inspired by a generation that popularized the sport in the 1940s and 1950s headed by Jerry Vera', and Dzowa himself says that he was a fan of Vera's and the other Highlanders' stars. 'They were great footballers. They were complete players, endowed with top drawer skills, pace, eyi … eyi everything a player had to have. As youngsters we had good examples to emulate.'[5]

Jerry's great friend and admirer, Charlton Ngcebetsha, abandoned partnership politics when the NDP was banned in December 1961 and was succeeded by ZAPU. Charlton joined ZAPU, becoming a National Councillor. After the 1963 split he remained loyal to Nkomo. He remained closely in touch with Nkomo while the latter was in restriction in Gonakudzingwa and consulted him closely as he helped bring old ZAPU and ZANU factions together to form the African National Council in 1971. Charlton become first Secretary General of the ANC. He was arrested in 1972 and himself sent to Gonakudzingwa. Judith Todd draws a characteristic picture of him:

> During the time of the Pearce Commission, when thousands of people were locked up by the Smith regime, Arthur [Chadzingwa] was for some time held in a cell with Charlton Ngcebetsha. He helped the time pass by teaching Arthur cricket in a cell with no bat and no ball. Arthur said he got pretty good at shouting HOWZAT! … Charlton was quite irrepressible, and somehow, within a short time of his detention, the first edition of the *Gonakudzingwa Home News* hit the streets of Bulawayo.[6]

Charlton was released in 1975 and died suddenly in Bulawayo on 11 March 1977.

In the early 1960s J.Z. Moyo continued to lead the Makokoba Tenants Association and to protest at that township's neglect as well as to take an active role in national politics. He became National Treasurer of ZAPU and Financial Secretary of ZAPU's successor, the Peoples Caretaker Council. In 1963 he was sent to Lusaka as 'external representative' of the PCC. In 1971 he took over leadership of ZAPU while Nkomo was still in restriction. He became known as the most resolute proponent of the guerrilla war, and in April 1976 he was given full power over military affairs. On 22 January 1977 he called for increased military aid from the OAU. Hours later he was killed by a parcel bomb in his office in Lusaka. Joshua Nkomo records Moyo's death in his autobiography:

> All of us who lived through that war were hardened by it. Those who died were our closest friends: nowhere was safe. J.Z. Moyo was the man who came closest to negotiating unity between the Zipra and Zanla armies. He was very close to me indeed. One day in January 1977

---

5   'Dzowa Dynasty Part I – Paul Tsumbe Dzowa 60s Goal Scorer Supreme', 12 August 2008.
6   Judith Todd, *Through the Darkness*, Zebra Press, Cape Town, 2007, p. 262.

he received, in Lusaka, a parcel mailed from Botswana and addressed in the handwriting of one of his closest friends. He opened it and it exploded, killing him. Jason Moyo's death forced me back almost full time into the life of a military commander. As vice-president of Zapu and the senior man directly concerned with Zipra, he had provided a crucial link between the direction of the political and military wings of our movement. With him gone, I had to fill his place.[7]

Nkomo's own life has become so well known that the reader will need little reminding of it here. He was arrested on 16 April 1964 and spent the next ten years in Gonakudzingwa restriction area. By the time he was released on 3 December 1974 Bulawayo had become unfamiliar to him:

> I flew to Bulawayo. It was all unexpected: very few knew I was coming and there was no time to give warning of my return. But despite that there was a good turn-out to greet me with excitement. There was pushing and shouting, with people almost unable to believe that I was back ...
>
> Bulawayo had grown while I had been away, with new industries and new people moving in from the countryside to live in new townships on the edge of the city. I was almost a stranger. The shock of my release ... caught up with me – I was so unused to crowds and new companions that I could hardly speak. I just went home and collapsed into bed, exhausted.[8]

Soon Nkomo was out of Bulawayo again, based in Lusaka, travelling around the world to raise funds and arms for his guerrilla army, escaping assassination and abduction attempts, and negotiating with Ian Smith and Robert Mugabe. When he returned to Zimbabwe in 1980 he was greeted in Highfields by a crowd of over 150,000 people and went on to heroic triumph in Bulawayo.

Of all the characters I have been narrating, Hugh Ashton was the one who was able to work effectively in Bulawayo throughout the 1960s and 1970s. It was not easy for him in the early 1960s. Busani Mpofu writes in his study of Bulawayo between 1960 and 1980:

> As the Rhodesian Government came to be dominated by more conservative ... forces in the 1960s Bulawayo's Housing and Amenities Department came under fire from both the nationalists and the government.[9]

The old Advisory Board political culture in which Ashton – and Ngcebetsha – had invested so much crumbled away. From 1962 onwards many Board meetings had to be abandoned for lack of a quorum. In 1964 all the Boards dissolved themselves. The Boards and the Council agreed that there should be elected black councillors, but the Council offered four and the Boards demanded twenty. Ashton was not content to accept this stalemate, and importantly neither was Joshua Nkomo, who exerted his influence to back a compromise. In 1968 a single Joint African Advisory Board was formed for all the townships. It was divided into committees which mirrored the committees of the Council itself: the African chairs attended meetings of the relevant Council committees.

---

[7] *Nkomo: The Story of My Life*, pp.169-70. For obituaries of J.Z. Moyo see *Zimbabwe Review*, 6, 2, 1977.
[8] *Nkomo. The Story of My Life*, p. 153.
[9] Busani Mpofu, 'The Dynamics of Providing Social Services in a Colonial Urban Authority, Bulawayo 1960–1980', BA Special Honours dissertation, University of Zimbabwe, July 2003, p. 13.

Looking back in 1994 Ashton remembered that:

there was a time we had these discussions about African representation on the City Council and the Council was all for it and supported it in fact and we got as far as the Council offer of four seats for Africans out of twelve councillors at the time. But politics began to get a bit touchy. The Boards turned it down and said we want to take it over. The Council said no, no, that's too fast, too quickly. Discussions were never held and finally the Boards refused, they all resigned. For about four years there were no Boards. Every year we solemnly went through the process of calling for nominations, there were no nominations, so there was no Board. But eventually we had discussions with various people, Joshua Nkomo was one and others, and slowly [people stood] and then we formed a very strong Board with Nick Mabodoko and others. It played, I think, a very important part ... It helped enormously having done that, having a Board of that quality, when it came to the time of transition following independence. We got one of the best Councils in the country. When the African came into a position of authority he knew something of what it was all about.[10]

These modest advances were much disliked by the Rhodesia Front government. In Macintyre's time the Bulawayo Council had been despised by Huggins for being reactionary. Now it was despised by Smith for being too liberal. Busani Mpofu has two sections in his Honours dissertation – 'City/State Clash over African Represen- tation in Urban Local Government' and 'City/State Clash over Problems of Funding and Control of Africans'. He shows that in 1970 the Minister for Housing and Local Government stated that he had no intention of introducing direct African represen- tation on city councils; that existing African townships had to remain under white control and that any new ones had to be erected in African areas so that they could gain autonomy. Mpofu describes this statement as 'a direct slap in the face of the [Bulawayo] Council which firmly believed in direct African representation'. Worse was to come. In 1975 the government laid it down that no leases could be issued to urban Africans for longer than 99 years. All freehold schemes had to be withdrawn. This was a 'bombshell' to the Bulawayo Council which protested that it could not go back on its word.[11]

Ashton had left South Africa to come to Bulawayo because he disliked *apartheid*. Now in the 1970s he had to live with Rhodesia Front separate development. His nerve, and that of the City Council, held. They planned for what they realized was an inevitable transition to majority rule. In 1977 delegates were sent to examine the post-colonial experiences of Nairobi and Lusaka. The lessons learned helped Bula- wayo adjust. In June 1981 the old 15-man Council was replaced with a 23-seat body, fifteen councillors elected from the western African townships and eight elected by the central and eastern districts. Six former members of the Joint African Advisory Board became councillors. 'Unlike most cities', writes Mpofu, 'black majority rule in 1980 found the Council ready for transition.'[12]

Nkomo's triumphant return to Bulawayo and the establishment of an African Council brought the city back to life. African politics revived with canvassing for the 1980 election in which ZAPU won all the Bulawayo, and Matabeleland, seats. Trade unionism revived with a rash of strikes. Dorothy Masuka and other artists came back

10 Interview between Mark Ncube and Hugh Ashton, 1 June 1994, National Archives, Bulawayo.
11 Busani Mpofu, 'The Dynamics', pp. 18–29.
12 Mpofu, p. 29. Ashton's memory is still honoured in Bulawayo. When it was urged in 2008 that the White City Stadium be renamed the Bulawayo Council proposed that it be called the Hugh Ashton stadium instead.

to Bulawayo and 'township music/jazz was revived'.[13] Eddison Zvogbo, as Minister of Housing, declared that all long-term urban tenants should now have freehold. Even the Tenants Association of Makokoba now owned their houses. It seemed as if many of the long-term aspirations of black Bulawayo had been achieved. The young Yvonne Vera came of age at this new moment of pause and expectation.[14]

But the old city/state tensions survived and, indeed, intensified. An efficient, totally ZAPU city council was hard for Mugabe's ZANU/PF government to accept. Government ministers tried to rally ZANU/PF support in the city. At a rally in Stanley Square in November 1980 Enos Nkala – ZANU/PF's main Ndebele leader – called upon party supporters to form vigilante groups 'to challenge PF/ZAPU on its home ground'. Other speakers complained that 'only in Bulawayo did police commanders not meet visiting ministers' – as Home Affairs minister, Joshua Nkomo was in charge of the police.[15] Both Nkomo's ZIPRA guerrillas and Mugabe's ZANLA had been brought into the city and housed together in Entumbane township. Now in two violent outbursts it seemed as if the days of *Zhii* might have returned. Fighting broke out between the two guerrilla forces on 9 and 10 November 1980. At least 55 people were killed and 2,000 homes damaged. Then between 7 and 10 February 1981 more violent fighting erupted. This time there were at least 197 dead and 1,600 homes damaged. Violence spread into the townships. There were echoes of the faction fights of December 1929 as ethnicity once again became a divisive issue. Yvonne Vera's grandmother in Luveve, after all her years in Bulawayo, could still only speak Shona, and feared for her life: she certainly could not pronounce the Sindebele word, with all the clicks, which gangs were demanding for safe passage.[16]

The Gukurahundi violence of 1983 and after mainly affected the Matabeleland and Midlands countryside. Nevertheless the city of Bulawayo was punished for its loyalty to Nkomo and for its efficiency. At one moment all its firemen were arrested; at another all its rubbish collectors. ZAPU was swallowed up in the Unity Agreement of 1987. But the structural tension between city and state continued. In the years 2000 to 2008 the Bulawayo Council was dominated by a new opposition, the Movement for Democratic Change. As I wrote in 2007:

> Since 2000 the Zimbabwean state has radically intervened in urban local government. Elected mayors have been dismissed; whole municipal councils have been sacked; commissions appointed by the state have attempted to run cities. A whole series of state authorities – governors for both Harare and Bulawayo, district administrators for the townships – have been inserted above

---

[13] Joyce Jenje Makwena, *Zimbabwe Township Music*, p. 44.

[14] In 1980 Yvonne was a boarder at Luveve Secondary School. In November 1981 she was doing Form 4 there and participated in an essay competition about Bulawayo – 'Know Your City'. 'The participants had to tour the city of Bulawayo for six days before they could write the essay.' Yvonne came second. In 1982 she went to Hillside Teacher Training College as one of its first African students. Ericah Gwetai, *Petal Thoughts. Yvonne Vera*, Mambo Press, Gweru, 2008. Yvonne's mother's book reveals how much *Butterfly Burning* drew upon Yvonne's family history.

[15] Norma Kriger, *Guerrilla Veterans in Post-war Zimbabwe. Symbolic and Violent Politics, 1980–1987*, Cambridge University Press, Cambridge, 2003, p. 77.

[16] When I first urged Yvonne to read *Breaking the Silence*, the CCJP's report on the Fifth Brigade and the killing of thousands of Ndebele in the 1980s, she was at first reluctant to do so. She asked me: 'Does it describe what happened to Shona-speakers in Bulawayo in 1980 and 1981?' In fact it does not. Nor has anything else been written about the impact of the Entumbane violence in the townships. It deserves a treatment at least as full as my accounts of December 1929 and of *Zhii* in this book. In 1981 I was researching in Makoni district in Manicaland. Fugitive Manyika, fleeing from the violence in Bulawayo, spread terrifying stories of Ndebele vengeance.

and into the cities ... [ZANU/PF violence in Bulawayo rose] to a height on 16 November 2001 when the City Hall was stormed and ransacked by war veterans searching for the mayor, headed by a man who until recently had been Minister of Home Affairs. The Municipal Fire Brigade was stoned and hundreds of council employees beaten.[17]

Meanwhile, through all this, Makokoba remained crowded and poor, and full of sport, music and drama. In the 1990s it maintained its own football team, the Makokoba Warriors. In 1989 a group of young singers and artists founded NASA – the Nostalgic Actors and Singers Alliance. Ten years later NASA was re-named Siyaya, still 'firmly rooted in Makokoba'. Siyaya describes Makokoba as the 'oldest town with the newest of ideas'; one of its hit shows and discs is called *Kokoba* Town:

> In times of happiness people of Kokoba Town sing and dance, in times of sadness they also sing and sometimes dance. Music in this place is a necessity and not a luxury. The music will tell you rhythmic African stories before you hear or see them.

It might be a description of *Butterfly Burning*! Siyaya organizes an annual *Ibumba* Festival in Stanley Hall and Stanley Square. For December 2009, they say, 'Stanley Square will be transformed into a family and recreation place', with markets and side-shows.[18]

Every so often someone would suggest that the old township should be knocked down so that the valuable space so near to the city could be developed, but this was always countered by an appeal to Makokoba's historic role in the city's – and nation's – political and cultural life. In 2005, though, during the slum clearance Operation Murambatsvina, Makokoba *was* attacked, and characteristically resisted. Fire returned to the township. As the BBC reported on 15 June 2005:

> Police have fought running battles with residents of one of the oldest townships of the second city, as they demolished illegal structures. The BBC's Themba Nkosi says that Makhokhoba in Bulawayo was the centre of resistance to colonial rule. One woman stripped naked in protest after police destroyed her shack ... Our correspondent in Bulawayo says that even the well-respected traditional doctors in Makhokhoba township were not spared as riot police ordered the healers and their patients out of their shacks before setting them on fire.

> Most of the traditional doctors lost their herbs and supposedly magic charms. Makhokhoba has been a vibrant and colourful township for many decades. From the shacks of this township have come some of Bulawayo's top actors and theatre actors ... The police then moved on to flatten houses in Mzilikazi township next door to Makhokhoba. It is a totally chaotic situation with people running in different directions. I witnessed police in Mzilikazi removing belongings of those who had fled their dwellings as they were being demolished. Many told me they are now homeless.

Yet Makokoba maintains its nostalgic appeal. During 2005 the late William Phiri wrote a series of columns in the *Chronicle* about his memories of life in the townships:

> There is something magnetic about Bulawayo's first township, eLokayo, Old Location, Makokoba [he wrote on 9 November 2005]. The way a lightbulb attracts a moth at night, eLokayo has drawn the attention of all kinds of artistes and writers.

---

17 Terence Ranger, 'City versus State in Zimbabwe: Colonial Antecedents of the Current Crisis', *Journal of Eastern African Studies*, 1, 2, July 2007, pp. 161-2.
18 In 2002 Siyaya staged a performance of my book, *Voices From the Rocks*. I saw it first in Sheffield and then at the 2003 Book Fair in Harare. I regret that it has not been staged in Makokoba!

He went on to publish feedback from his readers about life *emalokishini*. Mr D. Mumba remembered Christmas in the early 1950s – the 'sweets, sadza and beef' in Stanley Square', the varied dances, cowboy films at the bioscope, dressing up as cowboys and Indians afterwards with 'wire guns for shooting'. 'Life was grand in the 1950s.' Themba Nyoni recalled boxing in Stanley Square and music shows in Stanley Hall. 'Going across to Lobengula Street was the most daring adventure. Life was hard, but they were the most enjoyable times of my life.'

It was this nostalgia for the townships, and Makokoba in particular, to which Yvonne Vera appealed during her time as Director of the National Gallery in Bulawayo. The launch of *Butterfly Burning* in 1998, with music by the revived 1950s township jazz group, the Cool Crooners; her 1999 exhibition of township photographs, *Thatha Camera*; her exhibition of decorated township bicycles; her planned exhibition of Lobengula Street in the glory days of its Indian stores – all spoke to the history which I have been re-telling in this book. Her successors have continued with the theme – an exhibition of township hairstyles, with Makokoba barbers available to cut visitors' hair; the forthcoming exhibition of memories and memorabilia of Highlanders football club. All this gives the black Bulawayo of the twenty-first century – the townships and the city both – an extraordinary sense of its past and the way in which it has made the present.

Selected Bibliography

Alexander, Jocelyn, JoAnn McGregor and Terence Ranger, *Violence and Memory: One Hundred Years in the 'Dark Forests' of Matabeleland*, James Currey, Oxford, 2000.

Ashton, Hugh, *African Administration in Bulawayo*, City of Bulawayo, 4 September 1957.

— 'The Economics of African Housing', *Rhodesian Journal of Economics*, 1969.

Barnes, Teresa. *'We Women Worked So Hard': Gender, Urbanization and Social Reproduction in Colonial Harare, 1930–1956*, Heinemann, Portsmouth, NH, 1999.

Bhebe, Ngwabi, *B.Burombo: African Politics in Zimbabwe, 1947–1958*, College Press, Harare, 1989.

— *Simon Vengayi Muzenda and the Struggle for and Liberation of Zimbabwe*, Mambo Press, Gweru, 2004.

Bonner, Philip and Noor Neiftagodien, *Kathorus: A History*, Longman, Cape Town, 2001.

Bozzoli, Belinda, *Theatres of Struggle and the End of Apartheid*, International African Library, 29, Edinburgh University Press, Edinburgh, 2004.

Burke, Timothy, *Lifebuoy Men, Lux Women: Commodification, Consumption and Cleanliness in Modern Zimbabwe*, Duke University Press, Durham, NC, 1996.

Burnham, F.R., *Scouting in Two Continents*, Heinemann, London, 1926.

Chadya, Joyce and Koni Benson, '*Ukubhinya*: Gender and Sexual Violence in Bulawayo, Colonial Zimbabwe, 1946–1956', *Journal of Southern African Studies*, 31, 3, 2005.

Chikowero, M., 'Subalternating Currents: Electrification and Power Politics in Bulawayo, Colonial Zimbabwe, 1894–1939', *Journal of Southern African Studies*, 33, 2, 2007.

Chipembere, Ennie, 'Colonial Urban Policy and Africans in Urban Areas, with special focus on Housing, Salisbury, 1929–1964', draft PhD thesis in Economic History, University of Zimbabwe, February 2007.

Cobb, J.M., *General Survey of the Living, Working and Housing Conditions of the Coloured Community in the Municipal Area of Bulawayo*, Bulawayo, 1931.

Coplan, David, *In Township Tonight! Three Centuries of South African Black City Music and Theatre*, Jacana Media, Johannesburg, 2007.

Dangor, Achmat, 'Another Country', *The Guardian*, 25 September 2004.

Davis, Alexander, *The Directory of Bulawayo and Handbook to Matabeleland, 1895–6*, Bulawayo, 1896, reprinted by Books of Zimbabwe, Bulawayo, 1981.

Dlamini, Jacob, *Native Nostalgia*, Jacana, Auckland Park, 2009.

Fraser, Robert, 'Postcolonial Cities: Michael Ondaatje's Toronto and Yvonne Vera's Bulawayo' in G.V. Davis, P.H. Marsden, B. Leadent, M. Delrez (eds), *Towards a Transcultural Future*, Rodopi, New York, 2005.

Gargett, Eric Stanley, 'Welfare Services in an African Urban Area', PhD dissertation, University of London, 1971.

Gray, Richard, *The Two Nations: Aspects of the Development of Race Relations in Rhodesia and Nyasaland*, Oxford University Press, London, 1960.

Guchu, Wonder, *Sketches of High Density Life*, Weaver Press, Harare, 2003.

Gussman, B.W., *African Life in an Urban Area*, two volumes, Bulawayo, 1952–3.

Gwetai, Ericah, *Petal Thoughts. Yvonne Vera. A Biography*, Mambo Press, Gweru, 2009.

Hinfelaar, Marja, *Respectable and Responsible Women: Methodist and Roman Catholic Women's Organisations in Harare. Zimbabwe, 1918–1985*, Utrecht, 2004.

Hove, M.M., *Confessions of a Wizard*, Mambo Press, Gweru, 1985.

Hyatt, S.P., *The Old Transport Road*, Melrose, London, 1914.

Ibbotson, Percy, *Report on a Survey of Urban African Conditions in Southern Rhodesia*, Bulawayo, 1943.

Jackson, Lynette, 'Uncontrollable Women in a Colonial African Town: Bulawayo Location, 1893–1958', MA thesis, Columbia University, 1987.

— *Surfacing Up. Psychiatry and Social Order in Colonial Zimbabwe, 1908–1968*, Cornell University Press, Ithaca, NY, 2005.

Johnson, David, *World War II and the Scramble for Labour in Colonial Zimbabwe, 1939–1948*, University of Zimbabwe Publications, Harare, 2000.

Kaarsholm, Preben, 'Si Ye Pambili (Which Way Forward): Urban Development, Culture and Politics in Bulawayo', *Journal of Southern African Studies*, 21, 2, 1995.

— 'Instability, Migration and Violence: Notes on a South African Peri-Urban Situation', in Bodil Folke Frederiksen and Fiona Wilson (eds), *Livelihood, Identity and Instability*, Centre for Development Research, Copenhagen, 1997.

Kriger, Norma, *Guerrilla Veterans in Post-war Zimbabwe: Symbolic and Violent Politics, 1980–1987*, Cambridge University Press, 2003.

Lunn, Jon, *Capital and Labour on the Rhodesian Railway System, 1888–1947*, St Antony's/Macmillan, London, 1997.

Macmillan, Allister, *Eastern Africa and Rhodesia: Historical and Descriptive, Commercial and Industrial Facts, Figures and Resources*, Collinridge, London, 1931.

Makwenda, Joyce Jenje, *Zimbabwe Township Music*, Storytime, Harare, 2006.

Maylam, Paul and Iain Edwards, *The People's City. African Life in Twentieth-Century Durban*, University of Natal Press, Durban, 1996.

Mbembe, Achille and Sarah Nuttall (eds), *Johannesburg: The Elusive Metropolis*, University of Witwatersrand Press, Johannesburg, 2008.

McNamee. J.P., *Report on Native Urban Administration in Bulawayo*, Bulawayo, 1948.

Moyo, Ortrude Nontokela, *Trampled No More: Voices from Bulawayo's Townships about Families, Life, Survival and Social Change*, University Press of America, Maryland, 2007.

Moyo, Temba, and Ole Gjerstad, *The Organizer. Story of Temba Moyo ((Life histories from the revolution. Zimbabwe, ZAPU)*, LSM Information Centre, Richmond, VA, 1974.

Mpofu, Busani, 'The Dynamics of Providing Social Services in a Colonial Urban Authority, Bulawayo 1960–1980', BA Special Honours thesis, Economic History, University of Zimbabwe, July 2003.

— 'The Struggle of an "Undesirable" Alien Community in a White Settler Colony: The Case of the Indian Minority in Bulawayo, Colonial Zimbabwe, 1890–1965', MA thesis in Economic History, University of Zimbabwe, March 2005.

Msindo, Enocent, 'Ethnicity in Matabeleland, Zimbabwe: A Study of Ndebele-Kalanga Relations, 1800s–1990s', PhD thesis, Cambridge University, 2004 .

— 'Ethnicity not Class? The 1929 Bulawayo Faction Fights Reconsidered', *Journal of Southern African Studies*, 32, 3, 2006.

— 'Ethnicity and Nationalism in Urban Colonial Zimbabwe: Bulawayo, 1950 to 1963', *Journal of African History*, 48, 2007.

Musemwa, Muchaparara, 'A Tale of Two Cities: The Evolution of Bulawayo and Makokoba Township under Conditions of Water Scarcity, 1894–1953', *South African Historical Journal*, 56, 1, 2006.

— 'Disciplining a Dissident City: Hydropolitics in the City of Bulawayo, Matabeleland, Zimbabwe, 1980–1994', *Journal of Southern Arican Studies*, 32, 2, 2006.

— 'Early Struggles over Water: From Private to Public Water in the City of Bulawayo, Zimbabwe, 1894–1924', *Journal of Southern African Studies*, 34, 4, 2008.

Ndlovu-Gatsheni, Sabelo, 'For the Nation to Live, the Tribe must Die: the Politics of Ndebele Identity and Belonging in Zimbabwe', in Bahru Zewde (ed.), *Society, State and Identity in African History*, Forum for Social Studies, Addis Ababa, 2008.

Ndubiwa, Michael, 'African Participation in Housing and Management in Rhodesia. The Bulawayo African Advisory Board', MA thesis, University of Zimbabwe, 1972.

Nehwati, Francis, 'The Social and Communal Background to *Zhii*', *African Affairs*, 59, 276, 1970.

Nkomo, Joshua, *Nkomo: The Story of My Life*, Methuen, London, 1984.

Nyairo, Joyce and James Ogude (eds), *Urban Legends, Colonial Myths: Popular Culture and Literature in East Africa*, Africa World Press, Trenton, NJ, 2007.

Nyathi, Pathisa, *Masotsha Ndlovu*, Longman, Harare, 1998.

Opara, Chioma, 'Not a Scintilla of Light: Darkness and Despondency in Yvonne Vera's *Butterfly Burning*', *Tydskif vir Letterkunde*, Spring, 2008.

Parpart, Jane and Miriam Grant, 'Constructing Difference and Managing Development: Material and Discursive Visions of "Progress" among African Elites, Bulawayo, Zimbabwe, 1953–1980', *Labour, Capital and Society*, 37, 2004.

Phimister, Ian, *An Economic and Social History of Zimbabwe, 1890–1948*, Longman, London, 1988.

Phimister, Ian, and Brian Raftopoulos, '*Kana sana ratswa ngaritswe*' (If the grass is burning, let it burn): African Nationalists and Black Workers – the 1948 General Strike in Colonial Zimbabwe', *Journal of Historical Sociology*, 13, 4, 2000.

Phiri, William, 'Religion in Makokoba', *Chronicle*, 26 April 2005.

— 'Growing Up in Makokoba', *Chronicle*, 9 November 2005.

Potts, Deborah, 'Restoring Order? Operation Murambatsvina and the Urban Crisis in Zimbabwe', *Journal of Southern African Studies*, 32, 2, 2006.

Primorac, Ranka, *African City Textualities*, Routledge, Abingdon, 2009.

Raftopoulos, Brian and Alois Mlambo (eds), *Becoming Zimbabwe*, Weaver Press, Harare, and Jacana, Cape Town, 2009.

Raftopoulos, Brian and Ian Phimister (eds), *Keep On Knocking: A History of the Labour Movement in Zimbabwe*, Baobab Books, Harare, 1997.

Raftopoulos, Brian and Tsuneo Yoshikuni (eds), *Sites of Struggle: Essays in Zimbabwe's Urban History*, Weaver Press, Harare, 1999.

Ranger, T.O., *The African Voice in Southern Rhodesia, 1898–1930*, Heinemann Educational, London, 1970.

— *Chingaira Makoni's Head: Myth, History and the Colonial Experience*, Indiana University, Bloomington, IN, 1988.

— *Are We Not Also Men? The Samkange Family and African Politics in Zimbabwe, 1920–1964*, James Currey, London, 1995.

— *Voices From the Rocks. Nature, Culture and History in the Matopos*, James Currey, Oxford, 1999.

— 'Bicycles and the Social History of Bulawayo', *Thatha Bhasikili. An Exhibition of Adorned Bicycles in Bulawayo*, National Gallery, Bulawayo, 2001.

— 'Pictures Must Prevail: Sex and the History of Photography in Bulawayo', *Kronos*, 27 November 2001.

— 'Dignifying Death. The Politics of Burial in Bulawayo, 1893 to 1960', *Journal of Religion in Africa*, 34, 1, 2004.

— 'The Meaning of Urban Violence in Africa: Bulawayo, Southern Rhodesia, 1890–1960', *Cultural and Social History*, 3, 2006.

— 'City versus State in Zimbabwe: Colonial Antecedents of the Current Crisis', *Journal of Eastern African Studies*, 1, 2, 2007.

— 'Myth and Legend in urban oral memory, Bulawayo, 1930–1960', in Ranka Primorac (ed.), *African City Textualities*, Routledge, Abingdon, 2009.

— 'Reclaiming the African City: The World and the Township', in Ulrike Freitag and Achim von Oppen (eds), *Translocality: The Study of Globalising Processes from a Southern Perspective*, Brill, Leiden, 2010.

Ransford, Oliver, *Bulawayo, Historic Battleground of Rhodesia*, Balkema, Cape Town, 1968.

Ruzingwe, Blessing, 'Makokoba: Poor looks, rich history', *Chronicle*, 5 March 1999.

Samkange, Stanlake, *The Mourned One*, Heinemann Educational, London, 1975.

Samuelson, Meg, 'Yvonne Vera's Bulawayo: Modernity, (Im)mobility, Music and Memory', *Research in African Literatures*, 38, 2, 2007.

Scarnecchia, Timothy, *The Urban Roots of Democracy and Political Violence in Zimbabwe. Harare and Highfield, 1940–1964*, University of Rochester Press, Rochester, NY, 2008.

Shutt, Alison and Tony King, 'Imperial Rhodesians: The 1952 Rhodes Centenary Exhibition in Southern Rhodesia', *Journal of Southern African Studies*, 31, 2, 2005.

Sibanda, E.M., *The Zimbabwe African Peoples Union, 1961–1987. A Political History of Insurgency in Southern Rhodesia*, Africa World Press, Trenton, NJ, 2005.

Simone, Abdou Maliq, 'Between Ghetto and Globe: Remaking Urban Life in Africa' in Arne Tostensen, Inge Tvedten and Mariken Vaa (eds), *Associational Life in African Cities: Popular Response to the Urban Crisis*, Nordic Africa Institute, Uppsala, 2001.

Stuart, Ossie, 'Good Boys, Footballers and Strikers: African Social Change in Bulawayo, 1933–1953', PhD thesis, London University, 1989.

— 'Players, Workers, Protestors: Social Change and Soccer in Colonial Zimbabwe' in J. McClaney (ed.), *Sport, Identity and Ethnicity*, Berg, Oxford, 1996.

Thornton, Stephen, 'A History of the African People of Bulawayo', draft PhD thesis, Manchester University, 1980.

— 'The struggle for profit and participation by an emerging petty-bourgeoisie in Bulawayo, 1893–1933', in Raftopoulos and Yoshikuni (eds), *Sites of Struggle*.

Todd, Judith Garfield, *Through the Darkness. A Life in Zimbabwe*, Zebra, Cape Town, 2007.

Vambe, Lawrence, *From Rhodesia to Zimbabwe*, University of Pittsburgh Press, Pittsburgh, PA, 1976.

Van Onselen, Charles and Ian Phimister, 'The Political Economy of Tribal Animosity', *Journal of Southern African Studies*, 6, 1, 1979.

Vera, Yvonne, *Butterfly Burning*, Baobab Books, Harare, 1998.

— 'Introduction', *Thatha Camera, The Pursuit for Reality,* National Gallery, Bulawayo, 1999.

— *The Stone Virgins*, Weaver Press, Harare, 2002.

Vickery, Ken, 'The Rhodesia Railway Strike of 1945, Part 1: A Narrative Account', *Journal of Southern African Studies*, 24, 3, 1998.

— 'The Rhodesia Railways African Strike of 1945, Part 2: Causes, Consequence, Significance', *Journal of Southern African Studies*, 25, 1, 1999.

West, Michael, *The Rise of an African Middle Class: Colonial Zimbabwe, 1898–1965*, Indiana University Press, Bloomington, IN, 2002.

White, Luise, 'Whoever saw a Country with Four Armies?: The Battle for Bulawayo Revisited', *Journal of Southern African Studies*, 33, 3, 2007.

Wild, Volker, *Profit not for Profit's Sake. History and Business Culture of African Entrepreneurs in Zimbabwe*, Baobab Books, Harare, 1997.

Yoshikuni, Tsuneo, 'Notes on the influence of town-country relations on African urban history before 1957: experiences of Salisbury and Bulawayo', in Raftopoulos and Yoshikuni (eds), *Sites of Struggle* .

— *African Urban Experiences in Colonial Zimbabwe. A Social History of Harare before 1926*, Weaver Press, Harare, 2007.

Zeleza, Paul Tiyambe, 'The Spatial Economy of Structural Adjustment in African Cities', in Zeleza and Kalipenia (eds), *Sacred Space and Public Quarrels: African Cultural and Economic Landscapes*, Africa World Press, Trenton, NJ, 1999.

Zhou, T., 'A History of the Private Locations Around Bulawayo City, 1930–1957', MA thesis, History, University of Zimbabwe, April 1995.

Index

Advisory Boards, 2, 7, 10, 28, 31, 38 fn76, 108, 111, 112, 113, 117, 141, 169, 171, 172, 173, 174, 181, 183, 184 fn84, 185, 186, 188, 189, 190, 192, 203, 207, 208, 218, 220, 221, 239, 240, 242, 243 fn104, 245, 246

African Methodist Episcopal Church, 3, 64, 78, 81, 172, 183

Alexander, Jocelyn, 1

Alexandria township, 12

Anglicanism, 3, 28, 78, 133, 144, 172

Apostolics, 137, 181, 182

Apostolic Faith Mission, 27

Ashton, Hugh, 9, 10, 169, 171 fn10, 173, 174, 175 fn23, 176, 178, 180, 185, 186, 187, 188, 189, 204, 207 fn101, 208, 218, 219, 220, 221, 222, 230, 231, 232, 234, 238, 240, 242, 247

Asians, 47, 48, 65 fn30, 66, 225

Banda, Hastings, 197, 205

Bango, Grey, (see Trade Unions) 133, 135, 138, 152 fn88, 162, 163, 164, 166 fn139, 171, 200, 201, 202, 208, 209

Bango, R.M., 206, 208 fn104, 238, 239, 240

Bantu [Native] Mirror, 28, 42, 43, 48, 68 fn62, 88, 104, 109, 116, 132, 134, 135, 140, 141, 142, 143, 144, 152, 163, 172, 176, 177, 189, 191, 198, 202, 204, 205, 219, 221, 226, 235, 244

Bantu Co-operative Trading Society, 203 fn84

Bantu Voters League, 27, 46

Barbourfields township, 169, 183, 184, 187, 188, 194, 203, 205, 220, 223

Baring, Sir Evelyn, 126

Barnes, Terri, 70, 71

Beadle, T.W., 164, 168

beauty contests, 8, 98, 178, 179

beer (African), 30 fn47, 44, 45. 76, 80, 90, 175

beer-halls, 27, 44, 45, 46, 52, 105, 110, 113, 116, 122, 123, 127, 139, 182, 223, 224, 226, 229, 235

Bhebe, Ngwabi, 1, 164

bicycles, 7, 17 fn14, 43 fn97, 58, 80 fn100, 81, 100, 117, 137, 149, 174, 179, 182, 184,

Bikwapi, Manyoba Khumalo, (see Ma-Dhlodhlo and Sipambaniso), 26, fn13, 27, 29, 132 fn26, 133, 172

Borrow Street, 16, map 18

boxing, 4, 41, 88, 95, 100, 101, 103, 134, 136

Bozzoli, Belinda, 12

builders, 25, 36, 125, 131, 147, 202, 203

Bulawayo (Lobengula's) 4, 14, 15, 16

Bulawayo, (Grass Town), 6, 16, 20, 23

Bulawayo Chronicle, 2, 17, 37, 38, 54, 56, 57, 83, 89, 90, 92, 94, 98, 113, 114 fn22, 149, 157, 159, 161, 162, 219, 223, 225, 227, 231, 232, 235, 238, 239

Bulawayo City Hall, 2, 57, 223, 249

Bulawayo Club, 2, 4, 57, 69

Bulawayo Council, 1, 2, 3, 7, 10, 24, 31 fn54, 32, 35, 36, 45, 46, 51, 64, 65, 66, 69, 72, 73, 76, 79, 82, 107, 108, 109, 110,